MW01130419

Praise for

WORLD ON THE BRINK

"An urgent, thought-provoking warning about one of the biggest challenges facing America today. It also provides practical approaches and well-reasoned proposals that will enable the US to maintain its global leadership for the decades ahead. A must-read on the most important issue in the world!"

—General David Petraeus, US Army (ret.), former commander of the Surge in Iraq, US Central Command, and coalition forces in Afghanistan; former director of the CIA; and coauthor of *Conflict: The Evolution of Warfare from 1945 to Ukraine*

"Alperovitch has long been one of the smartest commentators I know on Ukraine and Russia. He warned that Moscow would invade Ukraine long before others and has consistently provided highly prescient observations. Now, however, he turns his sights on China, and warns of the swelling risk that it will invade Taiwan in the coming years and spark a crisis in America as a result—unless active measures are taken to contain this danger now. Deeply researched and provocative, this is a powerful call to arms for Washington's policymakers and a must-read for anyone watching global affairs, the twenty-first-century tech sector, and international business."

—Gillian Tett, columnist and editorial board, *Financial Times*; and provost, Kings College, Cambridge

"*World on the Brink* is a clear-eyed analysis of Cold War II and a game plan for winning it. Alperovitch is the ideal guide to this new era of competitive geopolitics with tech, computing, and semiconductor chips at its core. Drawing lessons from Cold War I and Putin's attack on Ukraine, Alperovitch shows just how dangerous a brink we stand on. Provocative and insightful, this is essential reading for understanding the American-made world order and the threats it faces."

—Chris Miller, *New York Times*–bestselling author of *Chip War: The Fight for the World's Most Critical Technology*

"Alperovitch's personal story and incredible entrepreneurial success is both the embodiment of the American Dream and a perfect vantage point to understand the biggest geopolitical challenge we now face—the rivalry of China and its state-led economic model. *World on the Brink* masterfully navigates the present-day issues in critical materials, semiconductors, military, and other cutting-edge technologies with insightful historical context and pragmatic solutions. This is the first book to read if you want to understand the geopolitical landscape, what choices must be made, and how that will impact all of us."

—James Litinsky, founder, chairman, and CEO, MP Materials

"The stakes of Cold War II could not be greater. Alperovitch, one of our nation's foremost experts on technology and national security, has skillfully crafted a game plan for freedom to once again be the victor. This is a book that needs to be read by all Americans."

—Rep. Mike Gallagher, chairman, Select Committee on the Chinese Communist Party

WORLD
ON THE
BRINK

How America Can Beat China in the Race for the Twenty-First Century

WORLD ON THE BRINK

DMITRI ALPEROVITCH

with GARRETT M. GRAFF

PUBLICAFFAIRS
New York

PublicAffairs
Hachette Book Group
1290 Avenue of the Americas, New York, NY 10104
www.publicaffairsbooks.com
@Public_Affairs

Printed in the United States of America

First Edition: April 2024

Published by PublicAffairs, an imprint of Hachette Book Group, Inc. The PublicAffairs name and logo is a registered trademark of the Hachette Book Group.

Print book interior design by Amy Quinn.

Library of Congress Cataloging-in-Publication Data

Names: Alperovitch, Dmitri, author. | Graff, Garrett M., 1981– author.
Title: World on the brink : how America can beat China in the race for the twenty-first century / Dmitri Alperovitch, with Garrett M. Graff.
Other titles: How America can beat China in the race for the twenty-first century.
Description: First edition. | New York : PublicAffairs, 2024. | Includes bibliographical references.
Identifiers: LCCN 2023042363 | ISBN 9781541704091 (hardcover) | ISBN 9781541704695 (trade paperback) | ISBN 9781541704152 (ebook)
Subjects: LCSH: United States—Foreign relations—China. | China—Foreign relations—United States. | United States—Foreign economic relations—China. | China—Foreign economic relations—United States.
Classification: LCC E183.8.C5 A68 2024 | DDC 327.73051—dc23/eng/20231220
LC record available at https://lccn.loc.gov/2023042363

ISBNs: 9781541704091 (hardcover), 9781541704152 (ebook), 9781541704695 (international paperback)

LSC-H

Printing 5, 2024

Contents

The two most powerful warriors are patience and time.

—*Leo Tolstoy, War and Peace*

Prologue

A Dispatch from the Future

November 13, 2028. The winter season in Taiwan—lasting from November till March—is great for surfers. It's no Bali or Hawaii, as the size of the waves and their consistency may vary, but the Northeast Monsoon, which brings the cold China Coastal Current water into the Taiwan Strait, where it meets the warm Kuroshio Branch Current coming from the south, is known to form some significant waves. The Taiwan Strait is only about a hundred meters deep—shallow enough that during ice ages and the time of glaciers the island of Taiwan was physically connected to the Chinese mainland; but even in the modern era the two-hundred-mile-long passage—which varies in width from about one hundred nautical miles down to just seventy nautical miles and is one of the most vital shipping routes in the world—is known for frequent storms, large swells, and blinding fog and bedeviled by annual summer typhoons from roughly May to October. Between the typhoons in the summer and the stormy high-wave winter season, there is no predictably perfect and easy time to launch a large-scale amphibious invasion of Taiwan, especially with the strait registering about 150 days a year of winds above twenty knots, rough seas for amphibious ships and landing craft. Any landing on Taiwan's windy, shallow, and rocky beaches during that time is fraught and risky. Which is why, in the end, China decided to forego a beach landing and attempt an air assault on the island's port and airfield facilities, the seizure of which would allow for rapid arrival of follow-on troops and logistical supplies to facilitate a successful occupation.

The operations planners in the People's Liberation Army (PLA) had had years to deliberate their invasion strategy, adjusting year after year as China's own military capabilities grew and advanced. In the end, due to the unpredictability of the rough Taiwan Strait waters and the heavy fortifications the Taiwanese had built up around potential beach landing sites, the PLA came up with an innovative invasion plan—the opening stages of which they'd practiced repeatedly as the late 2020s unfolded. For several years, China had engaged in full-scale military exercises—loading up vast armadas of military and civilian ships with tens of thousands of troops, equipment, and matériel and heading toward Taiwan, always stopping just short of the twelve-nautical-mile limit that marks the start of the island's territorial waters. They figured they could practice with some impunity because they knew Taiwan could never afford to respond aggressively. One of the island's greatest defense dilemmas had long been its inability to respond to hostile provocations and threats with force—lest it be accused of instigating a conflict. US officials had warned Taiwanese leadership for years that under no circumstances could they fire the first shot—they had to take the Chinese punch before retaliating. Portraying China as the aggressor would be a critical step in building the international case that Chinese leader Xi Jinping was alone responsible for starting any war. The stakes couldn't have been higher: after all, even if the Taiwanese fired first at the PLA armada after it crossed Taiwan's territorial boundary, Beijing could still dispute the shooting as unprovoked and claim that it occurred in international waters—muddying the geopolitical waters such that Taiwan risked losing key moral and diplomatic support around the world. Too many countries wanted the excuse—they would only be too eager to continue trading with China, the world's second largest economy, irrespective of the conflict. If Taiwan was to survive and rally the world to its cause, it couldn't afford to offer that excuse.

The final Chinese PLA plan counted on precisely that Taiwanese restraint when China's ships entered Taiwan's waters and closed in on the vital northwestern coastal Port of Taipei, a modern facility completed in 2012 that boasted forty-five hundred feet of so-called berth space, a substantial amount of space available for cargo offloading. There the PLA planned to leverage existing infrastructure to rapidly unload hundreds of thousands of troops and thousands of tanks, armored vehicles, heavy engineering equipment, weapons, munitions, and the logistics supplies needed for the conquest of the island. While Taipei wasn't the largest port in Taiwan, the rapid capture of its docks was essential to the success of the operation since other Taiwanese port facilities were too far away from the capital city. That distance and Taiwan's extensive array of steep mountains and winding rivers made the rapid transport of a large PLA armored force from any other port or beach to the capital all but impossible.

The operational plan called for moving eight modern Type 075 *Yushen*-class amphibious assault ships, each with more than thirty-thousand-ton displacement, right up to Taiwan's maritime border, while being protected by PLA Navy (PLAN) guided-missile destroyers. Xi Jinping's regime had rapidly constructed the *Yushen* ships specifically with this mission in mind; each was a highly capable delivery platform for air assault operations, carrying a mix of up to twenty-eight attack and heavy transport helicopters and eight hundred troops. In the early morning hours, once the final order was given, two hundred Z-8 and Z-20 transport helicopters, all backed up by Z-10 attack gunships, would take off from the landing docks and head for the Taipei port, as well as the Taoyuan International Airport, ten miles west, and the smaller Taipei Songshan Airport, located right in the center of the capital city, just three miles north of the Zhongzheng government district. The plan called for helicopters to make the journey in ten minutes. (Ironically, these aircraft were built based on legally acquired Western technology—the Z-8 came from an original French-licensed design, and the Z-20 from the UH-60 Black Hawk, which America had sold to China in the 1980s. The Z-10 was built with Pratt & Whitney engines and assisted by European Airbus and AgustaWestland transmission and rotor installation designs.)

The heliborne brigades of the PLA Air Force (PLAAF) Airborne Corps, China's equivalent to the United States' 101st Airborne Division, would assault, capture, and secure the port and airport facilities, in preparation for follow-on forces with armored vehicles that would land at the airfields on the Chinese Y-20 and Russian-made IL-76 troop transport planes. As those transport planes descended, dozens of large roll-on/roll-off (RORO) ferries and vehicle transport ships—all built with "national defense requirements" and appropriated from Chinese industry by the PLAN—would rush into the captured port and unload tens of thousands of troops and hundreds of additional tanks and infantry fighting vehicles. Anticipating that the Taiwanese might manage to destroy the port's infrastructure ahead of the Chinese landing, the PLA has spent years practicing rapid offloading of these vessels in ports with minimal cargo handling infrastructure, such as a lack of pier-side ramps or tugboat support. Simultaneously, PLA land-based missiles, rockets, and bombers, along with attack aircraft deployed from two Chinese carriers positioned off Taiwan's eastern coast, would pummel Taiwan's air bases in an attempt to take the island's relatively small air force out of commission before it could get into the fight—destroying runways, fuel depots, and maintenance infrastructure and targeting the island's prized fleet of F-16 fighter jets. Mainland-based precision-guided ballistic and cruise missiles, such as DF-17 hypersonics, together with long-range, truck-mounted PHL-16 multiple rocket launchers and kamikaze drones, would all target stationary radars, fixed weapons platforms, critical command, control, communications nodes, naval facilities, energy infrastructure, and TV and radio transmission towers to sow chaos and impede the highly centralized decision making of the Taiwanese military. American-built Patriot air defense batteries, as well as Taiwan's indigenously developed Sky Bow systems, troop barracks, and anti-ship batteries were also high priority targets.

Achieving the invasion's main political objective—the rapid assault and capture of key government installations in Taipei, including the

Presidential Office Building and the Ministry of National Defense—relied on assault forces delivered by dozens of fast Type 726 *Yuyi*-class air-cushioned landing craft (LCAC) racing up the Tamsui River. The wide but relatively shallow river snakes through the mountains that separate the beaches on Taiwan's western shore from the center of the city and empties into the strait in the Bali district right next to the Port of Taipei; its tributaries pass near most of the key government installations in the city. That geography meant that the LCACs—deployed from the *Yushen* amphibious ships sitting at the mouth of the Tamsui and powered by large gas turbines and capable of achieving speeds of eighty knots—could deliver a battalion of marines and armored vehicles directly into the heart of Taipei's government district in under fifteen minutes. The one-two punch of the fast boats advancing up the river while airborne troops landed via rotor- and fixed-wing aviation at the Taipei Songshan Airport would allow the PLA to rapidly bring the fight to Taiwan's seat of government. While the PLAN marines captured Taipei's government and communications centers, the armored and infantry divisions would arrive on the island's northwestern coast, unload at the port and nearby airport on the other side of the mountains from Taipei city center, and then drive onto the highways that encircle Taiwan, racing toward the key population centers and military bases and hoping to overwhelm defenses. Having exercised each element of the plan for years, including simulated fast LCAC-boat city assaults on the Pearl River near Hong Kong, Xi Jinping's military generals assured him that the plan would achieve a rapid conquest of Taiwan before the rest of the world, especially the United States, had a chance to intervene to save the island.

Xi Jinping chose November 13, 2028, as China's D-Day, loading up his invasion fleet and issuing his final ultimatum.

With little to show after years of so-called gray zone tactics aimed at nonviolently forcing Taiwan to choose political unification with the Chinese mainland—tactics that ranged from constant economic and military pressure to social and traditional media influence campaigns to bribing and blackmailing of politicians—Xi had finally concluded that only military force would bring about achievement of this long-desired objective. As the 2020s progressed, Chinese military planners had presented one alternative strategy after another, including a last-chance alternative to an all-out invasion: a naval and air blockade aimed at isolating the island, which was heavily reliant on food and energy imports, and forcing its surrender without a fight. But in meeting after meeting, presentation after presentation, war game after war game, the blockade seemed unlikely to succeed. Xi worried that America would undermine the blockade with its formidable underwater and surface naval fleet and air power; he also worried about the economic effects—how the rest of the world would react to a prolonged confrontation across the strait that would surely cause a humanitarian disaster on the island and supply chain disruptions beyond it, ripples that would impact China itself. The United States and its allies might even launch a counterblockade of Chinese maritime oil and gas imports, a move that could paralyze China before its own blockade took a decisive toll on Taiwan. Any Chinese naval blockade was also likely to provoke Taiwan to take the one step it had never yet formally done, declaring full independence and irrevocably changing the geopolitical status quo. And perhaps most crucially for Xi, the approach of laying a prolonged siege to the island ran counter to his strong preference for resolving China's Taiwan problem in a rapid and decisive manner—to rip off the Band-Aid and present the world with the fait accompli of Chinese conquest and the long-awaited integration of Taiwan into the People's Republic of China.

Thus, after spending that summer and fall in strategy sessions, briefings, and quiet lone contemplation at Beidaihe (the Communist Party elite's seaside retreat) and in the party's Zhongnanhai compound in Beijing, Xi had settled on an invasion. As he concluded, if he was to take the step of mobilizing the military, risk a conflict with America, and cause a potential global backlash, it was best to go all the way and try to end it as quickly as possible. Victory, he'd been told by his generals and military advisers, would be swift and the Taiwanese resistance would be quickly vanquished. They had assured him that China's decades-long investment in new military systems, weapons, and training would be decisive. It wasn't even clear to Xi and the

Communist Party's Central Military Commission that the Americans would ultimately choose to fight for Taiwan once they saw the might of the China invasion fleet, once they calculated the price of the war in tens of thousands of American lives. Even if they did fight, the US military was far away—nearly five hundred miles away on Okinawa or seventeen hundred miles away in Guam. "We can hold them at bay long enough while our airborne assault units quickly secure key critical infrastructure resources on the island, and our landing force rapidly crosses the strait and secures the rest of the country to create a sense of fait accompli," Xi's top military adviser had promised in the final briefing the previous week. Xi believed the time for hesitancy was over. The time to act was now. As he saw it, victory would be his and his place in history assured; his ascent into the pantheon of Chinese historical leaders would be unmatched.

For the West, the warning signs had been there all year, but the distracted United States had failed to heed them until it was too late. The groundwork for the invasion had begun in the fall of 2027, when Xi Jinping was reelected as the leader of the Chinese Communist Party (CCP), entering his third decade in power. At seventy-five, he was the oldest Chinese leader since Deng Xiaoping. That fall, in his speech to the National Congress of the Chinese Communist Party—always the party's most important event—Xi proclaimed that the next five years would be the time when China would finally achieve its dream—his dream—of "national rejuvenation."

Taiwan, meanwhile, had held a quadrennial presidential election in early January, resulting in the victory (and May inauguration) of a pro-independence, center-left candidate from the island's Democratic Progressive Party (DPP)—a political shift and repudiation of the Kuomintang and the pan-Blue coalition that had sought to preserve closer ties between the Chinese mainland and the Republic of China. Xi saw the election as the final nail in the coffin of China's desire to bring about unification with Taiwan without resorting to the use of force. The relations between Taipei and Beijing had deteriorated steadily since the 2016 election of President Tsai, also of the DPP, as successive DPP candidates for presidency repeatedly proclaimed,

"Taiwan does not need to declare independence because it is already an independent nation," a line that enraged Beijing.

And yet as the warning signs had gathered in the Pacific, the United States had found itself preoccupied—the 2028 Summer Olympics in Los Angeles had presented a captivating pageantry of nations, full of soft-focus TV feature stories and host-nation pride. The Olympic festivities had merged into wall-to-wall coverage of another contentious and fraught fall presidential election building up to the November 7 Election Day, a contest that piled on top of thirty-four Senate contests—including fierce, expensive battles in battleground states like Pennsylvania, Arizona, and Nevada—that had consumed the national media attention. As in many election years, Congress itself had adjourned for the fall in early September and its members spent much of the summer on the campaign trail.

As was customary, the outgoing presidential administration had begun transition conversations with both major party nominees, but the truth was most of the experienced government hands had left for the private sector earlier in the year. The White House, Pentagon, and State Department were shorthanded and org charts were riddled with "acting" officials meant to serve out just a few weeks longer.

Throughout much of the year, some of those acting officials had tried to raise warnings about Taiwan. Boeing was finally on track to complete the delivery of four hundred Harpoon anti-ship missiles in early 2029, missiles Taiwan had originally ordered in 2023. Beijing had warned in a January statement that the delivery of these missiles to Taiwan was unacceptable to China and would present a major threat to its naval forces—something the PLAN had said it couldn't and wouldn't tolerate.

Throughout late summer 2028, even as the Olympics dominated the news coverage, media reports in the *Washington Post* and the *New York Times* had cited anonymous intelligence community sources pointing to significant troop buildups at PLAN's East Sea Fleet port facilities of Ningbo, Xiamen, Xiangshan, and Zhoushan. Satellite photos showed new temporary housing being built to house substantial numbers of PLA ground forces. (Some pundits had pointed out that the reporting in many ways mirrored the prescient intelligence community warnings from 2021 and 2022 about Russia's invasion of Ukraine, but it was a tough year to get Americans to pay attention to an island on the other side of the world.) Open-source satellite imagery had tracked the movement of a dozen of Chinese amphibious assault ships and destroyers from the South Sea Fleet ports to Xiamen, the port facing Taiwan across the hundred-mile strait.

Whereas in 2021 and 2022, a constant stream of world leaders and US officials had shuttled among European capitals and Moscow to discuss Russia's worrisome military buildup along the borders of Ukraine and try to discourage Vladimir Putin from launching an invasion, in 2028 Beijing had remained beyond reach. Xi and the CCP resisted any and all efforts at international dialogue—rejecting meetings, summits, or visiting delegations that might deescalate the crisis. China kept characteristically silent as these troubling developments unfolded; over and over again, the Foreign Ministry spokesperson had responded to queries with a simple "We do not comment on internal Chinese national security matters that should be of no concern to foreign parties."

The morning after the US election—even before the presidential winner was known or the balance of the US Congress could be predicted—the outgoing White House national security adviser held a press conference to announce that the United States had developed "high-confidence all-source" intelligence indicating that China was planning to launch an invasion of Taiwan in the coming weeks. The national security adviser revealed that the United States was sharing that intelligence with NATO allies, Japan, Australia, and Taiwan; she added that China had begun moving heavy weaponry—tanks, armored vehicles, artillery systems—as well as logistics such as food rations, water, and munitions to naval port facilities in the East China Sea for loading onto ships. PLAN had also started absorbing large civilian cargo ships and China's armed coast guard vessels under its command. Meanwhile, the United States was also moving another aircraft carrier battlegroup to the region—the USS *John F. Kennedy* (CVN 79), the world's biggest warship, was coming from its port in

San Diego and scheduled to arrive in ten days, the White House announced, to complement the USS *Ronald Reagan* (CVN 76) currently streaming toward Guam; a third carrier, officials whispered to the press, the USS *Theodore Roosevelt* (CVN 71), would probably be able to deploy by the end of the month.

That afternoon, from Beijing, the Chinese foreign ministry spokesperson denied the "White House lies" and proclaimed that "China is a peace-loving nation, and it's America that continually wages wars of aggression." He also said that Taiwan remained an internal China issue of vital importance to the Chinese people and that China expected all nations to abide by their One China principle commitments and not violate Chinese sovereignty.*

The BBC and French BFM-TV both reported on November 9 that Chinese ambassadors appeared to have fanned out across European capitals denying that China was preparing an invasion. At the same time, the news channels reported that each ambassador brought with them a highly detailed and customized presentation showing the economic ties, trade, and key import/exports between the respective European countries and China, as well as a historic recounting of the One China principle. The ambassadors all privately delivered a seemingly boilerplate and coordinated communication that should any war break out in the Taiwan Strait, it would be the fault of the Taiwanese secessionist government and their American enablers—a situation, they implied, that it would be best for Europe to stay out of. They all expressed their hope for continued peaceful development of economic ties between China and its European partners.

It was only around 3 p.m. on Saturday, November 11, that the US presidential election had a declared winner, once CNN announced

---

* The One China principle is a unilateral and not widely recognized position held by the Chinese Communist Party that the People's Republic of China is the sole legitimate sovereign state under the name of "China" and that Taiwan is an inalienable part of it. The One China *policy*, on the other hand, is a US diplomatic position of strategic ambiguity on the issue that merely "acknowledges that all Chinese on either side of the Taiwan Strait maintain there is but one China and that Taiwan is a part of China"—but importantly does not endorse the Chinese position.

that the leader in preelection polls had climbed over the 270 electoral vote mark. (Other networks followed suit shortly.)

And then, at noon Beijing time on Monday, November 13, 2028—around 11 p.m. the evening of Sunday the twelfth in Washington, DC—having completed its military buildup and with its forces poised to invade, China issued an ultimatum to Taipei demanding that the DPP president sign an agreement to voluntarily and peacefully join the People's Republic of China or face immediate consequences.

It took less than an hour for Taiwan to publicly reject the blackmail threat, and the Taiwanese president spoke on national radio and television shortly after 6 p.m. Taipei time (5 a.m. Washington time). Four minutes into the president's remarks, the internet across the island went offline, television screens across Taiwan went blank, and the radio stations went silent. Notably, though, the electrical power stayed on at the Tainan Science Park, where the high-tech chip fabs of the Taiwan Semiconductor Manufacturing Company continued to churn away.

Earlier that night, a phone rang in the Situation Room at the White House, as did another in the sensitive compartmented information facility (SCIF) installed in the Madison, Wisconsin, hotel where the president-elect had set up the transition headquarters. As the incoming national security adviser went to wake the president-elect, in DC, the outgoing national security adviser went to wake the president, replaying in her mind on the way up the stairs to the Executive Residence the years of the Pentagon's own war-game assessments of the terrible costs of potential war with China over Taiwan.

Tens of thousands of American personnel would be killed within days, while hundreds of aircraft and dozens of naval ships would be lost. In addition, air bases—such as Kadena Air Base on Okinawa, Marine Corps Air Station Iwakuni on Japan's main island, and Andersen Air Force Base on Guam—would be bombed, and worse, ballistic missiles might even target sites in the continental United States, like Naval Air Station North Island on Coronado in San Diego Bay and Whiteman Air Force Base in Missouri, the base of the long-range B-2 bombers. The Office of the Director of National Intelligence has also long warned that Chinese cyberattacks would almost certainly be launched against America's energy and transportation infrastructure; this was a conflict that would be felt in every corner of the US economy. And then there was the risk of a nuclear exchange, the probability of which was hard to estimate but couldn't be dismissed. This was no limited conflict, like Iraq or Afghanistan, or even a large-scale war like Vietnam or Korea.

No, the national security adviser thought, *should the president and America decide to defend Taiwan, war with China would be unlike anything the country had experienced since World War II.*

Introduction

I was in high school in Chattanooga, Tennessee, in the mid-1990s, when my father and I started my first company. My dad had been a nuclear physicist and applied mathematician in the Soviet Union working on designing nuclear power plants but couldn't find a job in the US nuclear industry, which had been in the deep winter and not building new nuclear reactors since the Three Mile Island scare in 1979. Instead, he'd ended up getting a job as a programmer in the energy sector, which was fine in terms of putting food on the table for our family but not work he found particularly stimulating. He got interested instead in the relatively nascent field of cryptography, and we launched a small company working in encryption and developing secure communications. My dad focused on the algorithms, while I took care of the business side. The company didn't end up doing extremely well, in part due to both of us having little time to dedicate to the business—him with a full-time job and me still in school—but for a high school kid, it was an amazing experience.

It opened my eyes for the first time to the broader emerging challenges of the digital world that people were just starting to appreciate in the '90s. I quickly realized that encryption and cryptography weren't the ultimate solution to securing our data and computer systems; rather, they were just *part* of the solution—if someone stole your keys, it didn't matter how good your code or algorithms were. No matter how mathematically ingenious your solutions might be, if someone got your key, it was still game over. I realized that cybersecurity (or "information security" as it was called back then) was a cat-and-mouse game between attackers and defenders, where no one had a permanent advantage and where both sides would be in a constant battle trying to defeat the other and protect—or steal—the crown jewels.

And that was my first big insight into the world of business and geopolitics. Understanding your adversary was essential—how they thought, what they valued, what they considered success or defeat. That realization led me to Georgia Tech, where I earned the school's first graduate degree in cybersecurity, and then into startups. I joined a small, two-hundred-person company right after finishing college in 2003 and stumbled into a specific corner where the adversary's innovation was happening at breakneck speed: spam.

Coming out of college, I interviewed with a company called CipherTrust that was focused on building secure encrypted email. They were interested in my background in cryptography, and I remember asking the CEO, Jay Chaudhry (now the CEO of another cyber company with a $30-plus billion market cap), in the interview process, "What's the product today and where is it going?" He explained that his company was temporarily refocusing the product development on email spam, which at the time was less than 10 percent of email—a minor nuisance. He said, "We've paused our work on encryption, and we're going to spend a quarter or two focused on spam, and then we'll go back to working on the thing that our customers really want—email encryption." I ended up joining the research team whose job was to "solve" the spam problem. Needless to say, we never went back to encryption. Within roughly a year, spam went from being 2 percent of email traffic to being 90 percent of email traffic—it became the problem every company was trying to solve.

Initially, spam was merely annoying—flooding inboxes with emails promoting Viagra and porn—but soon our adversaries learned it had more lucrative uses. The problem quickly evolved into phishing, botnets, and all other nefarious activities that we see today. It all happened within about eighteen months. And I had a front-row seat to watch the threat evolve in real time.

Much of the world's spam was emanating from criminals in Russia and other former Soviet republics in the early 2000s, and as I researched and worked to block the latest tactics, I watched our adversaries learn and adapt. The spammers weren't very focused on operational security back then, and using my Russian-language skills I could read their public discussions on web forums about what they were doing and how they were evolving their tactics to defeat the latest defenses we created. This wasn't, I realized, about learning how to block a particular email in an inbox—there were people on the other side learning from each of our moves. We evolved. They adapted to our countermeasures. I realized that collecting intelligence and understanding what an adversary's motivations are and where they're headed is fundamental to cybersecurity. It was a lesson that I would carry forward as my own work in the industry evolved from fighting spam to combatting intrusions and countering hackers.

It was a lesson, too, that I would carry with me as I moved from looking at criminal gangs just trying to steal a buck to confronting nation-states tapping into our economic advantage, stealing national security secrets, and destabilizing our political system. Cybersecurity is unique, too, as a science because it's one of the few applied sciences where the problem is human-made—there is a sentient opponent on the other side watching and adapting to everything you do. Unlike say in medicine, where one day a particular disease might be cured, you are never *done* in cybersecurity: as long as there are people, criminal organizations, and nation-states that wish to do us harm, you will always need to stay vigilant and evolve your defenses. It is also the only realm of national security where we ask the private sector to directly take on foreign adversaries; during World War II, we never asked Ford Motor Company or Shell Gasoline to develop their own strategy for defending against and defeating the Nazis, nor during the Cold War did we ever push MGM or R. J. Reynolds to build their own fighter jets or tanks to secure their corporate headquarters from the Soviet military. And yet today, day in and day out, America's companies are on the front lines of cyber battles, defending their networks against the intelligence services, militaries, and criminals operating out of China, Russia, Iran, and North Korea—a lesson that many companies, from Sony Pictures to Colonial Pipeline, have learned the hard way.

That lesson was one I learned early in my cybersecurity career. One particular moment stands out in my own digital battles over the last two decades: Operation Aurora.

Few back in 2009 were thinking about how nation-states were targeting organizations in cyberspace. The internet's problems at the time mostly revolved around relatively small-time criminals involved in email spam, credit card fraud, bank account compromise, and identity theft. Cybersecurity companies focused on the technical side of such problems, such as limiting data breaches, patching software, and combating malware. But then in 2009 I found myself working for McAfee—one of the largest cybersecurity companies of the day—and running the investigation of a series of hacks targeting Google and about two dozen other US companies by an entity that appeared linked to the Chinese government. Here we had a nation-state posing a specific risk to private US companies across a range of industries, from technology and manufacturing to defense.

I realized that much of my industry was getting it wrong: they talked about the Google hack as if it was some specific piece of malware or technical tool that had been discovered. For me, though, a light bulb went off: *This is not about malware. This is not about how they got in. This is not about the technical details of the attack*. It's about the *who*. The state of China had been hacking into Google to steal emails of Tibetan dissidents and others in order to collect intelligence on people in China—thefts that could potentially have life-threatening consequences for those activists. More broadly, China was stealing the intellectual property of American industry. The *who* was fundamental to the *why*. Knowing who your adversary was told you what you needed to protect and how to defend yourself.

As my team and I examined the data from the intrusions into Google and other large companies, I felt like I was watching the world change before my eyes. Deep in the malware, I spotted the word

"Aurora," a word that instantly resonated with me from the Soviet history drilled into me during my school years in Moscow in the 1980s, and so I decided to name the hack Operation Aurora. *Aurora*, after all, was the Crimean War–era cruiser stationed in St. Petersburg that in 1917 fired the shot to signal Lenin's Bolsheviks to launch the October Revolution. That shot changed the course of the twentieth century, and indeed of world history—leading to the establishment of the Soviet Union, the spread of communism around the world, and the launch of the Cold War—and I instantly felt that this hack marked another momentous and historic turning point. It was the first major hack of a private company that anyone had ever attributed publicly to a foreign nation-state adversary, an attack on the private sector by hackers from another country's intelligence services.

When I started pulling on the strings of that investigation, I realized there were many other related attacks taking place that few were paying attention to and no one was talking publicly about. In 2011 my team and I revealed Operation Night Dragon, a large-scale set of intrusions from China into Western oil and gas companies to steal data that would advantage Chinese state-owned enterprises in this sector. Six months later I unveiled another Chinese campaign—Operation Shady RAT, a name that played on the "remote access tool" the attackers used to gain access to compromised networks—that targeted seventy-one organizations, from US defense contractors to the International Olympics Committee over the course of more than five years. I was finding large-scale cyber espionage attacks everywhere. The realization of the scope of the Chinese intrusions into Western companies made me coin another phrase that has since become common cybersecurity lore—often quoted by the likes of FBI and NSA directors and CEOs of companies like Cisco: "There are only two types of companies—those that know that they have been hacked and those that don't yet know."

The Night Dragon hackers in particular were so sloppy that they left Chinese fingerprints all over the operation, including malware that had Chinese language sprinkled throughout. As we examined the targets, we could see the hackers had been stealing data, particularly data on new exploratory oil and gas projects that China wanted to compete on in Central Asia and elsewhere around the world.

I realized that the sloppiness might work to our advantage: maybe, for the first time, I could even find the individual people doing this. Indeed, as I dug in, I found that one of those involved in building Night Dragon's online infrastructure had carelessly purchased servers used to control the malware in his own name. I shared it with a few reporters when we published our findings. A Beijing-based reporter for the Associated Press called up our suspect, and amazingly enough, he casually confessed, "Our company alone has a great number of hackers [as customers]," telling the reporter in a telephone interview, "I have several hundred of them among all my customers."[1]

It was a stunning revelation: I had stripped away the supposed anonymity of the internet and found an individual in China who was helping to attack US companies and steal economic data.

The real-world ramifications for McAfee came quickly: the company had a small sales office in China and the Chinese authorities visited it hours after our public report was published. They turned the place upside down, panicked the staff, and threatened the company with a clear message: don't ever publish details about Chinese intrusions again. The McAfee leadership came down hard on me too—the company didn't want to risk its Chinese business, either in terms of financial losses or endangering its domestic personnel there. The CEO told me to knock it off with China. I listened—sort of.

In the next attack I dove into, we traced it back not to China but to North Korea. We found hackers who had actually launched a destructive attack, attempting to wipe out the computers of a South Korean bank. It was evidence to me that the problem wasn't just China: countries were beginning to understand that the cyber domain was a place where they could use leverage to coerce others and enforce their will.

The attacks, one after another, convinced me that our industry was missing the worldwide change taking place around us. Until our investigations, virtually no cybersecurity firm was focused on the details of the person behind the keyboard. Cybersecurity firms still focused on the tech: *How do we defend against a piece of malware? How do we patch against this specific vulnerability?* That mindset needed to change. This realization led me to want to launch a company focused on the adversary and change the way our entire industry thought about its work. The key questions to me weren't technical. They were strategic. The question wasn't how you stop the Night Dragon hackers from compromising your system; the challenge for the US government was "How do we stop China?" For that, there were both technical and nontechnical solutions. And at every stage of the cyber problem, intelligence would be fundamental. We had to understand our adversary in order to address the technical attacks, which meant attributing every attack as best as possible.

The realization led me to create a model for the company I founded after leaving McAfee, CrowdStrike, which would go on to become one of the biggest and most financially successful in the cybersecurity industry. Our mantra was simple: *you don't have a malware problem, you have an adversary problem.*

The same thought process applies on the global stage, too. As a nation, we don't have a cyber problem. We have a China, Russia, Iran, and North Korea problem. Solving each of them isn't about the technology, it's about the people and geopolitics. We must understand our adversaries—and ourselves—to know where our leverage exists around the globe.

And today, America's top foreign policy challenge is its China problem.

THERE IS A LONG PATH BETWEEN TODAY AND THE FICTIONAL EVENTS of November 13, 2028, laid out in the Prologue. We should hope that this fictional scenario never unfolds, but over the last two years, the West has seemingly woken up to the fact that there is a nonzero chance that we may end up in a scenario very much like the one I lay out, perhaps in 2028 or sometime after. We stand today at a critical inflection point for US foreign policy, America's role in the world, and the twenty-first century more broadly—a moment where the United States and its Western allies are confronting seriously for the first time the implications of the economic and military rise of China, reckoning with how Xi Jinping has accelerated the timeline of China's ambitions and what that means to our future and our allies, like Taiwan.

We are a World on the Brink.

The first two decades of America's foreign policy in the twenty-first century were defined, for better or worse—and largely, for the worse—by wars of choice. The next two decades are going to be defined by whether the United States can avoid a war with China, a conflict that neither country views as an optional or desired "war of choice," but one that nonetheless looms so clearly and whose stakes are so well-defined that the possibility of such a war will hang over nearly every engagement between the two great powers for the next decade.

It's common today to hear pundits and prognosticators talk about how America's influence is waning, about how the rise of China, authoritarian trends around the world, our humiliating military loss in Afghanistan, and Russia's invasion of Ukraine mean the globe's primary superpower now exists in a multipolar world, where its enemies are emboldened and where it is losing influence globally. Emerging from the COVID-19 pandemic, our country is supposedly weaker at home and abroad. The American Century is over, we're told; the twenty-first century belongs instead to China.

The truth is more complicated: Yes, the world has changed, but America still has no equal in the world. It's just been playing the wrong cards and following the wrong strategy. In fact, America's more powerful than many even in our country think it is. And, crucially, our adversaries are weaker than many believe they are.

China's period as a global superpower might not last a century—it might not even endure a generation. Instead, we're entering a period that may last as little as thirty years, before China's demographic and economic challenges overtake its apparent success. In fact, we're watching our two primary foreign adversaries—Russia and China—make ruinous decisions for their own countries, with Vladimir Putin's disastrous decision to invade Ukraine and Xi Jinping's economically destructive policies like Zero-COVID, tech industry crackdowns at home, and antagonistic wolf warrior diplomacy abroad.

Those stumbles follow nearly four decades during which China masterfully pursued a strategy of rising quietly—boosting its economic and military capabilities in ways that often were too subtle or seemed too small to provoke a strong Western response. But in recent years, an impatient Xi Jinping moved too quickly and too aggressively, waking the world to the China challenge before the country's development was complete and secure. The Russian invasion of Ukraine has crystalized attention too on the hunger Xi and the CCP leadership have for retaking Taiwan and "reuniting" China, a threat that until relatively recently had seemed both out of reach militarily and an almost anachronistic throwback to an era where big countries seized territory by force.

Today, I see an adversary who is behaving—and appears to be thinking—along the same lines that ultimately led Vladimir Putin to launch his large-scale invasion of Ukraine in 2022. When on December 21, 2021, I announced on Twitter, "I have become increasingly convinced that Kremlin has unfortunately made a decision to invade Ukraine later this winter," and laid out seven signals that to me indicated Russia wasn't merely bluffing, the argument came as a startling surprise to many inside and outside Washington, where it went against the grain of widely shared analysis. My thread received thousands of retweets and tens of millions of views. Today, the gathering clouds around Taiwan look worryingly similar.

But, whereas our runway before Russia's invasion was just weeks or months, recent developments around China's threatening buildup give us time to prepare. In fact, these new geopolitical signals, along with Xi's other recent leadership stumbles at home, present us with an important opportunity. We have a unique moment and capability to counter China in a way now that would have been impossible if the country had kept growing more quietly for ten or twenty more years. We must make the most of this small window of opportunity. It won't stay open for long.

These self-inflicted wounds provide the best opportunity the United States has had in three decades to refocus around the only foreign policy goal in the twenty-first century that really should matter: avoiding that hot conflict with China while ensuring our country remains dominant on the global stage. We are trying to do too many things in too many places and not focusing, intensely, on what should be the main priority of our foreign and domestic policy: winning. By this I mean preserving our unrivaled geopolitical and economic power, while averting a catastrophic war, one that would almost certainly cost us dearly in blood and our economic well-being.

Now, after decades of spreading ourselves too thin, in too many places, in nonstrategic ways, the United States is entering the most dangerous and destabilizing geopolitical period since the beginning of the Cold War (what I will argue in the pages ahead we should really call Cold War I): a generation in which China's economic and political power will peak before the PRC suffers the consequences of a coming demographic collapse, powered by the aftereffects of its one-child policy and amplified by the inevitable birth rate declines experienced by nearly all developed societies. During this dangerous generation we need to find ways to maximize our own economic and political leverage and navigate through it with our own strengths intact and enhanced.

Today there is no challenge on the geopolitical landscape equal to countering the rise of China and its potential disruption of the global security order that the United States has led and fostered since the end of World War II. This will be an unprecedented moment in our history. In our own near-century of global leadership, the United States has never really faced a true peer competitor. "For more than a century, no US adversary or coalition of adversaries reached 60 percent of US GDP," strategist Rush Doshi writes, but China has already surpassed that mark, all the way back in 2014.[2] As Doshi observes, "China's scale and its increasingly global ambitions are geopolitical facts, and the country seeks to set the terms for the twenty-first century in the same way that the United States set them for the twentieth."[3]

The threat goes to the center of the most basic of our global strategic goals and realities. As Elbridge Colby, the primary architect of the Pentagon's 2018 national defense strategy, writes, the simplest statement of the United States' foreign policy and security objectives is "to maintain the nation's territorial integrity and, within that territory, security from foreign attack; sustain a free, autonomous, and vigorous democratic-republican political order; and enable economic flourishing and growth."[4] This task is ours alone to fulfill. There is no one else to do it if we don't rise to the occasion—there is no other equal force to the United States on the global stage and no other geopolitical team equal to the Western alliance.

We are late waking up to this challenge from China; for much of this century, US companies thought the benefit of Chinese business outweighed the potential cost—I lived much of this firsthand in the cybersecurity field, as I watched Chinese government hackers pillage Western intellectual property while corporate leaders and boards looked the other way rather than risk losing access to the lucrative Chinese market. A C-level leader at a Fortune 500 company once told me, "We know China is robbing us blind. But we can't afford to get out of their market. Our only hope is that we would innovate faster than they can steal the results of our research." It was never a strategy with much of a chance of success. Competing with a country that is simultaneously robbing you blind while investing in indigenous research and development performed by a large, highly educated population was always a recipe for failure. It was really only during the final years of the Obama administration that American policy leaders began to think differently about China, a trend that accelerated and became more prominent under Trump and has largely continued under Biden. As late as 2016 President Obama argued America should root for a "successful, rising China," but that same year, the US Navy acknowledged it was entering a new epoch: "For the first time in 25 years, the United States is facing a return to great power competition. Russia and China both have advanced their military capabilities to act as global powers."[5]

Today, we see and understand a very different China, one that threatens the global community that has tried to keep a global war from breaking out for almost eighty years, and we realize that a confrontation with a nuclear-armed China is a real possibility.

A war between the West and China would be devastating, potentially costing tens of thousands or even hundreds of thousands of lives in a short time span and wreaking economic havoc that the world hasn't seen since the Great Depression. There is no small, contained war with China. Any such war is a naval war, a missile war, a space war, and a cyber war. It is also, almost certainly, one that pulls in allies and US territory almost from the start—it's hard to believe that any fight with the United States over Taiwan would not include preemptive or retaliatory strikes against our military facilities in Japan, Guam, Hawaii, and perhaps even the US mainland. It would, in many ways, be foolish for China, if it becomes convinced that the United States will come to Taiwan's defense as President Biden has now publicly promised on four separate occasions, to embark on any large military expedition without targeting US and allied assets located nearby. And in the event of such strikes, the United States would almost certainly retaliate with its own strikes on the Chinese mainland. Indeed, even if the Chinese do not target American territory in a first strike, should the United States decide to enter the war to preserve Taiwan's freedom it might have to choose to bomb Chinese air bases to neutralize the threat to US naval ships in the region—and such strikes would almost certainly provoke Chinese retaliation against the US mainland. Where and when such a conflict might end—between two nuclear-armed powers no less—is anyone's guess.

Stopping short of a shooting war must be the guiding imperative of US foreign policy, but the reality is we're already locked into a conflict that is something less than war but far from a harmonious cooperative peace. Everyone has their own less-than-war analogy—Henry Kissinger said we're in the "foothills of a Cold War," while Harvard professor Noah Feldman calls it a "Cool War" and international relations scholar Michael Doyle calls it a "Cold Peace."[6] But none of the analogies work quite as well as "Cold War II."

Cold War II is in some ways not quite the zero-sum ideological fight that the United States found itself in with the Soviet Union. And the United States and China are deeply commercially intertwined—a major distinction from Cold War I. We are entangled too by a whole host of other issues, where the United States and China need or want to work cooperatively, like nuclear nonproliferation, global conflict resolution, and climate change. But the primary underlying challenge is mostly the same: Who gets to define the global security order?

While it's easy to shorthand the current challenge as the "US versus China," the geopolitical landscape is vastly more complex. There are at least three highly independent players—the United States, China, and Taiwan itself—even before you get to our other perennial adversaries Russia, Iran, and North Korea, not to mention the countries populating the complex geopolitical geography of Asia, from Japan, South Korea, India, Vietnam, and the Philippines, among others, and the differing economic-driven priorities of the European Union and the United Kingdom. "Cold War II so far is much less global in its reach and the sides are less clear-cut," Doyle writes.[7] Thus far, we have failed to reckon with that multidimensional dynamic and how it will shape the geopolitical challenge to come.

From his earliest moments at the top of the Chinese system, Xi has made national rejuvenation and the China Dream a cornerstone of his platform. As he has said, "Everyone has an ideal, ambition and dream. We are now all talking about the Chinese Dream. In my opinion, achieving the rejuvenation of the Chinese nation has been the greatest dream of the Chinese people since the advent of modern times. This dream embodies the long-cherished hope of several generations of the Chinese people, gives expression to the overall interests of the Chinese nation and the Chinese people, and represents the shared aspiration of all the sons and daughters of the Chinese nation."[8] In fact, Xi has been even more blunt; according to a December 2023 NBC News report, he explicitly told President Biden during their San Francisco summit "that Beijing will reunify Taiwan with mainland China but that the timing has not yet been decided." We should take his own statements seriously.

Our goal today, one that extends the American Century for many decades to come, is simple: we have to make some smart decisions, increase our leverage, contain our adversaries, and wait them out, because—long term—we've got all the advantages, from strong and broad geopolitical alliances to economic might to a more durable and adaptive system of government. But doing so will require rethinking our domestic policies, our global alliances, and maximizing our leverage around the world. Beating China requires us to reframe our engagement with other lesser adversaries like Russia, North Korea, and Iran and to view our work with allies, and partners like India and Vietnam, through that same lens.

We've actually done this successfully before. During the Cold War—that is, Cold War I—strategists spoke of the "window of vulnerability," in the 1950s, and the "year of maximum danger," in 1983, when the superpowers briefly came very close to nuclear conflict. Yet, by patiently practicing deterrence—protecting Western Europe from Soviet invasion—and waiting out the inevitable economic-driven decline of the Soviet Union's power, we won the first Cold War. Today, we need just as careful and strategic an approach to this new conflict. China's success is not a foregone conclusion—nor is its failure. America's actions will help decide who wins the race for global leadership. If we make ill-considered choices, if we dilute our focus and attention into too many areas, and, in a worst-case scenario, allow the CCP to succeed in its quest to retake Taiwan, China can still emerge dominant and victorious in this century—a shift in geopolitical balance with profound ramifications for America's economy, its workers, and the global security order.

However, by playing our cards smartly, America can win the twenty-first century and come out stronger at home and abroad. The unrivaled dominance of the US technology and financial sectors is a source of unprecedented leverage for resolving America's global challenges and securing the nation's economic and geopolitical future for future generations. The weapons that are required to win in this new age of great power competition are not just people, drones, missiles, ships, and aircraft but sanctions and export controls, smart trade policy, effective domestic industrial policy, software, and hardware. Rethinking and reorienting America's place in the twenty-first century requires the nation to better think about, deploy, and maximize the incredible leverage it actually has over the global economy—from pop culture to the US dollar to semiconductors.

Over the next decade, the United States and its Western alliance have to walk an incredibly thin and delicate line: every morning, we want Xi to wake up and think, "Today's not the day to invade Taiwan," but also to imagine that tomorrow *could* be—after all, we don't want him to undertake a rash action, even if he believes the chances of success are low, because he has realized that the window to take Taiwan is about to close permanently. Stalling day by day is a winning strategy. Just as it was in Cold War I, time is on America's side in Cold War II. But we must use that time wisely.

Over two thousand years ago, amid the Third Punic War, Cato the Elder used to finish his speeches before the Roman Senate with his rallying cry, *delenda est Carthago*: "Carthage must be destroyed." Today, our rallying cry—the central organizing principle of American foreign, trade, defense, and industrial policy this century—must be *Sinae deterrendae sunt*. China must be deterred.

PART I

Cold War II, a New Era

CHAPTER 1

The Road to the Brink

SOMEDAY, WHEN THEY KNOW THE ENDING AND HOW THE COMING years and decades unfold, historians will debate when Cold War II started—what was this era's Churchill Iron Curtain speech in Fulton, Missouri, or the George Kennan "Long Telegram" of the US-China tensions? There's a good argument to be made that May 2014 should be considered the time when the United States took its first steps to acknowledging that it is already in Cold War II, the moment when the reality of years of growing tensions—and the outlines of years more tension to come—crystalized in a single month and both the United States and China took major steps to escalate and define the terms of their conflict.

On the US side, it was May 19, 2014, when the Justice Department launched a groundbreaking indictment of five Chinese soldiers working for the People's Liberation Army Unit 61398, one of its most prolific hacking units, for targeting US companies in a sweeping campaign of economic espionage. It was a hacking team that I knew all too well—the same one I had described with my Operation Shady RAT report, a team in the cyber industry we called "Comment Crew."

The unprecedented criminal charges marked the government's public acknowledgment of the devastating espionage campaign I'd been watching for years. For more than a decade, Chinese military and intelligence officers had been hacking US and other Western companies, stealing trade secrets and pillaging intellectual property. That economic espionage came at a real cost to American jobs, and even today most Americans don't realize the extent to which China's explosive economic growth has been supercharged by thefts of Western knowledge and the displacement of US industries.

The Justice Department charges were the latest move in a three-year-long effort to raise the specter of that Chinese threat and the danger, specifically, of Comment Crew. Amid my Shady RAT report in 2011, I had called out China for engaging in "a historically unprecedented transfer of wealth . . . negotiation plans and exploration details for new oil and gas field auctions, document stores, legal contracts, SCADA configurations, design schematics and much more has 'fallen off the truck' of numerous, mostly Western companies."[1*]

The frustrations of the rhetorical handcuffs I faced at McAfee led me to leave; I turned in my notice days after the release of the report and launched CrowdStrike a month later. Later, in 2013, the spotlight returned back to Comment Crew with a highly impressive seventy-four-page report by one of our primary competitors—a cybersecurity company called Mandiant—about a group they called APT1, their own name for Comment Crew. The APT1 report revealed that the hackers were part of PLA's Second Bureau of the Third Department of the General Staff, also known as Unit 61398, located in a white nondescript building protected by a military guard in Shanghai. A year later, the Justice Department indictment targeted that same team.

The Justice Department's message with the indictments was clear. China was violating international norms—countries may spy on one

* The explosive revelations took the world by storm—becoming a top news story in Western papers and television newscasts around the globe. Escaping the usual confines of geopolitical coverage of the *New York Times*, *Washington Post*, and CNN, the story even became the main feature in *Vanity Fair*.

another and companies may compete against each other, sometimes aggressively so, but countries shouldn't use government resources to target private companies to steal their intellectual property and trade secrets to help their domestic competitors.

China made two major moves of its own that May in 2014—each of which would, in retrospect, announce major new chapters of China's strategy to seize control of the South China Sea, bit by tiny bit. Early that month, Vietnam found that China's premier billion-dollar oil-drilling platform, a vessel known as *Haiyang Shiyou 981*, was setting up shop inside what Vietnam considered its own Exclusive Economic Zone, about 120 miles east of Vietnam's Ly Son Island. China, confronted, announced it was exploring drilling nearby and, in the days and weeks that followed, a fleet of Vietnamese and Chinese vessels, ranging from fishing boats to law enforcement and militia boats to coast guard cutters, began a tense showdown. "By the middle of May, Hanoi claimed that China had deployed 130 vessels to the scene; Beijing said Vietnam had 60 ships involved," wrote South China Sea expert Gregory Poling. Diplomatic protests spread, from Vietnam to the United States to Japan and even the EU, and China eventually pulled back—*Haiyang Shiyou 981* moved twenty miles closer to China on May 27.

That same month, on the other side of the South China Sea, another crisis erupted, as the Philippines publicized and protested a Chinese dredging effort at Johnson Reef, an all-but meaningless rock in the Spratly Islands of the South China Sea. The reef, which is only above the water at low tide, had been previously the scene of a deadly showdown in March 1988, when China and Vietnam were tussling over the Spratlys. After a Chinese group of four ships harassed Vietnamese ships in the area, Vietnamese troops landed and tried to erect their flag on Johnson Reef, only to touch off a battle with Chinese forces. Exactly how and what unfolded has long been in dispute, but when it was over, two Vietnamese transports were sunk, a tank landing ship was destroyed, and sixty-four Vietnamese personnel were dead. China had occupied the reef ever since, and in May 2014 photos began circulating of a giant dredging project by the Chinese-owned *Tianjing*, the largest dredging ship in Asia.[2] The operation, as it turned out, had been ongoing for months, creating a harbor and some twenty-seven acres of land. Later, it became clear that the dredging had also helped cover up a sophisticated poaching operation, whereby a Chinese fishing fleet from Hainan had pulverized the reef to harvest giant clams and then taken the clams back to China for market while the *Tianjing* moved in. "Everything about the operation was illegal under both Chinese and international law. But the *Tianjing* crew helped destroy the evidence and the scale of their poaching, which soon extended to dozens of reefs across the Spratlys and Paracels, wouldn't be known for years," Poling writes. That spring, the *Tianjing* also dredged at two other reefs and finally, on May 22, moved on to a fourth that would soon sprout thirty-four acres of newly created land for China's territorial ambitions.

Nine days later, Defense Secretary Chuck Hagel stood at the Shangri-La Dialogue security confab in Singapore and, along with Japanese prime minister Shinzo Abe, denounced China's "destabilizing, unilateral activities in the South China Sea." Stability, Hagel and others argued, rested instead in international cooperation. Hagel defended the system of alliances that the United States had helped craft over seventy-five years and pointed to the emerging defense ties between the United States and Vietnam—a remarkable turnaround, he noted, as he and Vietnamese defense minister, General Phùng Quang Thanh, had both joined their nation's military in 1967 when the two countries were locked in a bloody war.[3] Now, nearly a half century later, they were discussing cooperating together against a common threat. China's actions threatened this framework in the Pacific. As Hagel said, "The United States will not look the other way when fundamental principles of the international order are being challenged."[4]

It was the same message that the Justice Department had delivered in Washington that month with the hacking indictments: *China was trying to upend the international order, and the United States wouldn't let that stand.*

CHINA AND THE UNITED STATES ALMOST ENDED UP ON A VERY DIFFERENT path. On March 5, 1946, General George C. Marshall,

America's hero of World War II, stood on a remote airstrip in northwest China, a place called Yan'an, with Chairman Mao Zedong to proclaim a new age of cooperation. "An unprecedented era of progress awaits China," Marshall proclaimed. Mao, in turn, promised, "The entire people of our country should feel grateful and loudly shout, 'long live cooperation between China and the United States!'"

For Marshall, even amid a life of hard-won triumphs and conquests, a man who no less than Winston Churchill had called the "organizer of victory" in World War II, a man who had achieved the rare and distinguished rank of a five-star general—an honor bestowed upon just nine men in American history—that day in China was a particular achievement. He and his boss, President Harry Truman, believed they were securing a bright and collegial future for China, establishing a fledgling democracy on the Asian continent that would bring the nationalist Kuomintang government, led by Chiang Kai-shek, and the communist revolutionaries under Mao together under a single, united team.

It was a huge moment for the postwar era. After all, the conflagration that would come to be known as World War II had started not in Poland in 1939 but in China in 1937, where Japan's imperial desires first led to an attack on the mainland of a country then torn apart by a decade-long civil war between Chiang's nationalist Kuomintang government and Mao's communist forces, who had headquartered themselves around Yan'an in an area known as Revolutionary Base Area. As the United States entered the war and the tide in the Pacific turned against Japan, Franklin Roosevelt embraced Chiang, even inviting him to the Cairo Conference in 1943 to sit alongside himself and Churchill, the first non-Western leader to do so, and US aid in the Lend-Lease program helped sustain Chiang's fight. (At that conference, the allied leaders fatefully decided to return the island of Formosa, now known as Taiwan, which had been taken by Japan in 1895, to China.) As FDR saw it, "450,000,000 Chinese would some day [*sic*] be united and modernized and would be the most important factor in the whole East."[5]

During World War II, fifteen out of the sixteen Doolittle Tokyo Raider bombers crash-landed in China. US bombers repeatedly struck

Japan from Chinese airfields and Chinese forces fought more than half a million Japanese troops on the ground. The war in China and Japan's occupation had been especially brutal. A sixth of the nation's population was displaced and turned into refugees; some fourteen million Chinese were estimated to have been killed during the war and under Japan's occupation (a national toll only exceeded by the Soviet Union); and among the tens of thousands of Chinese prisoners taken by the Japanese throughout the conflict, only fifty-six survived the war.[6] While Chiang Kai-shek desperately pushed US officials to expand their commitment to the war, FDR made a strategic decision to achieve victory in Europe first. Furthermore, the US strategy of marines and naval forces island-hopping through the Pacific, bloody as it was, was in its own way a recognition that to fight the massed armies of Japan on the mainland of China would in fact have been even harder and bloodier. Despite the incredible bravery of US fighters like Claire Lee Chennault's mercenary Flying Tigers, the first-ever private military contractors to enter a war on behalf of the United States, and the heroic efforts of cargo pilots flying "the hump" over the Himalayas to resupply Chiang's fighters, the US effort was just a fraction of what it was in Europe. "The US could only keep the Nationalists on life support," concludes longtime China correspondent John Pomfret in his definitive history *The Beautiful Country and the Middle Kingdom*.[7]

Through the war, Mao's communist forces had taken advantage of the nationalists' focus on the Japanese invaders to steadily gain territory themselves, boosting their control of the country to nearly a third of China—momentum furthered by the surge of Soviet forces into China against Japan in the final weeks of World War II. A party that had just forty thousand members at the start of the war in 1937 now had over a million faithful, whereas Chiang ended the war with even less political backing in the United States than when he'd started and the *New York Times* speculated in May 1944 that the US public would favor shifting its official backing to the communists.[8] As Pomfret writes, "As World War II drew to a close, [the CCP] also reinforced the notion that the Communists would be responsible members of a coalition government and not dedicated to seizing absolute power later on."[9]

Many in the American foreign policy establishment wanted a stable, secure China, even with communists in the government, a view heavily influenced by John Stewart Service, one of State Department's "China Hands," who was the first American official to make contact with Chinese communist headquarters during World War II. After meeting with Mao, Service wrote in his June 20, 1944, report of his impression of the Chinese people: "They regard the Kuomintang—from their own experience—as oppressors; and the Communists as their leaders and benefactors. . . . From the basic fact that the Communists have built up popular support of a magnitude and depth which makes their elimination impossible, we must draw the conclusion that the Communists will have a certain and important share in China's future."[10*]

As Daniel Kurtz-Phelan traced in his book, *The China Mission: George Marshall's Unfinished War, 1945–1947*, Truman had dispatched the general to Asia to execute FDR's wartime vision and ensure China would stand as one of what FDR had called the "Four Policemen," the Big Four powers in the postwar world—something it could only do if the decade of conflict between Mao and Chiang ended and a firm central authority emerged that could administer the vast rural land and the even-then enormous population of a half-billion Chinese. "Truman's instruction to Marshall was to go to China, bring Chiang and Mao together in a single government, and avert war. American power would be used to create 'a strong, united, and democratic China,'" Kurtz-Phelan wrote.[11]

And, against seemingly the longest of odds, Marshall had succeeded. Over lengthy negotiations, shuttling between the two camps on a five-hour journey that required five different forms of transportation, he'd brokered a cease-fire in the Chinese civil war, lectured them on Benjamin Franklin and the US Constitution, and gotten them to agree to merge their forces into a single national army.[12] Marshall told Truman, "Peace will really reign over China." Mao agreed, telling

* But as China historian Rana Mitter writes, Service and his group "were not privy to intraparty discussions that made it clear Mao would never genuinely entertain an alliance with Washington. His ideological alignments were toward Stalin and toward a radical, violent, indigenous revolution."

his followers they were entering "a new stage of peace and democracy." The country needed an enormous amount of rebuilding after the harrowing devastation caused by the Japanese aggression and occupation, not to mention the looting by the Soviet Union, which had stolen nearly 70 percent of Manchuria's industrial equipment, seized as self-described war reparations.[13]

The move meant Marshall had succeeded in stopping in its tracks in China the march of communism—the scourge of the new, still-to-be-named Cold War. That very day, as Marshall and Mao celebrated, Truman and Churchill were half a world away in Fulton, Missouri, where Churchill was warning of the "iron curtain" falling across Europe. But there would be no such barrier in Asia, where the rumblings of the Cold War were yet indistinct. Or so it seemed.

As Kurtz-Phelan writes, "Once Marshall's plane took off over the mountains that morning, Mao would not meet another high-level American representative until Richard Nixon's visit twenty-six years later." Marshall's deal would unravel quickly. The civil war restarted. By 1949 Chiang and the nationalists were in full retreat, evacuating themselves, the government, about two million loyal nationalists, and three million ounces of gold to Taipei, on the island of Formosa (some nationalists went for a few years to Burma and Thailand, from which they continued to carry out guerrilla raids into communist-controlled China). In Taipei, they proclaimed that the Republic of China lived on and maintained that their government had rightful sovereignty over the mainland they'd left behind, even as the communists consolidated power and Mao established—at Beijing's Gate of Heavenly Peace on October 1, 1949—what he proclaimed was the People's Republic of China. It was a separation, a country, and an island that would bedevil both US presidents and mainland China's communist leadership for the next seven decades.

THERE'S PROBABLY NO INTERNATIONAL RELATIONSHIP IN THE WORLD that has more frustrated the United States over two-and-a-half centuries than that with China. For generations, American optimism and hope—and, in turn, Chinese optimism and hope—have been dashed upon reality, periods of warmth and alliance have been broken by betrayals and intense racism, and dreams of mutual economic development have sputtered amid geopolitical complications.

"What emerges across the centuries is a recurring theme of mutual non-comprehension and deep suspicion, often followed by periods of exaggerated hopes and expectations that then collapse in the face of fundamentally different political and strategic imperatives," writes Kevin Rudd, the former Australian prime minister and China expert.[14] "If there is a pattern to this baffling complexity, it may be best described as a never-ending Buddhist cycle of reincarnation," writes John Pomfret. "Both sides experience rapturous enchantment begetting hope, followed by disappointment, repulsion, and disgust, only to return to fascination again."[15]

Whereas the United States of America is a uniquely European creation, a country and culture created in response to what its Founders saw as correcting the worst aspects of the Old Continent and borrowing from the philosophies of the Age of Enlightenment, China spent its two formative millennia largely self-centered, conceiving of itself as the center of civilization. "Over the millennia, China also developed its own philosophical and religious traditions (Confucianism, Taoism, and Legalism) without reference to the wider world," Rudd notes. "China, therefore, as seen through the framework of its national historiography, had been a relatively successful self-contained, self-referential political, economic, philosophical, cultural, and religious system."[16]

China's power, wealth, and influence peaked in the eighteenth century during the high point of the Qing Dynasty, when the thirteen English colonies in North America comprised little more than an idea, wild forests, plantations, Native American settlements, and religious refugees.[17] For hundreds of years, few Westerners, mostly traders and missionaries, had ever even glimpsed China, but just as the United States was founded, change came to the Asian continent, too. "Until the start of the nineteenth century, the Chinese dealt with Westerners, to their own satisfaction at least, as inferiors who were fortunate if they even had contact with the Middle Kingdom," writes historian Margaret MacMillan.[18] Then the Industrial Revolution delivered a flood of superior technologies and an economic boom driven by enormous productivity gains and advanced weapons to the West and opened an era that China would remember as the Century of Humiliation, when China's ruling dynasty would disappear and the country would be nearly carved up among a flood of Western colonial impulses.

The history of the United States and China is tightly linked: trade with China, in fact, is built into the very DNA and founding myth of the United States. It was Chinese tea from what is now Fujian Province—a beloved treat in the American colonies—that was thrown off the ships *Dartmouth*, *Eleanor*, and *Beaver* by patriots into Boston Harbor on the night of December 16, 1773, the event that ultimately escalated into the American Revolution. Subsequently, imported porcelain became one of the first status symbols for the new country's elite—a trade good so associated and defined by its Asian manufacturer that it was shorthanded then and now simply as "china." The first postindependence, American-led expedition to China took off from New York on George Washington's birthday in 1784 when the three-masted *Empress of China* set sail for Guangzhou—a gleaming exotic city, known to the West as Canton, that at the time boasted a million residents, equal to a quarter of America's entire white population. China at the time was at its wealthiest and most prosperous, responsible for fully a third of all of the manufacturing in the world.[19] And when the *Empress* returned to the United States fifteen months later, after trading its cargo of beaver skins and ginseng for tea and porcelain, its load included a 302-piece dinner and tea set for Mount Vernon, decorated in Guangzhou specially for the Revolutionary War hero with the emblem of the Society of the Cincinnati.[20] The nation's first president was ironically the first target of Chinese-enabled intellectual property theft too: artist Gilbert Stuart took the captain of the trade ship *Connecticut*, John Sword, to court in 1802 and got an injunction prohibiting him from selling one hundred copies of

Stuart's famous portrait of Washington that Sword had procured in Guangzhou.[21*]

The most quintessentially American fortunes were built in the China trade. "The Astors, Greens, Russells, Delanos, Lows, and Forbeses plowed the proceeds earned in China into New England textile mills, Philadelphia banks and insurance companies, New York real estate, and railroads that laid the foundations for American power," Pomfret writes.[22] The Forbeses, in particular, developed close ties with the Chinese trader Wu Bingjian—who was known to his business partners as Howqua and was in the early 1800s the wealthiest man in the world—and eventually took over managing his estate for decades; when their descendent John Forbes Kerry was the US secretary of state, Pomfret notes, "a portrait of Howqua [hung] at the Forbes estate on Naushon Island just off Cape Cod."[23]

Over the decades ahead, American merchants, missionaries, doctors, and even the military developed a complex web of relationships across China; for example, an American opened the first Western hospital at 3 Hog Lane in Guangzhou.[24] US traders, including the grandfather of FDR, Warren Delano, helped feed and fuel China's opium addiction in the 1800s, undercutting the established British crop from India by funneling a fresh supply from Turkey; the Boston-based trader Perkins & Company alone snapped up as much as half or even three-quarters of Turkey's entire opium crop for the Chinese market.[25] (The tensions that would spill over into the midcentury Opium Wars led Delano to facilitate the first US military sale to China, handing over a nine-hundred-ton ship, the *Chesapeake*, that China hoped would help defend Guangzhou from the British.)[26]

The first US officials arrived in China in 1842, ready to force the Chinese trade open alongside the British victories of the Opium War

* Sword had purchased one of Stuart's portraits from the artist in 1801, then taken it with him to China to have it copied by Chinese artists in their then-popular reverse-glass painting technique, paying about $20 each—he intended to sell the copies after smuggling them back into the United States as his own personal property. Stuart, in court, argued successfully that the painting he sold Sword had come with restrictions against copying the image.

that would initiate the fall of China's greatness and open what would come to be known as the Century of Humiliation and Unequal Treaties.[27] The humiliations then were surely many—from the defeat of the Qing Dynasty in the First Opium War in 1841, which led to the British occupation of Hong Kong, to the Boxer Rebellion and punishing reparations payments to Western powers to conflicts against, variously, France, Russia, and Japan that all steadily robbed Chinese leaders of influence and control over their own millennia-old lands.*

As it turned out, that first mission in 1842—a naval squadron, led by Commodore Lawrence Kearny—ended up developing a friendly relationship with the local officials, and Kearny hosted Chinese admiral Wu Jianxun aboard his flagship frigate, the USS *Constellation* (Wu's first-ever glimpse of a modern Western navy), and laid the groundwork for what would soon be a thriving arms trade. By 1865 Asia's largest weapons plant, the Jiangnan Arsenal, was entirely the product of American manufacturers. "Its translation department was the largest in China and with its focus on western technology represented China's first attempt at collecting industrial secrets—by fair means or foul—from the West," Pomfret writes.[28] This was also the period when large numbers of Chinese began to flock to the United States for the first time. Chinese immigrants helped to settle the West and build the transcontinental railroad, confronting overwhelming racism and deadly labor practices along the way. In the mid- and late 1800s, Chinese immigrants comprised a tenth of California's population and a third or more of the population of states like Idaho and Montana. Their numbers worried US officials enough that they enacted the first-ever immigration restrictions focused on a particular ethnicity, but the restrictions couldn't dampen the Chinese interest in the American Dream. "The brighter aspects of free soil, free labor,

* Secretary of State John Hay famously warned as he rolled out the Open Door policy—which aimed to prevent the "carving of China like a melon"—that "the inherent weakness of our position is this: We do not want to rob China ourselves, and our public opinion will not permit us to interfere [if others do]."

and free gold overshadowed the dark side of exploitation, injustice, and discrimination," historian Liping Zhu writes.[29]

Through the latter half of the 1800s, as China retrenched and the American economy soared, US missionaries helped build the modern Chinese educational system, as YMCAs spread through major cities, and pushed for cultural reforms, including the end of the brutal tradition of binding women's feet and the infanticide of female babies.[30] In the wake of the Boxer Rebellion, the United States, beginning to assert itself across the globe for the first time, was part of the alliance of Western powers that signed a new protocol with the Qing Dynasty and sent a new military force to Tianjin, and by 1905, Chinese students were, in turn, studying at West Point.[31] (The Fifteenth infantry regiment in Tianjin, Pomfret notes, "became known for its outstanding commanders, such as George Marshall and Matthew Ridgway, and for the highest rates of alcoholism and venereal disease in the service.")[32] Chinese immigrants—and, notably, their food—continued to remake the United States; hemp seeds, so-called Meyer lemons, and new breeds of spinach, all from China, remade American agriculture.[33]

Chinese politics seemed to grow evermore entangled with the United States. The Revive China Society—the forerunner of what would become the Chinese nationalist movement—was actually founded in Hawaii, in 1894, as Sun Yat-Sen, revered both as Father of the Nation in today's Taiwan and Forerunner of the Revolution in the PRC, and his fellow Chinese patriots launched a revolutionary movement that would eventually overthrow the Qing rulers and lead Sun to be elected the first president of the Republic of China in 1911, an election Sun learned he won while in Denver, Colorado, on a fundraising mission to the United States.[34] Woodrow Wilson called the revolution that overthrew the last imperial dynasty in China "the most significant, if not the most momentous event of our generation," and the United States was the first country to formally recognize the new government.[35] The Rockefeller Foundation poured new money into China, with the intent of jump-starting an educational and scientific explosion, and John Dewey's educational pragmatism swept the Chinese elite.[36]

While often wrapped in gauzy rhetoric about freedom, these Western moves were almost all crassly commercial—even the US effort to preserve China's territorial integrity against European colonialism through the Open Door policy was really a move meant to block other countries from stomping out US business interests in China.

And then there was Wilson's betrayal.

President Wilson's desire to preserve his beloved League of Nations led him to break his lofty promise of self-determination and side with Japan as the Treaty of Versailles was negotiated to end World War I, forcing upon China territorial concessions forever remembered as a unique betrayal by a supposedly loyal ally. "In the long history of Chinese disappointment with the United States, America's failure to stand up for China at Versailles occupies a central place," Pomfret writes. "When Wilson broke that promise, he sent the Chinese on a quest for alternative ideologies. . . . America's inability to recognize the wave of the future in China opened the door to a country that would grow into its biggest foe: The Soviet Union."[37] As China historian Rana Mitter points out, "Versailles showed that the west's supposed desire for international justice and order was yet another sham. Many of China's youth turned to nationalism, or in some cases Marxism, for salvation."[38]

Within months of the Treaty of Versailles, a Changsha teacher in his midtwenties named Mao Zedong—a man who had long admired the United States and hoped it would onc day team up with China to defeat Japan—turned his back on America, forming the Russia Studies Society. In 1921 he attended the first national congress of the Chinese Communist Party.[39]

Beginning in the 1930s, the Japanese invasion of China, its imperial aggression, and the onset of World War II splintered the little control the Chinese nationalist forces had over the country, giving the CCP the chance to solidify control over more of the countryside than it had even been able to dominate before. It was the start of the national unraveling that would lead to George Marshall's desperate and unsuccessful mission in 1946 and launch the modern era of US-China relations.

Of course one of the first complexities of this new period of relations between the United States and China is that it's really always been an issue more accurately of US-China-Taiwan relations, a balancing act across three distinct governments, each subject to their own political constraints, shifting tides, and attentions. The policy of the United States toward the PRC and the Republic of China is really the story of four US presidents: Franklin Delano Roosevelt, who sought to boost China's global stature and treat it as a great power; Harry Truman, who as Marshall's peace deal unraveled was accused of "losing" China amid the opening chapters of that Cold War and then in 1950 found US troops fighting desperately against Chinese forces in Korea; Richard Nixon, who reopened the door to China; and Jimmy Carter, who normalized the diplomatic relations with the PRC, revoked recognition of Taiwan, and opened up trade, laying the foundation for the economic growth that China has experienced since then—and creating a ticking time bomb underneath the US-China-Taiwan relationship in the process. Understanding their individual and collective legacy and what they can teach modern policymakers about how to handle China today is vital.

FDR and Truman's efforts to secure a role for China in the wake of World War II had seemed a noted departure from a century of on-again, off-again Western meddling on the Asian continent—a moment where China was to be treated as an equal and not as a mere business opportunity. But whatever chance FDR, Truman, and America ever had to bring peace and democracy to China—and historian Odd Arne Westad has long argued that it was always a fanciful quest—that postwar engagement didn't last. While Marshall's name would become synonymous with an ambitious, world-transforming investment in rebuilding Europe, the United States never made a similar commitment to China, a decision that would infuriate Chiang Kai-shek and surely contributed to his government's collapse in the civil war that followed.

Truman spent much of his presidency ignoring Taiwan and scaling back the US commitment to Chiang's nationalist KMT party (although he provided $400 million to Chiang in 1948 to try to forestall his loss in the civil war, arguably too late) and in 1950 proclaimed that the United States would not provide "military aid or advice to Chinese forces on Formosa"; still, in his final years in the Oval Office, as the Korean War engulfed the peninsula and the broader region, he came to recognize Chiang's government in Taipei as an increasingly important ally. The CCP had whipped up anti-American fever at home among its subjects, and Mao's forces had massed 150,000 troops in Fujian ports to attempt a cross-strait invasion in a fleet of wooden motorized junks. As the North Korean invasion kicked off the Korean War and the United States contemplated the loss of Taiwan to the communists as well, Truman ordered the Seventh Fleet into the Taiwan Strait to prevent any invasion. "The fighting in Korea caused an overnight reversal of US policy toward Taiwan: from abandoning the island to CCP takeover to guaranteeing Taiwan's protection through US military deployment," notes Asia-Pacific security scholar Denny Roy.[40] Later, the United States forged a defense treaty with Chiang, one that importantly kept Chiang from launching his own cross-strait invasion of the mainland without US permission.[41]

For decades to come, Truman, Eisenhower, and their successors maintained that Generalissimo Chiang's government in Taipei was the "true" Chinese government. "American presidents referred contemptuously to the Reds and insisted that the capital of China was Beiping and not Beijing, because that is what their allies in Taiwan still called it," MacMillan wrote.[42] The US government turned forcefully against the Chinese communist leadership, applying sanctions to what Eisenhower's secretary of state John Foster Dulles saw as the "godless Chicoms" even stricter than those levied against the Soviet Union.[43] In 1958 Mao's communist Chinese forces shelled the nationalist-held Taiwan Strait islands of Quemoy and Matsu and brought the world to the brink of its first serious nuclear crisis. All told, Dwight Eisenhower threatened the use of nuclear weapons against the PRC a total of eight times (although he vetoed the Pentagon's actual proposed use of them) and visited Taipei personally in his round-the-world tour in mid-1960, receiving what the *New York Times* called "one of the most tumultuous receptions of his career."[44]

Through the years, a powerful conservative China lobby in Washington ensured that US support for Taiwan never wavered and helped Chiang's government hold on to the "Chinese seat" at the United Nations, at the International Olympic Committee, and in other international bodies. The United States led the opposition at the UN to an annual resolution offered by Albania to expel Taiwan and admit Mao's China to the body instead, but year by passing year, global support for the resolution grew—at one point, the United States had to dispatch a Navy plane to bring the Maldives delegate to New York to secure the vote for Taiwan. Finally, the United States maneuvered to get the measure marked an "important" question, which meant it had to be decided by a two-thirds vote in the UN.

Meanwhile, behind a door now firmly closed to the West, Mao's communist government launched on the mainland a brutal, generation-long cultural and economic modernization effort, one that saw upwards of fifty million people die in purges and famines that accompanied failed policies like the Great Leap Forward and the Cultural Revolution.

At the same time, Richard Nixon—long one of the nation's leading anticommunists—arrived in the White House thinking about how to reopen China to the world. As he said in 1967, "We simply cannot afford to leave China forever outside the family of nations, there to nurture its fantasies, cherish its hates and threaten its neighbors. There is no place on this small planet for a billion of its potentially most able people to live in angry isolation." He sensed an opportunity as relations between China and the Soviet Union splintered, Mao came to reckon with the geopolitical isolation of his country, and the United States found itself over a barrel as it tried to bring to an end the ruinous Vietnam War. "The times were ripe for each side to make a move toward the other. In both countries there were influential voices saying that the advantages of a relationship, even a cool one, outweighed continuing nonrecognition," MacMillan writes in her history, *Nixon and Mao.* *[45]

---

* Often lost in the telling of the Nixon-China story is just how remarkable and controversial the move was as well for Mao, who felt himself increasingly ideologically

Secret talks between Kissinger and Chinese premier Zhou Enlai, brokered by Pakistan—which along with North Korea, North Vietnam, Romania, and Albania was practically China's sole ally in the world—led to a small breakthrough in what came to be known as ping-pong diplomacy: a US table-tennis team playing in a World Table Tennis Championship in Japan was invited, last minute, in April 1971 to visit China too, the first significant friendly contact between American and Chinese citizens since 1949. Nixon followed up with a stunning surprise announcement of the ongoing secret talks with China led by Henry Kissinger and that he would journey himself to Beijing for direct talks in 1972.

Even as the China-US talks continued, though, the United States found the world's backing of Chiang and Taiwan unraveling; despite massive efforts by then–UN ambassador George H. W. Bush, the United States lost a vote to have Taiwan occupy the UN's China seat, failing in the end to even garner the support of the United Kingdom or Canada. The vote came even as Kissinger was in Beijing for the second round of talks, negotiating a careful statement with Zhou: "The United States acknowledges that all Chinese on either side of the Taiwan Straits maintain there is but one China." As Zhou told Kissinger, "That place is no great use to you, but a great wound to us."[46]

In Beijing for his historic visit in February 1972, Nixon jotted down the three things Mao clearly wanted: "1. Build up their world credentials, 2. Taiwan, 3. Get US out of Asia." Both sides understood that Taiwan would be their main stumbling block, and as they talked, Nixon scribbled himself another note: "Let us not embarrass each other." The United States was in a delicate moment. Nixon and Kissinger were willing to scale back support for Chiang and to stifle any attempt by Taiwan to move toward full independence, but Nixon needed to get through reelection before the United States could move

---

split from a post-Stalinist Soviet Union, with which he had engaged in armored border clashes with along China's Manchurian border as recently as 1969. Mao's own physician confronted the leader, asking, "How could we negotiate with the United States?" only to have the Chinese leader reply, "The United States and the Soviet Union are different. The United States never occupied Chinese territory."

to normalize diplomatic relations. Nixon danced around it as best he could. "This is one China, and Taiwan is part of China," he said in his first private meeting with Zhou. In the end, Zhou agreed that they could wait to resolve the issue.[47] As he left China in February 1972, seemingly triumphant, Nixon declared, "We have been here a week. This was the week that changed the world."[48]

Chiang, rightly, saw Nixon's move as—yet another—calculated betrayal. In his diary, he called the US president "Ni Chou," *Nixon the clown*.[49]

Despite Nixon getting the historical credit for "reopening China," neither he nor his successor Gerald Ford took the ultimate step of restoring diplomatic relations with communist China and reversing America's recognition of Taiwan. That step would be undertaken six years later by Jimmy Carter and his hawkish national security adviser Zbigniew Brzezinski, who was preoccupied with building an anti-Soviet coalition. "I believed that the normalization of relations between our two nations would advance the cause of peace in Asia and the world," Carter said later. "The People's Republic of China comprised about one-fourth of the world's total population and played a major role in international affairs. That reality needed to be officially recognized by my country."[50] He found a willing partner in Deng Xiaoping, who had eventually succeeded to the leadership of China after the internal party struggle following Mao's death in 1976.

Again, Taiwan and the Republic of China was the main sticking point; again, the United States and China succeeded in maintaining a positive relationship by setting it aside and focusing on other less controversial issues first. "We recognized that for the People's Republic of China, its relationship with Taiwan was considered a domestic issue," Carter recalled, and in the end, the United States and China found a way to dance around it again.[51] After months of secret negotiation, the United States and the People's Republic of China announced on December 15, 1978, that they would recognize one another and establish official diplomatic relations; the recently disgraced Nixon himself attended the resulting state dinner at the White House in January 1979 when Deng Xiaoping visited Washington, DC.

Deng Xiaoping arrived at Andrews Air Force Base, to be met at the airport by Vice President Walter Mondale. He was keen to use American know-how and investment to jump-start his economy back home—goals that he knew hinged on achieving so-called Most Favored Nation (MFN) trading status, meaning China would be treated as favorably as any other US trade partner when it came to import tariffs and other trade barriers. MFN status, in turn, hinged on whether a country allowed freedom of emigration—a cudgel the United States used during the Cold War against the Soviet Union. As Carter recalled, Deng joked, "We'll qualify right now—if you want us to send you ten million Chinese tomorrow, we'll be glad to do it." Carter joked back that he'd send Deng ten thousand journalists in exchange.

Under Carter, the United States issued a formal statement outlining its new One China policy: "The Government of the United States of America acknowledges the Chinese position that there is but one China and Taiwan is part of China." As part of the agreement, the United States committed to ending the mutual defense treaty with Taiwan, brokered during Eisenhower's presidency, but said it would "maintain cultural, commercial, and other unofficial relations with the people of Taiwan."[52] The shift in position upset Congress—particularly Senator Barry Goldwater—and the legislature passed in 1979 the Taiwan Relations Act, which would become the guiding force for the United States and codified America's relationship with the island through an unofficial nonprofit, wholly controlled by the government, called the American Institute in Taiwan that would serve as the de facto US embassy for the country. The act stopped short of a full defense guarantee but did provide for American sales of weapons to Taiwan and required the United States to "maintain the capacity of the United States to resist any resort to force or other forms of coercion that would jeopardize the security, or social or economic system, of the people on Taiwan," another wonderfully ambiguous promise.[53]

On one level, Carter and Brzezinski's efforts, building on earlier work of Nixon and Kissinger, were a diplomatic and bureaucratic masterwork, a position that embraced a certain "strategic ambiguity" whereby the United States acknowledged the Chinese position without necessarily agreeing itself. Yet it was a position that would deliver decades of further heartburn to Carter's successors.

The effort by Nixon and Carter to reestablish US-Chinese diplomatic relations coincided almost exactly—and again, not coincidentally—with the "reform and opening-up" moment as China's incredible economic success story began to transform Mao's rural, agrarian country into what a half century later would be Xi Jinping's global industrialized superpower. The Great Leap Forward had meant to push China into the future, but it had failed spectacularly and lethally, delivering years of famine and leaving the country lagging ever further behind the West. Perhaps as many as forty million Chinese died, a number larger than the entire population at the time of Canada, Spain, or South Korea. By 1979, notes journalist Evan Osnos, "the People's Republic of China was poorer than North Korea; its per capita income was one-third that of sub-Saharan Africa." Deng changed course, radically, saying famously and not very communist-like, "Let some people get rich first, and gradually all the people should get rich together." In 1978, at a party event known as the Third Plenum of the Eleventh Central Committee, Deng Xiaoping launched "a new Long March to make China a modern, powerful socialist country."[54]

Specifically, he pushed what Zhou Enlai had called the "four modernizations," efforts to reform, modernize, and accelerate agriculture, industry, defense, and science and technology, endeavors that in the party's mind would lead to "xiaokang," a "moderately prosperous society." He needed US help with just about every aspect of the modernization effort. "Chairman Mao and Zhou Enlai brilliantly sold the impending rapprochement as an act of celestial benevolence, bestowing warm relations on the barbarians from the land of the flowery flag [the United States]," Pomfret writes, but "in reality, China's leadership needed America at that point far more than the reverse."[55]

And China got what it needed: American investment poured back into China, while the Chinese visiting the United States were fascinated by the technological lifestyles and modern conveniences they discovered in the West as tourists.* US military aid and weapons sales began to flow once again, including a half-billion-dollar deal to upgrade the Chinese Air Force, a terribly myopic decision we are now regretting.[56] Peking University historian Yuan Ming concludes, "The American factor was, in the end, the all-encompassing factor in China's modernization."[57]

It would be a huge transformation for China—and the world beyond. "After over a century of decline, occupation, civil war, state repression, and socialist revolution, China finally did manage to catapult itself into an era of stunning dynamism and economic growth," Orville Schell and John Delury write in their exemplary exploration of China's quest for "wealth and power." China's modern era is defined, they argue, by "the abiding quest for *fuqiang*, 'wealth and power,'" a phrase that has become shorthand for the ancient credo *fuguo qiangbing*, "enrich the state and strengthen its military power." Importantly, it's a phrase—and sentiment—that emerged during an era not of China's rise, but of its fall, a longing that grew during the Century of Humiliation when the once-powerful China saw itself in global retreat. Thus, while we generally translate the phrase as "wealth and power," Schell and Delury write, its meaning is rather closer to "prosperity and strength."[58]

"These two characters have repeatedly stood in for the profound desire among China's cognoscenti to see their country restored to the kind of greatness their ancestors had once taken for granted," they write. "What 'liberté, egalité, fraternité,' meant to the French Revolution and to the making of modernity in the West, 'wealth, strength, and honor' have meant to the forging of modern China."[59]

China's era of wealth and power was just beginning. And it would avenge that Century of Humiliation. As the *Wall Street Journal*'s China-focused reporter Chun Han Wong writes, "The 'Century of Humiliation' forms the spine of the People Republic's founding mythology, where the party emerged as China's rightful rulers by avenging its indignities and restoring its honor."[60] But one thing wouldn't

* One of those visiting the state of Iowa as part of a corn industry delegation in 1985 was a certain youthful man called Xi Jinping.

change: a half century later, Taiwan would still be a sticking point between the United States and China.

The end of Cold War I shaped today's showdown in ways big and small. As the Iron Curtain collapsed between the West and the Soviet Union, China's age of economic reform was accelerating. Deng Xiaoping's efforts to undo the policy mistakes and human suffering of the Cultural Revolution remade daily life—bringing a version of capitalism into the economy and rising standards of living for hundreds of millions of Chinese people.

As general secretary of the Chinese Communist Party from 1982 to 1987, Hu Yaobang helped drive some of the reforms and tackle the resulting official corruption; then, in 1987, as student protests mounted, pushing for more openness and press freedom, Deng ousted him out of office, Hu resigning with a humiliating "self-criticism." The resignation, though, made him even more popular with those who wanted reform; following his death in 1989, there was public pressure for a state funeral, setting in motion the biggest challenge to the Communist Party's rule in decades. The protests began as a pressure campaign to mark Hu's memorial service but quickly came to encompass a wider set of complaints about party corruption, the pace of economic reform, freedom of speech and the press, and more. On April 22, 1989—over a month before the momentous start of the fall of communism in Eastern Europe—tens of thousands of students marched on Tiananmen Square, the iconic central square in Beijing marked by the Gate of Heavenly Peace, the front gate of the historic fifteenth-century Imperial City. As the spring progressed, tensions escalated; the square was occupied by hundreds of thousands of Chinese—students and not—perhaps even a million participated. Hunger strikes spread; martial law was declared on May 19. In a national address, Premier Li Peng said, "We must adopt firm and resolute measures to end the turmoil swiftly, to maintain the leadership of the party as well as the socialist system."[61] An effort the following day by the army to retake the square was blocked by protesters and thus began a multiday standoff.

"You had these . . . touching moments of the people appealing to the army to join them, and feeding them, and giving them water, and saying, you know, 'Could be your son. Could be your daughter,'" recalled journalist Orville Schell, who was in Beijing at the time. "These sort of doe-eyed, puzzled soldiers—who were mostly country people, weren't experienced with big city life—just wondering what was going on here. And not wanting to hurt anybody."[62]

A group of Beijing art students constructed a thirty-three-foot-tall Goddess of Democracy, a Chinese Statue of Liberty, made from Styrofoam and plaster, her torch of liberty rising before the imperial gates and the famous portrait of Mao that looked over the square. Feeling an increasing political threat, the Communist Party began to move more decisively. On June 3, another wave of troops—much larger than the first—began to converge on the square and, after overcoming numerous hastily erected blockades throughout the city, the army massacred the student protesters. To this day, no one knows how many died as the military cleared the square and the streets leading up to it; the official government death toll was just two hundred civilians and several dozen government forces, but many human rights groups said the death toll stretched into the thousands. Citing someone who was a "close friend" on the Chinese state council, the British ambassador to China confidentially estimated the toll closer to ten thousand.[63]

The showdown inside China, which Westerners glimpsed through only snippets of coverage, was crystalized in one of the most famous pictures of the century—perhaps one of the most famous pictures of all time—of a lone, grocery-bag-carrying protester in a white shirt halting a column of army tanks in their tracks. The bravery of that figure in the face of seemingly unstoppable government power inspired Americans, and public opinion in the United States, which had been increasingly pro-China, turned overnight.

But President George H. W. Bush, a former American head diplomat in China himself, didn't want to undo the fresh warmth and engagement of the 1980s. Bush, despite saying that "throughout the world we stand with those who seek greater freedom and democracy," opted out of a harsh response to the attacks on democracy protests, insisting that it was not the time "for an emotional response, but for a reasoned, careful action that takes into account both our long-term interests and recognition of a complex internal situation in China."[64*] Six months later, the Berlin Wall fell; the Warsaw Pact that had aligned against NATO and the West in Europe was dissolved just fourteen months later.

Then Bill Clinton arrived, ready to criticize China where Bush wouldn't. Accepting the Democratic nomination in New York on July 16, 1992, Clinton laid out his New Covenant for the country and promised "an America that will not coddle tyrants, from Baghdad to Beijing."[65]

It seemed like the beginning of a new era.

IF *US POLICY TOWARD CHINA* IS THE STORY OF FOUR PRESIDENTS, the president who changed *Chinese policy toward the United States*—by contrast—is the story of a fifth: Bill Clinton. He came to office promising to push for reform but found himself wanting to follow through on his "It's the economy, stupid" campaign theme, under pressure from business leaders who wanted to take advantage of China's growing middle-class market. The growth potential was too huge to miss. China's economy soared 14 percent in 1992, the year Clinton was elected, and the year of his inauguration foreign companies signed a staggering eighty-five thousand deals with Chinese companies.[66] And there was still so much growth to gain: in 1996, while technology was ubiquitous in the United States enough that Americans were creeping online through AOL, Prodigy, and CompuServe, China still only had five telephone lines for every hundred people.[67]

Chinese leaders began to understand the tremendous leverage they had with Western business; the Century of Humiliation and Unequal

* The most lasting legacy of the Tiananmen Square massacre in US policy, as it turns out, was a Bush order meant to protect Chinese studying in the United States from the requirement to return after completing their studies: some fifty-three thousand students ultimately received green cards, a critical mass of students, many among them engineers, who contributed to the intellectual capital of Silicon Valley in the decades following.

Treaties had been reversed. Many of these new deals began to feature the hallmark of Chinese practices to come—forced technology transfer, unbalanced joint ventures—and the Clinton administration's push on human rights sputtered in the face of the focus on the economy and trade.

But if China began to flex its economic might in the 1990s, there was one aspect of American power that truly worried the Chinese government: the US military. Chinese military and political leaders had watched with astonishment as the US-led coalition barreled through the Iraqi military in Operation Desert Storm, obliterating an army that Chinese had considered its peer in just one hundred hours of ground combat. Then, in the mid-1990s, tensions again arose between Taiwan and China; after Taiwan's president gave a reunion speech at Cornell University, the PLA began to "test fire" missiles into the waters around Taiwan in July 1995. The United States responded by sending multiple US Navy ships through the Taiwan Strait, including the USS *Nimitz* carrier battle group that December. When China again tried to intimidate Taiwan ahead of its first-ever free presidential elections in spring 1996, the Clinton administration responded by dispatching not one but two carrier battle groups to the seas around Taiwan—the largest US naval force in Asia since the end of the Vietnam War. In this case, the intimidation backfired on China, which realized that it had no military might equal to a US carrier group. It quickly began a crash investment program in missiles and other naval assets that could contest the seas off its coast.[68*]

Another episode during the Clinton years helped transform the Chinese military balance with the United States: the 1999 Kosovo War—a conflict almost forgotten by Americans but very much

* "[The incident] helped launch the second phase of China's military modernization. One could draw a straight line from the PLAN's humiliation in 1996 to its near-peer status with the US Navy today," writes maritime strategist Gregory Poling. In 1998 a Chinese businessman purchased from Ukraine a stripped-out hulk of a never-commissioned and deteriorated Soviet Union–era *Kuznetsov*-class aircraft carrier named *Varyag* for $30 million, under the pretext of renovating it into a floating casino. The casino never materialized, and fourteen years later *Varyag* reemerged from the Dalian naval shipyard as *Liaoning*, China's first aircraft carrier.

remembered by the PLA. An internal Chinese military report, prepared by the vice chair of the Central Military Commission, Zhang Wannian, said, "The forces of Yugoslavia have provided a useful reference point for our army on the question of how an inferior equipped force can defeat a superior-equipped force under high-tech conditions," adding, "Serbian resistance . . . gives us a lot of inspiration. We should apply these revelations to preparations for military struggle."[69]

Then, in May 1999, during NATO's air campaign in that war, the United States accidentally bombed the Chinese embassy in Belgrade—a tragedy that Chinese propaganda quickly appropriated even as Chinese officials wondered conspiratorially just how much of an accident it actually was. "No one in China believed the bombing was an accident," John Pomfret writes. "From the top of the party to society's bottom rung, the Chinese had such a deep respect for American technology that they found it impossible to accept that the United States could make such a mistake." Speaking at an emergency Politburo meeting, Li Peng said the attack was "a carefully crafted plot of subversion" and that the incident "reminds us that the United States is an enemy."[70]

Enemy or not, the United States ended the Clinton years by fatefully gifting China its most desired goal: membership in the World Trade Organization (WTO), a move that would turbocharge the already growing Western investment and heat the Chinese economy red hot. Bill Clinton, who had arrived in the White House promising a tough on China policy, left office in the twenty-first century with China having not only embarked upon a massive investment in military modernization but also opening its borders to Western trade that would strengthen China dramatically while hollowing out American manufacturing and pillaging US intellectual property. Firms like Goldman Sachs, Morgan Stanley, and McKinsey rushed into China to provide the money and know-how necessary to build, build, build.

By the 2000s China seemed almost unstoppable. For every two-year period from 2008 to 2017, Harvard political scientist Graham Allison notes, "the increment of growth of China's GDP has been larger than the entire economy of India. Even at its lower growth rate in 2015, China's economy created a Greece every sixteen weeks and an Israel every twenty-five weeks."[71] Op-ed and magazine pages in the 2010s were dominated by stories proclaiming that the American Century of the twentieth century would be supplanted by the Chinese Century in the twenty-first. In a 2015 *Vanity Fair* essay entitled precisely that—"The Chinese Century"—Nobel Prize–winning economist Joseph Stiglitz noted, "2014 was the last year in which the United States could claim to be the world's largest economic power," and in 2018, the *Economist* proclaimed that "although America remains the lone superpower, China has already replaced it as the driver of global change."[72]

The accompanying leap in wealth and quality of life was nothing short of fantastic, lifting hundreds of millions into the middle class: in just a generation, China went from having 90 percent of its population living on the equivalent of less than $2 a day, the global poverty line, to just 3 percent.[73] It was an unparalleled historic economic revolution that came during a period of global peace enforced by the US-led security order. In the end, Pomfret notes, "More than perhaps any other nation, China has benefited from the Pax Americana—the system of free trade, secure waterways, and globalized financial markets built by the United States and its allies after World War II."[74]

In 2005 Robert Zoellick—then deputy secretary of state—outlined the modern history of the US-China relationship, saying, "Seven U.S. presidents of both parties recognized this strategic shift and worked to integrate China as a full member of the international system. Since 1978, the United States has also encouraged China's economic development through market reforms. Our policy has succeeded remarkably well: the dragon emerged and joined the world. Today, from the United Nations to the World Trade Organization, from agreements on ozone depletion to pacts on nuclear weapons, China is a player at the table." Now, Zoellick cautioned, it was time "to urge China to become a responsible stakeholder in that system."[75]

It was not to be. China, as it turned out, had little interest in playing responsibly by international rules promoted by the United States. Nor did it have any interest in building a democratic society. The hopes of generations of American leaders and foreign policy establishment that the reopening of China and its economic integration with the West would produce domestic reforms collided with the CCP's authoritarian vision for China. Today, China scholar Liz Economy writes, "China is an illiberal state seeking leadership in a liberal world order."[76] To understand how China has used its newfound wealth and power to alter the geopolitical balance across Asia, it's best to start with an atoll about 130 nautical miles west of the Philippine island of Palawan.

MISCHIEF REEF, IT TURNS OUT, IS WELL-NAMED. LEGEND HAS IT that the reef, part of the Spratly Islands, was named after a British trading ship, the *Mischief*, from the nineteenth century, but the reef was where in 1995—just around the time of the Taiwan Strait Crisis—China began tiptoeing into the strategy it would use to seize, develop, and militarize large portions of the South China Sea.

Much like Taiwan, the hundred reefs, atolls, and islands of the Spratlys had changed hands multiple times in the twentieth century—they'd started as a French naval base, for its colony in Indochina, then were seized by Japan in World War II, and today lie well within the Philippines Exclusive Economic Zone. Despite their emptiness, they're considered strategic because they supposedly sit both atop large oil and gas deposits and astride key shipping lanes coming up from the Malacca Strait; roughly a third of all global maritime commerce passes through the South China Sea and about 60 percent passes through Asia.[77] Although China's closest territory, Hainan Island, is seven hundred miles away, the communist Chinese government claims that its ties to the islands date back to its wide-ranging explorer Zheng Ho in the fifteenth century. And so, just three years after the US military closed up shop in Subic Bay, its last base in the Philippines—the end of a ninety-four-year-long presence that included both a brutal colonial era and Douglas MacArthur's proud, triumphant return in World War II—China moved in on the reef.[78]

On February 8, 1995, China raised its flag over Mischief Reef—an operation watched over by a fleet of eight Chinese ships, including armed military vessels—and began constructing octagonal sheds on stilts atop the reef, which is about nine kilometers by six kilometers wide and too low-lying to be technically called an island.[79] China claimed at first that the shelters were for fishermen, but in November 1998, a Philippine military reconnaissance plane discovered that the sheds were being upgraded to concrete barracks-like structures, complete with a three-hundred-meter pier. In 2014 the occupying Chinese forces began a massive land reclamation effort, with a fleet of dredging craft building up the reef and adding more than a thousand acres of land. By 2016 the once-uninhabited reef housed a blossoming base complete with an eight-thousand-foot runway and antiaircraft defenses.

Mischief Reef became the textbook example China repeated across the region. Over those two decades, countries across the South China Sea began to see a familiar pattern: first China would place buoy markers on inhabited reefs, then construct concrete markers, then—left unchallenged—temporary facilities, and finally permanent ones. If and when the Philippine Navy destroyed the encroaching markers, China never protested, preferring patience and taking advantage of the overstretched Philippine Navy, waiting for it to turn its attention elsewhere. Often the Philippine Navy found that the Chinese "fishermen" it arrested in and around the uninhabited Philippine-claimed South China Sea reefs were wearing matching tracksuits and lacked any of the calluses on their hands common to those engaged in actual commercial fishing.[80]

China saw the effort as key to securing what it called the "nine-dash line," a geopolitical demarcation line that actually started with eleven dashes—in 1946, Chiang Kai-shek's Republic of China published a map of the South China Sea denoting what it saw as China's territorial claims, which it said included all of the Paracels, Pratas, and Spratly Islands as part of the settlement at the end of World War II. Later, communist China, under Premier Zhou Enlai, removed two of the lines around the Gulf of Tonkin following a treaty with Vietnam, leaving a total of nine dashes across the maritime map that ever since it has tried, with varying efficacy, to enforce as its own.*[81]

The claims of the "nine-dash line" are as sweeping as they are historically unjustified. According to the final agreements of World War II, both the '43 Cairo and the '45 Potsdam Declarations, in which the great powers set out their terms for the surrender of Japan and return of the territories it had conquered, China never got the claims it said it did later. Moreover, the idea that China "controls" the South China Sea as far as the "nine-dash line" indicates, pushing right to the boundaries of the other neighboring countries, goes against the recognized international claims to offshore control—normally, countries are only able to assert a twelve-mile territorial limit, as well as a broader set of special rights to use and explore marine resources out to a two-hundred-mile limit, known as the respective country's Exclusive Economic Zone (EEZ). The EEZs, established by the 1982 United Nations Convention on the Law of the Sea (UNCLOS), which China ratified, are meant to protect a country's right to the sea floor, while the surface is considered international waters.

At 3.5 million square kilometers, the South China Sea—roughly bordered by Taiwan, the Philippines, Malaysia, Indonesia, and the Indochina peninsula (including Vietnam, Thailand, Laos, and Cambodia)—is more than double the size of the Gulf of Mexico and about a million square kilometers larger than the Mediterranean. And, according to the Chinese government's historic (and legally unfounded) claims, it controls about two million square kilometers of the sea, pushing China's claims right up to the borders of Vietnam, Malaysia, and the Philippines.

In 2012 China and the Philippines clashed at another coral atoll called Scarborough Shoal, and the Philippines filed a formal grievance under the terms of the UNCLOS. In 2016 an international tribunal at The Hague declared China's claims invalid, rejecting both its historic claims to the islands as well as the idea that China's settlements on the

* According to a US State Department analysis, the lines barely moved over the years from 1947 to 2009.

Spratlys created an extension of China's Exclusive Economic Zones. China effectively shrugged and kept building. "This is a bundle of fairy rope the West has tossed out at a strategic moment in a vain attempt to terminate China's development," proclaimed China's official Xinhua News Agency.[82] And using the Chinese name for the Spratlys, the head of the Chinese Navy, Admiral Wu Shengli, told his US counterpart, "We will never stop our construction on the Nansha Islands halfway . . . no matter what country or person applies pressure."[83]

Three of the Spratly Islands—Mischief Reef, as well as two others—came to boast operational military bases, with airfields, missiles, and radars, as does one in the Paracels. The effort involved has been massive; at key points in the Subi Reef construction, another China-occupied Spratly Islands reef, the project involved more than seventy ships. A half-dozen other reefs and atolls have less developed facilities too, and in the spring of 2018 China also announced on its Weibo microblogging site that it had successfully landed a long-range Chinese bomber at Woody Island, its largest base in the Paracels.[84] The airfields give its patrol and fighter planes a wide range of operations across the South China Sea. That summer, the incoming head of US Indo-Pacific Command, Admiral Philip S. Davidson, announced, "In short, China is now capable of controlling the South China Sea in all scenarios short of war with the United States."[85]

While the US Navy has regularly—despite Chinese protests—conducted so-called freedom of navigation patrols nearby to demonstrate that it considers the surrounding waters international territory, month by month and year by year, China has successfully written itself a new reality in the South China Sea. "[Early on, people were] pretty dismissive of those island bases—'Oh, we'd be able to scrape them clean with Tomahawk [missiles] in the first hour of the conflict,'" says Thomas Shugart, a defense expert at the Center for a New American Security. "I don't think people see it that way anymore."[86]

While the United States wasn't looking—and while it wasn't inclined to pick a fight with China anyway—China managed to slowly but decisively slice off large portions of the South China Sea. "That's the long game that they often play," the US Navy's Seventh Fleet

Commander Vice Adm. Karl Thomas told the *Wall Street Journal* in 2022. "They will build a capability—it's there and they'll just incrementally increase their presence."[87]

The battle—or, more accurately, the lack of a battle—over the islands is in many ways a microcosm of the modern China challenge, America's failure to read China correctly, and its failure or disinterest in acting earlier to counter its rival's rise. Obama administration officials, though, argue that they didn't have much choice in the matter; the administration didn't have anything meaningful to offer China as a carrot to stop its South China Sea expansion efforts, and the stick—the threat that United States would actually provoke a military confrontation over uninhabited coral reefs—just was "utterly unrealistic," recalled Daniel Russel, who was assistant secretary of state for East Asian and Pacific Affairs from 2013 to 2017. As he says, "We could have made this the absolute be-all and end-all of the relationship, and in effect double-dared the Chinese to enter into military conflict with the US over this at the cost of any hope of progress in any other area of the relationship."[88] Of course, that hope of progress in other areas didn't materialize either.

These were, in many ways, the "salami tactics" that Nazi Germany used to seize territory ahead of World War II—taking little bites of territory or engaging in violations of the Versailles Peace Treaty, no single move initially large enough or consequential enough to provoke a reaction, yet over time cumulatively adding up to creating a new fait accompli. "Salami tactics, we can be sure, were invented by a child," said strategist Thomas Schelling. "Tell a child not to go in the water and he'll sit on the bank and submerge his bare feet; he is not yet 'in' the water. Acquiesce, and he'll stand up; no more of him is in the water than before. Think it over, and he'll start wading, not going any deeper; take a moment to decide whether this is different and he'll go a little deeper, arguing that since he goes back and forth it all averages out. Pretty soon we are calling to him not to swim out of sight, wondering whatever happened to all our discipline."[89]

"China has steadily militarized the contested waterway while squeezing out its neighbors. US policy has failed to halt, or even markedly slow, that process," Poling writes.[90] Targeting these islands today isn't necessarily all that straightforward either; while it's easy to hear "coral reef" and "atoll" and think small, the islands China has chosen and built up are generally quite large. Analysts point out that from one side to the other Mischief Reef is approximately the size of the Washington, DC, I-495 Beltway—hardly an easy target for a missile strike, even before you consider the distance the United States would have to attack from and that China built many of the facilities precisely to withstand such an attack, either through hardening or even burying certain facilities.[91]

Indeed, at almost every turn and policy front, the depth, breadth, and scope of China's threat to the global security order and international rule of law is almost impossible to capture. The clearest way, though, is to use the party's own guiding principles—principles not just incompatible with but specifically opposed to the world that the United States has spent the last two centuries trying to create. In 2013 the Communist Party circulated what came to be known as Document number 9, which China scholar Elizabeth Economy described as "paint[ing] the CCP as in the midst of an intense struggle with Western liberal values that had begun to take hold in certain sectors of Chinese society." It focused on what have come to be known as the "seven no's" or the seven perils, which Economy describes as "universal press freedom, civil society, citizens' rights, the party's historical aberrations, the 'privileged capitalistic class,' and the independence of the judiciary. It represents both a confirmation and an expansion of the 'five no's' that then National People's Congress Standing Committee Chairman Wu Bangguo articulated in 2011: no multiparty politics, no diversification of the party's ideology, no separation of powers, no privatization, and no federal system of government."[92] Months after Document number 9 came out, the world got a clear indication of how China would act beyond its borders as well: it announced the creation of a new Air Defense Identification Zone (ADIZ), executing on a longtime goal of the PLA that would create a "Great Wall in the Sky" where planes passing through would be subject to interception by Chinese flights.

The ADIZ, though, was just as offensive as the island-building campaign: it encompassed about two-thirds of the East China Sea and overlapped with long-standing zones established by Japan, South Korea, and Taiwan—lines largely drawn by the US military after World War II—and led to protests by those governments. Japan called the new Chinese rule "profoundly dangerous acts that unilaterally change the status quo in the East China Sea, escalating the situation, and that may cause unintended consequences."[93] Looking back, this was a key moment—China's salami tactics were succeeding in changing the state of the Pacific, and no one had a good plan to counter them. As the *Wall Street Journal* concluded, "The U.S. missed the moment to hold back China's buildup in part because it was focused on collaborating with Beijing on global issues such as North Korea and Iran, and was preoccupied by wars in Iraq and Afghanistan."[94]

It's easy if you're China to look at the West and think this is its moment of opportunity to upend the global security order—that the West is weakening and the postwar liberal democratic system is unraveling. In the late 2010s the European experiment appeared under pressure in the wake of Brexit and the United States was riven by partisan polarizations and bitterly divisive elections. These events, contrasted with China's own steady quarter century of governmental investments and growing economic and military clout, provided "a period of historical opportunity." A year after the United States and United Kingdom were transformed by the election of Trump and Brexit, Xi outlined in a three-and-a-half-hour October 18, 2017, speech to the Nineteenth Party Congress his vision for a national rejuvenation that would raise it to "world-class" status by the hundredth anniversary of the Chinese Community Party in 2049, a "new era" that "sees China moving closer toward the world's center stage."[95] Chinese government thinkers and officials that year would begin to embrace and discuss what they called "great changes unseen in a century," moves that signaled a shift in power from the West to the East, as a country that had quietly bided its time to claim power now saw opportunities aplenty. "The West's subsequent response to the coronavirus pandemic in 2020, and then the storming of the US Capitol by extremists in 2021, reinforced a sense that 'time and momentum are on our side,' as Xi Jinping put it shortly after those events," Doshi writes. "China's leadership and foreign policy elite declared that a 'period of historical opportunity' had emerged to expand the country's strategic focus from Asia to the wider globe and its governance system."[96]

They weren't necessarily wrong. We were, for too long, distracted and disoriented.

CHAPTER 2

Distracted and Disoriented

VLADIMIR PUTIN HAS LONG WANTED THE WORLD TO THINK he's a great reader of Russian literature—he knows that authors like Dostoyevsky, Tolstoy, and Pushkin represent how so many people around the world have come to learn about and love Russia, its culture, and its history. Russia, he says, is a "reading nation," telling one gathering of writers in 2010, "Literature has always been an essential intellectual component of the Russian mentality and a true brand of our country."[1] One of my most enduring memories of studying Russian literature in school in Moscow was having to write an essay about the deep meaning behind Tolstoy's very long and elaborate description of an oak tree in *War and Peace*, an assignment I certainly did not relish at the time.

As I watched Russia mass a military force on the border of Ukraine in the fall and early winter of 2021, I began to suspect that Putin was specifically thinking of a different Russian playwright, one I'd read in my childhood in Moscow, Anton Chekhov, who offered what is perhaps the most famous piece of playwriting advice ever: "If in the first act you have hung a pistol on the wall, then in the last one it should be fired."

Putin wouldn't be building up such a large force on Ukraine's border if he didn't intend to use it, I thought. On December 21, 2021, I took to Twitter with that startling argument: "I have become increasingly convinced that Kremlin has unfortunately made a decision to invade Ukraine later this winter." I laid out seven signals that to me indicated that Russia wasn't merely bluffing, from its nonsensical haphazard diplomatic ultimatums to its expanding propaganda efforts to cyber intelligence gathering in Ukraine. The Twitter thread, which at the time represented a major departure from the public consensus of what's known as "The Blob," the professional foreign policy community in Washington, took off like a rocket—receiving thousands of retweets and tens of millions of views.

A few weeks later, I got a telephone call from Jake Sullivan, President Biden's national security adviser. He said he agreed with my reasoning and conclusions regarding the likely inevitability of Russian invasion of Ukraine and wanted to talk through the administration's strategy—the US government was pushing to do whatever it could to influence Putin's decision making and deter war. High-profile negotiations were about to start in Geneva between the State Department and the Russian Foreign Ministry, perhaps the last chance to try a Hail Mary and stop a conflict that would cause untold casualties and economic destruction—in Ukraine and beyond—and dramatically remake global geopolitics. Unfortunately, while Jake and I talked, it didn't seem like there was much that the United States could do to discourage Putin's plans.

And yet the more I watched the administration's public statements, the more I realized how incoherent and contradictory the US policy around Ukraine actually was. President Biden (correctly, in my view) had publicly and forcefully taken off the table the idea that American troops would go in to fight Russia in Ukraine, but the administration continued to insist that they were in favor of Ukraine joining NATO at some unspecified later time—a policy consistent with one President George W. Bush had announced at the NATO Bucharest summit in 2008 to the consternation of our French and German allies. There was an obvious and worrisome contradiction in these statements. If the North Atlantic alliance voted to admit Ukraine, the United States and its allies were signing up for the vaunted and central so-called Article 5 commitment, the solemn promise that an attack on any NATO member was to be considered an attack on all, a pledge that the United States would defend Ukraine's territory as if it were our own. And yet, here in 2021 was President Biden repeatedly and explicitly refusing to do just that. At the time, I asked Jake that very question: *If the United States was unwilling to send Americans to fight and die in Ukraine now, why would it be more willing to do so in the future?* What would change in the future that would make American mothers and fathers accept sending their sons and daughters off to fight in Ukraine? Was our abstract commitment to let Ukraine join NATO just empty talk, an autopilot-like continuation of a fourteen-year-old policy from three presidents ago? Was it a policy that no longer served American interests? And, if so, given that Ukraine's possible future accession to NATO membership appeared to be one of the key pretexts for Putin's threats of an invasion, would it make sense to take it off the table to at least deny him the propaganda talking point? Jake made it clear, though, that President Biden, as he had made abundantly clear publicly, was not willing to go there, despite the administration's desires to do everything possible to try to stop this invasion.

I was incredulous—not because I necessarily believed then (nor do I believe today) that NATO expansion was the main driver of Putin's decision to launch his war of genocidal aggression, but because it seemed clear that the administration really didn't believe committing American lives to defend Ukraine was ever going to be a risk worth taking. And President Biden was hardly alone in that view; virtually no one in the US political system believed that was the wrong decision. And yet, by continually talking about the US support for Ukraine's eventual accession into NATO, they were also implicitly saying that they *could* risk the lives of American troops to defend Ukraine at some unspecified future date. The policy was incoherent. It was a moment that crystalized for me a nagging worry about American foreign policy since the 1990s.

No one was willing to debate and state firmly the true geopolitical interests of the United States. America had no idea what it wanted.

Today, we still don't.

On one level, Russia's illegal invasion of Ukraine has turned into a huge tactical and strategic success for the United States. For the cost of less than $100 billion in military aid, we were able to assist brave Ukrainian forces in decimating the Russian military—killing over a hundred thousand troops, destroying thousands of pieces of armor, air defense, artillery, and aviation, and even sinking the symbolic target of the flagship of the Russian Navy's Black Sea Fleet, the heavy cruiser *Moskva*. In other words, for the equivalent of what the Pentagon normally spends in about seven weeks in current "peacetime," we worked with allies across Europe to render the Russian military incapable of large-scale offensive ground combat operations for probably a generation. Putin's Russia has been decisively isolated from the West economically and politically; its energy sector, a critical driver of the Russian economy and a long-held Sword of Damocles hanging over Europe, is in dramatic retreat, with countries across Europe moving rapidly to free themselves from Russian oil and gas coercion. Sanctions, intense domestic inflation, and supply chain paralysis seem likely to doom Russia to anemic growth for many years to come.

Meanwhile, NATO and Europe seem stronger than ever. The North Atlantic alliance itself—long rudderless in terms of purpose, mission, and the ever-diminishing military capability of our European allies—has been reinvigorated with renewed energy, expanded defense spending commitments, and the new applications by Finland and Sweden to be full members. All the while, we have managed to avoid any much-feared escalation into a broader NATO-US-Russia confrontation. And, most importantly—thanks in no small part to our provision of key intelligence and military systems—Ukraine lives. Ukraine has managed to survive as a country, preserve its government, and even restore much of the territory it had lost to the Russians in the early days of the war.

Yet, despite all of these tremendous successes, big and little, our end goals with this conflict remain frustratingly undefined. The administration keeps talking about supporting Ukraine "as long as it takes" but what is the "it" that we are trying to achieve? The United States and our allies remain confoundingly ambiguous about whether "it" represents the full return of every inch of Ukrainian territory, back to the pre-2014 boundaries, or whether some territorial concessions to Russia are acceptable in pursuit of a peace settlement. Our ambiguity means that our definition of victory in this conflict is essentially being left to Ukraine, which itself has issued contradictory statements on its ultimate desired outcome. That's not a successful recipe for a winning grand strategy.

But this pattern of vagueness is, unfortunately, par for the course in US foreign policy. In fact, if we look at the history of US wars over the last century, we see a tragic history of repeatedly entering conflicts without clearly defined plans and objectives to achieve—wars like Korea, Vietnam, Iraq, and Afghanistan, wars that cumulatively have killed a hundred thousand US troops and destroyed many more American and foreign families. In all of those cases, we fought to a loss or stalemate, as decisive tactical military victories on the battlefield were stolen by a lack of political focus and strategic success. Those conflicts, all now infamous in American history, stand as a sad testament to the disconnect between America's unparalleled capabilities and our lofty ambitions and the true perils of not having a realistic strategy and upfront definition of victory. Now, the undefined objectives of the Ukraine conflict—not a conflict where America is fighting with its own forces, but still one where we have plenty of money, military-industrial capability, and international prestige on the line—have the potential of becoming yet another "forever war" that saps our defense budgets and undermines weapons systems for years to come.

The biggest problem with the US approach to Ukraine, though, is that we've thought about it ever since 2021 as exclusively a Russia issue. As Rob Joyce, the head of cybersecurity at the National Security Agency, has famously said, "Russia is a hurricane. China is climate change."[2] We've spent so much time focused in recent years on Vladimir Putin's hurricane that we've lost sight of how we should be focused on the Russia-Ukraine conflict in terms of how it will impact our future with China. Russia today is a shrinking, weakening power, capable of upsetting apple carts and the international order but hardly influencing the world beyond that. It remains a formidable nuclear threat and can be an existential threat to neighbors like Ukraine and Georgia, but it's by no means the existential threat to democracy and the Western world that the Soviet Union was at the height of the Cold War. Instead, it has manifested as a geopolitical distraction just at a time when a truly existential threat is peering just over the world horizon: China.

WE'RE USED TO THINKING FROM HISTORY BOOKS THAT THE COLD War started sometime in 1945, '46, or '47—perhaps when George Orwell first coined the term in reference to the world living in the shadow of nuclear weapons (1945), or when Winston Churchill coined the term "Iron Curtain" in his speech in Westminster College in Fulton, Missouri (1946), or potentially when Moscow-based US diplomat George Kennan sent his "Long Telegram" back to Washington arguing that the Soviet Union could never see "permanent peaceful coexistence" with the West (1946), or perhaps when Harry Truman announced his new doctrine pledging American "support for democracies against authoritarian threats" (1947). But the truth is that America, so big and geographically removed from most of its adversaries, has a bad habit of not realizing when other countries have already gone to war with it.

There's a good argument to be made that the Soviet Union entered the Cold War with the United States in 1920—a cold war, in fact, that grew out of a now mostly forgotten hot war, an episode that not coincidentally involved another ill-fated and unsuccessful foreign intervention. Most Americans do not realize that there was a time when the United States was in an actual war in Russia, but in the waning months of World War I, President Woodrow Wilson in fact dispatched a total of about thirteen thousand troops to Siberia. The deployment came after the collapse of the Russian empire, the Bolshevik revolution of 1917, and the ensuing Russian Civil War, as the Allied powers decided to intervene militarily in support of the White Russian forces in 1918. Ultimately, many other Western countries contributed troops—including Japan, Canada, Great Britain, Czechoslovakia, France, Italy, Greece, and Romania—and the forces fought across the Far East (Vladivostok), Far North (Arkhangelsk), Siberia, the Caucasus, Crimea, and Odessa.

America's two primary forces, known as the American Expeditionary Force, Siberia and American Expeditionary Force, North Russia, were nominally meant to secure Allied supplies and help ease the way for the fifty-thousand-strong Czechoslovak Legion to get to the Western front in Europe; many of the US troops came from the Army's 339th regiment, which largely comprised men from Michigan, because US leaders imagined them particularly hardy for the cold of Siberia. The US forces fought alongside the White Russians against the Bolshevik Red Army. The mission lasted some two years, with US policymakers citing, variously, the need to prevent German strategic expansion in the north and east against a weakened Russia, the need to get Russia back into World War I (the Bolsheviks had pulled out of the war after signing a peace treaty with Germany in the spring of 1918), and the need to contain the spread of communism and territorial ambitions by some allies like Japan, who wanted to build a buffer state in Siberia. No one was ever really clear what the forces were doing there or why, and, perhaps not surprisingly, the mission failed spectacularly. The United States finally pulled out its forces in 1920—as did most of the other Western countries. All told, about four hundred US troops died in Russia without achieving anything lasting.

It's an episode that America forgot—but the Russians didn't. Today you'd be hard-pressed to find any mark of America's brief foray into Russian Revolution outside of Troy, Michigan, where a large marble polar bear memorial stands guarding the graves of fifty-six AEF soldiers. The Russian Bolsheviks, though, felt that a valuable lesson had been reinforced for them: the capitalist powers were intent on destroying communist regimes. Immediately following the Western withdrawal from Russia, the Bolsheviks went to work on promoting their long-held Marxist concept of world revolution, a global struggle of the working class against capitalism, and built up the institutions that would carry it out—including the Communist International (Comintern) in 1919 to coordinate that fight. From its start the Soviet Union, formed in 1922 when Vladimir Lenin consolidated the Bolshevik rule over Russia's neighboring lands, saw itself as facing an existential and unavoidable struggle with Western capitalism.

Key to this effort would be the Russian secret police and intelligence apparatus, beginning with the Cheka, the precursor to the infamous KGB. Felix Dzerzhinsky, the founder of the Cheka, focused almost immediately on foreign intelligence, creating a Foreign Department in December 1920 with the mission of uncovering any interventionist plots or economic blockade plans against the Soviet Union—plots Russia long imagined were being schemed by their capitalist adversaries—as well as gathering information about foreign military alliances, and, notably, the theft of industrial intellectual property and trade secrets.* Espionage against the bourgeois enemy was hardly the only focus of the newly formed Soviet Union. As Mikhail Frunze, one of the top Red Army commanders during the Russian Civil War, put it in his official 1921 Red Army military doctrine, "Between our proletarian state and the rest of the bourgeois world there can be only one state of long, stubborn, desperate war not for peaceful life, but to their death; war that requires colossal endurance, discipline, firmness, inflexibility and unity of will."[3]

The entire Soviet system right up until World War II was based on the premise that conflict between itself and the capitalist states was highly likely, if not inevitable. In fact, one of the main contributing factors to Joseph Stalin's paranoid Great Purge of 1936–1938—a purge

* The Cheka would evolve into the Cold War–era KGB and, later, after the collapse of the Soviet Union, the modern-day domestic intelligence agency FSB and the foreign intelligence–focused SVR. The Cheka's Foreign Department originally had six centers that said a lot about how Russia viewed the world at the time: (1) Northern, focused on the Baltics and Scandinavia; (2) Poland, which was considered the number one immediate threat to the Soviet Union in 1920; (3) Central Europe, with residences in Berlin and London; (4) Southern Europe and the Balkans; (5) Eastern, focused on a wide swath from Turkey and Iran to Japan and China; and (6) America, with residences in New York and Montreal.

that resulted in the deaths of almost a million people across the Soviet Union—was his conviction that everyone around him was a Western spy. Stalin would disregard reports from his exceptionally well-placed spy networks in the United Kingdom and the United States that continually reported to him that the West had no active intelligence assets in the Soviet Union and execute his own operatives under the charge of being agents of Western imperialism (usually British) or of his sworn archenemy Leon Trotsky.

By and large, the West remained quite oblivious to the existence of this "cold war" throughout the 1920s and early 1930s. In the late '20s, Secretary of State Henry Stimson famously disbanded the World War I code-breaking effort, known as the American Black Chamber, and proclaimed, "Gentlemen don't read each other's mail."[4] Diplomatic relations between the United States and the Soviet Union were established in 1933, and US and German industrialists flooded into the Soviet Union to help build numerous factories and heavy industry, including the now destroyed Azovstal metallurgical facility in Mariupol, which was based on the world's largest steel mill, the Gary Works plant, in Gary, Indiana. Virtually the entire Soviet automotive industry was built by Western firms, starting in 1929 with the Ford Motor Company, which helped to establish GAZ—which would later produce the famous Volga limousines that would ferry around the Soviet leadership—to manufacture cars built on Ford Models A and AA, as well as the Fordzon-Putilovets tractors built under the Ford license at the Kirov plant in Leningrad, a deal negotiated by the famous American industrialist (and later owner of Occidental Petroleum) Armand Hammer. Hammer himself had established a factory to produce pencils in Moscow, which was later nationalized by the Soviets. In 1930, under the direction of designer Andrey Vasilenko, the Soviet Union illegally reverse engineered a combine harvester from Holt Caterpillar (later Caterpillar) to produce an indigenous Soviet harvester, Kommunar, which enabled the Soviets to entirely stop importing combines from the West.

Eventually—and necessarily—the Soviet Union put its animosity with the West on hold during World War II to confront a common and much more dangerous threat to civilization. During that war the Soviet Union was an indispensable ally of the West in the fight against fascism, and as late as the famous Yalta Conference revealed, the United States believed that peaceful collaboration between the two nations would be critical to building a more secure global order in the aftermath of the war. But those moments represented only a strategic pause, and by the end of the war, America finally recognized the new global rivalry with the Soviet Union, as Moscow instituted communist coups across eastern European countries only recently liberated from the Nazis, which it now controlled with an iron fist.

By the time the United States broadly recognized the now-capitalized Cold War with the Soviet Union in 1947—the year, not coincidentally, that the United States ultimately founded its first civilian peacetime intelligence agency with the creation of the CIA—the Soviet Union had been working against the capitalist West for two decades. Naming the state of affairs that existed between the two powers was largely just a political formality.

THE PARALLELS OF THIS HISTORY WITH OUR CURRENT COMPETITION with China are remarkably similar. It's only been in the last few years that American policymakers and corporate leaders have begun to realize China is more of a threat than an opportunity—a realization that, much like with the first Cold War, seems to be arriving in C-suites and foreign policy circles decades after China firmly set its sights on the United States.

In terms of its formal policy, the United States has shied away from formally recognizing its entry into a new cold war, opting instead for a policy of "strategic competition" with China. Standing along Xi in 2015, President Obama said, "I believe it is in the interests of the United States to see China grow, to pull people out of poverty, to expand its markets, because a successful and stable and peaceful China can then serve as an effective partner with us on a range of international challenges."[5] And even in the final year of his presidency, President Obama said the United States should hope for a "successful, rising China," rather than a China that felt weak and threatened.[6] It's a mindset that has carried forward as his onetime vice president assumed the presidency himself. In November 2022 President Joe Biden explicitly eschewed a "cold war" framing, arguing that "there need not be a new Cold War" between the United States and China.[7]

Similarly, some commentators have argued that it's a mistake to use the label "cold war" to describe this conflict. In particular, these skeptics argue that the United States and China are far more economically integrated and technologically interdependent than the United States and the Soviet Union were at any point during the twentieth century. Moreover, they point to the pressing need for America and China to collaborate on shared challenges like climate change as proof that a full-fledged cold war is unlikely to unfold between the two countries.

While there's some truth to these points, they overlook the most compelling arguments in favor of the "new cold war" framing—namely, that the leaders of the Chinese Communist Party are themselves approaching the conflict in these terms. One of the most important lessons from Cold War I is that it only matters to some extent whether *we* recognize we're in a cold war. China has a voice in this too. When one looks at the common definition of a "cold war"—a state of conflict between nations that does not involve direct military action but is pursued primarily through economic and political actions, propaganda, acts of espionage or proxy wars waged by surrogates—it becomes hard to argue that's not already the situation we face with China (and have faced for decades prior). In the lead-up to the Chinese Communist Party's Twentieth Party Congress in 2022, Chinese president Xi Jinping repeatedly referred to the coming of a "great struggle" in China, a term that harkens back to Mao Zedong's twentieth-century conflict with the capitalist West. He called on the party to "to carry out a great struggle with many new historical characteristics" and reject "thoughts and actions to avoid conflict." Indeed, this is not a new recent idea from him. It first appeared in October 2017 as part of his report to the Nineteenth Party Congress, predating the Trump trade war (2018) and Biden's export control war (2022), indicating that this is not simply a reaction to Western anti-China measures.[8]

One of the things that the United States struggled with in the run-up to the invasion of Ukraine was that Putin actually meant what he said in the summer and fall of 2021—that his complaints about Ukraine, his fears about NATO expansion, his manifesto outlining why Ukraine should not exist, all in the end actually were part of his reasoning for invading Ukraine in February 2022. His warnings and reasoning, it turned out, were public all along, it's just that they seemed so irrational, so crazy, and so out-of-bounds that Americans and especially Europeans struggled to accept them. As Emily Horne, the spokesperson for the National Security Council, related on the one-year anniversary of the invasion, "One thing that has struck me throughout this process—and certainly struck me throughout the fall of '21—is that a lot of the times Putin and Russia were saying very plainly what their intentions were and what they wanted to do. And the West often had a very difficult time understanding that and hearing that. He made the case for what ultimately transpired very clearly in that manifesto in the summer of '21."[9]

That unexpected public clarity is one reason why it's worth understanding China's current geopolitical strategy, in particular, understanding what and why its leaders have been saying in recent years. It is enormously hard for Westerners to penetrate Chinese decision making. Rush Doshi, who assembled one of the largest troves of official Chinese government statements in his own research, wrote, "Some of the key Party institutions in foreign policy—the General Secretary's office, the Politburo Standing Committee, the Leading Small Groups (many now called Central Commissions), and the Central Military Commission—publish virtually nothing directly and are extremely challenging to study given the secretiveness surrounding their activities."[10]

And it's not just foreign policy. Almost every aspect of the country's leadership, decision making, internal debate, budgeting, procurement, and development process is a black box.[*11] All of the normal

* As Rush Doshi noted when he was assembling his database of official Chinese statements, "While the memoirs and selected works of several Central Military Commission

documents and tools that exist in open Western democracies—from organizational charts and legislative appropriations bills to tell-all memoirs by former officials—don't really exist, or are locked tightly behind China's closed doors.

Even at a pretty granular level, decisions are opaque. As Dean Cheng, a longtime China security watcher, says, the United States has been puzzled at really basic levels by China's recent investments in space systems, satellites, and space exploration. "No one has a good estimate of China's space program budget," Cheng says. "China's space program is more opaque than the Soviet space program—which was pretty opaque. We don't even know how they buy a satellite—who gets a say, how long it takes."[12]

That opacity makes it all the more critical to analyze its growth and goals. "The Party believes its official speeches and texts are of critical importance, and for that reason, many of the most astute observers of China have long taken them seriously," Doshi writes.[13] But figuring out what the lengthy, dry, and euphemism-filled documents actually say and what they mean is hardly an easy chore; China scholar Simon Leys, who devoted more than half a century to studying the country and its politics, once compared reading official party documents as "akin to munching rhinoceros sausage, or to swallowing sawdust by the bucketful," explaining it required "crack[ing] the code of the Communist political jargon and translat[ing] into ordinary speech this secret language full of symbols, riddles, cryptograms, hints, traps, dark allusions, and red herrings."[14] Nevertheless, China's ambitions have been there to see for anyone who was paying attention; in the early 2010s, Harvard political scientist Graham Allison asked Lee Kuan Yew, the founder of modern Singapore, whether China's goal was to replace the United States and become the predominant power in Asia. "Of course," he said. "Why not? They have transformed a poor society by an economic miracle to become now the second-largest economy in the world." But "unlike other emergent countries, China wants to

(CMC) vice chairmen whose terms ended as late as 2002 are available, not a single volume is available for who served after that period."

be China and accepted as such, not as an honorary member of the West. The Chinese will want to share this century as coequals with the United States."[15]

China has spent two hundred years trying to reclaim the glory, power, wealth, and prestige it enjoyed at the peak of the Qing Dynasty. It was Chinese statesman and philosopher Sun Yat-Sen—the man who was the first leader of the nationalist Kuomintang party—who in 1894 founded the *Xingzhonghui*, roughly the "Revive China Society," language that was later adopted by the Chinese Communist Party and leaders from Mao onward, a push that Jiang Zemin, the Chinese leader in the 1990s, would call the effort to "rejuvenate China."[16] As Jiang said, the CCP has "shouldered the great and solemn mission of national rejuvenation since the day it was founded"; speaking at the eightieth anniversary of the founding of the CCP, he explained, "In the 100 years from the middle of the 20th century to the middle of the 21st century, all the struggles of the Chinese people have been to achieve wealth and power for the homeland . . . and the great rejuvenation of the nation. In this historic cause [of rejuvenation], our party has led the people of the country for 50 years and made tremendous progress; after another 50 years of hard work, it will be successfully completed."[17]

And just as the 1910s and 1920s saw a dramatic reconsideration of the West and the United States by Russia, in the late 1980s and early 1990s China's view of the US threat evolved. China's adversarial view of the United States, the West in general, and its own place in the world was reinforced in the wake of what Rush Doshi calls the "traumatic trifecta": the uprising and massacre in Tiananmen Square in 1989, the Gulf War in 1991, and the collapse of the Soviet Union in 1991. As Doshi explains, "The Tiananmen Square protests reminded Beijing of the American ideological threat, the swift Gulf War victory reminded it of the American military threat, and the loss of the shared Soviet adversary reminded it of the American geopolitical threat."[18]

The wind-down of Cold War I and the subsequent collapse of the Soviet Union reoriented China. For years, it had seen war with the neighboring Soviet Union as a real possibility, and ever since Nixon's reopening had successfully triangulated to play the US-Soviet rivalry to its own benefit, but by 1985 Deng Xiaoping declared that threat effectively over and a new era was emerging.[19] Instead, in the years ahead, Deng came to see the United States as its primary enemy. As he said in 1989, "I [had] looked forward to the end of the Cold War, but now I feel disappointed. It seems that one Cold War has come to an end but that two others have already begun." To him, "the Western countries are staging a third world war without gunsmoke—by that I mean they want to bring about the peaceful evolution of socialist countries towards capitalism."[20]

By then, China saw probable war with the United States as its biggest challenge. "China had lost its strategic leverage," wrote scholar Kai He, and "given US policies on human rights and Taiwan, the US as the sole superpower posed a very serious challenge to China's internal and external security."[21] It was a message that American business and political leaders didn't take to heart. Instead, as China sought actively to acquire weapons that would deny the United States access to the waters around its shores and sought economic ties with the United States that would entangle the two countries and minimize the chances for successful economic reprisals, America's politicians welcomed China into elite international clubs, like the World Trade Organization, and CEOs flocked to China, sensing opportunity in its billion new customers and consumers—opportunities that, for too many Western companies, would never arrive or prove short-lived.

The Chinese military had expected that Iraq's large forces would stall the US-led coalition liberating Kuwait, perhaps even drawing the United States into a quagmire, only instead to watch US troops rout Iraq in just one hundred hours. It was such a rude wake-up call to China that America's military was far stronger than they'd given it credit for and not a force that they could hope to match anytime soon that Jiang Zemin, then the party general secretary and chair of the Central Military Commission, personally participated in a series of studies about lessons from the Gulf War.[22]

In the years since, China, Doshi argues, has pursued an organized and careful strategy of displacement, one that began in the 1990s by emphasizing how to "blunt" Western power while China itself remained weak, and then proceeded in the following two decades to enter a "building" stage, where it could more directly take on America and its allies in the Pacific—investing in military, economic, and diplomatic tools and partnerships that would allow it to better flex its growing power capabilities. That Chinese strategy, known as *Tao Guang Yang Hui*, roughly translated "to hide one's capabilities and bide one's time," was a smart attempt, Doshi says, "to encourage Chinese self-restraint at a time when its relative power was low."[23]

For instance, instead of attempting to match the United States weapon-for-weapon, China invested in what it called *shashoujian*, or "assassin's mace" weapons, cheap, mass-producible asymmetric weapons that could counter the very strengths of the US military—like anti-ship missiles and maritime mines that could target the naval fleets necessary to wage war close to China's shores. Beginning around the Gulf War, China underwent a huge modernization program for its submarines—retiring its outdated Soviet-era submarines and bringing roughly seventy new submarines into operation. But *how* it made that investment is almost as interesting as the project itself: it invested in low-tech diesel submarines, since as one officer said, "the price of a nuclear submarine can buy several, even more than ten, conventional submarines." Moreover, it equipped them with YJ-18 anti-ship ballistic missiles with a range of four hundred kilometers—it was, from top to bottom, an aircraft-carrier-killing fleet.[24] These weapons, military leader Zhang Wannian declared, would be key to "fulfilling unification," official jargon for retaking Taiwan, as "only after developing our own *shashoujian* . . . will China have the ability to take the initiative in strategy."[25]

On the economic front, the global political controversy over the crackdown and massacre at Tiananmen Square led Chinese leaders to realize their trade links with the West were more tenuous than it may seem. Suddenly, China's Most Favored Nation trading status—renewed annually since 1979 without controversy—was in jeopardy with the US Congress. The Tiananmen Square protests kicked off an era when a whole host of other more controversial subjects were thrown into the trade debate. "What was discussed was not whether

China allows freedom-of-emigration; instead it was human rights, religion, family planning, Taiwan, Tibet, nuclear nonproliferation, trade deficits, labor reform products, and other irrelevant questions," former foreign minister Li Zhaoxing recalled in his memoirs. "China had to beg the United States. China must be obedient, otherwise it will be punished by the United States Congress."[26] It was a worrisome new twist for a country on the economic rise, one that the Chinese government suddenly saw as a major geopolitical threat. Gaining membership in the WTO with the market access benefits that would bring suddenly became paramount—and, incredibly, the United States basically caved on this issue. "By the early 2000s, it was clear that China had played its weak hand well," Doshi writes. "China had bought itself stable market access abroad, which in turn made multinational companies more willing to invest in and export from China—setting off a virtuous circle of explosive growth in China while accelerating deindustrialization and increasing unemployment in the industrialized world." In two decades, China's economy would soar from 10 percent the size of America's to 70 percent.[27]

Across the board, the contemporary relationship with China looks a lot like US relations with the Soviet Union in the 1920s and 1930s. By now, we've also experienced decades of espionage, including the theft of intellectual property and trade secrets on an unprecedented scale, thefts enabled and supercharged by cyber, the new power espionage tool. For the last thirty years, China has also been reforming and building up its military, with the doctrinal focus on confronting the United States in the Indo-Pacific—not unlike what the Soviet Union was doing in the 1920s and 1930s, except with its primary enemy at the time being the United Kingdom. While this antagonistic activity was taking place, US and European businesses, entrepreneurs, and financial investors were setting up subsidiaries in China, facilitating the transfer of key knowledge and intellectual property, transfers often forced by coercive rules instituted by the Chinese government meant to boost local industry. These huge Western-led investments, all done to lower cost of goods production by tapping into the cheap Chinese labor market, as well as optimistically with the hope of opening up vast Chinese markets to US and Western companies, enabled China to build up its economic power and benefit from licensed, coercively shared and outright stolen technology, not unlike their predecessors had done in the Soviet Union pre–World War II. They also helped China to create huge, global, and powerful domestic champions like Huawei, Baidu, Tencent, and Alibaba.

The parallels do not end there. While internet and press freedom advocates talk about the "Great Firewall" that isolates the news and media ecosystem inside China, Xi Jinping's government is pursuing ambitious plans beyond its borders to build a "sphere of influence" that are not wholly unlike Soviet Union's efforts during Cold War I. (In 1997, Zbigniew Brzezinski defined a Chinese sphere of influence simply "as one in which the first question in the various capitals is, 'What is Beijing's view on this?'")[28]

At the core of the Chinese influence machine is the organization called the United Front, created by the CCP in the 1930s following Mao's identification of it as one the CCP's "three magic weapons," alongside armed struggle and party-building. It came into its present form immediately following the end of World War II in 1946, with the newly created United Front Work Department (UFWD) being given the mission, according to the Department of State, "for coordinating domestic and foreign influence operations, through propaganda and manipulation of susceptible audiences and individuals."[29] According to historian Michael Hunt, the CCP's Central Committee tasked the UFWD with "establishing links with other Asian communist parties, as well as overseas Chinese," and from the very beginnings of communist China, Mao pursued a policy of Asian regional leadership, one supported and even encouraged by Stalin.[30] Liu Shaoqi, Mao's lieutenant in the early days of the PRC, proclaimed shortly after returning from Moscow in 1949 that the road traveled by China under Mao's direction is "the road the peoples of many colonial and semi-colonial areas should traverse in their struggle for national independence and people's democracy."[31]

Following the Sino-Soviet split in the 1950s, Mao's ambitions expanded, as he saw an opportunity to unite "oppressed people" across

Africa, Latin America, and Asia "to create a powerful new international front against the two imperialist superpowers," Hunt writes.[32] This work included support for Maoist guerrilla insurgencies and communist parties around the world, including the Malayan Communist Party that fought against British colonialism in the 1950s, Maoist rebels in Congo in the 1960s, the Eritrean Liberation Front independence movement in Ethiopia the 1960s, the Dhofar Liberation Front Marxist insurgency in Oman in the 1960s and 1970s, Thailand's Communist Party fighting against its government in the 1970s, and the People's Liberation Army in Namibia fighting in the South African Border War in the 1970s.

While Chinese attempts to export its Maoist ideology and support for regime-changing insurgencies ended following Mao's death, the UFWD continued on, refocusing its efforts on the Chinese diaspora. According to the US State Department, as Chinese students started to "attend western universities in the late 1970s, the CCP facilitated the establishment of Chinese Students and Scholars Association (CSSA) chapters on Western campuses to monitor Chinese students studying abroad and ensure their views remained in line with that of CCP beliefs," activities that not only continue to this day but have gotten even more brazen. Today, such groups "actively wor[k] to inhibit debate and interactions between Chinese and non-Chinese peers to keep the former from learning new perspectives or attempting to challenge CCP dogma, while PRC diplomatic posts often provide funding and guidance to CSSA chapters, even encouraging members to disrupt lectures or events on campus that question CCP ideology or positions."[33] Recently, Xi went even further by establishing a Mwalimu Julius Nyerere Leadership School in Tanzania, which opened its doors in 2022, where "Chinese teachers sent from Beijing train African leaders that the ruling party should sit above the government and the courts and that fierce discipline within the party can ensure adherence to party ideology."[34] These long-arm efforts continue beyond China's "thought police" to include its actual police too: Western countries realized in 2022 and 2023 that China had established more than one hundred overseas police stations, many operating in secret, that aimed "to monitor, harass and in some cases repatriate Chinese citizens living in exile." In April 2023 the Justice Department arrested and charged two men allegedly employed by the Ministry of Public Security, who had been operating an undercover police station in Lower Manhattan's Chinatown.[35]

In its own backyard, the Chinese government has been conducting a genocide against its Uyghur minority, recently consolidated its control over Hong Kong, and is adopting an increasingly aggressive posture toward Taiwan—control over which would be a critical stepping stone toward dominance in the Pacific. Finally, Xi has explicitly signaled the acceleration of a quiet arms race with the West, calling on the Chinese military to completely modernize its armed forces by 2035, moving it up from the original 2049 target, and, according to US intelligence, ordering it to be ready to invade Taiwan by 2027. Even accounting for the important differences in economic interdependence that the West has with China compared to its trade connections with the Soviet Union, these policies constitute the foundations of a new—if distinctive—cold war between the United States and China. While many pundits now talk out loud about America being in a new cold war or "Cold War 2.0," it's worth noting that much like the enormous differences between World War I and World War II—to include the underlying causes and makeup of coalitions—this cold war with China isn't entirely comparable to the last one. Nor is it a continuation of the original Cold War, which those who choose the "Cold War 2.0" label would seem to incorrectly imply. A better way to look at this would be to recognize that we're in Cold War II.

This Cold War II, between the United States and China, is inherently different from the one that unfolded between the Soviet Union and the United States, as the challenge from China is fundamentally different today from what we faced during the ideological competition that characterized much of the twentieth century. Most obviously, the United States and China have deep and massive economic ties, even if partial decoupling in critical technologies such as semiconductors and artificial intelligence is already in progress. Unlike the Soviet Union and Mao's China, Xi's China today has limited expansionist interests.

The Soviet Union, for much of its existence, was focused on the spread of communism around the world, not only ideologically believing that communism was the better system to govern the world but also practically appreciating that the more communist countries there were in the world (which would be its natural allies, although it didn't always pan out this way in practice), the safer and more powerful its position would be on the global stage. China, on the other hand, is currently not looking to change governments around the world, even if it is seeking to influence them and their population through UFWD operations, such as government-funded Confucius Institutes and CCP cells on Western college campuses, and traditional and social media propaganda operations worldwide.[36] The PRC ensnares countries within its economic sphere of influence with infrastructure investments (which often turn into debt traps in impoverished Global South countries), bribery of corrupt officials, trade enticements of access to the massive China market, and offers of sales of cheaper goods—from BYD electric cars to Huawei telecommunications infrastructure. The price that countries have to pay for such economic largesse is often viewed as minimal by growth-focused governments: ignore the Chinese human rights record and domestic authoritarianism, never criticize its foreign policy and—most importantly—never contradict its territorial claims on Taiwan, parts of India's Arunachal Pradesh state, Japan's Senkaku Islands, Vietnam's Paracel Islands, and large parts of the South China Sea.

For much of Cold War I, the long-term strategy of both the Soviet Union and the United States was to destroy each other's systems. The explicit goal of the US "containment policy" was based on the insights of George Kennan, who had argued that the "Soviet Union will not last" due to its unnatural system and that all that the United States had to do was wait it out for its ultimate failure. (Kennan would later become a critic of US policy and claim that his containment strategy never included the military dimension.) Similarly, the leadership of the Soviet Union, adhering to the Marxist-Leninist ideology, believed that capitalism was unnatural and temporary oppression of the worker class by the bourgeois and would eventually be replaced by communism.

All that Russian communists had to do was wait (or better yet, help to accelerate the processes) for the US government to self-destruct under the pressures of racial tensions and class struggle.

In Cold War II, both China and the United States believe that the two countries are here to stay. There are some in America who believe that the CCP may eventually collapse, but few are counting on that outcome. And their current goals in this competition are not destruction of each other's systems but a competition for influence around the world, first and foremost in the critical Indo-Pacific region. Neither believes that this struggle is existential like it was in Cold War I. Rather, it is a fight for global economic, diplomatic, and military supremacy—a fight about who controls the economic levers and has more influence in global institutions of the twenty-first century.

Finally, unlike Cold War I, the coalitions of each country are much less defined. For nearly the entire last half of the twentieth century, the world was divided fairly rigidly into three blocs: Western, Soviet, and Non-Aligned. Today, no such coalitions exist. China has few, if any, true allies like the Soviet Union did—not even Russia has the allies it once had, for that matter—and China doesn't even exercise any meaningful political control over its few entirely dependent states like North Korea. The United States faces its own complex geopolitical considerations. While it has strong allies in Europe and Asia, countries in those regions have their own economic entanglements with China and are pushing back on the notion that they should have to choose between trading with China and siding with the United States when it comes to partially decoupling their economies from China or denying China access to critical technologies. While there was never any question about which side NATO allies would choose in Cold War I, we can't be entirely sure which side our allies—even our closest allies—will choose on specific issues with China. Moreover, many countries—from Africa to Asia to Central and South America—are actively welcoming and encouraging Chinese investments and technology upgrades, as well as, increasingly, influence operations.

Confronting these realities and complexities requires a deeper, harder look at how we've organized ourselves, our government, our economy, and at our core strategies for the decades ahead. That's a process, unfortunately, that we haven't done well since the end of Cold War I, when we properly aligned decade after decade our politics and military and economic strengths to counter the Soviet communist threat. In fact, thinking strategically and long term has never been one of the strengths of the American system, given the constant changes in presidential administrations every four or eight years and the subsequent redrafting and rewriting of the national security strategies. After all, if it's truly a "national strategy," should it really change so frequently?

THERE'S A LIKELY APOCRYPHAL QUOTE ATTRIBUTED TO WINSTON Churchill that "Americans can always be counted on to do the right thing—after they have exhausted all other possibilities." And indeed America's history of foreign policy largely seems to be one of belatedly recognizing how it's viewed by others around the world; for decades, America's sheer size, industrial and economic might, and geographical isolation allowed a certain detachment from geopolitical realities, advantages that have been steadily eroded in the nuclear, digital, and terrorism age. Particularly overseas, clear articulation of realistic end goals is something that America often struggles with—a fact driven in part by politicians' obsession with lofty rhetoric about spreading our values and freedom around the world, words that cannot be matched by reality due to the fundamental limitations of US power and resources (and, perhaps, most of all, the limitations of American patience and domestic politics).

One of the few times in the modern era that America got this question of grand strategy right was during Cold War I, when there was a clear game plan for victory: containment until the unnatural Soviet Union collapses as an entity and its ideology of communism is resoundingly defeated by capitalism. It was a policy outlined in the earliest days of the conflict, as Kennan's "Long Telegram" famously provided a blueprint for the policy of containment that the United States adopted to constrain the expansion of Soviet influence during the latter half of the twentieth century. But in addition to serving as the seed of what would later become the Truman Doctrine, Kennan's telegram provided an incisive analysis of the ideological premises that undergirded the Soviet Union's Cold War mentality.

Chief among these premises was the belief that Soviet communism was engaged in a zero-sum conflict with Western capitalism, a conflict that could not be resolved by peaceful political means. As Kennan wrote, "[The] USSR still lives in antagonistic 'capitalist encirclement' with which in the long run there can be no permanent peaceful coexistence." As a consequence, Kennan wrote, Soviet leadership had internalized the necessity of "[seeking] security only in patient but deadly struggle for total destruction of rival power, never in compacts and compromises with it."[37]

This final point was key: even while the United States and the Soviet Union remained nominal allies during and in the immediate aftermath of World War II, Kennan recognized that the logic of Soviet power placed that country on a direct crash course with the United States. As a practical matter, Kennan argued, the USSR had already begun to prepare for this inevitable conflict, adopting policies "devoted to increasing in every way strength and prestige of Soviet state," chiefly through the development of "intensive military-industrialization," "maximum development of armed forces," and "great displays to impress outsiders." Kennan astutely recognized that these policies pointed toward conflict, not collaboration—no matter what the rhetoric coming out of Washington or Moscow implied.

No such articulation of end goals exists today in our relationship with China. America's current policy of "strategic competition"—a policy that has been embraced across the domestic political spectrum—is based on the notion that the United States and its allies can pursue two objectives at once: outcompeting China in areas of strategic importance while also collaborating with it on topics of mutual concern. But like all hybrid policies, this one is fraught with potential contradictions. When push comes to shove, which priority will take precedence—competition or collaboration? Moreover, this strategy requires a willing partner on the Chinese side and, thus far, on every issue of what many in the West think should be mutual interests for both countries—from climate change to the resolution of destabilizing conflicts like Russia's war on Ukraine—President Xi has refused to play ball. He demands, instead, to be paid first, which to him means the United States rolling back the export controls, sanctions, and tariffs that he sees, not inaccurately, as containing China's economic growth.

If anything, we learned the wrong lessons from Cold War I. Winning the first Cold War gave America and our leaders the mistaken notion that democracy was on the march—it was the "end of history" and the "universalization of Western liberal democracy as the final form of human government," as Francis Fukuyama declared—and there was a lasting and ultimately corrosive belief that America was all powerful and that we could do anything and everything. In the years that followed, the United States received some brutal lessons in the limits of its power and resolve—from the streets of Mogadishu in the Somalia intervention memorialized in *Black Hawk Down* to the failures of attempts to bring better governance to Haiti. More recently, our decades of failure in Iraq and Afghanistan have humbled us but have not permanently disavowed us of the mistaken notion that America can do anything we put our mind to. American strategy has been rudderless ever since 1991—jumping to intervene from one crisis to another around the world to confront enemies both real and exaggerated.

Even the fight against terrorism over the last twenty years was highly nebulous in terms of its end state (how do you defeat a tactic?), and the promotion of democracy as a strategy was haphazard and dubious as a recipe for success. I recall vividly participating in debating strategies for fighting terrorism in my international affairs classes during my graduate degree work at Georgia Tech as my personal horror and shock in the aftermath of the 9/11 attacks was rapidly displaced by amazement and admiration of the US military's rapid dismantlement of the al-Qaeda and Taliban power base in Afghanistan. And then shifting again into disbelief as America's grand strategy to defeat terrorism morphed into the amorphous mission of "spreading democracy" and "institution building" in Afghanistan. These were admirable and lofty goals no doubt, but I couldn't help but wonder even back then whether the United States was capable of achieving them in a place we understood as little as Afghanistan, the country that had sapped the last energies of the Soviet Union, the country of my birth. And then we barely let the dust settle from that invasion before embarking on the ultimate war of choice in Iraq, with similarly nebulous goals and shifting missions. And after twenty years, we've largely abandoned both countries with little to show for our investment of trillions of dollars and thousands of American lives lost and many more families destroyed by the scourge of PTSD.

Still too often today US foreign policy seems based on blind hope: Iran and North Korea will voluntarily give up their nuclear weapons programs if only we let the economic sanctions do their work long enough; China and Russia will embrace rule-of-law capitalism and transform themselves into friendly Jeffersonian democracies that follow the rules-based international order; our allies in Europe and the Middle East will always choose us over accommodation with our geopolitical competitors. In the twenty-first century, we've too often refused to acknowledge realities on the ground all over the world and accuse leaders of other countries of being irrational if their decisions and actions go against the grain of our vision for the evolution of the world's order.

Envisioning the path forward for American democracy and Western values requires a clear-eyed assessment that global actors are rational, even if the reasons for their actions are not consistent with Western democratic priorities and views of the world. Evaluating the best tools, levers, and pressure points to maximize US influence requires understanding—sharply and coldly—what matters to "us" and what matters to "them." It requires envisioning—and articulating—what matters most to us in our global relationships and what our desired and achievable end state actually is. This involves much more clear articulation of our key foreign policy goals, as well as longer-term strategic thinking, than America typically manages to accomplish, with its frequent continuing budget resolutions, regular fights over the debt ceiling, biennial congressional elections, and quadrennial presidential shifts. We need to reengage with the long-term strategy, like we successfully did during Cold War I and in efforts like the Marshall Plan. Right now, unfortunately, we have goals—support Ukraine "as long as it takes"—without a larger and longer-term vision or strategy for victory.

It should now be clear that it is time to scale down our ambitions for a worldwide liberal order, and it is time to get tough with China, the only global adversary who can truly challenge us and displace us as a global economic and military superpower. We need to unite the country and our leaders behind a single, straightforward goal: navigating the most dangerous period we've confronted since the 1940s, the period of maximum danger when the balance of power between the United States and China in the twenty-first century will be decided.

The United States can't do everything—be the world's policeman, solve every crisis, and every war. No one can. This does not mean we should pull back across the world and become isolationist Fortress America, but it does mean matching our ambitions to the limits of our power. It means that we have to accept more of the world as it is than we might wish it to be and admit that we do not have the power to make every country a democracy, end conflict everywhere, or even prevent states like North Korea and Iran from going nuclear. But we *can* do a lot if we prioritize and marshal our resources in the pursuit of our most critical objective, if we understand and articulate what that objective is.

We need to focus on one thing: winning. Winning the peace, winning economic competitions, winning the technological race, winning allies.

Winning will require focus. Winning also requires discipline and realism and allies.

Winning will require making some hard choices. Take Ukraine as an example. There is a rightful celebration of Ukraine's survival against Russian genocidal aggression but there is little discussion of what realistic victory looks like. There is certainly hope that Ukraine can recover all the territories it has lost to Russia since becoming a country in 1991, but that should not be the only bar for victory of US objectives. If one looks at it objectively, Russia has already lost. Its military has been decimated in Ukraine. Its weapons and munitions stockpiles are depleted and will take a decade or more to rebuild even in the best of economic conditions, much less under the severe sanctions and export controls that are curtailing Russia's economic growth and limiting its ability to procure advanced Western technologies at scale. The United States has been able to reinvigorate the NATO alliance and give it a new (or old) purpose. It has been able to articulate more clearly the threat that China poses to Taiwan—given the territorial grabbing example that Putin has just provided the world in Ukraine. By all accounts, we have already won and Russia has lost. And yet, because of the lofty rhetoric many will consider anything short of Ukraine regaining all of its territories, a goal that might not be militarily achievable, a loss not just for Ukraine itself but for its primary supporter—the United States.

Countering Russia in Ukraine, instead, should be viewed through the lens of what is our main challenge for the next twenty-five years: countering China. Avoiding a conflict with China and avoiding ceding our global economic, diplomatic, and military dominance to it should be the primary critical objective of US foreign policy, a goal that will be even more challenging to achieve than defeating the Soviet Union was during the Cold War. We have to marshal all of our resources in the accomplishment of that task and do our best to avoid or minimize the nonessential distractions.

CHAPTER 3

The Taiwan Dilemma

So what made me so convinced in December of 2021 that Russia was going to invade Ukraine before the end of winter of 2022, months before they actually did it and with many respectable foreign policy pundits at the time predicting the exact opposite? And, more relevant for today, what does Putin's decision to invade Ukraine say about why Xi Jinping is likely to attempt to invade Taiwan in the coming years?

For me, it started with Ukrainian president Volodymyr Zelensky's background as a comedian. Many years before he entered politics, Zelensky had spent an early part of his career participating in comedy shows on Russian television—shows like the iconic *KVN* (Club of the Funny and Inventive), a marquee comedy program that has been one of the most popular shows of Russian and Soviet television since the early 1960s. It's sort of a mix of *Saturday Night Live* and the comedy improv *Whose Line Is It Anyway?*, with teams of college-age youth competing before judges with skits often themed to current events and politics. *KVN* was an institution in Russia, one of the few programs that had showcased non–party approved humor on Soviet television—or at least until it ran afoul of censors in the 1970s and been banned until Gorbachev's perestroika brought it back in 1986. The TV format spawned franchises and local competitions all over the country—and later, even, the world, as émigrés from the former Soviet Union in places like the United States, Israel, and Australia formed their own amateur teams. Many universities created their own KVN teams and competitions; my mother and her cousin had participated in one during their college years, and I had captained an amateur KVN team in my middle school class in Russia. Putin even attended a number of recordings of the show in person, one of which featured a team captained by a young man called Vladimir Zelensky, who would later go by President Volodymyr Zelensky.

Zelensky had helped lead several highly accomplished Ukrainian teams in the late 1990s, and when he was elected as president of Ukraine in 2019, I immediately recognized that Moscow was likely intrigued by the prospect his presidency had created. He was a familiar face, steeped in Russian culture, and a native Russian speaker who at least back then had struggled to speak Ukrainian well. He was elected on a platform of ending the war in the Donbas that had been raging since 2014 and making peace with Russia. There were a lot of signs initially that he likely seemed a man that Putin could do business with. But by 2021 the indicators coming out of Moscow made it quite clear that Putin had run out of patience that Zelensky would do his bidding. As Zelensky's term unfolded, he faced a fractured political landscape, one riven by an eight-year war against Russian proxies and intelligence services in the Donbas that had cost thousands of Ukrainian lives. There was no peace to be had with Putin, only capitulation, and, in fact, Zelensky pushed steadily in what the Kremlin saw as an anti-Moscow direction.

Just before Zelensky's inauguration in May 2019, the Ukrainian Rada—its parliament—had passed a law giving priority to Ukrainian language in the public sphere, making it the language of choice across government services, media, and education. The law caused an outcry from Russian officials, who claimed to be standing up for the interest of Russian-speaking citizens of Ukraine. Moreover, Moscow waited in vain for Zelensky to implement the so-called Minsk Agreements that had been pushed on his predecessor by Putin and the big European powers in the fall and winter of 2014–2015. The agreements required Ukraine to grant local self-governance to the breakaway Donbas provinces in exchange for a ceasefire, and—not surprisingly—they proved very unpopular in Ukraine, where they were judged (correctly) as a wily Russian attempt to further weaken and divide their country. And while Putin himself broke the agreement—it required him to withdraw his armed mercenaries from occupied Ukraine, something he had no intention of doing—to him, it was a lesson that diplomats and diplomacy weren't going to solve his Ukraine dilemma.

But perhaps Zelensky's most "egregious" act in Putin's mind was when the Ukrainian government went after Viktor Medvedchuk, a leader of the pro-Russian party in Ukraine and Putin's man in Kyiv. In the 1970s Medvedchuk was a defense lawyer who was appointed to defend several Ukrainian dissidents being prosecuted by the state for "anti-Soviet" activities and who, according to contemporaries, instead did everything possible to ensure their conviction. He turned politician in the 1990s and simultaneously—as is not uncommon in the post-Soviet landscape—became a very rich man, owning an over three-hundred-foot megayacht (with a twelve-meter-long swimming pool), a Gulfstream jet, a Bell helicopter, and even a replica of a Pullman dining train car that he had given his wife for her birthday. In 2003 he started to actively court a close relationship with Vladimir Putin, convincing him to even become a godfather to his daughter a year later. Putin allegedly came to believe that no question involving Ukraine could be solved without Medvedchuk, so when the Ukrainian government initially sanctioned Medvedchuk in February 2021 and put him under house arrest in May of that year, Putin likely lost faith that Zelensky could ever be a partner in his attempt to bring Ukraine back into Russia's sphere of influence.

But it wasn't just Zelensky.

I've spent much of my adult life now as a careful observer of Vladimir Putin, and I feel like I know him—or at least I know people *like* him—from growing up in Russia. By 2021 I had watched Putin's rise warily for almost a quarter century. As his profile on the world stage grew and he consolidated power and turned the clock back on freedom and democracy in Russia, I instinctively felt like I understood his mindset and understood his toxic imperialist appeal to the Russian people—though I of course found it repugnant. He was much older than I was, but we had both lived through the same wrenching dissolution of the Soviet Union, and growing up in Moscow, I'd known kids just like him: *dvor bullies*.

Life in the Soviet Union changed very little from World War II through the end of Cold War I; the technological marvels and rapid expansion of the middle class that the United States experienced during the same time period was tempered inside the Iron Curtain. In Putin's generation and mine, many Muscovites lived in blocky Soviet high-rise apartment buildings, built together in squares that enclosed a courtyard known as a *dvor*. The *dvors* were the neighborhood gathering place, where kids would play unsupervised for hours—all day, sometimes, on weekends. Every neighborhood *dvor* had a bully, one tough kid who tried to rule by fear and intimidation.

That is Putin. He has spoken over the years about how growing up in the Soviet Union toughened him, and that experience led him to view the geopolitical map as a *dvor*. He believes being a bully solves everything—that playground cunning, always trying to find an advantage, trying to stab someone in the back while they're not looking will always achieve his desired outcomes.

As a leader, he tapped into something very elemental about the Russian psyche: grievance, victimhood, and imperialism. It is a common view among Russians that Russia had been a great empire whose greatness was stolen by the West.

I was eleven, living in Moscow, when the Soviet Union dissolved. As a kid it was hard to fully grasp the implications and the causes of your country disappearing. The system I had grown up in was falling apart, and it wasn't clear what was going to emerge.

What many in the West missed at the time is that many Russian citizens had mixed feelings about the regime's end and the fall of communism; certainly there was happiness about the collapse of a repressive, authoritarian regime and, especially, the dissolving of the fearsome and loathed security services—although, as we would later learn, the KGB would emerge in a new form with a new name all too soon. People celebrated the fantastic economic revolution that allowed Western goods like blue jeans and Coca-Cola and all the other trappings of the American middle-class life to arrive in Russian stores. But at the same time, there was an acute, gnawing feeling that the greatness of their country disappeared overnight. Great Britain, the empire upon which the sun never set, had faded over decades, giving the British people plenty of time to adjust to the new world landscape; the Soviet Union's greatness disappeared seemingly in weeks.

Psychologically, the empire's dissolution packed a lot of punch because the propaganda that Russian citizens had all experienced in school and on television during the Soviet era was very powerful. They were one of the world's two superpowers—the first country to send a satellite into space, the first to launch a man into orbit around the planet. The Russians had been told for so long that they were great and that their country and vision for the future would be triumphant that it unmoored them when, in fact, the empire crumbled like a house of cards.

The transition to economic and political liberalism was hardly smooth. Many Russians had the sense that the United States, the West, and their Wall Street and Fleet Street bankers had plundered Russia's economy, dancing on the grave of the Soviet Union as ordinary Russians saw their life savings and retirements evaporate amid rampant inflation and astounding corruption. (Often enough, it was Russians themselves who did the plundering and ended up becoming unimaginably rich oligarchs.) The transition devastated lives as much as psyches.

In August 1991, I lived through the country's first putsch, as former Soviet hardliners tried to overthrow Mikhail Gorbachev's government, holding him incommunicado at his vacation house in Crimea, and reformist leader and newly elected Russian Federation president Boris Yeltsin rallied Muscovites to defend the House of Soviets (often called the Russian White House), housing Russia's lawmakers. I'll forever associate that attempted coup with *Swan Lake*; the music from Tchaikovsky's ballet ran on a loop on state television in the hours of the coup, an ominous sign for all of us watching because the music had become the marker the Soviet Union used when leadership changed. In 1982 the ballet had aired on TV as government leaders debated who would lead the country after the death of Premier Leonid Brezhnev; it was a stalling tactic, meant to give messy succession discussions time to play out. The same public ritual had occurred when Brezhnev's successor, Yuri Andropov, had died in 1984, and then when his successor, Konstantin Chernenko, died in 1985. Now the chords of Tchaikovsky's music seemed to portend an end to Gorbachev.

My parents and I went down to see the demonstrations at the center of the city; there were already huge crowds surrounding the Russian White House where the opposition politicians were holed up—and tanks in the streets on the way to crush the resistance. The atmosphere was both tense and jubilant. Everyone felt that they were witnessing history in the making, but no one yet knew how this chapter would end. Boris Yeltsin, the new president of the Russian republic—which was still within the framework of the Soviet Union at the time—climbed atop one of the tanks (an image captured in one of history's most remarkable photos) and gave a defiant speech that contributed to the hardliners losing their nerve and ultimately giving up.

Two years later, in 1993, it was Yeltsin who used tanks to attack that same Russian White House, the seat of Russian parliament that by then was full of nationalist and reactionist politicians opposed to his policies. He then violated the constitution by dissolving parliament, leading to the deadliest outbreak of street violence in Moscow since the October Revolution. The West, determined to support the democratic reformer Yeltsin at all costs, looked the other way. Russia's slide toward authoritarianism and illiberalism can, unfortunately, be traced directly to that moment. The unconstitutional use of force against opposing politicians was ignored by most Russian democratic liberals and the West alike, sacrificed on the altar of expediency to avoid a return to power of communists and nationalists. But it was only a matter of time before at least the latter group was elected to power anyway.

What looked to the West like the miraculous march of freedom after the fall of the Iron Curtain didn't feel like a miracle to most Russians. For many people, the collapse made life in the 1990s much worse on a daily basis. Sure, there were Western clothes and new luxuries in the stores, but most people couldn't afford any of it. And there was an explosion of street crime. The Soviet Union had been relatively safe, in terms of crime—the draconian punishments and official monopoly on corruption of authoritarian regimes often lead to minimal petty crime. But as the country collapsed, the doors to the prisons were opened and political prisoners and hardened criminals alike (one of them being a then-unknown Evgeny Prigozhin, the future leader of the Wagner Group and the Internet Research Agency) flooded back into society, creating an opening for the rise of powerful transnational organized crime groups. One thing I remember so vividly about those early '90s is the crime; life immediately felt very unsafe, with shootings in the streets, drugs, and organized crime exploding overnight. The law enforcement institutions, under their own pressure amid the government's fall, not only couldn't keep up but all too often became co-opted by the mafia.

When Putin came to power in 1999 and talked about rebuilding Russia, I understood viscerally the appeal of his message, even though I of course abhorred it. While I was living in the United States by then, I still talked to my grandparents back in Moscow, who, like many others, unfortunately voted for him. Most people in the West bought into the miracle of democracy and did not appreciate the disaster that the '90s bore for many Russians, as a small group of oligarchs grabbed all the wealth and the benefits of the economic liberalization while most of the country faced not an abundance of freedom but poverty. Putin tapped into this reality, telling the electorate, "I'm going to improve your lives and security and restore Russia's greatness." And in his first years in power, the rise of oil prices following 9/11 meant that life actually did get better for many Russians; the country's dependence on fossil fuels meant that the high energy prices translated into dramatically improved standards of living in Russia. Plus, Putin cracked down on visible street crime, making it clear early on that the only crime and corruption would be that sanctioned by his state. He also started to rebuild the Russian military and Russian power on the world stage.

In the 2000s I could see the grievance in Putin's statements and in the presentations he and his minions gave regularly in settings like the Munich Security Conference, the annual confab of presidents, prime ministers, foreign and defense ministers, various elected officials, and geopolitical experts: *We're here to make Russia great again (even if that exact slogan had not yet appeared on the geopolitical landscape). We're here to rebuild the empire that was stolen from us. The West backstabbed us, taking advantage of the weak leadership of Gorbachev, who let himself get snookered and allowed the West to break the country apart.*

Year by year, I had watched Putin warily, and even though I certainly never sympathized with him in any way, shape, or form, I absolutely understood how so much of the Russian people's support for him was genuine (and I think some parts of it remain genuine to this day). He was delivering on his promises to restore Russian power and greatness—to force the world and its neighbors if not to respect Russia, then to at least fear it. It was grotesque imperialism, but it worked.

By the end of the second decade of the millennium, I noticed a new dimension to Putin's rhetoric. By 2021 it was evident that we were witnessing an aging authoritarian leader who was determined to "fix" what he viewed as an unsolved problem: Ukraine, a country that he long believed didn't deserve to exist on its own, a space that by history and destiny he thought was meant to be part of Russia, a territory that was slipping away from his sphere of influence.

At the same time, it was quite clear to me that Putin—about to turn seventy and likely very mindful of his own longevity—was obsessed with his own place in history. He had long spoken admiringly about Peter the Great, the Russian tsar who came to power just two generations after a long lawless and anarchic period known as the Time of Troubles, when Russia had lost a third of its population and been occupied by the Polish-Lithuanian Commonwealth. Peter had restored Russian military strength, created a navy, modernized the country, expanded its territories through conquest, and established an empire that became one of Europe's Great Powers with his newly built city of St. Petersburg as its capital. It's not hard to see how Putin, who was born in St. Petersburg, then Leningrad, who also came to power after the unstable and chaotic period of the 1990s and had worked to rebuild the Russian military and expand its influence—and now its territory—would see himself as a worthy successor of Peter.* Putin clearly imagined himself restoring the old Russian empire—an empire that would be built on nationalism and patriotism, unlike the Soviet Union, which had been assembled on the quicksand of communist ideology.

The mortality clock, too, was no doubt weighing heavily on Putin's mind, particularly after his two-year period of self-imposed isolation during the COVID-19 pandemic. During this period, he mostly refused to see anyone who had not undergone PCR testing and a two-week isolation, and where his public meetings involved theatrics like huge spaces and comically long tables, which were so absurd that they became internet memes.

Put it all together and Putin's sense of urgency of getting Ukraine—that prize territory of the tsarist Russian empire, Russia's breadbasket, and a critical buffer state along the march of previous European invaders—back into Russia's orbit was acute.† Having given up on

* By contrast, Putin frequently bashes prior Soviet leaders—including Lenin, the founder of the Soviet Union and its spiritual and ideological leader, who he believes planted the seeds of Russia's dramatic loss of territory and population after the dissolution of the Soviet Union. In Putin's mind, Lenin's mistake was granting each republic its own recognition in the Soviet Union creation treaty—recognition that Putin feels was ill-considered because they had all been part of the Russian empire to begin with. (It's an obviously historically incorrect view given that many territories, such as Georgia and Azerbaijan, had preserved their cultural heritage and national aspirations. Some, like Ukraine, had even proclaimed their own short-lived states during the Russian Civil War, until they were reconquered by the Bolsheviks.)

† Russia is not entirely wrong to think that without the Ukrainian lands as a buffer, its capital is uniquely exposed to potential invasion—a fact underscored by the ability of the Wagner mercenary armored column of troops to get within a couple hours of Moscow in less than half a day from the border of Ukraine during their mutiny in June 2023. Putin is, however, mistaken in his claims that Ukraine's membership in NATO would make Russia less safe. Even setting aside the fact that NATO is a defensive alliance, Russia, of course, already shares land borders with six NATO countries: Estonia, Latvia, Lithuania, Norway, Poland, and the recently joined Finland. If NATO had any interest in

Zelensky and lost his puppet Medvedchuk to the wheels of Ukrainian justice, if Putin wanted to get Ukraine back, he would have to rely only on himself and what he—as it turned out mistakenly—thought was the might of the rejuvenated Russian military.

Putin's obsession since coming to power was to Make Russia Great Again, even if he didn't resort to that explicit slogan or to marketing it on hats. He early on consolidated his power over domestic Russian territory, brutally suppressing the insurgency in Chechnya and bringing it back into the fold of the Russian Federation, as well as doing away with elections of regional governors (choosing instead to appoint them directly from a cadre of loyalists).

Across the 2000s Putin invested in huge military modernization programs, taking advantage of high oil and gas prices—which finance a large part of Russia's budget—and creating new weapons platforms like the T-14 Armata fourth generation tank, Su-57 fifth generation stealth fighter, and air-launched Kinzhal ballistic missile (which the Russians market as "hypersonic" even though it has not demonstrated ability to significantly maneuver at greater than Mach 5 speeds—the common definition of a hypersonic weapon). He also attempted to move away from the military's long-term reliance on low-quality draftees and convert it instead into a professional contractor force.

That newly equipped and better-trained force, in turn, became part of Putin's efforts to interfere in the affairs of other independent states, from the takeover of Crimea and parts of eastern Ukraine to saving dictator Bashar al-Assad from defeat by Sunni and Kurdish insurgents during the Syrian civil war. He involved Russian paramilitary forces in conflicts in Libya and parts of Central and Eastern Africa, helping out friendly dictators in order to spread Russian geopolitical influence (and grab some of their natural resources), and worked to raise the country's prestige abroad by bringing the Olympics, World Cup, and Formula 1 to the Russian Federation.

---

invading Russia—which it doesn't—it has plenty of opportunities to do so already. And it is, of course, absolutely reprehensible to want to compensate for perceived and imagined threats by invading sovereign border countries.

Throughout, Putin's goal above all else has been for the United States—the world's only superpower—to treat him and his country with the respect he believes he and Russia deserve, welcoming them as equals, just as FDR treated Stalin during World War II. A major part of achieving that goal has involved reestablishing a "sphere of influence" where neighboring countries would be heavily influenced, if not fully dominated, by the Kremlin.

Except for the three Baltic states that cast their lot with the EU and NATO, most of the other former Soviet republics—the Central Asian states of Kazakhstan, Kyrgyzstan, Tajikistan, Turkmenistan, and Uzbekistan, as well as Armenia, at least prior to Russia abandoning it in its recent resumptions of territorial conflicts with Azerbaijan—have largely aligned with Moscow. Furthermore, by 2021 Putin's policies had led to the effective reabsorption of the third biggest former Soviet state, Belarus, into Russia's sphere of influence. (Belarus is led by a fellow authoritarian president, Aleksandr Lukashenko, who had agreed in 1997 to enter into a federal Union State with Russia but for decades stalled implementing the agreement until 2020, when Putin assisted him in suppressing democratic protesters following a rigged election and thereby dramatically reduced Lukashenko's room for independent maneuver.) Thanks to multiyear military and intelligence interference efforts in Georgia following Putin's short military campaign against the country in 2008, Russia has been able to get the Georgian government to exercise more of a pro-Russian line as well. Azerbaijan also keeps relatively warm relations with Moscow, while Moldova continues to be divided with Russia supporting its breakaway province of Transnistria.

All of these investments, escapades, and promising geopolitics, though, only got Putin so far. In his view, the restoration of Russian global influence could not be accomplished without Ukraine, which had been the second-biggest republic after Russia in the Soviet Union, being brought back under his control—if not outright rule. All in all, aside from the forever-lost Baltic states, it was Ukraine that kept Putin up at night as "the one, the most important one at that, that was trying to get away."

Indeed, by 2021 Putin specifically felt that Ukraine was slipping further and further from his grasp, in no small part because of his own previous actions.* Culturally and politically, the country was aligning west, toward Europe. It had been steadily investing in its military—its spending had nearly tripled since 2014—and increasing numbers of US and other NATO military trainers were helping to build up and reform the Ukrainian military, which was in the meantime increasing stockpiles of modern Western weaponry, such as the Javelin antitank missiles first provided by the United States in 2018. Ukraine also had a robust military-industrial complex, as it had retained many Soviet-era factories. (Notably, by the time of the invasion, Ukraine had managed to produce small quantities of Neptune anti-ship missiles, which it later used to sink the *Moskva* cruiser, the flagship of the Russian Black Sea fleet, and was getting close to fielding short-range Hrim-2 ballistic missiles.) These developments made Putin realize that the longer he waited to invade, the harder the task would be, further amplifying his decision to go sooner rather than later.

Putin, buoyed by his military's performance in Syria, was also highly confident in its abilities and the investments he'd made since coming to office to modernize the fighting force. President Obama had derisively predicted Syria would be a quagmire for Russia, but with a relatively light level of involvement of his air and naval assets, augmented by the paramilitary Wagner Group and special forces on the ground, Putin was able not only to hold back the rebels but to reverse dictator Bashar al-Assad's fortunes and restore most of the country back to his control. Putin also believed the lightning-quick operation by Russian military intelligence Spetsnaz forces to take over Crimea in 2014, amid little Ukrainian resistance, showed that Ukraine would be no match for his forces.

* Not the least of Putin's problems with Ukraine was that his illegal seizure and annexation of Crimea in 2014 had removed Crimea's nearly 2.5 million mostly Russian-speaking people—a population that had much historical affinity for Moscow—from participating in Ukrainian elections. The removal of those voters, plus the growing antagonism toward Russia among the Ukrainian populace sparked by Putin's aggression, ensured that pro-Russian candidates would be unlikely to ever again win nationwide elections at the Ukrainian ballot box.

At the same time, the Russian president was convinced that the Western backlash against Russia for this latest aggression would be minimal, just like it had been for the takeover of Crimea or the invasion of Georgia in 2008. Sure, there might be pro forma sanctions, but Putin had spent years de-dollarizing the Russian economy and believed it was now resilient against sanctions because of his orders to implement "import substitution" of critical goods. The Russian government had even created an indigenous payment network (SPFS) to serve as an alternative to international bank messaging system SWIFT and another (Mir) to replace the Visa and Mastercard credit card networks.* Putin also doubted that Europe, hobbled by its reliance on Russian gas, had the stomach to enact the most severe sanctions. (In 2021 Germany, Europe's biggest economy, imported over 55 percent of its gas and a third of its oil from Russia.) Putin simply could not imagine that Germany and other European countries dependent on Russian energy would be able to decouple from these fossil fuels so rapidly. To be fair, Putin was not making a bad bet. As I found out while attending the Munich Security Conference in February of 2022, mere days before the invasion, many European political and business leaders in attendance were not only convinced that Putin would not invade but could not contemplate getting off Russia's fossil fuel needle for years to come. Ironically, the shock of their disbelief being proved wrong by the invasion itself likely played a huge role in shaking up the European community and convincing it to lean in aggressively and to rapidly reduce the continent's energy dependence on Russia.

By 2021 Putin was not only all-powerful politically at home but also stunningly isolated. Years into his ever-tightening grip on the Kremlin, he had no one left among his government advisers capable of challenging the above-described assumptions and convincing him that the invasion could turn out a blunder of enormous proportions. His self-imposed COVID isolation meant he saw very few people in

* This may have been the only assumption about the war that Putin got somewhat right. Western observers have been surprised by the relatively limited impact of sanctions on the Russian economy thus far—with GDP dropping by just a little over 2 percent in 2022 and resuming growth again in 2023.

person and had largely surrounded himself with loyalist yes-men who would not dream of challenging him: most of them were even more nationalist and hawkish than he was, constantly egging him on. Even if someone did offer a contradictory opinion, he would confidently dismiss it, believing he knew better. One of the stories I heard from a well-placed source in Russia was that when Putin was considering seizing Crimea in 2014, he had some of his economic team come to him with concerns about the impact that Western sanctions would have on the Russian economy. Putin dismissed them with a telling line: "My job is to reunite Crimea back with Russia. Your job is to make sure we don't suffer any serious consequences for it. I'll do my job. You do yours."

Exchanges like this underscore that Putin is a confident—and hereto largely successful—gambler. In the days following the Ukraine invasion, I found it astonishing to see how many foreign policy experts in DC, stunned that they had been wrong about whether Putin would invade, expressed their profound shock by explaining, "He has changed." No. The truth is he has always been this person. One of his very first acts as Russian prime minister in 1999 was to launch the Second Chechen War, a war of choice that began only three years after the first one ended in such a humiliating disaster that it seriously endangered Boris Yeltsin's reelection campaign in 1996. It was an enormous gamble that he could win a war that Yeltsin previously lost and not lose popular support—and yet he did. Next, he gambled that he could punish Georgian president Mikheil Saakashvili in 2008 with a war without suffering any major consequences for it—and he pulled that off as well, with no one even bothering at the time to kick Russia out of the prestigious G-8 club of leading Western nations. The Crimean and Donbas adventures in 2014, not to mention the intervention in Syria, were also great gambles that proved highly successful—with very limited downsides for Putin personally. Finally, his regime's cyber-led interference in the US presidential elections in 2016 had made him look all powerful on the world stage. Each of these acts entailed major risks that could have backfired badly, but he had always lucked out.

Putin's whole life story, in fact, has been one of enormous luck. He was at the right place and the right time when the Soviet Union fell apart and his employer the KGB was in disarray, a disarray that allowed him to be picked up as a mentee by the powerful mayor of St. Petersburg Anatoly Sobchak and eventually rise to the influential post of deputy mayor of Russia's second-largest city. Then, after Sobchak lost his reelection campaign, Putin used his St. Petersburg connections to get a job as deputy head of presidential administration in Moscow, a post that later led to an appointment heading the FSB intelligence service in 1998, becoming prime minister in 1999, and, finally, being anointed as Yeltsin's successor at the turn of the millennium. It's hard to think of anyone else being luckier in their meteoric career progression to become leader of Russia in the last hundred years. It must have given him great confidence that he was born under a lucky star and his gambles would always work out.

But the Ukraine invasion, as we now know, was the gamble—his biggest yet—that looks to have broken the streak.

I mention all of this not only because it helps explain the unexplainable—why Putin took such a huge seemingly unnecessary gamble, one that has come at incredible cost to his country in blood and treasure—but because in this case, I believe that what's past is prologue.

As Putin did with Ukraine, Xi seeks to do with Taiwan.

WHY CHINA IS LIKELY TO INVADE TAIWAN

When I look at the situation in China, I unfortunately see very similar dynamics playing out there: an authoritarian leader, Xi, with few internal checks on his power, who—like Putin—has recently turned seventy and faces a ticking actuarial and political clock and who—like Putin—has also publicly proclaimed that the Taiwan problem cannot be pushed onto future generations, clearly implying that he is intent on "solving" it in his lifetime. I see a leader who—like Putin—has continued a decades-long upgrade to his nation's military, views the target of his desire as an illegitimately independent territory, and sees it slipping culturally and politically further away from Beijing.

The parallels are strong and all worrisome, perhaps none more so than the fact that China likely sees a window closing on Taiwan unification. Not unlike Ukraine in the case of Russia, Taiwan is also slipping further away from Beijing's grasp. Over the last seventy-five years, the Taiwanese have built their own independent identity and most consider their island an independent country, even if it hasn't formally proclaimed independence. In fact, Taiwan in recent decades had even successfully made one of the most challenging political evolutions in the world, transitioning relatively peacefully from an authoritarian dictatorship with one-party military rule to a competitive multiparty democracy.

In a July 2023 poll, only about 1 percent of the Taiwanese demonstrated a desire for unification with the mainland as soon as possible and another 6 percent claimed they might want to see it at some unspecified future date (perhaps when they think the CCP may no longer be in power).[1] Taiwan has remained separate now for long enough to develop its own cultural and political identity. Indeed, whereas Chiang Kai-shek arrived on the island in 1949 with the expectation and hope that his administration would one day return from the Republic of China as the legitimate government of all of China, entire generations have been raised to see themselves more as Taiwanese than Chinese. Polls indicate that over 60 percent of the population consider themselves Taiwanese and another almost 33 percent consider themselves both Taiwanese and Chinese; today, only a small minority of the island's residents—about 3 percent—identify themselves as Chinese first and reject the Taiwanese identity. In October 2023, I attended a National Day celebration parade in Taipei, and the immense pride people on the street expressed in their Taiwanese identity was palpable. It became quite clear to me that even if China were a democratic country, not ruled by the brutal CCP dictatorship, few people in Taiwan would have any interest in a unification that gave up their sovereignty to the mainland. Just like people everywhere, they love and want to preserve their own nation and not be beholden to anyone else.

China's own actions have also made a future peaceful Taiwanese unification less likely. The brutal crackdown in 2019 and subsequent destruction of the "one country, two systems" promise to Hong Kong—the principle that Hong Kong (and later Macau) would become a part of China but would keep their democratic system until 2047, fifty years following reunification—make any similar overture or promise to Taiwan seem laughable. If Xi reneged on that promise to Hong Kong after less than half the expected time had elapsed, why should the Taiwanese expect anything different? Moreover, they have seen the cost to Hong Kong of China's crackdown in terms of fraying of Western business ties, disappearance of free speech, and the right to protest and democracy and now have a clear understanding of how their own daily lives might be impacted if the island reunites with the mainland. Who in their right mind would trust Xi's word now?

This evolution in public opinion is particularly worrisome for Beijing, which tracks sentiment on Taiwan very closely. If you're sitting in the decision-maker ranks of the CCP, you have to be increasingly pessimistic about Taiwan becoming voluntarily absorbed into mainland China. The imperative to use force, or at a minimum coercion, looms large.

Just like Putin, Xi is obsessed with his legacy, trying to emulate Mao and join him in the CCP's pantheon of great and historic leaders. Along with Mao, he has been anointed as one of the four "core" leaders of the Communist Party, "a recognition by party members that they had become central to the party's functioning and, by extension, to the fate of China and its people," according to Xuezhi Guo, an expert on Chinese politics.[2] Also like Putin, Xi has isolated himself at the top of the Chinese decision-making hierarchy by purging all opposition within the party and consolidating power and becoming, as Kevin Rudd put it, "numero uno, dos, and tres. All else is detail."[3] Another top Australian sinologist, Geremie Barmé, makes the point even starker: "Xi has outdone Mao. He has more titles and more power than Mao."

In China, Xi holds three roles simultaneously. First, he is the head of state, a title that is translated overseas as "president" but in China denotes "state chairman," a nod to Mao's traditional leadership role. Simultaneously, Xi is general secretary of the CCP—the paramount leader of the country's sole political organization—and chairman of the Central Military Commission, which makes him the commander in chief of China's armed forces, police, and militia.

The consolidation of power around Xi marks a distinct turn from China's recent history, one that's important to consider both in the context of his own personal history and that of China. It wasn't that long ago that China's regime seemed to be developing into a relatively normal, albeit authoritarian, functioning government, one with routine transfers of power that marked it as being larger than any cult of personality. In 1982 Deng Xiaoping, who had taken office amid the chaos that followed the death of Mao, pushed through a new constitution that, via its article 79, placed term limits on the presidency—two consecutive five-year terms—but those limits seemingly never applied to him and he controlled the reins of power until his own death in 1997.* But in the years ahead, both Jiang Zemin and Hu Jintao dutifully abided by the term limits, and there was every hope as Xi Jinping assumed the national trinity of titles in 2012 and 2013 that China had entered a new era of mature, if not democratic, governance.[4] Writing as Xi took office, Nicholas Kristof hailed him as a "reformer" and stated, "Here is my prediction about China: The new paramount leader, Xi Jinping, will spearhead a resurgence of economic reform, and probably some political easing as well."[5]

History turned out differently. "Xi started reversing this trajectory almost immediately," his biographer Chun Han Wong wrote, and by the time the Nineteenth Party Congress convened in 2017, it was clear he was setting the country on a different course from the one predicted.[6] In February 2018 the government announced a plan to remove the article 79 term limits from the Chinese constitution. As Wong wrote, "The proposal shocked many Chinese. Their country may have attained the trappings of capitalist modernity—sleek skylines, glitzy

* He accomplished this, in part, by allowing junior allies to hold the technical titles of president and general secretary, while he served "only" as the head of the Central Advisory Commission, a newly established body that was designed in theory to provide political assistance and consultation to party leadership but in reality held all the authority and power.

consumer brands, and high-tech infrastructure—but their politics was backsliding toward what many considered a bygone era."[7]

Xi has proven himself a crafty political player, one clearly on track to be China's ruler for at least an unprecedented fourth term, perhaps even for life, and a figure who has defined (and redefined) what China calls its "fifth generation" of Communist Party leadership. Much of Xi's story is a quintessentially Chinese one, albeit one that began with great relative privilege. His father was chief of the CCP's propaganda department under Mao, reportedly involved in the infamous UFDW work and suffered, like many other individuals, from various purges and exiles amid the failure of Mao's Great Leap Forward. At one point the senior Xi was sent away from the family for seven years, and Xi himself, thirteen when the Cultural Revolution began, recalls being jailed multiple times growing up for appearing to be "anti-revolutionary."[8] His mother was forced to denounce him publicly and turned him away one night when Xi escaped political detention and came home seeking food and shelter, for fear her other children would be taken away by the state.

At fifteen, Xi was among some seventeen million urban Chinese sent to the countryside to work as part of a vast Mao "reeducation" effort. ("Everyone was crying, there wasn't anyone on the train who didn't cry," Xi recalled in a 2004 television interview.) According to Wong, "Xi lived in a cave dwelling, shared with others, and typically rose at 6 a.m. to do menial farm work."[9] After years of hard work—during which he demonstrated a seemingly insatiable love of reading books—he ended up at Tsinghua University just as Mao died and afterward, with his father's connections, began his own political rise. Henceforth, his career would take him from village secretary to military aide to deputy party secretary in Zhengding, a county in the north China province of Hebei, to (by age thirty-two) vice mayor of Xiamen, and then onward to municipal party boss in Fuzhou and eventually the number one provincial official in Fujian (recall that Fujian is the province on China's southeast coast that looks across the Taiwan Strait at Taiwan). There, he got some of his first geopolitical exposure to the Taiwan issue, overseeing a reserve antiaircraft artillery division.[10]

By the turn of the millennium, Xi was clearly a figure on the rise, albeit hardly an exceptional one; in 2002, he became the head of the province of Zhejiang. "Zhejiang was a pacesetter in the party's embrace of private business," Wong writes. "He traveled abroad to drum up investment and greased the wheels for foreign businesses, helping American companies like Citibank, FedEx, McDonald's, and Motorola set up or expand operations in Zhejiang. In a prelude to his future campaigns to promote higher-end and strategic industry, Xi blacklisted 'backward' manufacturing sectors, which were made to either upgrade their technology or leave the province."[11]

As the party elite began considering the loyal ranks for its fifth-generation leader, the field of candidates was made up of just two individuals: Xi and Li Keqiang, the governor of Henan, the central province that lays claim to being the birthplace of the Han Chinese civilization some three thousand years ago. "Many fellow princelings favored Xi. They believed the party must be led by born-red officials who would never renounce their revolutionary lineage, as opposed to apparatchiks of humble stock—such as Mikhail Gorbachev—who might one day betray the party," Wong wrote.[12] In October 2007 both men were promoted to the Politburo as expected, with Xi outranking Li by a single position, a difference sufficient to indicate, though, that Xi had been tapped to eventually lead China when Hu Jintao left office. Li, an economist, would become the number two, the premier of the People's Republic, but rise no further and die of a heart attack in 2023.

In the years since taking office—and in the years since he began to extend his own presidency beyond tradition and law—Xi has crafted something close to a cult of personality, one that tries to link him and the rule of the CCP to China's long history. Former Australian prime minister Kevin Rudd remembers sitting at the opening ceremony of the 2008 Beijing Olympics—China's $43 billion coming-out ceremony as a global superpower—and watching, fascinated, with other world leaders, including George W. Bush, as the hosts put on an elaborate visual and audio history of China. "The visual collage of Chinese traditional civilization and culture, with not a single reference to Mao, the Communist Party, or the People's Republic. The intended impression for the world was civilizational continuity, with the current Communist leadership simply forming yet another dynasty of the eighty-three dynasties that had preceded it," Rudd recalled.[13]

The new Politburo standing committee under Xi "comprises a secretary of his, some advisers and some buddies, all flunkeys, or courtiers and viziers at best. Xi has purged China of the factional style of politics that has existed literally for 2,200 years. At no point—except for the year 1966 arguably—did Mao ever have absolute power. Even at the height of Mao's power, he couldn't get rid of the people he needed to run the country." Today, Xi has his own inspirational and education ideology-focused mobile app, Xuexi Quiangguo, roughly translated as "Learn from Xi to Strengthen the Nation." The app offers both carrots (points) and sticks (quotas) to encourage use by party members, and as Wong reports, "The chore became vexing enough for some users to devise work-arounds, using custom-made software to simulate app usage."[14]

There is no power in China but Xi, whose opinion stands as not just first among equals but first, last, and only. The decision to invade Taiwan, not unlike Putin's decision to invade Ukraine, will be made by one man, driven by his oversized ego: Xi Jinping.

One might think that Russia's disastrous failure to conquer Ukraine—and the wide-ranging consequences of the economic and diplomatic isolation from the West it has suffered as a result—would give Xi some pause in attempting his own military adventure. While that is possible, we can't rely on such wishful thinking alone. For one, the Chinese have an arrogant attitude toward Russia and its capabilities. In nearly every area—economic power, domestic political control, the mastering of advanced technologies, global diplomatic clout, the proliferation of domestic titans of industry—China has long ago bypassed the Russian Federation. It's not a stretch to imagine that Xi looks at Putin's failures in Ukraine and rather than seeing lessons for caution, simply assumes that he and his own reformed military would do much better, that where Russia is weak and easily bullied by the West, China is too strong and powerful to be confronted in the same way.

There are reasons, though, that Xi should actually be *more* wary about his capabilities as compared to Russia. Xi knows well that the Chinese military is highly inexperienced. Whereas Russia has been engaged in brutal scorched-earth combat regularly over the last generation, most notably in Chechnya and eastern Ukraine, long preceding this most recent invasion, China has not seen serious combat for forty-five years, the last time being its disastrous invasion of Vietnam in 1979. There is no one serving in the PLA who has fought or led in combat, small border and maritime skirmishes with India and the Philippines notwithstanding.[*] Yet, if Xi assumes that he can deter the United States from coming to Taiwan's defense, he very well might shrug off any concerns about his military's performance. And indeed, when I asked a senior Pentagon official what lesson they think China is extracting from Russia's war on Ukraine, I got a surprising response: "They learned that America will not go to war with a country that's armed with nuclear weapons."

WHY TAIWAN MATTERS

There are five reasons that Taiwan matters to Xi—and thus to China. These are history, destiny, security, geography, and ego.

History. Xi, most simply, sees Taiwan as a historical part of China. For generations, in fact, CCP leaders have seen Taiwan as special among all the various lost and former territories of previous Chinese empires.

In their telling, the island was annexed by the Qing Dynasty in 1683 and remained a part of the Chinese empire for the next 212 years, until the empire ceded the group of islands Taiwan was part of to the Empire of Japan following the loss of the First Sino-Japanese War in 1895.[†15] And it is true that Chinese people on both sides of the strait consider Japan's fifty-year occupation of the island to have been illegal and part

* Then again, Taiwan isn't in much better shape: Taiwan's military has also not seen serious combat since the Battle of Yijiangshan Islands during the First Taiwan Strait Crisis in 1955.

† An American, John W. Foster—the grandfather of both future secretary of state John Foster Dulles and first civilian CIA director, Allen Dulles—helped negotiate the treaty that handed Taiwan over to the Japanese.

of the Century of Humiliation, the period from the First Opium War of 1839 through the end of World War II when Western and Japanese powers dominated China. During this period of various lost wars and resultant unequal treaties, China ceded Hong Kong to the British; gave Taiwan, the southern part of current Liaoning Province, and suzerainty over Korea to the Japanese; and gave up to the Russians Outer Mongolia and parts of Manchuria, land that is now the Russian territory of Primorsky Krai, with its regional capital of Vladivostok.

For a hundred years, first the Chinese nationalists and, later, the Chinese Communist Party have been demanding to restore what they consider to be illegally seized lands back to Chinese control. And the second part of the twentieth century saw most of them returned, as the communists reconquered the de facto independent Tibet in 1951 and achieved the transfer of Hong Kong and Macau from British and Portuguese rule in 1997 and 1999 respectively. Taiwan, for its part, briefly reverted back to mainland rule in 1945 following Japan's surrender in World War II, to be governed by the nationalist Chiang Kai-shek and his KMT party, but then, following KMT's defeat at the hands of Mao's communists, Chiang Kai-shek and two million of his loyalists established a nationalist dictatorship on Taiwan and, in the eyes of the CCP, the island was lost yet again.[*16] True, there were other disputes that China has been unwilling to give up on—with Bhutan, India, Japan, Vietnam, the Philippines, Indonesia, and Malaysia—but Taiwan stands out as chief among the lingering wounds.

Destiny. Beyond its historic territorial relevance to China—an issue that the CCP has certainly shown itself to be flexible on occasion—the Taiwan question is considered unfinished business from the civil war by Beijing. Mao, after all, did not conclusively defeat Chiang

* The communists officially abandoned their designs on two historic parts of China: Mongolia, whose independence Chiang Kai-shek was forced to recognize under Soviet pressure following World War II (independence reaffirmed by Mao after his takeover of China in 1949), and the roughly five hundred thousand square miles of Manchuria and other territories that had been seized by Russia in the nineteenth century, which were finally officially accepted as Russian in the border demarcation agreement signed by Chinese and Russian foreign ministers in 2005 in Vladivostok.

Kai-shek's nationalists in 1949 but instead allowed them to escape and establish the government in Taiwan and lay claim to their competing vision of the Republic of China as the country's true legitimate government. Mao did try on several occasions to depose Chiang and capture Taiwan, viewing it as a bridgehead waiting to be exploited by his American enemy, but his plans for a full-scale invasion in 1950 were derailed by the Korean War.[17] Today, three-quarters of a century later, the island is still a thorn in the CCP's political side, as the party's victory will remain incomplete until that last "counterrevolutionary" outpost is defeated and brought into communist China's orbit.

Security. The presence of US forces on Taiwan until 1979 had long encouraged Beijing's obsessive desire for "liberation" because, to China, Taiwan was always part of a larger security equation. In 1950 Chinese ambassador to the UN Wu Xiaquan had cited and endorsed a perhaps apocryphal quote from former Japanese prime minister Tanaka Giichi, who allegedly said, "To conquer the world, one must first conquer Asia; to conquer Asia, one must first conquer China. To conquer China, one must first conquer Manchuria and Mongolia. To conquer Manchuria and Mongolia, one must first conquer Korea and Taiwan."[18]

China's worst fears were seemingly confirmed in the Korean War, in which it saw the US defense of South Korea against North Korea's invasion as an attempt to annihilate the buffer state, unify the peninsula, and secure a US-aligned government along the Chinese border—the American counteroffensive that brought US forces right up to the Chinese border was a provocation never really understood by Douglas MacArthur, commander of the allied war effort, that resulted in the massive Chinese intervention in support of North Korea and years of brutal fighting. Today, China views both South Korea and Taiwan as American vassal states and sees Taiwan's inclusion in the US-led Western sphere as a potential threat and further evidence of attempts to "contain China."

It's easy to discount the insecurity and fear that undergird Xi's (and the CCP's) desire for Taiwan, but the geopolitical reality is that America often underestimates the degree to which our adversaries' actions are driven by fear of our power and potential actions. For decades a widely held view persisted that the root cause of the Cuban Missile Crisis and the fateful decision by Soviet leader Nikita Khrushchev to place nuclear-armed missiles on the island in 1962 lay in Soviet strength and aggression, more specifically by Khrushchev's perception of young president Kennedy's weakness at their first summit in Vienna in June of 1961, compounded by the disastrous Bay of Pigs invasion attempt by CIA-funded Cuban exiles. Recently declassified Soviet documents reviewed by Cold War historians Sergey Radchenko and Vladislav Zubok prove the opposite, however. It wasn't American supposed *weakness* that drove Khrushchev to this dangerous and provocative move. Instead, he took the opposite lesson from the Bay of Pigs: he was driven by the fear that what the US-backed invasion demonstrated was not that America *couldn't* overthrow Fidel Castro's communist regime, but that it *wanted* to do so and *could* and *would* likely try again in the future. He feared that such a successful invasion by Kennedy or a subsequent US administration would endanger his hold on power in the Kremlin, as he would be blamed by hardliners for this failure, or that China would take advantage of a future loss of Cuba to challenge the Soviet Union for primacy and leadership of the communist world. "Our whole operation was to deter the USA so they don't attack Cuba," said Khrushchev to his top political and military leaders on October 22, 1962, according to the minutes from the recently declassified Soviet Communist Party archives. Khrushchev's reading, of course, was profoundly erroneous—the last thing that Kennedy wanted after the Bay of Pigs catastrophe was to go at it again—but the Soviet premier's terrible (and paranoid) understanding of American political dynamics led him to misread the situation and nearly provoked the end of human civilization in the process (and ultimately did bring about the demise of his own hold on the reins of power in the Kremlin).[19]

It may similarly take decades, if ever, for us to see the classified documents from Xi's China, Kim Jong Un's North Korea, or Khamenei's Iran and to understand thereby how much of these regimes' bellicose policies and nuclear weapons buildups are being driven by of fear, either of American action or of appearing politically weak domestically, but the answer is almost surely more than we realize right now. While

America's leaders traditionally convince themselves of our peaceful and benevolent intent, it's easy to see how China, Iran, Russia, and North Korea might view the world differently as they look out at the world's reigning superpower, one who has a history of regime change operations and has effectively surrounded each of their countries with a network of partners, allies, and military bases.

The leaders of nations are historically terrible at understanding their adversaries' thinking, in part because leaders—convinced of their own peaceful intentions but wary of the nefariousness of others—tend to underestimate how their own actions will be viewed by others while overestimating the aggression of foreign adversaries. History again and again tells us that fear is a powerful motivator for all sorts of aggressive actions—including Japan's bombing of Pearl Harbor, which stemmed from the empire's intent to prevent the United States from interfering in its conquest of Southeast Asia.

Thus, it is highly likely that China's policy toward Taiwan is driven at least in part by insecurity and fear that US containment of China could cause the CCP to lose its hold on power. Since Chiang Kai-shek's retreat to Taiwan, the island has been viewed by the CCP as a geopolitical, military, and political threat—an "alternative China" that for decades has also served as a base for American forces and now represents a rival political system that is increasingly open, democratic, and prosperous. We should not underestimate the degree to which the CCP is concerned about the potential of Taiwan to be used as a platform and information weapon to destabilize China, even if that may seem like a totally absurd scenario to us.

Geography. As China's power and military capabilities grew following first Nixon's overtures and then Carter's "reopening" of the country after 1979, and as it became less concerned about a possible US invasion that could snuff out the communist regime, a new (and old) narrative emerged about Taiwan's strategic position. Namely, Taiwan was cast as the gateway to the Pacific and key to unlocking China's role as the predominant power in Asia.

The waters around China in the East and South China Seas are very shallow; in the Taiwan Strait, the average depth is just 330 feet and in the South China Sea near China's coasts, it's usually 1500 feet or less. In contrast, the depth on the western side of Taiwan drops down to 13,000 feet right off the coast, as the Eurasian continental shelf ends. The shallowness of China's internationally recognized waters is a major problem for Chinese submarines leaving mainland ports to go out on patrol: before they can get to the deep waters where they can disappear and evade US detection, they must go past the choke points of the First Island Chain, which includes Taiwan and sits at the intersection of East and South China Seas. Across the First Island Chain, from Japan to Taiwan to the Philippines, various choke points are controlled by US security partners. Thus there is almost no path for China to project meaningful naval power into the eastern Pacific without breaking free of the First Island Chain, which is under the control of nations that view China with at best suspicion, if not outright fear. Beyond the concerns of the submarines and the surface fleet navy more broadly, though, stands the issue of the trade routes. China is uniquely dependent on global trade—its economy relies on energy and food imports, as well as manufactured goods exports, many of which are transported via the vital Strait of Malacca, one of the busiest shipping channels in the world and one that is often patrolled by US Navy warships. Chinese leaders for decades have worried about what CCP leader Hu Jintao had called the "Malacca Dilemma," referring to the lack of alternatives China has to trade routes that aren't dominated by America and its allies. Occupation of Taiwan and the consequent displacement of the United States from the Western Pacific would provide China with more alternative secure routes for trade with the rest of the world.

Ego. Lastly, an important element of Taiwan's importance to Xi is his own legacy. Over his last decade in power, Xi has positioned himself as one of the great historic leaders of modern China—on par, according to the Communist Party's telling of his story, with the founder of the PRC, Chairman Mao. And what better way to put himself on par—perhaps even exceed—the greatness of Mao than to achieve the goal that Mao himself could not and complete the conquest of Taiwan?

Mao had often discussed the inevitability of Taiwan being unified with the mainland. In a conversation with the newly appointed

Finnish ambassador to China in 1955, he said "that China will not give up on taking over Taiwan, because the island belongs to them, be it then war with America as a consequence."[20] But ultimately Mao recognized that he was powerless to accomplish the conquest in his lifetime. In a private conversation with Khrushchev in 1959, Mao admitted, "The issue of Taiwan is clear, not only will we not touch Taiwan, but also the off-shore islands, for 10, 20 and perhaps 30 years."[21] Xi will cement his place in the pantheon of Chinese—and perhaps global—history if he manages to complete Mao's vision and bring about the "Chinese Dream," a concept Xi himself coined immediately after becoming the leader of the CCP in the fall of 2012.

In his very first speech as general secretary of the CCP, Xi outlined how, in his estimation, previous leaders had "failed one time after another" in modernizing the country. In contrast to them, he set as his North Star the achievement of the "great rejuvenation of the Chinese nation," with unification with Taiwan a critical part of that dream. Specifically, in this address given at the CCP Congress in 2017, Xi proclaimed that "realizing the rejuvenation of the Chinese nation is a dream shared by all of us as Chinese. We remain firm in our conviction that, as long as all the sons and daughters of the Chinese nation, including our compatriots in Hong Kong, Macao, and Taiwan, follow the tide of history, work together for the greater national interests, and keep our nation's destiny firmly in our own hands, we will, without doubt, be able to achieve the great rejuvenation."[22] In the years since, his government, the Chinese media, and other institutions have come to adopt the same aspirational language.[*23]

As of this writing, it is clear that Xi is getting impatient. Whereas Deng had instructed the Chinese people to "hide your strength, bide

* "The rejuvenation narrative is a well-understood and powerful one in China," writes China scholar Liz Economy. "It evokes memories of the country as the Middle Kingdom demanding tribute from the rest of the world; China as a source of innovation, creating paper, gunpowder, printing, and the compass; and China as an expansive, outward-facing power, with Ming dynasty Admiral Zheng He commanding a naval fleet of more than three hundred ships and sailing throughout Asia to the Horn of Africa and the Red Sea."

your time," Xi has overturned that three-decade policy and effectively turned it into "show off your strength, waste no time." In 1990, following the global backlash against China for its Tiananmen Square crackdowns, Deng released a twenty-four-Chinese-character strategy that became a guiding principle for Chinese foreign policy. Thirty-three years later, Xi rewrote it with his own much more aggressive—and impatient—twenty-four characters:

Deng Xiaoping Strategy, 1990		**Xi Jinping Strategy, 2023**	
冷静观察	Observe calmly,	沉着冷静	Be calm,
稳住阵脚	secure our position,	保持定力	stay determined,
沉着应付	cope with affairs calmly,	稳中求进	seek progress and stability,
韬 光养晦	hide our capabilities and bide our time,	积极作为	be proactive and achieve things,
善于守拙	be good at maintaining a low profile,	团结一致	unite (under the banner of the party),
决不当头	never claim leadership	敢于斗争	and dare to fight

Translation courtesy of Moritz Rudolf, a fellow at the Paul Tsai China Center of the Yale Law School, https://x.com/MoritzRudolf/status/1633667867836030977?s=20.

All of these pieces—history, destiny, security, geography, and ego—come together to drive Xi's relationship with both his own citizens and the world beyond. "The past is inscribed in China's mental terrain in a calligraphy so powerful that it determines most of its approaches to the present. History therefore influences Chinese ways of seeing the world in a more direct sense than in any other culture I know," writes historian Odd Arne Westad.[24]

Suffice it to say, though, that Xi's reading of the shared history of China and Taiwan is not, exactly, how the Taiwanese see it. Nor is it a history and story that the rest of the world should entertain. It is therefore worth spending some time unpacking the narrative.

Neither history nor "destiny" really back up Xi's view of Taiwan. In fact, the great irony of China's current geopolitical focus on "reuniting" Taiwan to the mainland is that the island has never really belonged to China. It is a dichotomous and complex island, one that's both not quite Chinese but also not *not* Chinese. "Since the early 1600s, the efforts of Taiwanese settlers and pioneers, mostly from China, to create their own nation on the island have been suppressed or smothered by a succession of colonial administrations," writes Jonathan Manthorpe in his political history of the island.[25] Across its four-hundred-year modern history, Taiwan has always been wrapped in a certain level of geopolitical intrigue. Even the way its existence was first publicized to the West and Europeans in the sixteenth century is part of one of history's great espionage capers.

In the 1500s the Portuguese ruled Europe's connection to Asia; Vasco da Gama's four ships and 170 crew had discovered the first sea route to India in 1498 and soon the country established what was known as the Portuguese State of India, based in Goa. For decades, the Portuguese brutally fortified the path to the Indian Ocean and explored Asia, reaching Ceylon in 1505, establishing a key port in Malacca (in modern-day Malaysia) in 1511, exploring to Guangzhou, in China, in 1517, and making it all the way to Japan in 1542. Along the way, they built a hugely profitable—and highly envied—trading network of spices, from cinnamon to saffron, and other goods from all manner of cultures. By the end of the century, Portugal had become the wealthiest country in the world. But in an age before the widespread availability of maps, none of Europe's other maritime powers understood how or where to sail to penetrate these mysterious lands. The Portuguese route maps to Asia, called *roteiros*, or "rutters," were closely guarded secrets, at least until a Dutch functionary named Jan Huygen van Linschoten arrived as an aide to the archbishop of Goa. There, over a period of five years, he carefully copied by hand the prized *roteiros* and made notes about what goods came from where and the alliances the Portuguese used to maintain their trading network. Upon his return to the Netherlands in 1592, he published a three-volume work called *Itinerario* that blew open the secrets of the Portuguese empire. It included not only the *roteiros* maps and key landmarks but also detailed information on the trading networks—where to obtain what spice at what cost—and strategic observations about where the Portuguese network was weakest. The first Dutch expedition to Asia left the same year *Itinerario* first appeared, 1595. "Within five years, Portugal's supremacy in Asia vanished as Dutch and English traders, with van Linschoten's handbook as their guide, swarmed all over the East," writes Manthorpe. "It was a signal moment in Europe's relationship with Asia and changed the entire balance of power in as profound a way as the acquisition of the secrets of the atom bomb by agents of the Soviet Union in the mid-twentieth century."[26]

Within a few short years, the Dutch had moved decisively into places like Indonesia (which van Linschoten had singled out as Portugal's weakest link) and colonized Taiwan in 1624, a place they knew by the name van Linschoten had popularized: Ilha Formosa, beautiful island. It was the name the West would predominantly use for the island for much of the next four hundred years.

Across nearly two millennia, Taiwan has been an island mostly of only *attempted* conquest, with chapters of colonization by the Portuguese, Spanish, Japanese, and ultimately Han Chinese. The first record of Chinese contact with the island dates back to 230 AD, when an expedition from the Wu Dynasty during the era known as the Three Kingdoms found it full of indigenous Austronesian people, what the explorers back then termed wild barbarians; the first Chinese maps called it *I Chou*, "a barbarous region to the east." It took hundreds more years for explorers and cartographers to understand that Taiwan and modern-day Japanese Okinawa were separate islands, and it wasn't until 605 AD that Chinese explorers returned to Taiwan, thinking it was Okinawa. In 607 AD a force of a thousand Chinese soldiers fought local tribes in three brutal, costly battles. Notably, its commander, General Chen Ling, returned to the mainland "convinced that taking possession of Taiwan would not be worth the necessary investment in blood."[27]

The island and its native population sat largely unmolested for a thousand years, until da Gama arrived with the Portuguese and, later, van Linschoten's espionage led the Spanish and Dutch to establish colonies. "The Dutch undertook the first serious effort at developing Taiwan," writes Denny Roy, in his history of the island. "Establishing a government over much of the island, the Dutch organized labor, created mines and plantations, and introduced new crops and tools." The colonial economic growth lured more mainland Chinese and, according to some estimates, this community comprised as many as fifty thousand individuals on Taiwan, which was also populated by a about two to three thousand Dutch soldiers, officials, and traders.[28] Parts of the island, though, remained the purview of pirates, many of whom had sought safe harbor from the Chinese mainland in the wild island's nooks and crannies, and one of whom—the so-called pirate prince Koxinga—defeated and ousted the Dutch colony and established a kingdom on Taiwan in 1661 that lasted for twenty years.

After a successful mainland Chinese naval campaign by the Qing Dynasty against Koxinga's Kingdom of Tungning in 1683, the mainland rulers—who had little actual interest in the island—asked the Dutch if they'd be interested in repurchasing their former colony. Only when the Dutch refused did the Qing Dynasty assume control itself, loosely ruling the western part of Taiwan for the next two hundred years, until the forced handover to the Japanese in 1895. The island became known for its tea and camphor exports; specifically, in the nineteenth century, Taiwan was the world's leading supplier of the lucrative and strong-smelling camphor oil.

It was hardly a stable or welcome occupation. "A backwater on the fringe of the Chinese Empire, Taiwan was not a prestigious post for mainland administrators," Roy writes. "Not surprisingly, insurrections against the mainland authorities were frequent." By one calculation, there were 159 "sizable" rebellions on the island in just the two hundred years of Qing rule—including, most famously, the 1787 rebellion led by Lin Shuangwen, who raised an army of three hundred thousand.* Island scholars refer to the Qing years darkly, joking, "Every three years an uprising, every five years a rebellion."[29]

---

* Qing forces eventually captured and executed Lin Shuangwen, as well as his leading rebels, and—in a punishment common at the time—castrated more than forty sons of the rebels under the age of fifteen.

Even at the occupation's peak, no more than the western third of the island was under the control of the Qing, and pirates continued to roam freely along much of the coast, leading to protests by the British, French, Japanese, and even the US governments in the 1800s. In 1867 indigenous Taiwanese tribes killed the survivors of the American barque *Rover*, when it wrecked on the island's southern tip. The Qing leadership told the United States that they lacked any control over the indigenous territory; the imperial court refused any responsibility for the remainder of the island beyond its western parts and gave the United States the all-clear to avenge the attack itself. And so America's Asiatic Squadron landed a force of nearly two hundred sailors and marines from the USS *Hartford* and USS *Wyoming* on Taiwan that June; the US force fared poorly in the heat, lost a senior officer to sniper fire from the tribes, and withdrew hastily. A second invasion force the following month—this time with mainland Chinese troops but a US envoy overseeing the operation—was more successful and reached an agreement with the tribes that they would no longer kill white shipwreck victims. That agreement, though, didn't extend to Japanese mariners, and in 1871 a massacre of the crew of a Japanese shipwreck led to a Japanese invasion of the southern part of the island and a campaign against the tribes.*[30]

Even as the nineteenth century ended, it was clear Taiwan had established its own identity distinct from the mainland. "The people who became known as the Taiwanese came to Taiwan to get away from the conditions in China. Taiwan became a place where Chinese individuals and communities could make a fresh start," Roy writes.[31]

Most recently, Taiwan hasn't belonged to "mainland China" in any meaningful sense since the end of the 1800s, after which the island was a Japanese colony for a half century and then functionally an independent country for nearly seventy-five years now. Mao himself said in 1936 that Taiwan was not part of the China empire's "lost territories" and that

* As a result of these invasions and colonies, as well as Chiang Kai-shek's import of two million Chinese in 1949, Taiwan's indigenous groups are now less than three percent of the overall population of the island, but intermarriage over generations and hundreds of years means that today an estimated seventy percent of Taiwanese have aboriginal blood.

he supported its independence, just as he did that of Japanese-occupied Korea. As he told American journalist Edgar Snow, an eager scribe for Mao's view of the world, "It is the immediate task of China to regain all our lost territories, not merely to defend our sovereignty below the Great Wall. We do not, however, include Korea—formerly a Chinese colony—but when we have re-established the independence of the lost territories of China, and if the Koreans wish to break away from the chains of Japanese imperialism, we will extend them our enthusiastic help in their struggle for independence. The same thing applies to Formosa."[32*]

Indeed, when Chiang Kai-shek's mainland nationalist government first took control of the island back from the Japanese in 1945, it was seen by the locals as just as oppressive and exploitative as the Japanese colonists. For example, in November 1945 the nationalists commandeered all of the island's garbage trucks to haul the property they confiscated as war loot back to the docks for export to the mainland. (The Taiwanese response became famous: "Dogs go and pigs come."[33]) Vicious fighting on the island between the KMT and the Chinese communists resulted in thousands of deaths, and it was only as Chiang Kai-shek's forces lost control of the mainland that they began to view the island as a refuge rather than, effectively, as war loot.

Chiang Kai-shek's retreat to the island in December 1949 with his two million Kuomintang nationalists and the army began with years of instability and oppression, and in the first decade or so, both sides—Mao on the mainland and Chiang on the island—harbored aspirations of a cross-strait invasion that would depose the respective enemy and unite Taiwan and the mainland into "one China." But as the 1950s progressed, those ambitions, always more aspiration than reality, receded, and even as Chiang's forces continued a yearslong brutal campaign of terror against resistance on the island, land reforms on Taiwan kicked off a phenomenal period of growth and prosperity. Farmers saw their income double, worker productivity soared, and, in the 1960s, that newfound wealth provided the foundation for an

* Snow's 1937 book, *Red Star over China*, would be influential in raising the profile of Mao's communist movement and Zhou Enlai would call him "our best friend abroad."

era of industrialization that transformed Taiwan into the manufacturing powerhouse it is now.[34] Chiang died in 1975 and when his son and successor, Chiang Ching-kuo, passed in 1988, it created the space for political reforms and the unwinding of the one-party Koumintang military rule. In 1996 the island had its first open and fair election for president—the first free and competitive election in a predominantly Chinese society in the entire four-thousand-year history of China. Both of the leading candidates in that election were firm supporters of independence, and China was forced to protest by holding bellicose military exercises in the strait as the Taiwanese voted, to no avail. To the mainland Communist Party, the election and clear trend toward a push for internationally recognized independence were a strong signal that the chances for a peaceful, natural unification were receding.

As Taiwan's history shows, it has never been "Chinese" in the way we (or the island residents) would consider it. "The raw truth is that no government of China, neither the current Communist administration nor the previous Kuomintang regime, has a persuasive legal or moral claim to sovereignty over Taiwan," writes Manthorpe. "There has never been a Chinese administration that exercised control over both the mainland and Taiwan at the same time."[35]

Maps are stories—what you choose to feature, how you orient it, the scale—every choice that goes into making a map is an editorial decision that changes what the map conveys, who it is important and useful to, and whose narrative or history it tells. In that sense, it is easy to look at a traditional western map of China and miss the significance of Taiwan, the dot off its eastern shore. On a map showing all of China—the third-largest country in the world by size, a landmass larger than Europe, stretching across five time zones, some thirty-one hundred miles east to west and thirty-five hundred miles north to south—it's hard to understand why Taiwan matters. But if Xi is wrong about Taiwan's history, he is absolutely right that the geography of Taiwan matters to almost any future he—or future Chinese leaders—hope to build.

It might be better, though, to look at Taiwan on this map:

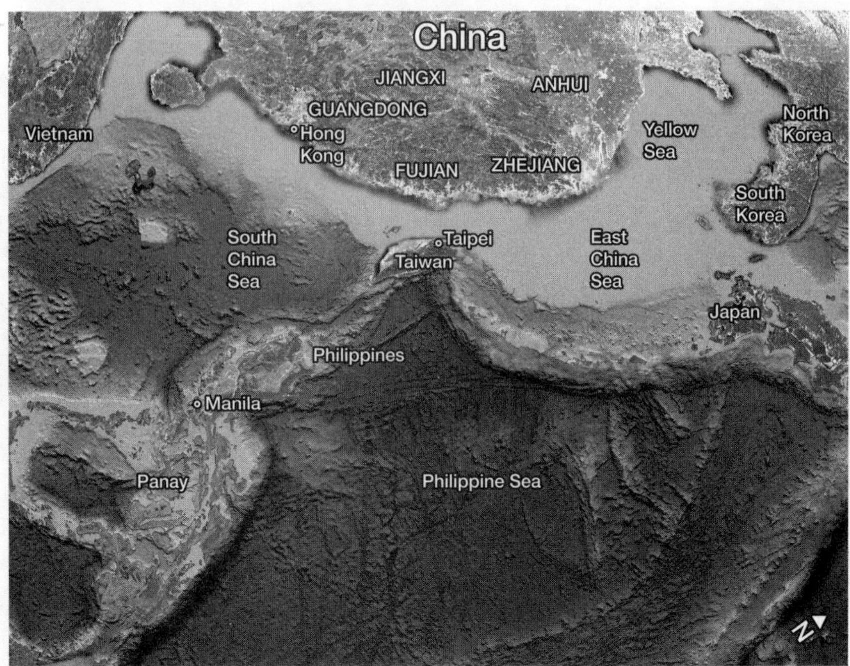

Data SIO, NOAA, US Navy, NGA, GEBCO. Image Landsat / Copernicus

To China, Taiwan isn't a tiny dot off the eastern shore. The island's geographic position is right smack dab front and center in the way that China thinks about itself—and has thought about itself for hundreds of years.

Today, it is easy to overlook the reality represented by China's most famous attraction, the Great Wall. The wall, built piece by piece by multiple dynasties across more than two thousand years, was meant to secure the empire's northern edge from the threatening and all-too-real invasions by nomadic tribes and horse-mounted armies of the Mongols and other enemies. China is today, and always has been, a country uniquely surrounded by hostile and, in the past, aggressive neighbors. It has land borders with a total of fourteen other countries, more than any other country in the world, and claims disputed maritime boundaries with another seven.

And it's hardly a friendly neighborhood. Writing in their book, *China's Search for Security*, political scientists Andrew J. Nathan and

Andrew Scobell describe China's understanding of the world as "a terrain of hazards, stretching from the streets outside the policymaker's window to land borders and sea lands thousands of miles to the north, east, south, and west, and beyond to mines and oilfields of distant continents." As the two scholars summarized in 2012, China's neighbors comprise "seven of the fifteen largest countries in the world (India, Pakistan, Russia, Japan, the Philippines, Indonesia, and Vietnam—each having a population greater than 89 million); five countries with which China has been at war at some point in the past seventy years (Russia, South Korea, Japan, Vietnam, and India); and at least nine countries with unstable regimes (including North Korea, the Philippines, Myanmar/Burma, Bhutan, Nepal, Pakistan, Afghanistan, Tajikistan, and Kyrgyzstan)."[36] Since the end of World War II, China has had border disputes with most of its neighbors, who today include four of the world's eight other nuclear powers (Russia, India, Pakistan, and North Korea).

Geography, it is said, is destiny, and the differing landscapes of China and the United States have long defined their historical trajectories. Unlike, say, the United States, whose border with Canada is the longest undefended border in the world and which shares a language, strong cultural similarities, and geopolitical alliances with Canada, China shares its neighborhood with large countries—like India, Japan, Korea, and Russia—that are not just culturally dissimilar but come from proud, long traditions of millennia-old civilizational empires themselves. In many ways, the US-Mexico relationship—hardly a warm or always productive one—is still more friendly and culturally and strategically aligned than almost any relationship between China and its neighbors. The border security picture from Beijing calls to mind the old saying "just because you're paranoid doesn't mean they aren't out to get you."

As international relations scholars Hal Brands and Michael Beckley write, "The perception of danger everywhere drives a strong impulse to expand: Only by pushing outward can China secure its frontiers, protect its supply lines, and break the bonds a punishing environment imposes."[37] That natural reaction to its neighborhood, though, only exacerbates the fear and distrust China's neighbors have of the People's Republic.

The role of the Great Wall in Chinese history is also worth remembering because of its relevance, strategically, to Taiwan. China, despite its giant landmass, has historically viewed itself as a maritime nation, one oriented toward the coast. The Great Wall was meant as a way, in effect, to close off the back door, to secure the northern border against threatening marauding armies. China's western border, meanwhile, was characterized by deserts and mountains—also inhospitable—and the south was distant, isolated by mountains and rivers. The "center" of China, for thousands of years, was its east, along and around the Yellow River. "In essence, China has had its back on the middle part of the Eurasian continent, and that orientation has had enormous consequences for the country as it has approached the rest of the world," Odd Arne Westad writes.[38*] And today, Taiwan, blockading China's unfettered access to the Pacific, represents as much of a threat to Beijing's global naval and trade ambitions.

Few countries in history have thrived on a global scale without being maritime powers. For example, Great Britain relied on the naval-economic link to dominate the eighteenth and nineteenth centuries, building a truly global empire on which famously the sun never set, an economic powerhouse Britain assembled despite having a much smaller population than the other two great powers of the time—France and Russia. This link between a strong navy and a strong economy was a lesson that the United States learned the hard way early in its infancy: when the newly independent colonies lost the far-ranging protection of the powerful British Navy, the North African Barbary States began to prey on US merchants in the Mediterranean. The US Congress, empowered by the newly ratified Constitution to levy taxes and maintain armed forces, invested in shipbuilding that eventually

* In the 1400s, as China's maritime trade flourished, the famous admiral Zheng He assembled a treasure fleet that included some of the largest sailing vessels ever constructed and over thirty years led seven far-ranging expeditions to Southeast Asia and beyond.

allowed the US Marines to storm Tripoli, an early triumph that inspired the famous lyrics of the "Marines' Hymn," and future presidents, from Millard Fillmore to Teddy Roosevelt, saw commerce and naval power as inextricably linked.

The eventual economic rise of the United States in the twentieth century is hard to separate from the global dominance of the US Navy. For the seventy years after World War II, the navy guarded and secured trade routes in every corner of the globe, protecting variously against Iranian speedboats, Somali pirates, Houthi missiles, and—not irrelevantly—Chinese aggression in the Taiwan Strait, moves that made the world safe. We take for granted today that arguably one of the most consequential inventions of the twentieth century—the standardized shipping container, responsible for the rise in global trade that has brought so much prosperity to the United States and Asia alike, among many other markets—would not have been very significant if the sea-trade routes had not been made safe for commerce.

Today, China is even more dependent on global trade than the United States but is only a few decades into any meaningful investment in its own naval fleet. Its global trade exists on a daily basis under the protective umbrella provided by the US Navy—a clearly fraught (and indeed long-term unacceptable) situation for a country that believes it deserves to once again become the world's greatest power.

Currently, around 70 percent of China's oil imports—mostly from the Middle East and Angola—pass through the narrow Malacca Strait, a five-hundred-mile-long passage between the Indonesian island of Sumatra and the Malay Peninsula that is the primary gateway between the Indian Ocean and the South China Sea. At its narrowest in the Phillips Channel, the trade passage is just 1.7 miles wide, making the Strait of Malacca one of the most significant natural strategic choke points in the world, right up there with Gibraltar in the Mediterranean, the Bosporus entrance to the Black Sea, or the Strait of Hormuz at the base of the Persian Gulf—all choke points, it's worth noting, also patrolled and secured by the US Navy or NATO allies. And both ends of the Malacca Strait pose potential problems for China: the eastern side would be easy for India, hardly China's closest friend, to control if it desired, and its western edge is secured by Singapore—a key US partner and frequent host to US warships, albeit one that also maintains very friendly relations with China.

China is all too aware that the alternatives to the Malaccan passage, like the Sunda or Lombok straits, have their own geopolitical or security complications, not to mention that they are much longer and thus costlier routes. To mitigate its long-term reliance on the Malaccan passage, China has invested in projects like a Kazakhstan-China oil pipeline and another pipeline running from the Bay of Bengal to China's southern Yunnan Province. It hopes, furthermore, to develop easier access to Pakistani ports like the deep-water facilities at Gwadar through the Belt and Road Initiative, but for the foreseeable future there remain few good options if, someday, the United States decides to close the Strait of Malacca to Chinese ships. An aspiring great power simply cannot allow itself to remain in a position to be blackmailed in such a way, just like early America could not allow itself to be blackmailed by the Dey of Algiers.

Xi recognizes this threat well. In 2013, his first year in power, he proclaimed the "great significance" of "building China into a maritime power," a goal he saw as "important . . . for promoting China's economic development in a sustainable and healthy way, safeguarding national sovereignty, security, and development interests, realizing the objective of building China into a well-off society in an all-round way, and realizing the great rejuvenation of the Chinese nation."[39] To Xi, "The ocean's function for national economic development and opening up to the world has become more important, the ocean's place for defending national sovereignty, security, and development interests has become more prominent, the ocean's role for the civilized building of our nation's ecology has become more apparent, and the ocean's strategic position for international, economic, military, and technological competition has clearly risen."

In the last two decades, China has begun investing in a so-called blue water navy, acquiring aircraft carriers, cruisers, and other modern oceangoing naval vessels, rushing submarines into service by the literal dozens, building destroyers at a rapid clip, and even starting to establish naval bases on the African coast. But all of that ambition and the PRC's impulse to protect and secure further-flung trade routes is bottled up by geography—the lack of deep waters along the Chinese coastline and the western side of the First Island Chain.[40] There's a good reason that Douglas MacArthur, in a different era, called Taiwan an "unsinkable aircraft carrier and submarine tender." As he said, "The geographic location of Formosa is such that in the hands of a power unfriendly to the United States it constitutes an enemy salient in the very center of that portion of our position now keyed to Japan, Okinawa, and the Philippines."[41]

MacArthur's statement in 1950 is significant, too, in reflecting how countries far beyond the United States and China have material geopolitical interests in Taiwan as well. Taiwan represents a strategic crossroads not only for China but for two other key regions of the eastern Pacific: Japan and Southeast Asia. While we're used to shorthanding Taiwan's location as "off the Chinese coast," a slight twist of the viewpoint shows it as the final, dominant island in the chain stretching up to Japan through Okinawa, what Manthorpe calls "the period dot at the base of the question mark formed by Japan's island chain." Viewed yet another way, it could be the northernmost island of the seven-thousand-island Philippines archipelago. As Manthorpe says, "In the full panoramic view, Taiwan's geographic position presents three different realities at once. It is an offshore extension of China, the southernmost reach of the Japanese chain, and the northernmost stretch of Southeast Asia."[42]

Given Taiwan's strategic importance to the region, the United States, and the world, it is also worth imagining a scenario in which Taiwan does fall prey to Chinese takeover—either by military force or coercive threat. In fact, I did just that at a war game I ran with participation of US and EU officials, as well as of representatives from regional countries, at the Munich Security Conference in 2023. Sitting at a large round table in an ornate dimmed dining room of the historic Bayerischer Hof hotel—the usual location of one of the top geopolitical gatherings of the year—I presented the potential Taiwan invasion scenario, playing it out step-by-step and asking each of the "countries" to respond to each new development.

The players, all experienced international diplomats, politicians, and national security experts, pretended in turn to represent the United States, EU, Japan, and other relevant countries as they discussed various response options. Development by development, we laid out a scenario like that in the Prologue to this book, exploring how China might someday squeeze Taiwan and what tools the world community would have available to respond. When, at one point in the game, it became clear that the United States might fail to save Taiwan and that China might succeed in its objective to seize and subjugate the island, the reaction of the rest of the world—as represented by the players at the game—was shocking.

When Taiwan "fell," the international players, all purportedly representing US allies, immediately told me, as the showrunner of the game, that they now perceived the geopolitics of Asia—and perhaps the entire world—to have just been indelibly altered. They calmly said that they would now consider China the leading power in the Indo-Pacific and would reorient their foreign policies to accommodate that reality. It did not mean that they would break their alliances or trade relationships with the United States, but they would, they warned me, treat the failure of the United States to deter and ultimately stop the Chinese takeover of Taiwan as a cataclysmic event that signaled the permanent US decline as a Pacific power. Even though they all knew that America did not have a treaty obligation to defend the island, they made it clear that our prestige and credibility was tied more to that objective than many Americans might appreciate.

Indeed, public statements from various US political leaders over the last two decades have contributed to a feeling of a broader commitment to Taiwan than might be gathered from carefully worded and ambiguous diplomatic communiques. Consider President Clinton in 2000: "We'll continue to reject the use of force as a means to resolve the Taiwan question. We'll also continue to make absolutely clear that the issues between Beijing and Taiwan must be resolved peacefully and with the assent of the people of Taiwan."[43]

Or President Bush in 2001: "I have said that I will do what it takes to help Taiwan defend herself, and the Chinese must understand that."[44]

Or President Obama in 2008: "I will do all that I can to support Taiwan's democracy in the years ahead."[45]

Or President Biden's response in 2022 to a journalist's question of whether US forces would defend Taiwan: "Yes, if in fact there was an unprecedented attack."[46]

Beyond muddled and contradictory public statements and policy declarations, the participants in my Munich war game understood that if China had Taiwan in hand, there would be a fundamental new geopolitical reality: China would be free of the geographic blockade of the First Island Chain and could project power across the vastness of the Pacific Ocean and establish control of the key trade routes. The PRC would be a power that everyone in the region would have no choice but to reckon with, a reckoning made all the more fraught because their faith and trust that, if push came to shove, America would step to their aid decreased drastically as a result of the takeover. It would be a titanic regional rebalancing, one where, the participants insisted, they would have no choice but to seek accommodation with China and take its interests into account, including at the expense of America's.

And there is more. All of that critical geography, maritime trade routes, naval access, and physical realities obscure another key reason why the United States should care about Taiwan. For as much as Xi may worry about the oil passing through the Malacca Strait or his submarines passing through the First Island Chain, Taiwan is also key to the manufacture of the *new* oil of today's tech-enabled economy: semiconductor chips. They are simply irreplaceable in the modern world, the building blocks of today's computing-dependent life, and Taiwan—thanks to the Taiwan Semiconductor Manufacturing Company (TSMC) and its founder Morris Chang—makes more of them, more reliably, and with more advanced technology than just about anywhere else on the planet. China has no alternative to Taiwan's chips, and neither—currently—does the United States.

It's not an overstatement to say that the geography and strategic relevance of Taiwan is such that the outcome of China's battle for control of the island will define the geopolitics of the twenty-first century. No less an authority than Chang himself recognizes this, telling the *New York Times* at age ninety-two in the summer of 2023 that China's ambitions are fully limited by the Western dominance of chip technology. "We control all the choke points," Chang said. "China can't really do anything if we want to choke them."[47]

CHAPTER 4

They Are Weaker Than We Think

Our Adversaries' Realities at Home and Abroad

WORKING IN CYBERSECURITY, I NEVER EXPECTED—OR intended—to get a front row seat to the wildness of a presidential campaign. Most days, my work, while heavily driven by the rhythms of international geopolitics, was about as far removed from domestic US political news as possible. Then, in late April 2016, my cybersecurity company CrowdStrike received a seemingly routine telephone call that would change my life.

The incident started like all others: we received a call from a law firm hired by an organization that believed their computer systems had been breached by an unknown actor and they needed our help figuring out who did it, what happened, and how to stop it going forward. Such inquiries from potentially hacked organizations (and their law firms) were routine; we received them weekly, many due to the aggressive posture that the FBI had started to take in the early 2010s to actively notify companies of potential intrusions based on information that the intelligence community may have picked up as it was tracking adversary activity online. Indeed, that was precisely how this incident started: the FBI had repeatedly notified the Democratic National Committee (DNC) over a period of eight months that hackers affiliated with the Russian government had successfully penetrated the political party's network. It took months for the DNC to take the warnings seriously.

As our team worked over the course of the next month and a half to investigate and remediate the intrusion, we found that it wasn't just one hacker. Two separate Russian intelligence services had targeted the DNC; both the civilian foreign intelligence service, known as the SVR (roughly their equivalent of the CIA), and the military intelligence service known as the GRU had been inside the networks of the DNC after initially compromising its sister organization, the Democratic Congressional Campaign Committee (DCCC).

The DNC chose to publicly disclose their breach to the *Washington Post* on June 14, 2016, a revelation that initially went relatively unnoticed but over the course of months went off like an explosion in US politics, one that would become the opening salvo of a series of questions and revelations about Russia's role in arguably the craziest and most unpredictable election in US history. The country and political system seemed torn apart by conspiracy theories and accusations of foreign influence in our election, most of them underpinned by that fateful revelation of the Russian hack-and-dump of emails they had stolen from the DNC, DCCC, and the personal email account of John Podesta, the chairman of Hillary Clinton's campaign. They were also stoked by the later investigation and indictments of Russian internet trolls and GRU operatives by the Department of Justice for attempting to influence the election.

In the subsequent months, I watched from the sidelines as Russia's hacking efforts went largely unpunished. In the years after, I then watched numerous investigations and revelations of Moscow's efforts to interfere in the 2016 election turn Russia, its internet trolls—run by a shadowy figure who would become a geopolitical household name amid the war in Ukraine, Wagner chief Evgeny Prigozhin—and Vladimir Putin into what seemed to me to be an all-powerful, manipulative caricature. The idea that Russia was this ten-foot-tall bogeyman, capable of brainwashing voters and upending American democracy with a few carefully crafted tweets and memes, seemed ludicrous to me. What I saw was something different and more mundane. The Russian intelligence services had been bumbling their way through the Democratic Party networks, rival services seemingly unaware of each other's presence, operating noisily and ultimately getting picked up by the US intelligence community.

Moreover, after they stole various emails and documents from those networks, their original distribution plan failed miserably. They first created a WordPress blog site, using the invented identity of a supposed Romanian hacker, and started publishing the stolen documents. Few in the media paid attention. Then they created a Twitter account to try to amplify the leaks further, also to little result. As the Justice Department's indictment later explained, it was only when the founder of Wikileaks Julian Assange reached out to the Russian operatives via a Twitter direct message to ask for their archive of stolen material to distribute through his site that they realized they could achieve much greater reach by laundering the data and publishing it on another highly visited site with a proven reputation of leaking US government secrets. These weren't James Bond masterminds; they were closer to Johnny English, bumbling their way to some nominal success.

To me, the vast gap between the press coverage of the Russian interference and the reality I saw was an important reminder that the public perception—and too often the pundits' perception—of our adversaries gives them way more credit than they actually deserve.

In fact, neither Russia nor China is anywhere near as powerful as we've made them out to be over the last decade. Nor are we as powerless as it seems to affect their behavior in ways that would serve our interests. It's critical, instead, to recognize the reality of what both Russia and China now face at home and how their own domestic political calculations will drive and shape their engagement with the world beyond the next generation.

RUSSIA

Russia under the leadership of Vladimir Putin has confounded, confused, and outplayed the United States on the global stage for much of the last two decades. Taking advantage of high oil and gas prices in the aftermath of 9/11, Putin's regime invested in strengthening Russia's security state, rebuilding the economy, raising the standard of living, and snuffing out Islamist insurgency in Chechnya, bringing that breakaway republic back under the Kremlin's control. These actions, not surprisingly, have earned Putin deep loyalty from and popularity with the Russian public. He has consolidated power at home by repressing all meaningful free press, political opposition, and Russian civil society and centralized the country's private sector among a select group of powerful and loyal oligarchs whose fortunes rely on his continued patronage.

I recall vividly the spring of 2001, just a little over a year after Putin had become president of Russia following the sudden New Year's resignation of Boris Yeltsin, and the striking images that emerged when Putin seized the only independent nongovernmental TV news channel, NTV, from an opposition oligarch and handed it over to the state-owned Gazprom energy company. The story had played out over the course of weeks on Russian television, with NTV's journalists trying to rally support among the Russian population and issuing desperate appeals to Putin to save their station from confiscation, but it all proved for naught. Putin played along—he even invited representatives of the station for a meeting at the Kremlin to "hear" their concerns, but NTV was seized in an early morning raid some weeks later, nevertheless. Having consolidated his control over much of the media and removed most prominent opposition voices, he then proceeded to consolidate control over politics and business. Two years after NTV was subjugated by the state, the powerful oligarch Mikhail Khodorkovsky was arrested and jailed on fraud charges, and his oil company,

Yukos—at the time one of the largest in Russia—dismantled and sold into pieces after Khodorkovsky dared to protest the government's allocation of state energy resources to Putin's personal friends. In 2004 Putin eliminated the elections of regional governors, opting to replace the voting process with a patronage system where he would personally appoint the governors; in doing so, he turned a potential avenue for opposition into a tool to reward loyalists. Along the way, he has managed to loot and sock away probably billions of dollars of wealth for himself, his family, and his friends, using his oligarch friends' "wallets," front companies, shell corporations, and opaque ownership structures to do everything from building a billion-dollar vacation and bunker complex on the Black Sea to cornering the market on Russian vodka through the distiller Kristall, which appears to be controlled by Putin himself.

Externally, Putin largely worked quite successfully to tie many of the former Soviet republics closer to Russia as well as punish those that openly defied him, like Georgia in 2008 and Ukraine since 2014. The attempts by the West to counter or penalize actions like Russia's seizure of Crimea in 2014 were weak, late, and ineffectual. Crimea became a vacation destination for Russians and a major Russian military hub (massively expanding on the Sevastopol naval base that Russia had leased from Ukraine since 1991) he'd long hoped it would be, at an almost negligible cost geopolitically.

His adventure in Syria to prop up dictator Bashar al-Assad, a move that President Obama famously proclaimed would turn into a quagmire for Putin, proved to be much more successful than the United States anticipated. Instead of a costly debacle, the Putin regime combined a ruthless disregard for human rights and indifference to war crimes and effectively used the dispensable lives of the Wagner Group for ground force operations, along with a devastating carpet-bombing campaign by the Russian Air Force, to turn the tide in the civil war and largely restore Syria back to Assad control, allowing the dictator to survive long enough to be welcomed back into the Arab League in 2023.

Furthermore, Putin has successfully expanded Russia's influence by building close relationships not just with anti-Western countries—such as China, Iran, Venezuela, and North Korea—but also with many countries that traditionally have been part of US coalitions or have stayed nonaligned, such as Turkey, Saudi Arabia, India, South Africa, and Brazil. And of course, the attempt at interfering in the 2016 election with email hacks and trolls on social media succeeded beyond Putin's wildest imagination—not so much because these efforts changed any substantial number of votes, they very likely didn't—but because they activated existing US political divisions, amplifying and exacerbating them and helping to fracture the Western coalition, upend American and European politics, and allow Putin remarkable freedom of movement on the world stage.

These accomplishments are all the more surprising because Russia generally and Putin personally face a notably weak hand at home. The Russian Federation is home to an aging, shrinking population and a sclerotic fossil-fuel dependent economy, one that was headed south even before the disruptions of the COVID-19 pandemic and the commerce-crippling series of ever-expanding western sanctions, export controls, and international business flight that followed the 2022 invasion of Ukraine. In short, Putin has done the best that he can to paper over a failing, shrinking country and prop up an unhealthy economy, but his time as a world power player is running out. Understanding the realities of the next quarter century of Russia's trajectory requires understanding both the grave, self-inflicted wounds from the Ukraine war and the country's long-term demographics.

Putin's problem at the start of 2022 was that he believed his own propaganda. He'd poured billions into what he thought was a successful military modernization program, and previous successes in foreign interventions, as well as exaggerated divisions among Western allies, led him to overestimate Western weakness and underestimate American and European resolve. Those decisions led to the dramatic miscalculation on Putin's part to engage in a regime-change and territorial border changing operation in Ukraine, a costly, bloody war that has quickly exposed fundamental and surprising weaknesses—surprising first and foremost, almost certainly, to him personally—in his military, even as it has rapidly unified the West against him and brought down punishing and destabilizing sanctions against the Russian economy.

It is important to recognize why Putin chose to invade Ukraine in the first place. In the wake of the invasion, Putin—and too many other Western pundits—claimed the war was provoked by the expansion of NATO. Over the last quarter century, multiple rounds of negotiations have seen eastern and central European states that had formerly been part of the Soviet-led Warsaw Pact ascend into the major Western alliance, bringing it for the first time right up to Russia's borders. Furthermore, the fateful resolution by George W. Bush at the Bucharest NATO summit in 2008, adopted against the protests of the French and Germans, to one day admit Ukraine and Georgia into NATO seemed likely to expand the alliance's presence along Russia's borders even more significantly. Putin, the theory goes, felt threatened by the continued expansion of the Western alliance and the betrayal of the supposed post–Cold War promise that NATO would expand "not one inch" to the east—a promise that, despite its prominence on Russia's list of grievances, was never actually formally given by the United States or NATO in the 1990s.

The truth of Putin's motives is more sinister. What drove him into a ruinous and genocidal war of choice was his imperialistic ambition and the belief that Russia had a right to control countries on its periphery, especially those, like Ukraine, that had been part of the Russian empire and later of the Soviet Union. In the West we often think of Putin as the embodiment of a reincarnated KGB—the fact that he spent the 1970s and '80s as a mediocre midlevel KGB agent is usually referenced in the opening lines of his biography—but it's probably more accurate to think of him as an international gangster.

His primary professional formative window wasn't just with the KGB intelligence service but also the six critical years he spent in the 1990s working as the key adviser to St. Petersburg mayor Anatoly Sobchak. Back then, as the Soviet Union melted away and the once centrally controlled communist state lurched toward something resembling a free-market economy, Russia was engulfed in *razborki*—gangland warfare between increasingly powerful organized criminal groups that took advantage of the disorder to establish control over many key industries across Russia, buying many politicians in the process. Nowhere was this crime, corruption, and greed more prominent than in St. Petersburg, which was known at the time as *Banditsky Peterburg*, Bandit Petersburg, a name and period that even inspired the creation of a highly successful Russian criminal TV series in the early 2000s.

In his lofty position in the city government—Putin eventually rose to be the deputy head of city administration in 1994—it would have been impossible for him not to come into regular contact with St. Petersburg's organized criminal elements, as a number of journalistic investigations have indeed alleged. In those Russian Wild West days, he was responsible for such crime-attracting activities as supervision of gambling/casino businesses, registration of business ventures, and granting of export licenses. He adopted—and later took to another level—gangland tactics, perfecting and expanding corruption and protection rackets on a national and even international scale. His efforts to tame and transform Russia's oligarch class into his own lackeys, so that their fortunes became effectively his own personal wallets, were little more than a more ambitious version of local mafia extorting neighborhood businesses to pay protection money, albeit on the grandest possible scale.

But along with criminal tactics, Putin adopted the gangland demeanor, language, and way of thinking. Occasionally, he lets his inner gangster lingo slip, such as when he proclaimed that Russia in 1999 would kill the Chechen terrorists "in the outhouse" or when he quoted a Russian punk rock lyric about rape in reference to Ukraine ("like it or not, it is your duty, my beauty") during a press conference with President Macron weeks prior to the 2022 invasion. Like a gangster, he reacts violently when he feels he's being denied something he considers rightfully his, or when he senses that it is slipping away.

Putin invaded Ukraine because, simply, he believes Ukraine belongs to him as Russia's ruler—that it is not a real country and should instead be a part of Russia, or at least under its control in its sphere of influence—and he feared that it was slipping away to the West. The invasion had less to do with the Ukraine's future NATO membership than it did with Putin's sense that Ukraine deserved punishment for flirting with the West—for daring to aspire to join NATO and the EU, for having competitive democratic elections, for hosting Western military trainers and requesting their weapons, for divorcing from the Russian Orthodox Church, and for promoting Ukrainian history, culture, and language and diminishing the role of Russia in Ukrainian society. It was the geopolitical equivalent of a mafia thug beating up his girlfriend for flirting with another man out on the town—to show her and everyone else the consequences of betraying him. Putin felt he needed to show Ukraine, and the world, the price of perceived treachery.

He thought, wrongly, that the easy solution was to take out his anger on Ukraine by launching an illegal war of aggression, one that is now proving to be so ruinous that it may very well lead to a permanent decline in Russia's power. Putin thought the invasion of Ukraine would be a cakewalk, that his reformed and rebuilt military would make easy work of the Ukrainian forces and that the population—which in his mind consisted of displaced and dislocated Russians to begin with—would welcome him as a liberator. Military plans seized from captured Russian armored vehicles by Ukrainian forces suggested that Moscow aimed to achieve its military objectives within a few weeks. And when that initial plan to capture Kyiv and install a puppet government failed, he once again resorted to thuggish behavior, launching a destructive missile and drone campaign to burn down the Ukrainian energy infrastructure and destroy the country's economy. Like a mafia capo who has realized that his girl will never return to him, he tries to have her beaten to death rather than let anyone else have her.

But the very things that had long helped Putin scramble the hard way to the top of Russia's unforgiving political environment combined in 2020 and 2021 to undermine his most daring move yet. Always paranoid, Putin had become evermore isolated during the extended COVID-19 pandemic. Strangely fearful about the possibility of getting sick, skeptical of his interlocutors, and isolated from even his most trusted allies and advisers, Putin lived in an ever-shrinking world. As the Ukraine war began, US intelligence officials came to realize to their astonishment that they knew more about the invasion plans than did many in the Russian military. "It's our impression that the basic decision to invade and a lot of the planning was in a circle of probably no more than three or four people around Putin," CIA director Bill Burns reported.[1]

Instead of a tidy short war that reunited Ukraine with Mother Russia, Putin achieved little more than a costly, grinding, brutal quagmire. The military's modernization comprised not much more than bureaucratic Potemkin village constructions, hobbled by corruption and mismanagement, and its weakness and underperformance on the battlefield surprised even US officials. "The Russians thought that they had an effective competent army to execute combined arms maneuver," General Mark Milley, the chairman of the Joint Chiefs said. "As it turned out, they couldn't do it. They stumbled around and they couldn't pull it together."[2]

In a year, Russia is estimated to have lost something like 30 percent of its entire military power, suffering not just enormous losses in tanks, infantry fighting vehicles, artillery systems, air defenses, aircraft, and munitions but also devastating losses among the resource most challenging for Russia to replenish: young, working-aged men. An entire generation's worth of modern war matériel has been destroyed, and Russia has been forced to dip deep into antiquated and mothballed armor and tanks. While some of these losses have been important symbolically and had real impacts on national morale, like the sinking of the Black Sea flagship cruiser *Moskva*, the day-to-day attrition of Russia's military might has been astounding. According to US intelligence, Russia has lost more than 60 percent of its corps of thirty-five hundred operational tanks, including huge percentages of its most advanced machines.[3] At Russia's 2023 Victory Day Parade, an event Putin usually uses to showcase the country's best weaponry, a lone T-34 tank crossed Red Square—a piece of armor that was cutting-edge eighty years ago.

Moscow faces international isolation unlike anything it has experienced since the Bolshevik Revolution of 1917, and the country's economic power is further diminishing by the day. Sanctions and export controls on Western goods flowing to Russia are only part of that shrinkage; the longer-term prognosis isn't good either, as the world transitions away from fossil fuels and pursues climate-change goals that will move countries away from the lucrative oil and gas extraction that has powered Russia's modern economy. In the interim, Russia's dramatically reduced share of the large European market for its natural gas and oil makes it even more reliant on China for sales; the PRC, of course, is determined to extract a very hard bargain and purchase Russian resources at low prices. Putin's Russia, which was long used to having the upper hand in the world's energy markets, instead finds itself at the mercy of the globe's buyers of last resort.

The wide-ranging international sanctions are having significant effects. While Russia's GDP growth increased moderately in 2023, it will very likely be stunted by sanctions, asset seizures, and export bans in key areas such as chips. Even though China is helping to circumvent the Western ban on semiconductors, the shortfall of critical chips and advanced machinery will ultimately limit Russia's ability to produce large quantities of modern weapon systems. Under the best of circumstances, rebuilding its military after the losses in Ukraine would take a decade or longer, but it is entirely possible that with the international sanctions and export controls it could turn into a generation-long effort and that the huge stockpiles of weapons Russia has lost on the battlefield are irreplaceable.

The ban on aviation parts and aircraft means the Russian Federation's ability to transport goods and people across the country's vast landmass—spread across eleven time zones—is diminishing by the day as the United States and Europe crack down on the illicit smuggling efforts of suppliers in Turkey and Central Asia; if sanctions continue long enough, similar problems will likely hit the Russian railway system too. The effect of these shortages is more profound than a first glance might reveal. Taken together, the Russian government's ability to project power and influence even inside its own massive country is shrinking—a unique challenge given that Russia has always been a multinational, multiethnic society that has been kept together in no small part by strong oversight from Moscow.

The Russian economy has so far managed to weather the full brunt of Western sanctions and export controls with surprising resilience, in large part due to the highly competent management of Elvira Nabiullina, the head of the Russian Federation's central bank, who is widely considered one of the best central bankers and economists in the world. Yet even she is not capable of pulling miracles out of her hat. In response to a record-setting fall in the value of the ruble during the summer of 2023, Nabiullina hiked up interest rates to a whopping 16 percent, levels that are hardly conducive to economic growth. In October 2023, in response to the precipitous fall in ruble's value against the dollar, Putin instituted capital controls, mandating exporters in natural resources sectors to sell their foreign currency reserves and thus boost Russia's currency. With another myopic short-term fix, Putin has added on to Russia's long-term problems, further destroying the ruble's reputation and encouraging more capital outflows. The long-term growth prospects for Russia remain dim, exacerbated by the exodus of Western capital, technologies, and investments from the country.

If the Western sanctions remain in place, the Russian economy will stagnate and wither with time and be forced to increase its reliance on Beijing, a prospect that few in Moscow relish. Russia has already begun diverting energy and mineral exports from hostile European markets to China. Russian consumers are increasingly relying on Chinese imports to replace Western products that are no longer accessible. The Chinese renminbi is now playing a major role in transactions on the Moscow Stock Exchange, a role that will only expand with time. In effect, the stability of the Russian economy will rest on injections of Chinese cash and goods, a dynamic that will allow Beijing a great deal of leverage over Moscow.

Taken together, Russia's own miscalculations and the sweeping, coordinated actions of the West following the invasion in the spring of 2022 have doomed Russia's economic growth over the medium to long term, cutting the country off from key financial markets and systems, paralyzing important supply chains, freezing Western investment and participation in day-to-day business, and strangling critical portions of the economy. Russia, for the moment at least, has been cut off from the future.

As I wrote with Cold War–era historian Sergey Radchenko shortly after Russia's invasion, in almost every way, "Putin's land-grabbing imperialistic misadventures will leave Russia a poorer, sadder, more repressive, more insecure, and ultimately less attractive place to live."[4] This makes the other reality facing Russia even more brutal.

Even before Russian tanks crossed the Ukrainian border, setting off events that would lead to the death and physical and psychological maiming of hundreds of thousands of Russia's men, Russia was facing a demographic peril. In the years since the breakup of the Soviet Union, Moscow has lost nearly half the population it used to rule over. In 1991 the population of the Soviet Union was just shy of 300 million people, larger than the US population of 250 million. In 2023, thirty-two years after the former republics broke away, the Russian population stood at just about 146 million and was shrinking rapidly.

In 2020, Russia's population shrank by half a million; the downward trend has since continued. Amid the turmoil of the Ukraine war and mass mobilization, the country suffered a new massive brain drain as young men fled to avoid being mobilized for the military's brutal and treacherous fight. Estimates of the mass out-migration range as high as a million Russians who fled overseas in the immediate wake of the announced mobilization in September 2022.[5] The *Economist* estimates that since 2020, Russia "has lost around 2 million more people than it would ordinarily have done, as a result of war, disease and exodus. The life expectancy of Russian males aged 15 fell by almost five years, to the same level as in hurricane and coup-torn Haiti."[6] In the years ahead, due to the continued declining birth rates and a shrinking life expectancy driven by disease and alcoholism, Russia may lose over half of its population, bringing it down to just sixty-seven million—roughly a fifth of the current US population—before the end of the century. That means that in a few decades, the United Kingdom might be more populous than all of Russia. The path to reversing those population trends, meanwhile, looks difficult at best: since coming into office, Putin has rolled out measures aimed at increasing the domestic birth rate, but even though these have contributed to a slight uptick in the birth rate from the low point of 1.25-children-per-woman in 2000, it still remains below the 2.1-children-per-woman replacement rate that Russia desperately needs.

Any real population stabilization and growth would require vast immigration into the country, something Russia has almost no meaningful experience with. The country's entire foreign-born population is about five million, roughly 3 percent of the overall population—measured against, for example, the roughly forty million immigrants in the United States, who make up about 14 percent of its population—and its economic and geopolitical woes, coupled with the threat of working-age males being conscripted into the military, hardly make it an enticing prospect for potential migrants. Calculations by Moscow's Higher School of Economics show that the Russian Federation would need to attract over a million immigrants a year for the next eighty years to avert the worst-case scenario of population shrinkage, a goal that seems fanciful for the foreseeable future.[7]

Given its declining demographics, a stagnating economy, and a decimated twentieth-century military, Russia's potential to present a threat to the United States or even its own neighbors in Europe and Asia will dramatically diminish in the coming years. While it will remain a powerful nuclear force with a huge ballistic missile arsenal—in essence its last remaining power play—the Russia of the next quarter century seems likely to more closely resemble North Korea, another dictatorship armed with nukes, in terms of stature, prestige, and power on the world stage than the swaggering G-8 superpower it was at the beginning of this century.

Far from the geopolitical force that American politics seemed to indicate Russia to be in the wake of the 2016 election, the country seems more on the path to being a "larger and northern North Korea" than a true near-peer adversary. Both can still play a role of spoiler and cause us periodic problems on the geopolitical stage, but neither country presents a major challenge to American global power.

CHINA

If we think of America as fundamentally an idea—the promise, however imperfect and long-stressed, that all people are created equal and endowed with inalienable rights, a country where all can rise according to their talent and industry and not their social station—China is best understood in its modern incarnation as a political party. Its state is inseparable from the Chinese Communist Party, an institution that grows ever less ideologically "pure" even as it grows more powerful and authoritarian. Where Mao once offered his infamous *Little Red Book* of communism, Xi offers an ideology of more naked control and tyranny.

Xi's promise of a national rejuvenation and a Chinese Dream is meant to secure and fulfill decades (centuries even!) of long-desired economic advancement for an enormous population that has long lived and suffered economically far below its potential. The CCP has offered a deal to the Chinese people—it will run everyday life in the country with an authoritarian fist, limiting speech, the media, religion, and even basic commerce and capitalism, in exchange for a range of policies that will deliver a rising economy, a steadily improving quality of life, and, internationally, a respected China that ranks as a global superpower. That bargain, however Faustian, succeeded remarkably for forty years, but today increasingly feels unbalanced and precarious. Just as China emerges atop the world stage, almost every aspect of its success is under threat.

At its heart, just as in the case of Russia, understanding China is about understanding the trends of its population—a population that for much of the last two millennia has been among, if not the, largest of any country in the world. That size—and the sheer length and historical breadth of Chinese civilization—has long made China a world-shaping force. In fact, its relative weakness in the postwar twentieth century was more a historical anomaly than the normal state of play.

In the thirteenth and fourteenth centuries, in the era of the Yuan and Ming dynasties, China was home to as much as 20 or 30 percent of the world's population and ranked alongside Italy as the wealthiest country in the world. In the fifteenth century, it was a globe-leading innovator: when Christopher Columbus became the first European to glimpse the Americas, Chinese explorers like Zheng He sailed on treasure ships that dwarfed Columbus's flagship *Santa Maria*, exploring east through Southeast Asia to India to the Red Sea. And, although such retrospective projections are at best only estimates, economists like Macquarie Securities' Viktor Shvets believe China had the largest economy in the world through the sixteenth and seventeenth centuries.

The Industrial Revolution robbed China of that leading position in the world economy. "Most of the relative and absolute decline occurred from the 18th century onwards, coinciding with the accelerating pace of industrial revolutions, which ushered the modern age of much faster productivity growth rates," writes Shvets.[8]

As the world industrialized, China for centuries struggled to keep up with modern standards of living. In the wake of World War II, China was responsible for less than 4 percent of the world economy, compared to America's 26 percent, even though it had a population of half a billion in 1950, dwarfing the 150 million people in the United States. (George Kennan, the architect of the US Cold War strategy of containment, labeled China dismissively in 1948 as amounting to little more than a "vast poorhouse."[9]) Even as late as 1990, China's then-1.1 *billion* accounted for just about 5 percent of the global economy.

Its rise as an economic power over the last generation has come as hundreds of millions of Chinese have moved into the middle class and become modern consumers. Since the rapprochement with the West under Richard Nixon, which, to recall, was followed by normalization of diplomatic relations and establishment of economic ties under Carter in 1979, it was able to effectively harness that vast labor pool to become the world's factory—first producing simple goods and, more recently, increasingly, climbing up the value chain and becoming a producer of highly sophisticated products, like iPhones and semiconductors.

The resulting explosion of economic growth and modernization was unparalleled in world history; by the measure that economists love, so-called purchasing-power parity, China's GDP per person increased tenfold in three decades from the 1990s to the 2010s. In the decade after the 2008 global financial crisis, China alone accounted for almost half of the growth of the world's GDP.[10] Along the way, more than seven hundred million Chinese consumers who had been living in extreme poverty moved to the middle class. Numbers like that and change that rapid make it almost impossible to grasp the sheer scale of China's voracious growth. (It was growth, though, that came at a tremendous cost—fueled by a rapacious pillaging of the country's natural resources and pollution of its environment, to the point that the Chinese capital's routine smog became a major backdrop of the 2008 Olympics.) Its rising manufacturing prowess—accompanied by its rampant and rapacious intellectual property theft and economic espionage—allowed China to build and field increasingly capable military systems while transforming into a global trading behemoth. China's military investment accounts for over 30 percent of the world's total increase in defense spending over the previous decade, and today roughly two-thirds of the globe already engages in more trade with China than with the United States. Through its various overseas investment vehicles and its audacious trillion-dollar Belt and Road Initiative—meant to remake trade channels and create a modern-day equal to the "all roads lead to Rome" of yore—China has become the world's number one lender.*

Just as it peaks as a modern economic and military power, though, China is facing historic and unavoidable challenges. As much as many pundits warn of the Chinese Century ahead, China's continued success is far from assured. Significantly, these weaknesses of our nation's primary adversary in Cold War II are reminiscent in certain ways of the weaknesses of the Soviet Union in Cold War I. After all, part of the challenge of Cold War I memory is that we know how it ends. Understanding that the Soviet Union collapsed relatively quietly and peacefully due to its own inherent internal contradictions obscures now how

* China is also, of course, one of the top foreign buyers of US Treasury bonds, owning slightly less than $900 billion of US debt in 2023, as part of its efforts to carefully manage the exchange rate of the renminbi, moves that help ensure the power of its export market.

truly threatening the USSR seemed and how worried US policymakers were across decades about the Soviet Union's might. "We may one day look back on China as we now view the Soviet Union—as a formidable foe whose evident strengths obscured fatal vulnerabilities," Hal Brands and Michael Beckley predict.[11]

When we consider that the Chinese economic and political boom is being powered by four things—workers, capital, resources, and willing trading partners—all four categories increasingly appear exhausted.

First and foremost, China faces a ruinous population decline, one so precipitous and unavoidable that it will *also* be without parallel in the modern world. The country faces an inevitable ticking time bomb as a result of the CCP's One Child policy, instituted in 1979 as China faced what its leaders thought would be calamitous population growth and widespread food scarcities.

China's leaders in the late 1970s believed they were on a dangerous and unsustainable overpopulation trajectory, but in solving one problem they unintentionally doomed future leaders to confront a different, equally impossible challenge. Decimated by war and famine, the country's population had nearly doubled in size following an official policy in the 1950s and 1960s that pushed families to have more children, resulting in growth that became seemingly unsustainable. Even though the draconian One Child policy was steadily rolled back—even by the late 1980s it applied technically to just about a third of the country—the official policy remained in place into the 2010s. It lasted long enough that when it was rolled back and China began desperately *encouraging* more births, the country's population trend collided with what sociologists call the "fertility trap," whereby rising standards of living, the integration of women into the workforce, better health care, and access to birth control have seen birth rates steadily drop in nearly all modern developed countries.

Today, Chinese women *could* have more children but no longer *want* to.[12] It doesn't help that, according to a Beijing think tank, China is (on average) the second-most expensive place in the world to raise a child, after just South Korea, outpacing even the United States and Japan. "With such calculations, I can barely imagine a second child and any family that wants a third is just amazing," one Chinese mother wrote on the Weibo microblogging site.[13]

In 2021 China saw just 7.5 births per 1,000 people, its second record-low year in a row, and it has one of the lowest fertility rates in the world, with just 1.3 children per woman—a fraction of the birth rate of 3.6 children per woman that existed at the inception of the One Child policy.[14] The collapsing birth rates are such an immediate crisis that China in 2021 began cracking down on divorce and hospitals are turning away men seeking vasectomies. "The fundamental policy is that China needs more childbirths," one hospital director told the *Washington Post* in 2021.[15]

The United Nations reports that India has already overtaken China as the most populous nation, and that China's population is likely to shrink in the immediate future—the first time it has done so since the Great Famine of 1959 to 1961—and its population will age quickly, a shift with its own major economic, political, and military ramifications. Today, the median age in China is already approaching forty, compared to just under thirty in India. By 2100 even the most conservative projections show that China's population might shrink by half, even as its working-age class plummets in size. By midcentury, people over sixty-five are expected to outnumber those who are younger. These numbers inspire panic in Chinese officials; an aging population places enormous strain on social safety nets.

It's not a coincidence that China's meteoric economic rise coincided with the peak of a huge working-age bubble. Growth comes from having workers—lots of workers. China in the 2000s had roughly ten working-age adults for every elderly person over sixty-five, a recipe for explosive growth and a strong social and family safety net, as its working-age population peaked at nearly a billion people. But that working-age population began to shrink by 2011, just as China became the world's leading economy, and the math ahead is inescapable. The World Economic Forum estimates that "while there are currently 100 working-age people available to support every 20 elderly people, by 2100, 100 working-age Chinese will have to support as many as 120 elderly Chinese."[16]

That reversal creates tough math. "Countries with shrinking working-age populations have found it nearly impossible to produce strong economic growth," Morgan Stanley's Ruchir Sharma wrote in a 2016 study of what he called the "demographics of stagnation."[17] "A one-percentage-point decline in the population growth rate will eventually reduce the economic growth rate by roughly a percentage point," he continued. Consider the instability and change that will come as China shifts from a country accustomed to averaging 7, 8, or 9 percent annual growth or more—the official government estimates are often in the mid-teens, but most economists dismiss those official numbers as inflated—to a country whose GDP may very well begin *shrinking*. The demographic retreat, moreover, will be fast. By 2050 China's population will have fallen by a hundred million people, the equivalent of losing an entire Egypt or Vietnam. Increased competition for workers will drive further labor cost increases, accelerating the already significant flight of manufacturing companies to destinations across Asia and the Pacific with cheap labor and unburdened by US tariffs.

It's easy to think about population loss only in terms of economic numbers, but for a country like China—or any country really—a shrinking population reshapes the social and cultural fabric, rewriting the entire national spirit, its fundamental zeitgeist. It changes the national mood, the way people think of their country, and even the way they experience their own lives. Anyone in China under fifty has never known a time when China was not a rapidly rising power, increasing its global swagger as its economy modernized, gleaming new buildings rose, and infrastructure improved in the blink of an eye.

These titanic changes, which will be experienced in raw numbers by the nation as a whole, and in spreadsheets and briefing graphs by its political leadership, will be acutely felt by each individual family in living arrangements and around holiday dinner tables. A society long built on extended families and huge networks of aunts and uncles will confront an era where two-fifths of those under fifty will be only children by the 2050s. In 2020 the average thirtysomething in China has *fifty* living cousins, but projections by Nicholas Eberstadt and Ashton Verdery in *Foreign Affairs* show that "in 2050, the average young Chinese person under the age of 30 will have only a fifth as many cousins as today . . . and almost one in six will have no cousins at all."[18] That's a profoundly different human daily experience. A society that for generations has relied on children and grandchildren to support the elderly—and where the government's own social safety net remains woefully inadequate—will have to find other means of financial support as China confronts what Eberstadt and Verdery call "the great graying."

"It amounts to a radical change in a society historically defined by the importance of filial ties," they write. "Material advances notwithstanding, the shrinking, aging, and more atomized China of 2050 may be a profoundly pessimistic place. . . . The coming transformation of the Chinese family is for now likely a blind spot for the CCP—and has all the makings of a 'strategic surprise,' with the potential to throw Beijing's great plans into disarray." The CCP has thrived over the last half century because day by day, year by year life in China has gotten better and more prosperous. What happens when that bargain is no longer clear? And how likely will Chinese parents support military adventures knowing that their only child may perish in them?

That profound and by-now-unavoidable population collapse will remake the country and ripple through every facet of China's economy, politics, and geopolitics. As it considers the future of its military, for instance, Chinese leaders are surely cognizant that its fighting-age population has actually peaked and is already in decline.[19] And yet the coming collapse is only a single piece of the increasingly serious and complex domestic and international picture the country faces.

The Chinese economy in many ways is being sustained on a financial house of cards, driven by enormous government spending; some economists believe that nearly all of the country's growth in the last ten to fifteen years has come from increasing government spending, a pattern that will become unsustainable at some point. Debt has spiraled at private firms and the banking system's immature oversight systems almost surely don't capture the real risk. As Reuters reported in 2023, "Officially, non-performing loans at China's commercial banks total around 1.5 trillion yuan (over 200 billion dollars). But some analysts say the bad debt is as much as 14 times higher because lenders use various methods to conceal the true figure."[20]

Massive unplanned expenditures amid the Zero-COVID lockdowns added to mountains of debt held by local governments. Local debt now totals roughly $9 trillion, a little more than a third of the total US federal debt. S&P Global now estimates, "Two-thirds of local governments are now in danger of breaching unofficial debt thresholds set by Beijing to signify severe funding stress, with their outstanding debt exceeding 120% of income [in 2022]."[21]

China's far-reaching central controls might in theory enable it to weather a debt crisis better than, say, the United States did in 2008, avoiding what economists call a "Bear Sterns Moment" or "Lehman Brothers Moment," when the collapse of a single firm brings down a whole interlocking system.[22] But it is not clear how deftly the Chinese government will be able to continue its delicate economic ballet and plate-spinning—many of the highly skilled Chinese economists who have been responsible for managing the country's miraculous growth over the last two decades and adroitly limiting the effects on China of the global financial crisis (and in some ways, benefiting from it) are now rapidly retiring as Xi Jinping is sidelining the old "growth at all costs" guard amid an increasing focus on security and "order maintenance." Arguably the existential risk to China from debt isn't just an outright default; rather, it's a forced slowdown in growth, as local governments defer spending, trim workforces, delay infrastructure projects, or otherwise curtail and pare back the very spending that has helped prop up the economy nationally. Already government workers from teachers to garbage collectors are complaining about their wages being cut, complaints that have even led to protests in major cities like Wuhan and Dalian.[23] Some are not even getting paid at all.

Beyond the government's money, though, China's economy has benefited enormously from a credit-fueled real estate boom that appears increasingly shaky. A major part of the Chinese success story of the past half century has been its urbanization, as tens of millions of people flocked to cities from the countryside, creating huge demand for housing and development as a country that was 80 percent rural as late as the 1970s became 65 percent urban. Today, China boasts more than a hundred cities with over a million residents.

Amid that huge economic and urbanization shift, the very idea of private homeownership is actually only a generation old in China. It was only in 1980 that Deng Xiaoping allowed people to purchase their own homes; the housing sector was only commercialized by then-premier Zhu Rongji in 1998. Party leaders have spent the last decade becoming increasingly concerned with how an asset once viewed as a necessary shelter has become a key tool for profit, fueling rapid price increases. "Houses are built to be inhabited, not for speculation," Xi told the Nineteenth Party Congress in 2017.[24]

Today, housing continues to play an outsized role in the economy, and it is significant that the uncertainty and lockdowns of the COVID-19 pandemic precipitated a dangerous market downtown.[25] In fact, real estate comprises a whopping 30 percent of China's GDP, while it never exceeded 13 percent of US GDP at the height of the financial crisis. Part of the problem was that whereas China's megacities thrived, urban construction in smaller cities dramatically outpaced demand. Whole cities were built to house urban residents who may now never arrive; Kangbashi, in Inner Mongolia, was once projected to house a million residents and today has barely one hundred thousand, leaving its vast prebuilt infrastructure all but deserted.[26] The collapse of the Evergrande Group, China's second largest property developer, led it to walk away from Lu'an, where it had begun to build twenty-six-story residential towers, a $9 billion theme park, and a $4 billion electric-vehicle plant.[27] "For the past 15 years house prices in China mainly went up. They have spent the past six months sagging like a termite-weakened floor," the *Economist* wrote in early 2023.[28] Now the housing boom has started to crash and a potentially catastrophic collapse may be in store for the Chinese financial sector, which might make the US 2008 housing recession look like a minor bump in the road. Tens of millions of prebuilt homes and apartments sit empty across the country, speculative investments once anticipated to deliver major profits that may crash the housing sector instead.

It's also easy to oversell both China's economic success and how much further it still has to go. It is true that China has gone from an extremely poor country to one dominated by the middle class—one of the most miraculous improvements in standards of living in history—but it's a middle class that's still not close to the definition of the term that would be familiar to developed Western economies. It is also one that has come at a real human cost to the population.

For instance, China might be catching up to the United States on a GDP basis—although it's still nearly 25 percent lower—but the overall size of its economy is driven by the simple size of its consumer base, not its wealth. China's per capita GDP is just a sixth of the United States': $12,500 per citizen versus about $70,000 per citizen. On the global stage, China sits around seventieth in terms of per capita GDP, on par with Costa Rica or Malaysia, hardly countries most Americans would consider wealthy. "I think it's very unlikely that . . . China will get to U.S. levels of GDP per capita—that's our measure of wealth—for at least the next 50 years, if ever," Simon Baptist, global chief economist at the Economist Intelligence Unit, told CNBC in 2021.[29]

Furthermore, along the way to greatness, China has poisoned itself. "According higher priority to growth and job creation than to environmental protection has had highly negative and increasingly resented impacts on health and quality of life," Thomas Fingar and Jean Oi wrote in their analysis of China's rise, *Fateful Decisions*.[30] Air pollution has been an all-too-visible indication of China's environmental challenges; the haze in major cities has been notorious for more than a decade, when it was the subject of a dispute between the Chinese government and the US Embassy in Beijing, which had been tweeting out hourly air quality reports, and when a smog cloud led to the cancellation of hundreds of flights at the Beijing airport. By one NIH estimate, air pollution kills about 1.6 million Chinese a year.[31] And while as of 2023 the country has made some progress cleaning up pollution, it still faces a lengthy (and expensive!) effort to restore its air and water quality, much of which is considered unfit for human consumption. More than half of Shanghai's water is considered unfit for any purpose—let alone drinking!—and in the northern port city of Tianjin, just 5 percent of its water is drinkable.[32]

Overseas, China's attempts at global engagement and multilateral alliances have faltered, too. In 2013 Xi Jinping launched the vaunted Belt and Road Initiative, arguably the most ambitious global infrastructure project ever undertaken, one that aimed to pour Chinese money into projects on continent after continent to create a "New Silk Road" that would put China at the center of the Asian and global trading routes. (The project broadly started as an effort to build a land-based Silk Road Economic Belt and a Maritime Silk Road, hence the "belt" and "road.") What Xi called "a project of the century" had both domestic and international aims, as infrastructure efforts across Asia and Africa and elsewhere would ease and boost trade with China, knitting together rail and maritime networks with Chinese cities while aiding the global expansion of domestic firms like Huawei, whose cutting-edge telecommunications systems would form the backbone of new cellular and internet technologies in developing countries. Altogether, the effort led to projects in a stunning 147 countries, as money went to projects big and small, ranging from creating a $62 billion China-Pakistan Economic Corridor to building railways in Laos, constructing ports in Algeria, and even creating six hydroelectric dams in Bolivia.*

All told, China appeared ready to spend as much as $8 trillion, a quarter of the US total federal debt—much of that money came in the form of Chinese-owned loans that financed the foreign projects—and in its first years, it appeared a masterclass in global diplomacy and friendship-building (and friendship-buying). But what was seen even a few years ago as a giant geopolitical success story today feels more uncertain now that China has invested about a trillion of those planned dollars. China is starting to learn the same lesson that Russia had learned with the large network of Ukrainian collaborators they had on their payroll before the war—many of whom ultimately chose to melt away rather than risk their life supporting Russian aggression. You can

* Italy was the only G-7 country to sign on to the project but pulled out in 2023.

rent people but you can't buy them. Loyalty, of people or countries, is not available for permanent purchase.

Countries on the receiving end of the initiative have become warier of the accompanying debt and are recoiling at the quality of the Chinese-led construction projects. Malaysia actually announced in 2018 that it was shelving two of the proposed projects it had agreed to engage in with the Chinese, with the Malaysian prime minister telling Chinese officials, "We do not want a situation where there is a new version of colonialism happening." As a Singapore business professor told the *Global Trade Review*, "the debt model that Beijing has been pushing for to emerging countries, it's increasingly seen as a honeytrap that has backfired."[33]

Just as concerning for many local officials, though, is that the Chinese-led work itself isn't that good. "We are suffering today because of the bad quality of equipment and parts [in Chinese-built projects]," Ecuador's former energy minister told the *Wall Street Journal* in 2023.[34]

According to the *Wall Street Journal* investigation, countries around the world have been finding problems as China's grand promises materialized into subpar realities. Pakistan had to shut down a four-year-old hydroelectric plant after finding cracks in the tunnel that brought water to the facility, a shutdown that cost the country about $44 million a month in higher electrical rates. Uganda identified five hundred defects in a brand-new Chinese-built hydropower facility—some of them shockingly basic. For example, the Chinese construction firm never built the boom meant to keep floating debris from clogging the plant's intake valves. In Angola, a new housing complex was beginning to fall apart just ten years after it was built. In Kenya, a rail link connecting the coastal city of Mombasa with Uganda, Rwanda, and South Sudan—a project that was supposed to be one of the flagship Chinese infrastructure efforts in East Africa—was left incomplete after China pulled the remaining $4.9 billion in funding. Today, the rail link ends in a small village seventy-five miles west of Nairobi.[35] Perhaps the best evidence of the world's growing uneasiness with taking Chinese BRI investment is the declining participation in Beijing's global influence-flexing Belt and Road Forums: the number of heads of state attending the 2023 forum dropped to just twenty-three, down from a high of thirty-seven in 2019.

But despite this bad PR, developing countries still face a stark reality. Without significant alternative financing sources being available, the Chinese Belt and Road Initiative, warts and all, often remains their only option for upgrading their infrastructure and increasing economic opportunity.

At its most basic level, the Belt and Road Initiative began as an attempt to confront one of China's most fundamental weaknesses: its unchangeable geography and resource reserves. In this it stands in sharp contrast to the experience of the United States. While a range of factors led to the United States becoming the most powerful and wealthiest country in the world (perhaps even ever in history)—massive immigration-driven population growth, an innovation culture, rule of law and respect for property rights, and historically unprecedented access to capital to turn innovative ideas into highly successful companies—quite possibly the biggest single factor is its favorable geography.

Indeed, the United States was able to mature and grow into a world power largely untroubled by geopolitics for more than a century. Separated from the rest of the world by two giant oceans and bordered by two largely nonthreatening neighbors, the United States is one of the few major countries in the world that had the luxury since 1815 to only engage in wars of choice, not of necessity. Moreover, Americans have been self-sufficient in the production of food and energy for much of the country's existence, allowing us to feel safe and secure until the fateful events of Pearl Harbor in 1941 shattered our innocence. That attack heralded how the evolution of new technologies, such as aircraft carriers and submarines—and later, jet planes, nuclear weapons, and ballistic missiles—overcame the distance of the oceans and made us more vulnerable. Even so, after World War II, the United States effectively alone among the world's developed powers had not been devastated by fighting or wartime bombing campaigns. Its industrial might was now unparalleled, creating the circumstances for the incredible economic run in the decades that followed.

In contrast, China has no such luxuries today as it seeks to flex its new superpower status. A country that a half century ago was still largely agrarian has tipped into becoming the world's biggest food importer, capable of only producing 65 percent of its domestic needs. It is also the largest importer of coal and oil in the world, with much of that energy passing through narrow sea routes controlled by the US Navy, and despite rapid military modernization and much Sturm und Drang about how China has the "world's largest navy," the country has few so-called blue-water ships capable of defending its trade routes far from Chinese shores. Furthermore, despite massive investments in renewable energy sources—a sector that has been particularly boosted by state subsidies and massive intellectual property theft targeting Western wind turbine and solar panel manufacturers—China is not expected to reach energy self-sufficiency until at least 2060.

Moreover, the questions about China's rising bellicosity and the promises of the Belt and Road come just as China's arrogant and antagonistic self-styled wolf warrior diplomacy has embittered potential allies and strengthened the resolve and resistance of regional neighbors. Abandoning the standard niceties of diplomacy, Chinese representatives abroad have adopted an increasingly confrontational and antagonistic stance in their statements and policy positions—a combative posture nicknamed wolf warrior diplomacy, after the hit Chinese action film series *Wolf Warrior*, the latest film of which carried the tagline, "Whoever attacks China will be killed no matter how far the target is." In 2019, protesting Sweden's honoring of a Hong Kong dissident, the Chinese ambassador to Sweden told one interviewer, "We treat our friends with fine wine, but for enemies we got shotguns." More recently, China's ambassador to France, Lu Shaye, has become a particularly forceful example of this style—with notably egregious comments attacking Canada as white supremacist for protesting the Uyghur genocide, announcing that Taiwan would be "reeducated" after unification, and even questioning the sovereignty of post-Soviet states—a comment so absurd that it doesn't even square with Chinese policy, which recognized the independence of these states in 1991.[36] ("During a moment when the Global South is trying to hedge between the great powers, this was about the dumbest possible thing a Chinese official could have said," foreign policy strategist Daniel Drezner wrote.[37]) The cumulative effect internationally of such controversies and aggression has accomplished almost the exact opposite of what is traditionally considered diplomatic success: there are very few countries now where even 50 percent of the population view China favorably.

These political and geopolitical factors combine together to mark one of the most consequential shifts in China's global position: the rest of the world today is wary of China in a way that it never has been before. "Today, the business community is no longer standing up for engagement with China," former State Department official Susan L. Shirk writes in her book *Overreach: How China Derailed Its Peaceful Rise*. "The growing global perception is that friendship with China is no longer unconditional."[38] China's economic leaps over the previous generation came in no small part because of Western assistance and cooperation; today, that friendliness is receding. "The CCP is losing access to the open, welcoming world that assisted its ascent," Hal Brands and Michael Beckley note.[39] It is no small irony that it is the United States, more than any other nation, that has propelled and enabled China's rise and now finds itself racing to build a global alliance and network that can check Chinese power.

Add to all of this the financial and environmental precariousness and rising societal divisions that have been amplified by the misguided Zero-COVID strategy of 2020–2022, policies that led to increasing labor protests and highlighted the stark rural-urban divide, rising wealth inequality, and endemic elite corruption, and the current leadership of the ruling CCP faces an amazingly complex political environment and challenges to domestic political stability.

China's continued rise and economic, political, and geopolitical success is certainly not preordained, and the Chinese Century is hardly a guarantee. This fact is only underscored when one considers that the condition of the United States and its Western alliance is stronger—or at least can be stronger—than is commonly believed.

CHAPTER 5

We Are Stronger Than We Think

America's Strengths at Home and Abroad

IN NATIONAL SECURITY CIRCLES, YOU HEAR A LOT OF TALK ABOUT the power of the Five Eyes—the uniquely close, historically unprecedented and long-standing intelligence and security alliance between the world's five leading English-speaking countries, the United States, United Kingdom, Canada, Australia, and New Zealand. The relationship pulls together those countries' intelligence agencies, law enforcement entities, and defense capabilities into an international partnership so close and unique that personnel are cross-posted internationally, and the information sharing is so broad and far-reaching that it has a special marking, FVEY, which denotes US classified documents that can be shared among the group's members. On September 12, 2001, after a nationwide grounding of all civilian aviation in the wake of the 9/11 attacks, one of the only planes to fly into the United States was a special jet carrying the British head of intelligence, coming to Langley, Virginia, to visit his CIA counterpart and provide whatever support he could to a country in crisis.

To understand just how close and special the Five Eyes relationship truly is, though, you need only to look to another terror threat two years later. In December 2003 the NSA and US intelligence were picking up repeated so-called chatter pointing to a possible nuclear attack by al-Qaeda on Washington, DC. "Intelligence said there was very likely" a nuclear device that "could affect command and control systems in Washington," a former US official told the *Daily Beast* when the incident finally became public in 2017. "The concern was that it would be catastrophic." That Christmas Eve, NSA director Gen. Mike Hayden called his British counterpart at GCHQ, the UK's signals intelligence agency, and told him that if an attack was to knock out Washington, DC, he had instructed the US signals intelligence operation to report instead to Cheltenham, where the UK agency is headquartered.[1] "If we go down, you run the show," Hayden told his UK colleague David Pepper.

The story is a remarkable testament to one of America's most important and unique strengths: its unmatched series of alliances and global influence. It's a key part of what best be thought of not just as the "Five Eyes," but the "Five I's," the collected strengths and attributes that together explain why the United States and its Western alliance remains better positioned than China and its other adversaries to triumph in the twenty-first century: America's resilience and strength come from an unparalleled combination of *immigration*, *innovation*, *investment*, *influence*, and *ideas*. Together, those interlocking and mutually reinforcing strengths remind us that whereas pundits often overstate the strength of adversaries, many of them are also used to underestimating the United States' own strengths.

It's easy to watch the news these days and sell America short—to see the country as politically polarized, awash with violence, suffering from failing infrastructure, and enduring a dysfunctional government. But it's a lot harder to sell America short if you're one of its immigrants.

IMMIGRATION

"Immigration" in today's politics can often seem like a four-letter word—a curse rather than a blessing—but it's worth remembering why so many people from all over the world want to come here. First and foremost, we remain the beacon of opportunity and upward mobility for the world, the result of an enormous economic advantage that helps our workforce and the culture of innovation.

The American Dream remains a global aspiration—there is, by contrast, no widely recognized or emulated "Russian Dream" and while Xi has built his regime around rejuvenating the desire of a Chinese Dream, it's a concept that resonates only domestically and not even universally within his own country (just ask the Uyghurs). Our historic openness to immigration and entrepreneurship has provided us with an essential source of human capital and human spirit. In fact, in many cases, the best talents of Russia and China still come to the United States to learn and grow—an experience I know firsthand, as I was born in Moscow in the Soviet Union before my parents emigrated to the United States for my dad's work.

My parents had caught the American bug in 1990 when they had a chance to visit as part of a post-Chernobyl collaboration between US and Soviet nuclear scientists. (My dad was part of a program to jointly develop realistic computer simulators for nuclear power plants that could better train operators of civilian nuclear power plants and help avoid the next nuclear disaster.) Initially, I had remained in Moscow with my grandparents—the Soviet regime would not let my parents travel abroad with me in tow for fear that they would not return—but after their brief stint visiting and working in America, my parents knew that this was the country they wanted their son to grow up in. Thus, we left the country of my birth in 1994, as the Soviet Union unraveled, with a total of three suitcases' worth of our life's belongings, and following years of hardships and overcoming the huge challenges of navigating the overly complex US immigration system, I found myself a young teenager going to high school in Chattanooga, Tennessee, in the mid-1990s.

It was then—somewhat bored in school, as I had skipped three grades of math classes and still found the subject relatively easy—that

I caught the entrepreneurial bug. My dad was somewhat bored at his programming job too. And thus my first startup was created—working in the nascent field of cryptography and developing secure communications on the growing global network called the "internet." It taught me invaluable lessons in entrepreneurship and put me on a path that changed the course of my entire life.

That experience led me to pursue a formal cybersecurity education in college. Eventually I graduated as the first master's student in the then-inaugural degree in "information security," before it was called cybersecurity, from Georgia Tech, and embarked upon a career in the field. (It was then when I also caught my geopolitics bug, fulfilling my policy coursework degree requirement with international affairs classes—everything from nuclear nonproliferation to counterterrorism.) I joined startups that were solving cutting-edge problems in the field. Less than eight years later, having worked my way up from an entry-level engineer and scientist at a small startup to a vice president at McAfee, one of the largest cybersecurity companies in the world at the time, I found myself eager to go back to trying entrepreneurship once again.

By then, I'd worked on the Operations Aurora, Night Dragon, and Shady RAT hacks, getting a glimpse into the nation-state espionage from countries like China as it pilfered intellectual property from Western industries—and I knew there was an opportunity to build a better company to address the cyber threat unfriendly nation-states posed to Western companies. That startup, CrowdStrike, is now itself one of the largest cybersecurity companies in the world, employing over seven thousand people worldwide. In 2019 I stood with my coworkers on the floor of the NASDAQ stock exchange to ring the opening bell and take our company public.

I knew that the success that I had achieved in America as an immigrant would have been infinitely harder to replicate anywhere else in the world, likely even impossible. America's unequal access to capital allowed us to raise an unprecedentedly large investment in 2011 based on nothing more than an idea and our reputations in the industry. Our extensive talent base made it easy for me to seek out and recruit some of the world's best engineers and researchers in a matter of weeks. Out of the initial launch team of nine people, three of my recruits were immigrants themselves. Shortly after taking CrowdStrike public, I decided that it was time for a new mission and challenge—giving back to the country that has given me these incredible opportunities and founding a nonprofit, Silverado Policy Accelerator, to help promote policies that can keep America at the forefront of innovation and competitiveness in the twenty-first century.

This country is still the place where people come to make a better life for themselves and for their children, as my parents did for me. America is not (and never has been) a perfect meritocracy—the piercing research of economist Raj Chetty has opened the country's eyes to how too often an American's place in the economic hierarchy is determined by their zip code—but it still offers a level of social mobility all but unequaled around the world. Specifically, no country can boast the same degree of upward mobility for its immigrants as the United States: a whopping 13 percent of American billionaires are immigrants to this country.[2]

That upward mobility stems in part from how welcoming America continues to be, despite our often fierce political disagreements on the polarizing issue of immigration: people arrive on our shores and can become "American," not just formally with the granting of US citizenship but culturally welcomed and assimilated. In a generation or two (or less!) families of all cultures, religions, races, ethnicities, and languages can be thoroughly "Americanized." I was Russian—a teenager in Moscow—and in barely a quarter century, by age forty, I was an American entrepreneurial success story, fully American, and given opportunities to help senior leaders across the US government. It's easy to overlook how stunningly rare that accomplishment is elsewhere in the world. An American moving to Russia would be viewed with suspicion their entire life, and a white person moving to China will never be considered "Chinese," no matter how well he or she might speak the language; someone moving to France from overseas will struggle to be considered culturally "French" even if they spend decades living there.

Moreover, people continue to come to the United States in no small part because of the quality of America's higher education. China does have its share of good universities. For example, Tsinghua University stands widely regarded as the flagship university in China; in recent years, it's been ranked as the top university in the Asia-Pacific region. Most Americans, though, don't realize that the flagship of Chinese education ironically traces its roots to President Theodore Roosevelt and the Boxer Rebellion. In 1900, as the Qing Dynasty battled an anti-imperialist uprising, an eight-nation alliance that included the United States successfully interceded, sending forty-five thousand troops to quell the civil war. When it came time for China to pay reparations, Roosevelt believed that the approximately $30 million due the United States was too high and, with the approval of Congress, converted about a third of the payment to underwrite Chinese scholarships to study in America. The Tsing Hua Imperial College was, in turn, founded in 1911 as a preparatory school where returning Chinese graduates helped teach future students who would be sent to America.

Today, with fifty thousand students—about sixteen thousand undergrads and thirty-four thousand grad students—Tsinghua is about the size of the University of Texas at Austin, and its leafy thousand-acre campus in Beijing, filled with brick and granite buildings and domed architecture, wouldn't look out of place at MIT or the University of Virginia, a landscape befitting the royal garden where the school was founded over a century ago. Today, while Westerners do study at Tsinghua—about four thousand international students are enrolled there—it's not exactly a household brand and aspirational dream for millions of American high schoolers.

And yet visit Harvard Square on any given day and you will see a constant stream of buses disgorging Asian tourists who stand in line to have their photos taken on the steps of Widener Library and to rub the foot of the John Harvard statue for good luck. Harvard has about eight thousand international students, including about eighteen hundred from China, out of a total student population just half the size of that of Tsinghua. Harvard remains the dream school for aspiring Chinese families and even the families of its elite.

It's a testament to one of the easiest-to-overlook strengths of the American system: the reach and pull of American higher education remains unparalleled globally, despite unwise forays into culture wars. On almost any ranking system, the United States and the United Kingdom dominate the globe's best schools, creating a huge magnet for the world's top talent to come to the United States to study and, visa vagaries permitting, even stay in the country to work after graduating. According to the *US News & World Report*'s ranking, eighteen of the world's top twenty-five schools are American—Tsinghua ranks twenty-third, sandwiched between two Illinois schools, University of Chicago and Northwestern—and the other six schools are all Canadian or British. The more widely used international ranking by the British firm Quacquarelli Symonds features twelve US schools among its top twenty-five, alongside only two Chinese schools: Tsinghua and Peking University.

There's a reason that Xi Jinping, who himself graduated from Tsinghua, sent his only child, daughter Xi Mingze, to Harvard to study (under an assumed name)—and he's hardly alone. Two of Xi's three immediate predecessors as leaders of the CCP, Zhao Ziyang and Jiang Zemin, both had grandchildren who attended Harvard.[*3] On this point, plenty of Chinese citizens have agreed with their leaders. Over the last twenty years, a flood of Chinese students has remade the US higher education landscape. Chinese students became the largest cohort of international students in the US in the late 2000s, overtaking traditional leaders like Canada, India, and South Korea, in part because Chinese parents saw the US colleges providing a more well-rounded, higher quality, and more prestigious education than Chinese universities.[4] About three hundred thousand Chinese students now study in

* The extent to which the children of China's elite study overseas is indicative of the corruption endemic to the party; as the *Washington Post* reported in 2012, "the son of one party leader, who officially made just $20,000 a year in salary, attended Harrow School, an exclusive private academy in London with annual fees of about $48,000; then Oxford, which, for overseas students, costs more than $25,000 a year just in tuition; and the Kennedy School, which, according to its own estimates, requires about $70,000 a year to cover tuition and living expenses."

the United States each year, representing roughly a third of the million international students that flock to US campuses annually.*[5]

While there are lots of headlines and studies about US students falling behind international peers, the American workforce remains uniquely well-educated and literate. The United States issues about fifty thousand PhDs a year, including forty thousand in science and engineering, and globally, the country ranks fourth in the percentage of its workforce with PhDs, behind Slovenia, Switzerland, and Luxembourg. (Notably, from 2011 to 2021, Chinese students earned about fifty thousand of those PhDs.[6])

China knows it has to catch up with American achievements in education and is racing to do so; research by Georgetown's Center for Security and Emerging Technology predicts that Chinese universities will in 2025 produce more than seventy-seven thousand STEM PhD graduates per year, roughly double what they graduated in the mid-2000s.[7] About half of those graduates come from the forty-two schools that are known as the country's Double First Class (DFC) universities, which are heavily supported by the government.

But the American education system also benefits immensely from the philanthropy of its citizens and alumni. In 2021, having become concerned about the lack of quality cybersecurity graduates coming out of America's colleges, I created the Alperovitch Institute of Cybersecurity Studies at the Johns Hopkins School of Advanced International Studies (SAIS), which aspires to produce the best master's degree and PhD students in the field, along with cutting-edge research at the intersection of cybersecurity, intelligence, and strategic studies. The institute is located in a stunningly beautiful new building on prime real estate of Pennsylvania Avenue in the nation's capital—between the White House and the Capitol. That building came about

---

* These foreign students have been a key help to the business models of US schools, since they usually pay full price—in effect helping to subsidize financial aid for US students. In fact, full-freight-paying Chinese students have become so important to the University of Illinois at Urbana-Champaign that in 2017 it took out an insurance policy to cover the roughly $60 million in annual tuition Chinese students paid—an unexpected move that proved smart when COVID-19 hit just three years later.

through another generous donation of a Johns Hopkins alum—Michael Bloomberg.

Unfortunately, it is true that the success and quality of our top colleges is not reflected across our K–12 education system, which generally remains abysmal and lagging much of the developed world. It remains a key challenge for America to solve—to not just import the world's intellect but also do a better job of providing a high-quality education to a broader population of the citizens who have been born and raised here. But be that as it may, the strength of America's higher education helps to power an incredible world-leading economic engine and continuously renew and reinvent our spirit of innovation.

INNOVATION

Our economy remains the envy of the world—home to the world's largest and most important companies and the place where cutting-edge innovation and invention happen, to be in turn protected and underpinned by a robust rule of law and system of intellectual property protections, from trademarks and copyrights to patents and stringent enforcement of laws against theft of intellectual property and trade secrets.

This is where people want to invent things. There is simply nowhere on earth where it's easier to start a company, get it funded, recruit highly talented people, and have an enormous single market to sell into.

It's worth noting that it's also easier to fail in America than it is elsewhere—the bankruptcy system and ability to conduct layoffs with relative ease are critical to encouraging entrepreneurs and companies to take chances and risks in the first place. Europe's capitalist spirit and drive for innovation has long been stymied in part because of how onerous and expensive it can be to close a business line and terminate workers, which discourages risk-taking and growth-centric approaches in business.

Even hiring workers is easy in America. Most employees in the United States whom I recruited to work for me at CrowdStrike were able to join us a mere two weeks after turning in their notice to their previous employer—and hiring them from all fifty states was a relative breeze. On the other hand, while hiring people in the United Kingdom, I was frustrated to have to wait for months for new employees to join us because they were sitting out their mandatory fully paid "garden leave," unable to contribute productively to us or their previous employer. Setting up processes—legal entities, ensuring employment law and tax compliance, banks and fund transfers—to hire people across the European Union was as painful and costly as it sounds.

America's entrepreneurial drive is secured by some of the world's most robust and best-enforced intellectual property protections—protections that mean innovators know they can profit from their inventions and defend their insights against encroachment, theft, and appropriation by others. And, even beyond the protections of individual parts of the law, America's economy is backed up, more broadly, by the general rule of law—leading businesspeople in Russia and China have seen in recent years how capriciously the leadership of those countries, with their contrary "rule by law" system, can undermine and steal away even the most successful companies.

"For decades, Chinese leaders have pledged to build robust legal institutions that can deliver good governance and social stability," Xi's biographer Chun Han Wong writes. "But as China's economy took off, its fledging legal system struggled to keep up with the social distensions kicked up by widening wealth gaps and the spread of corruption."[8] Efforts by legal activists to push China toward a more Western-style independent judiciary have failed—and actually led, not a little bit ironically, to the imprisonment of many of those same activists—as China has instead settled on what George Washington University professor Donald Clarke calls "a system for the maintenance of order and the political primacy of the Chinese Communist Party, not for the delivery of justice."[9] There is no law in China but the dictates of the Communist Party, which means, in short, there's no law but Xi's whims. It is a more organized, tech-driven, and less in-your-face regime than Mao's bloody reign, but it is nonetheless arbitrary and driven by political winds. In meaningful ways, China has tangibly regressed under Xi's tenure: as of 2020 Chinese police no longer pledge in their service oath to "promote social fairness and justice" but instead promise to "defend political security" and "firmly uphold the absolute leadership of the Chinese Communist Party."[10]

You can start a great company in Russia or China, become wildly profitable and successful, and it all can and will be arbitrarily taken away should the government decide that you've crossed an invisible line. In Russia, we need look no further than at the case of oligarch Mikhail Khodorkovsky, believed at one time to be the sixteenth wealthiest man in the world, the force behind the oil giant Yukos. Early in Vladimir Putin's rule Khodorkovsky saw his business empire crushed and himself driven into exile after Putin perceived Khodorkovsky threatened to become a meaningful political rival. In China, Jack Ma had built by 2020 arguably the biggest Chinese brand in the world, Alibaba and his fintech company Ant Group, becoming the toast of the global tech conference circuit and the wealthiest man in China; then, just days before an Ant Group IPO anticipated raising $37 billion that would have been the world's largest public offering, Ma criticized Chinese financial regulators and Xi Jinping personally quashed the IPO.[11] Ma, usually outspoken and voluble, all but disappeared from the world stage for three months and did not appear in public from November 2020 until January 2021, during which period rumors swirled about whether he was under house arrest or detention. The explanation for the high-profile falling-out was clear: "Xi doesn't care about if you made any of those rich lists or not," said a senior Chinese official. "What he cares about is what you do after you get rich, and whether you're aligning your interests with the state's interests."[12]

Given the American tradition and protections for innovation and businesses, it is no accident that the United States is home to some of the world's biggest and leading companies across technology, energy, pharmaceutical, automotive, industrial, agricultural, and financial sectors. It's why the United States has more businesses than anywhere else on the planet, the key driver of our economic growth, employment, and innovation. And it's not a coincidence that the combination of America's immigration, education, and innovation has helped US companies and entrepreneurs invent the modern world. Other countries would be thrilled to have engendered just one of the incredible world-shaping inventions that have come from the United States in recent generations, from the personal computer to the internet and Google to the iPhone to stealth technology to reusable rocketry.

But to invent these incredible technologies you need investment capital—often lots of it.

INVESTMENT

America's innovation engine begins with easy and abundant access to capital. Wall Street remains the financial center of the world, the US dollar the world's most important currency, and US Treasury bonds the world's safest investment, occasional political panic over debt limit raises and resultant rating agencies' downgrades notwithstanding.[*13]

Nowhere else is it easier to start a business with a bank loan; the United States has almost ten thousand banks and credit unions—about one for every thirty-five thousand people in the country. In addition, America has thousands of venture capital, private equity, family office, and private credit firms ready to provide crucial capital to new and existing businesses. And even though there remain troubling broad gender and racial inequities in terms of who and what gets funded, the country has more capital ready to deploy than any other market in the world.

To recruit talent to build CrowdStrike, we needed funding and lots of it. Over the course of the company's history and through its IPO, we ended up raising almost $1.1 billion. The return on that money for our investors was a stake in what would turn out to be one of the world's largest cybersecurity companies; at the market peak, CrowdStrike was worth over $66 billion. I know I could not have built such a company anywhere else in the world.

---

* The absurdity of US debt downgrades from AAA to AA+ was best highlighted by the *Bloomberg* financial columnist Matt Levine: "If I were a ratings agency my rating on US government debt would not be a semi-arbitrary collection of As. My rating would be 'this is US government debt.' For good and for ill, people mostly know what that means!"

In America, we were able to succeed because of the access to capital, the ability to scale quickly, and the ease of acquiring customers in the large, diverse, and robust US economy.*[14] It's easy to overlook how critical this final factor is for the growth of a company: there is no other place in the world that presents as large of a single easy market for sales as the United States. For all the talk of Europe as a "single market," it's only true in some respects—any company that attempts to sell in Europe quickly realizes that it is not selling in "the EU" but in twenty-seven different countries, plus the UK, each with their own languages, cultures, sales and marketing models, and laws and regulations. In comparison, selling solutions to companies in Alabama (a market roughly the GDP of Portugal) is no different than selling them in California (roughly the GDP of the United Kingdom) or Illinois (roughly the GDP of the Netherlands).

That power and scale of American companies and capital, in turn, contributes to increasing our influence and power around the world.

INFLUENCE

For eight decades since the end of World War II, the United States has built a dominating network of military allies and economic partners without parallel in world history. In the postwar era, the US-led NATO secured Europe, the US-led Bretton Woods agreement secured the global economy, and the US-driven WTO liberalized global trade and contributed to unprecedented levels of economic prosperity over the last three decades. Crucially, the global economy remains centered on Wall Street and the US dollar; doing business all over the

---

* Unfortunately, that capital has not always been used just to propel forward American innovation and to serve our national security. Too much of it has gone to grow the industrial capabilities of our adversaries: first the Soviet Union during the early stages of Cold War I, Nazi Germany during the 1930s, and now China in the midst of Cold War II. On a recent trip to Taiwan, I nearly fell off my chair while having dinner with a Taiwanese-American former senior Goldman Sachs banker in Asia, who nonchalantly informed me that during the late '90s and early 2000s, they had provided the early financing to launch Semiconductor Manufacturing International Corporation (SMIC)—now China's largest chipmaker—Alibaba, their largest e-commerce company, and even Huawei, China's largest telecommunications provider.

world requires moving through the banking system that the United States dominates and controls.

The US dollar, despite all the hand-wringing from pundits, remains unassailable. For all the concern expressed about the decreasing share of global foreign exchange reserves being held in US dollar–denominated assets—the share of US dollar reserves did drop from a high of 72 percent in 2000 to 58 percent today—the true picture is more complicated, because that "fall" from 2000 represented more of a historic anomaly than the twentieth-century norm. In fact, the share of the US dollar reserves in 1990 was just 56 percent—about where it is today—but over the 1990s, there was a temporary movement to a higher allocation to dollars mostly attributed to the disappearance of national European currencies like the German deutschemark and the French franc ahead of the introduction of the euro in 1999. Once the euro arrived and emerged as a trusted currency, foreign reserves rebalanced again. If one were to expand the graph of foreign reserve currency mix across three decades of data, it becomes immediately apparent that the US dollar's share has barely changed—and if anything actually has slightly gone up!—because there remains no meaningful alternative to the security and power of the US dollar. Foreign reserves of Chinese renminbi remain below a miniscule 3 percent—just up slightly from 1 percent at the end of 2016 when it was included by the IMF in the so-called Special Drawing Rights (SDR) basket. The reason for China's currency struggle is simple: the renminbi is not freely convertible and no one trusts the currency controls policy of the CCP. Other alternatives to the US dollar are similarly floundering. Cryptocurrency like Bitcoin and Etherium, with its huge volatility and near exclusive use by speculators and criminals, has demonstrated that it's not a viable reserve option. Neither are the other BRICS currencies—the Brazilian real, Russian ruble, Indian rupee, or South African rand—as all are either too weak or not convertible enough to be trusted as reserve currencies. Finally, gold is also not an ideal reserve asset. Unlike actual currencies it is not very liquid—it is heavy, bulky, and has to be physically moved in order to buy or sell it. And it doesn't yield a return, unlike government bonds denominated in dollars or other currencies.

Perhaps most importantly, countries heavily sanctioned by the United States, like Russia or Iran, who look at gold reserves as a way to escape freezing of their assets by the all-powerful US Treasury, as happened to Russia after its invasion of Ukraine, will be very disappointed once they realize that in order to use those reserves to control their monetary policy, they will have to first sell that gold to someone—and the primary buyers would likely be international banks concerned about running afoul of that same US Treasury.

Plenty of countries may have their concerns, some valid, about the US dollar—from runaway congressional spending and unsustainable federal debt levels to the weaponization of the global US dollar-dependent financial system—but as former treasury secretary Larry Summers aptly put it, "What other currency is preferable to the dollar as a reserve and trade currency when Europe's a museum, Japan's a nursing home, China's a jail, and Bitcoin's an experiment?"[15]

Across the board, there is—for now—no better global friend or worse enemy than the United States. No country can come close to our ability to project power, quickly, to every corner of the world, through air, sea, cyber, and space domains. Our military might is unsurpassed—the United States spends annually on defense an amount equal to that spent on the next ten largest militaries combined, and at least six of those other ten are US allies (and the seventh, India, is increasingly a partner)—and no military on the planet is more experienced than ours. The US military has over decades invested in a combat-ready force built to fight any foe, anywhere in the world, at any time.

While the Chinese military increasingly presents a formidable threat in the Indo-Pacific region, it has virtually no power projection anywhere else on the globe. China has no soldiers or generals on active duty who have fought in a modern war, the country having last been in a conflict against Vietnam—an engagement that did not go well for them—all the way back in 1979. Furthermore, it has really only used force against its own citizens in recent decades or in small-scale, low-stakes, short-duration skirmishes along the Indian border (sometimes in fights where the combatants are armed with nothing more than sticks and bricks).

The recent Russian experience suggests that this is a real liability for China. Russia has struggled in Ukraine because prior to 2022 it hadn't conducted large-scale, land-based military operations since Afghanistan in the 1980s or, even before that, Czechoslovakia in 1968—neither of which was against an advanced military power. As the Russian military has learned the hard way in Ukraine, it has no meaningful experience in modern combined-arms engagements and its top-down command-and-control system is too siloed and slow to adapt. For better or worse, the United States has been engaged in large combat operations and wars every decade since World War II. As Russia lacks similar experience, two decades of Russian military modernization have been negated by Moscow's self-inflicted, shot-in-the-foot invasion of Ukraine.

Moreover, the strong multilateral response to the Ukraine invasion underscored the depth and breadth of America's alliances around the world; European and Asian countries moved quickly in concert with the United States to levy sanctions, freeze bank accounts, and cut Russia off from the global economic and banking system. It is impossible to imagine China mustering similar resources outside of its own borders.

All told, our multilateral, trade, intelligence, and security alliances ring the globe—even beyond the Five Eyes alliance, we have a strong new emerging security alliance known as AUKUS, with the UK and Australia, and a newly evolving partnership known as "the Quad" in the Pacific with Japan, India, and Australia. Many of China's regional neighbors, like Japan and South Korea, are among our closest military allies, and in Europe, NATO is set to actually grow even stronger with the new applications for membership from Finland and Sweden thanks to Russia's war on Ukraine.

In sharp contrast, China and Russia lack any meaningful global allies. Russia's only real partnerships in the Ukraine fight are Belarus, Iran, and North Korea, and even they have not sent their troops into Ukraine. North Korea, hardly a world-leading power, is also China's closest ideological partner, but the two countries are not even formal allies and view one another with wariness and distrust.

Our global influence is aided too by a uniquely friendly domestic geography. Very much unlike our adversaries—China, Russia, North Korea, and Iran all face complex regional tensions, enemies, and the need for heavily defended borders—we have no natural close enemies. Our country's geographic advantages translate into plentiful space for housing and population growth, abundant natural resources, fertile land, and a robust (if aging) national infrastructure for coast-to-coast transportation and commerce. That security accorded by natural terrain, in turn, allows us to focus much of our military spending on projecting power around the world, as opposed to the need our authoritarian adversaries have to allocate huge resources for domestic population control and deterrence of conflicts on their borders.

The US network of global influence, in turn, is enabled by America's constant ability to evolve, adapt, and produce new ideas, something that authoritarian and dictatorial regimes, highly dependent on the extraordinary capabilities of a select few rulers, tend to struggle with as the intellectual power of their regimes atrophies over time.

IDEAS

Today's political divisions often seem intractable, but it's easy to forget that our political system actually remains a source of strength, resilience, and opportunity for our country—one that none of our dictatorial and authoritarian adversaries can match.

Government in the United States was designed to have multiple centers of power. The framework the Founding Fathers left us did not depend on an "ultimate arbiter," a dictator or a sovereign; rather, it was a framework for what historian Joseph Ellis calls an "ongoing argument."[16] One of the lessons highlighted in Lin-Manuel Miranda's *Hamilton* is the remarkable structure of government that the Founders bequeathed upon us—one where political parties treat dissent and civil disagreement as not just acceptable but expected.

Indeed, the dramatic nature of the ultimately deadly Burr-Hamilton feud stems in part from how unique it was at the time of the Revolution. It was the only case of a Founder taking another Founder's life, and Henry Adams called it "the most dramatic moment in the early politics of the Union." More broadly, it was one of only a handful of times in our entire national history where senior political figures fought personally to inflict real wounds. By contrast, the French, Russian, Chinese Revolutions—and many others over the years—have all ended not with celebratory fireworks but in torrents of bloodshed and waves of multiyear reprisals and repression.

America developed a different tradition. Our system of political parties institutionalized channels for ongoing debate, discussion, and evolution. It's a remarkable accomplishment to disagree nonviolently—although not always civilly—as a society and a political system. As Ellis wrote, that structure "eventually permitted dissent to be regarded not as a treasonable act, but as a legitimate voice in an endless argument."[17] Our governmental institutions were purposefully set up as dueling power structures that would push us to be better. Yes, the government is far from perfect, politics can be nasty, and bureaucracy can be slow, but we are a country that is larger than any one party or one person.

Our representative democratic republic, our system of government, and our ability to disagree and debate internally without revolution have encouraged a level of stability and longevity that makes the United States and many of our Western democratic allies uniquely adaptive and form a key foundation of our global power.[18] That stability has been key to allowing the country to develop so many long-standing treaties, partnerships, and alliances.

This idea—of a country governed by the people, for the people, a land of meritocracy and opportunity where hard work is rewarded—is the central foundation of the American Dream, the dream that continues to be a beacon of freedom around the world, attracting immigrants to our well of intellect and spirit of innovation, and reinforcing our global integration.

The combination of these five incredible advantages has meant that for the last seventy-five years, countries that have chosen to play by Western rules the United States set through its military might, the multilateral institutions it established and continues to dominate, and its economic power, have gotten richer and more advanced, whereas others have tended to stagnate and wither. It is true that each of these five core societal, political, and economic strengths is indeed vulnerable and under threat in their own way in the modern era—China, for instance, is narrowing the gap on innovation, at least on paper, as Chinese schools today are minting far more PhDs than the United States and Chinese patent applications have surged. Still, if as an immigrant, entrepreneur, or investor you had to choose one system or the other today, the world at large is still clearly interested in choosing the American model.

Our challenge now, over the next thirty years, is to ensure that China doesn't end up being in the position to berate, bribe, and bully the rest of the globe into following its lead. We must, instead, remain the leader of a coalition of the world's most advanced and powerful countries. Given our advantages, the end of the American Century is hardly a foregone conclusion. The path toward securing that future, in turn, begins with a four-stage strategy that enables and defends the innovation of the United States and its Western allies and strengthens and focuses our approach to the rest of the world.

PART II

A Game Plan for Victory

CHAPTER 6

Step One—Enable Innovation

Across the past four decades, the United States has laid the foundation of its economy and national security atop an inch-wide piece of silicon: semiconductors, simply known to most as chips. Average Americans interact with hundreds of these Lego-sized technologies on any given day, in their smartphones, microwave ovens, cars, televisions, vending machines, grocery store kiosks, and TVs. Chips support the technologies that we can't live without—smartphones, airplanes, the modern electrical grid, and the internet itself—and the ones we count on to keep us living, such as MRI machines, water treatment plants, and advanced weapons systems. As our world grows increasingly "smart," semiconductors will help deliver the next generation of innovative technologies to drive our society and economy forward. The "intelligence" in artificial intelligence? Chips. Modeling of new medical treatments for diseases? Chips. Hypersonic missile advancements? Faster chips. It is often said that chips are the oil of the twenty-first century. In fact, even that statement may underrate the importance of semiconductors to the global economy, since, unlike chips, there are alternatives to oil. But there is simply no replacement in today's modern economy for semiconductors.

No one recognizes the importance of chips to the future more than China, which has spent the last decade fighting hard—and sometimes successfully—to advance its own domestic semiconductor know-how and manufacturing capabilities. Those tiny building blocks of computing have emerged even as a key part of the tension with Taiwan, both in terms of why it's critical to defend its freedom and in terms of the added benefit China would derive from controlling the island—in doing so it would benefit not just from its strategic geographic position as the gateway to the Pacific but also from its industry and knowledge.

Specifically, China would gain not just the freedom of maritime navigation that would come from controlling Taiwan but the tools, workers, and technology that make up facilities like TSMC's Fab 18, located in the twenty-five-hundred-acre Tainan Science Park, just outside Tainan City, a city of about 1.8 million people on Taiwan's southwest coast. (Tainan was originally established by the Dutch in thc early 1600s and then, after the defeat of the European colonists, remained the capital of the island for about two hundred years.) In fact, dollar for dollar and inch for inch, it's probably hard anywhere on earth to find pricier real estate than that owned by TSMC: when the company broke ground in 2018 on the facility that would become Fab 18, it announced that the 950,000-square-meter facility would cost about $17 billion, a price tag that would enable it to make some of the most advanced computer chips in the world. As chip historian Chris Miller observed, "In 2020, as the world lurched between lockdowns driven by a virus whose diameter measured around one hundred nanometers—billionths of a meter—TSMC's most advanced facility, Fab 18, was carving microscopic mazes of tiny transistors, etching shapes smaller than half the size of a coronavirus, a hundredth the size of a mitochondria."[1]

Altogether, add in TSMC's other fabs, including Fab 18's three neighbors in the Tainan Science Park and nearly a dozen other facilities scattered around the island at Hsinchu Science Park and other locations, and Taiwan alone is responsible for nearly 40 percent of new computing power manufactured every year worldwide.[2]

China knows just how critical access to these components will be in the years ahead; it has been investing heavily in its domestic semiconductor industry in an effort to expand its place in the global market and achieve maximal self-sufficiency. As early as June 2014, the Chinese government published a plan focused solely on the development of its integrated circuit industry, a plan that aimed at meeting 70 percent of its semiconductor demand domestically by 2025. (It's a long way from that goal at the time of this writing.) Top Communist Party leaders have emphasized the strategic connection between achieving a degree of self-sufficiency in chips and China's broader strategic objectives. In 2016 President Xi Jinping admitted, "The fact that core technology is controlled by others is our greatest hidden danger," and more recently, Vice Premier Ma Kai said—even more simply—at the 2018 National People's Congress, "We cannot be reliant on foreign chips."[3] China's Fourteenth Five-Year Plan, released in March of 2021, designates semiconductors as one of the seven areas that will be given priority access to government funding and resources.

To succeed over the next half century, the United States needs to prioritize two broad enablers of innovation—semiconductor chips and immigration—and protect its access to so-called critical minerals in order to carve out a global leadership role in the four areas of emerging strategic technologies: artificial intelligence and autonomy; biotech and synthetic biology; reusable and more efficient rockets, satellites, and spaceships; and climate-focused so-called green tech.

First, though, nothing happens without computer chips—a commodity that has both an important technological component and a geopolitical one.

Everything begins with the chips.

THE STORY OF ADVANCES IN COMPUTER CHIPS IS THE STORY OF A faster, more wired, more connected world, a world where for more than a half century, technology has advanced not linearly but exponentially.

Nothing happens in the world of technology without what the industry calls "semiconductors" or "integrated circuits," but what most of the world shorthands simply as chips. The basic building block of every computing device is a bit, which can represent a 1 or a 0. Far removed from the pretty interfaces, keys, and graphics we interact with on our computer, tablet, and phone screens, those commands, files, pictures, sounds, and videos are broken down into millions and billions of 0s and 1s, which help tell the tiny transistors embedded on chips whether to be on (1) or off (0).

The transistor itself was a postwar innovation that emerged from work by William Shockley at Bell Labs' famed facility in New Jersey. At first, it wasn't clear that the invention would mean much of anything to anybody; the *New York Times* placed IBM's June 1948 announcement of the breakthrough on page 46.[4] Shockley eventually went out on his own to perfect the new invention. In 1957 eight members of Shockley's lab—frustrated by the poor management and growing paranoia of the brilliant, Nobel Prize–winning physicist—announced they were leaving, and the so-called traitorous eight founded a company in Palo Alto known as Fairchild Semiconductor. Their timing, it turned out, was perfect. Three days after the launching of Fairchild, Sputnik rose from the Baikonur Cosmodrome site in Kazakhstan, shocking the world and igniting a fierce and overdue investment by the US government in science, the space race, and related military technologies.

The modern era of chips began in Silicon Valley (the very name derived from the material that serves as the base of computer chips) in 1961, when Fairchild Semiconductor launched Micrologic, a chip with just four transistors. America's space and missile races that decade were largely driven by the fast-improving technology. Prices cratered as the chips improved, too, which meant that computing power advanced quickly; one chip that sold for $120 in December 1961 cost just $15 by October 1962, ten months later.[5] The first major use cases were the space race and nuclear weapons delivery systems: the Apollo program and the Minuteman II ICBM project initially accounted for the majority of the entire country's chip manufacturing. Soon, however, the chips began to spread into other technologies. In the years ahead,

Fairchild's cofounder Gordon Moore realized that the number of transistors engineers could fit onto a chip was doubling roughly every year, and, as he recalled later, "I just did a wild extrapolation saying it's going to continue to double every year for the next 10 years."[6] The observation had profound implications, not just because of the computing power it projected but also because of the cost savings—as the complexity doubled, the costs halved too. As it turned out—with a minor adjustment in the 1970s, when the pace of the chips doubled in capacity every eighteen to twenty-four months instead of annually—what has come to be known as Moore's Law held effectively until 2010s, when the fundamentals of physics started to challenge the shrinking processes. Computers went from the size of a room to a wristwatch (and smaller).

Chips are arguably the fastest-evolving and fastest-moving hardware technology in the world, advancing at an exponential speed that has transformed nearly every aspect of modern life. The relentless advance of Moore's Law made those leaps possible, relying on engineering and science that increasingly appeared almost indistinguishable from magic as transistors and chips became more and more powerful. Today, as Scott Gatzemeier, a corporate vice president heading the US expansion of Micron Technology, explains, "crafting a two-nanometer chip is the equivalent of shooting a laser from the moon and hitting your fingertip on earth." Accomplishing that production magic requires processes that are unfathomably complex: the extreme-ultraviolet lithography machines that help "print" the chips, machines made solely by the Dutch powerhouse ASML, contain over one hundred thousand parts, ship in forty freight containers or four jumbo jets, and cost $100 million each.[7] As a report by Georgetown University's Center for Security and Emerging Technology calculated, "The production of a single computer chip often requires more than 1,000 steps passing through international borders 70 or more times before reaching an end customer."[8]

Over the last forty years, a series of distinct decisions by both industry and governments moved the center of gravity of chip manufacturing from the United States to Asia and, more specifically, to

Taiwan. Much of that trajectory was shaped by the ambition and energies of Morris Chang, a native of mainland China who had come to the United States for his education—he was the only Chinese student in Harvard's freshman class at the time—and who arrived at Texas Instruments just as the chip revolution took off in 1958.

Beyond their shrinking size and evolving complexity, the two main factors that drive the chips industry are scale and yield, that is, how large a number of chips can you manufacture at what level of reliability. Delivering chips at scale with high yield is the only thing that makes the fabulously expensive "fabs" profitable and requires having an incredibly rigorous process that can deliver yields above 90 percent. Over the decades, very few companies proved capable of marrying both the technical design and the process perfection required to make chips at scale profitably.

Taiwan began recruiting Texas Instruments in the 1960s, and in August 1969 the first semiconductor plant on the island began producing chips, a relationship that evolved in part at Chang's urging. For Taiwan, the idea of integrating its economy with that of the United States was a way to help boost security ties too, and other countries in the region followed suit. "Semiconductors recast the economies and politics of America's friends in the region. Cities that had been breeding grounds for political radicalism were transformed by diligent assembly line workers, happy to trade unemployment or subsistence farming for better paying jobs in factories," Miller writes. "From South Korea to Taiwan, Singapore to the Philippines a map of semiconductor assembly facilities looked much like a map of American military bases across Asia."[9]

With the rise of Asian manufacturing—and, in the 1980s, particularly the rise of Japanese chip manufacturers—the United States began to lose its long-standing semiconductor lead, a lead it partially gave up by choice. Much of the benefit of that choice accrued to the company Morris Chang founded in 1987, the TSMC. Chang had been recruited to Taiwan by its government two years earlier to lead its chip efforts; in his capacity as head of the island's Industrial Technology Research Institute, he recognized an opportunity to build a plant that could manufacture chips designed by others.

The Taiwanese government provided nearly half the necessary startup capital for TSMC, and it took off in short order. TSMC has succeeded in turning itself into the world's most valuable semiconductor manufacturer (and perhaps the world's single-most indispensable company) because the United States and other Western countries let it thrive; a generation ago, the US chip industry largely decided it wanted to get out of the business of making legacy commodity chips to concentrate on higher-end applications and chip design. Into this void stepped Chang, who raised his hand and said, in essence, "I'll do it." TSMC soon found itself flooded with customers keen to purchase those "giant" legacy chips—a business that has proved amazingly profitable. Whereas building an "advanced" chip fab might cost $10 billion to $20 billion—and then require retooling every three to five years to achieve the next technological milestone—a "legacy" fab might cost only a billion dollars and require fewer updates. Sure, the margins on legacy chips are lower, but over the course of a generation and given the scale—the majority of all chips are not advanced—the profit adds up.

With the cash and crucial process engineering experience from its legacy operation, TSMC took on the role as the maker of everyone else's chips and established itself as the industry's most important partner, one that could set standards up and down the supply chain. With time, it was able to eventually move into the market for more advanced chips too. "The geography of chip fabrication shifted drastically over the 1990s and 2000s," Miller writes.[10] "US fabs made 37 percent of the world's chips in 1990, but this number fell to 19 percent by 2000 and 13 percent by 2010." That shift was accelerated by the rise and chips hunger of Apple. The US computer giant was looking for a new supplier and moving away from relying on Intel chips for iPhones and Macs, seeking instead to replace them with their own designed chips. In the process, it worked with TSMC to build the world's most powerful computer chips. As one industry executive put it to me, "Apple is the pipe cleaner for TSMC—their employees are embedded in TSMC's Taiwan fabs and are instrumental in helping the Taiwanese chips manufacturer master cutting-edge node technology, which

Apple gets first access to for its needs. After TSMC fully satisfies Apple's demand for the most advanced chips, it can begin to fulfill orders from all of their other customers." Without Apple, its expertise, and its huge chips orders—in 2022 Apple was responsible for nearly a quarter of TSMC's overall revenue—TSMC simply would not be TSMC.

As TSMC became a global powerhouse with a big assist from Apple, the number of companies that could manufacture leading-edge chips continued to dwindle. By the late 2010s, as the industry pushed the boundary past the 10-nanometer process into an even more advanced 7-nanometer process, there were really just three left standing on the technical cutting edge of producing logic chips: Taiwan's TSMC, South Korea's Samsung, and America's Intel. Yet even as the industry moved from the United States to Asia and the knowledge of the process narrowed, the global supply system seemingly became evermore integrated and banal. It wasn't too long ago—just a few years, really—that the world effectively took the progress and availability of chips for granted. Then US-China relations worsened and then, even worse, COVID-19 hit.

Many Americans thought of computer chips for the first time in the midst of the COVID-19 pandemic when they saw car dealership lots empty out—and then remain empty for months. Cars today are basically drivable computers; the average gasoline-powered car might have three thousand chips, with an electric vehicle requiring five to ten times that. If the car manufacturer is short just one of those chips, production stops. And so for months during the pandemic, chip shortage waylaid the automobile industry. In 2022 I attended the Munich Security Conference and was surprised to discover US congresswoman Elissa Slotkin leading an in-depth discussion on the security of the semiconductor supply chain. She told me afterward that during campaign events in her working-class Michigan district, she was often met by blue-collar workers from local car plants chanting, "Chips, chips, chips." I realized then that this highly complicated and technical issue had truly become mainstream.

COVID-19 induced supply chain disruptions that exposed the industry's tiny margin of error and brought to the public consciousness something that had long worried China. The most important ingredient of modern technology-run life belonged, exclusively, to the West.

CHIPS IN INDUSTRY PARLANCE COME IN THREE CATEGORIES: "LEGACY," "mature," and "advanced," the industry's phrase for the ever-evolving cutting edge. While there's no exact standard definition, the industry generally considers any chips smaller than 20 nanometers to be "advanced" and anything larger than 40 nanometers to be "legacy." Everything from around 20 to 40 nanometers is considered "mature." But the terms "mature" and "legacy" underplay how vital even those technologies are to our modern world—making it sound like they are yesterday's news, a 2,400-baud modem in a fiberoptic world, whereas they remain central to just about every device in our lives. A better term for them would be "foundational" chips because they will remain as important to our daily digital life as aluminum is a century into the construction of airplanes. Sure, many wouldn't consider aluminum to be exactly cutting-edge technology anymore (even though new aluminum alloys continue to be invented and driven further by innovation in material sciences), but try building an airplane without it—most aircraft today are still about 80 percent aluminum. Even the Boeing Dreamliner, the first commercial aircraft to be made out of carbon fiber, relies on aluminum for 20 percent of its parts. And so it is with "legacy" and "mature"—or rather, "foundational"—chips.

Basically every electronic device contains foundational chips—often dozens or even hundreds of them—and many devices contain a mix of advanced and foundational chips. For instance, every electronic device at a basic level requires power, either from a battery or an AC/DC plug, and those basic power regulators and converters are all comparatively giant, 200 to 300 nanometers long. Those chips and sizes have remained constant for a generation and aren't going anywhere anytime soon. Take, for example, the iPhone. It generally has three advanced high-end chips—Apple's own designed processor, aka the phone's brain, which is manufactured by TSMC; a memory chip, typically sourced from Micron or SK Hynix; and a 5G modem chip currently designed by

Qualcomm and manufactured by TSMC or Samsung. Yet it has dozens of foundational chips that actually make the phone work—chips that control the power management, screen, camera, Wi-Fi, accelerometer, Bluetooth, GPS, and many other functions. Without foundational chips, there is no cutting-edge iPhone, but the reverse isn't true. In fact, given how quickly chips are advancing, you can make a decent iPhone—circa 2018—without using any "advanced" chips.

Advanced semiconductor chips are critical to four main categories of products: advanced weapons systems like guidance systems for precision munitions; high-end electronics, like iPhones, laptops, and computers; gaming systems, like Xboxes and PlayStations; and cloud computing, that is the massive data centers run by giants like Amazon Web Services and Google Cloud, where the entire internet lives and breathes and where today the world's most sophisticated AI models are being trained on computer systems thousands of times more powerful than a regular desktop. In short, it's not hyperbole to say that in the twenty-first century nothing happens without computer chips—a commodity that has both an important technological component and a geopolitical one.

Understanding the geopolitics of the next half century requires understanding this simple fact: China, as large and economically powerful as it is, doesn't yet possess the ability or knowledge to build the sophisticated machinery one needs to manufacture chips, whether advanced or foundational.

Within this context, China is both pumping money into its foundational chip industry, hoping to gain market share while engaging in price dumping designed to boost it artificially. A Silverado Policy Accelerator report in the fall of 2023 found that "China's planned expansion of foundational chip production will position it as the largest supplier of 20 to 180nm semiconductors (excluding memory)" and that "Chinese (manufacturers) are offering prices that are 20 to more than 30 percent lower than non-Chinese competitors for some products." But its ambitions do not stop there—it now seeks to follow TSMC's lead and build a domestic capability to manufacture advanced chips. Such a technological breakthrough would also be a major geopolitical milestone, eliminating the reliance of the Chinese economy on imported semiconductors from the West.

The challenge for China, though, is that there are just three countries in the world that house the companies that produce the sophisticated equipment necessary for a modern fab—United States, Netherlands, and Japan. That means that a coalition of just these three countries can come together and prevent China from buying the equipment required to build its own domestic chip fabs.*

Advanced semiconductor manufacturing tools are the most sophisticated equipment that man has ever built—the process of etching out a 300-millimeter silicon wafer is enormously complex. Doing so at scale and with a high success rate, what's known in the industry as "yield," is even more challenging.† As already mentioned, there are only a few companies in the world that understand how to accomplish this and make the required tools. So far, China hasn't been able to reproduce much of that most sophisticated equipment domestically despite pouring hundreds of billions of dollars into the industry and enabling vast efforts at economic espionage and intellectual property theft.

The systems of these fabs are among the most delicate manufacturing processes in the world, as the chemicals, equipment, and clean-room facilities in which they're made comprise an intricate robotic ballet that would make the world's most accomplished plate spinner wince. A single momentary power dip can shut a facility for a week, and a multihour outage could sideline a plant for months and ruin the silicon wafers on which chips are being built. In July 2022 a chip fab in Japan was hit by lightning and the momentary voltage drop, which shut down 90 percent of the factory, caused it to lose two weeks of production—an impact that rippled through the global

* Doing so, by the way, comes at little economic cost to those countries over time: the global economy requires purchasing the same number of semiconductors, regardless of where they're manufactured, meaning that preserving the chips tooling industrial secrets in the West only shifts where the chips are made, not the size of the overall market.

† Even the most advanced machines, like those made by ASML in the Netherlands, which require vaporizing tiny bits of tin on a wafer in milliseconds, hit up against the known limits of physics and chemistry and might "yield" success rates around 90 percent, the minimum level to be considered profitable in the industry.

company and resulted in a global shortage that quarter of 10 percent of expected production. Given that it takes about twelve to twenty weeks to manufacture a single semiconductor wafer and that a power outage could force a fab to scrap all the current wafers under production, any natural or man-caused power disruption could have massive impacts on the global supply chain.

The fabs, though, are more than just machines—they're also about the people who work the machines. The equipment in a fab is so specialized that the companies responsible for the equipment will often have their own technicians on-site to maintain and optimize it, constantly updating their software and replacing parts. Without that constant care and feeding, even these very expensive high end white boxy pieces of machinery become a useless bulky waste of space.

And that's why any US strategy to avoid losing global influence and power to China requires both ensuring that China doesn't achieve a tipping point of domestic independence in the means of production of semiconductors and that it doesn't seize Taiwan and its valuable fabs and make the rest of the world dependent on China for chips. That's critical because, as important as chips are to today's world, they're going to be even more important tomorrow.

THE NEXT GENERATION OF TECHNOLOGIES—FROM ARTIFICIAL INTELligence to autonomous vehicles—will require even more powerful chips and an ever-growing reliance on a steady chip supply. That's why the seventh-ever company to crack the trillion-dollar market cap, after a hefty stock market run up in 2023, was NVIDIA, a firm far less known to the American public than its five other fellow American thirteen-digit peers: Apple, Microsoft, Alphabet, Tesla, and Amazon (the sixth company on the list is Saudi Arabia's oil giant Aramco).

NVIDIA's origin story is as well known in Silicon Valley as the garages where Google and HP once began. Named after the Latin word for envy, *invidia*, the company began in a Denny's, three decades ago, when its founders saw an opportunity to design chips for specialized, high-end applications like gaming. But it had long struggled with imagining chips that were actually more advanced than the world was ready for. The company's cofounder and CEO Jensen Huang, another Taiwanese-born immigrant to the United States, had called then-nascent PC gaming a "$0 billion market." (As late as the 2008 financial crisis, the company's market cap was just $5 billion.) Then, in the 2010s, NVIDIA hit on the next "$0 billion market": AI. The company had realized that its advanced graphics chips, known as GPUs, which it originally invented to accelerate PC gaming, were also perfect for the backbone of the systems required to train large-scale artificial intelligence algorithms. As those systems, like ChatGPT, took off in the 2020s, the much-in-demand-chips were designed almost exclusively by NVIDIA (and manufactured by TSMC). It was, the *Wall Street Journal* wrote, "as if miners during the gold rush depended on a single company for their supply of picks and shovels."[11]

Generative AI programs like ChatGPT are built on what are known as large-language models (LLMs), which require tremendous computing power to train and run; building a single LLM can require as much electrical output as it takes to power a small city for several months. And, again, China was going to get shut out of these cutting-edge tools. Realizing the power of AI, the US government decided to implement what national security adviser Jake Sullivan has called a "small yard, high fence" strategy against China—identify the key technologies that are necessary for establishing technological leadership over the coming decades and systematically prevent China from acquiring them.

On October 7, 2022, the world saw the first steps of the implementation of that strategy as the White House and Commerce Department announced the first set of export control measures designed to stop China from importing advanced chips, such as A100 and H100 from NVIDIA, important for AI training, as well as the semiconductor manufacturing equipment needed to make them. I was on a briefing call the White House put together the day before the announcement—along with other semiconductor experts the administration wanted to brief on their upcoming moves—and was pleasantly shocked by the sweeping nature of the export control measures. It was clear that the White House got it—chips were essential to global military balance and economic prosperity and preventing China from achieving superiority and independence in that field was paramount. A year later, on October 17, 2023, the administration published an update to those export control rules that closed many loopholes the industry had uncovered to continue selling advanced chips to China. What's more, they made it clear that the process of clamping down on workarounds will be ongoing—the United States is dead set on preventing China from acquiring this critical technology from the West. One element of export controls was particularly unprecedented: not only did they identify a set of technologies that could no longer be exported to China but they also announced that anyone with an American passport or permanent-residency green card would not be allowed to work in the Chinese semiconductor industry on advanced semiconductor manufacturing. It was a savvy appreciation by the US government of just how critical the American-trained workforce was to the Chinese semiconductor industry—an industry that, until then, American workers were helping build, just as a previous generation of Americans and immigrants to America had helped build the Taiwanese and South Korean chips industries.

The action to block China from purchasing the world's most advanced chips was a worst-case scenario come true for China. And it wasn't even the first time its extreme vulnerability has been the centerpiece of a US action against it.

China's current small share of the world's chip manufacturing capacity isn't for a lack of trying. Increasingly, China—particularly under Xi Jinping—sees its reliance on the West for chips as a critical national security issue. Without chips, China cannot be the leader in 5G, AI, aerospace, or biotech. "During most years of the 2000s and 2010s, China spent more money importing semiconductors than oil," Chris Miller writes. "All of China's most important technology rests on a fragile foundation of imported silicon."[12] China produces 36 percent of the world's electronics—such as smartphones, computers, telecom infrastructure—and is the world's largest manufacturer of electric vehicles, but it couldn't produce any of those technologies without access to chips.[13] In 2022 alone, China imported over $417 billion worth of chips, its largest goods import by a long shot—the second largest was crude oil at $360 billion.

China's ambitions to become more prominent in the semiconductor value chain crystallized in the late '90s and the country has poured billions since into attempts to build a chip industry, but it has found it difficult to execute the three-part recipe that helped found and grow semiconductor manufacturing in Japan, Taiwan, and South Korea: (1) use government funds and officially sanctioned private-sector investment to (2) make deals with Western manufacturers to jump-start domestic production and (3) lure back native engineers familiar with the US manufacturing process.

In 2000 China, with a substantial investment from Goldman Sachs, launched SMIC, which later became one of China's national champion companies, aiming squarely for the logic chips business then dominated by American companies Intel and AMD. It accelerated these efforts to reduce dependency on the West when President Xi became leader in 2012. In 2015 China issued its famous Made in China 2025 plan, in which it articulated its desire to become a leading producer of semiconductors, along with electric vehicles, 5G, AI, biotech, and aerospace technologies. China had correctly identified the right mix of technologies essential for dominating the key scientific fields of the twenty-first century: computing, medicine, green tech, and space. Semiconductors, of course, were the underpinning of all the essential ingredients in all of the other technologies comprising the Made in China 2025 goals. The Chinese leadership's hope was to reduce the country's share of chip imports from roughly 85 percent to just 30 percent.

The same year that the Made in China 2025 plan came out, Tsinghua Unigroup—an investment firm controlled by Tsinghua University that aims to turn scientific research into profit-making businesses—attempted to buy memory chipmaker Micron for $23 billion, but the US chip powerhouse said it saw the effort as "not realistic," given likely

US government objections. Having failed at buying Micron, Tsinghua proceeded to launch an indigenous competitor, Yangtze Memory Technologies (YMTC). The surprise takeover attempt was a wakeup call for the US government—the *New York Times* dubbed the effort "a new chapter in the emerging technological cold war between the two countries"—and caused a fundamental rethinking, by both policymakers and the US semiconductor industry itself, about how to view the world of chips. (Credit Suisse noted afterward that "U.S. regulators . . . are increasingly viewing semiconductors as a strategic industry."[14]) Notably, Commerce Secretary Penny Pritzker said in a major speech just days before the 2016 election, "It is imperative that semiconductor technology remains a central feature of American ingenuity and a driver of our economic growth. We cannot afford to cede our leadership."[15]

The result of China's push has been a partial failure; it has spent tens of billions of dollars in the last decade propping up its industry, trying to create manufacturers, design firms, and equipment makers. According to Chinese state media, in the first ten months of 2020, the country saw fifty-eight thousand new chip-related companies start—roughly two hundred a day—a stunning level of throw-the-spaghetti-against-the-wall government policy. Somewhere in that pile, China hoped, would emerge one or two companies that could one day grow to be the next Samsung or TSMC. "Something is bound to accumulate, whether it's equipment, talent or factories, right?" said one of those chip entrepreneurs, Liu Fengfeng. "If not you or the other guy, then it will be someone else who ends up using it. I think this might be the government's logic."[16]

So far—luckily for the West—China has little to show for its efforts in mastering manufacturing of advanced chips, in part because of fraud and corruption—problems that hinder the actual success of those efforts and also waste a lot of money—and, in part, due to the export control measures hobbling their industry.[17] (Underscoring just how little had been accomplished, one of Tsinghua Unigroup's creditors began bankruptcy proceedings against the firm in 2021.)

From 2014 to 2020, China's domestic chip manufacturing crept up only from 15.1 percent to 15.9 percent of its total—meaning it was still about 84 percent reliant on imported chips.[18] According to CSET, the country has control over just 2 percent of the core intellectual property for chips (as opposed to America's 54 percent) and just 1 percent of the necessary fab tools. One of its most successful sectors is in chip design, but there it still only has 7 percent market share, contrasted to the US 46 percent. But it's not all terrible news for China. Having spent tens of billions of dollars across every segment of the semiconductor industry, it has seen "an unprecedented 30 percent annual growth in sales since 2020," according to CSET. "Still, U.S. firms like Nvidia . . . , and Intel dominate the international AI chip design market, while South Korea's Samsung and the Taiwan Semiconductor Manufacturing Company (TSMC) remain the titans of global semiconductor fabrication. High barriers to entry, including a reliance on intrinsic knowledge and highly specialized equipment, have so far prevented Chinese companies from catching up."

However, one area where China has caught up is in foundational chips. According to a report from Rhodium Group, "data on announced fab investments as of March 2023 show that around 60 percent of worldwide manufacturing capacity for 20-45nm process nodes is located in China and Taiwan, with 27 percent in China alone. Once new fabs that are scheduled to come online are included, China and Taiwan together could account for close to 80 percent of 20-45nm foundry capacity globally over the next 3–5 years."[19]

One of the most critical vulnerabilities China faces, though, is its reliance on foreign citizens. Chip manufacturing, especially of advanced chips, isn't something you can just learn in a book; this incredibly complex process at the outer bounds of our knowledge of physics and chemistry requires apprenticeship and hard-won technical expertise. To the extent that China has made any progress, it is due to the help of experts from abroad, primarily Taiwanese citizens—including former employees of TSMC—as well as dual Chinese-American citizens and green card holders who had previously worked in the West and have come back to China to assist their industry. In fact, the founder of SMIC and China's "godfather of semiconductors," as he is known on the mainland, is Zhang Rujing, who fled the mainland as a one-year-old along with his KMT family in 1949, grew up in Taiwan, studied engineering at University of Buffalo and Southern Methodist University in Texas, and gained critical experience working for Texas Instruments in the 1970s.*[20]

At present, however, many of the US workers who have helped get the Chinese chip industry moving are facing a difficult choice—relinquish US passports and green cards or stop working for the Chinese chips industry. Given the lack of security in China against often arbitrary government arrests and crackdowns, it's not difficult to see that most would opt for the safety of American citizenship or residency. Hundreds of top engineers and dozens of C-level executives working in Chinese chips firms are naturalized American citizens.[21] Many have reportedly resigned their positions after the adoption of the October 7, 2022, rule, evidently deciding that no amount of money was worth risking being stuck in Xi's increasingly totalitarian state without the safety of an American passport.[22]

The novel and extensive weaponization of export control rules by the United States began in earnest under the Trump administration and accelerated under Biden. In the chips industry, in particular, the United States has now used the West's lead on chips twice in recent years against both Russia and China.

The United States had first begun to flex its export-control muscle in 2016, when it added Chinese telecom company ZTE to its so-called Entity List, a roster compiled by the Commerce Department of international companies and people who are restricted from trading with Americans. Traditionally, the list had been reserved for

* It is an ironic and unfortunate fact that the United States—the inventor of the industry and the place that had attracted so many talented immigrants over the last fifty years who had contributed to the success of the industry—has failed to keep that talent in the country and let it go overseas, to Taiwan and China, in particular, to help build up their industries. Similar to Zhang Rujing, Kim Choong-Ki, the godfather of the Korean semiconductor industry, who taught two generations of semiconductor engineers at the Korea Advanced Institute of Science, had also studied at Columbia University and later went to work for Fairchild Semiconductor, the US chips industry pioneer.

criminals, shady holding companies, and suspicious banks that fund nefarious activities like terrorism or drug trafficking, but in the 2010s the successive White House administrations saw the potential to wield it against Chinese companies as part of the geopolitical tech war. The designation bans US companies from doing business with targeted entities, except by explicit government permission, a ban that can include tech sales. In 2019 the Commerce Department's Bureau of Industry and Security added Huawei Technologies and hundreds of its affiliates to the Entity List, a watershed moment in global trade. No company as prominent as Huawei had ever been placed on the Entity List before.

Although it was a brand with almost zero presence in the US—partially due to the US government's long-standing security concerns about allowing a Chinese company to embed itself deep in America's telecom infrastructure—Huawei was one of China's gems. Founded in 1987, coincidentally the same year as TSMC, by Ren Zhengfei, it had grown by 2019 into the world's largest manufacturer of telecommunications equipment and the second-largest maker of smartphones. Ren had grown up in Guizhou Province, one of China's poorest regions, where his parents were middle school teachers. He was studying civil engineering in college when Mao Zedong's Cultural Revolution erupted. Far from a dissident, Ren joined the People's Liberation Army and became a member of the CCP in 1978. As he told reporters in 2013, it was a period when all "exceptional people" were expected to sign up with the party. "At that time my personal belief was to work hard, dedicate myself—or even sacrifice myself—for the benefit of 'the people,'" he said. "Joining the Communist Party was in line with that aspiration."[23]

Ren left the military in the early 1980s. After a lackluster start in business, he founded Huawei with $5,600 in capital. He based the company in the southern city of Shenzhen, which at the time was a small coastal town that had just been designated a special economic zone, as part of the economic liberalization reforms instituted by Deng Xiaoping.

Ren hit on his first commercial success with small telephone exchange switches that connected calls inside hotels. From there,

Huawei expanded into selling and manufacturing the brains of telephony. Most of its early customers were in rural China, in areas that were ill served by the giant European telecom companies just beginning to expand into the country.

In 1992 Ren led a delegation of company executives to the United States, where they visited Texas Instruments, IBM, and firms in Silicon Valley. "We recognized that our own methods of R&D are extremely backward," Ren later wrote. "We simply have a long way to go to catch up."[24] Back home, he pushed his engineers to create the next generation of telephone switches. Telephones were then still a luxury in China, but as the Chinese middle class began to prosper, Huawei was well positioned to grow.

Eager to become a global player, Ren hired IBM to tutor the company on management and operations. Beginning in 1998, Huawei started pitching its switching technology overseas. Just as it had first cracked rural markets in China, it initially looked to underserved countries in Southeast Asia, Africa, and Latin America. "We had to spend a lot of time covering how to pronounce our name," recalls David Wang, a longtime employee who served as the executive director of Huawei's board. "We're not 'Hawaii,'" the telecom emissaries would explain as they introduced their company name. "We're 'Huawei. Like 'how are we?' said fast."[25]

Ren fostered a corporate culture of militaristic zeal. "The market has no time for tears," he once told employees. "It respects only the brave. If Huawei intends to survive, it has to carve out a bloody path for itself." Today, walls throughout Huawei's buildings—and the cardboard sleeves on the campus's Illy coffee cups—show a battered Soviet IL-2 World War II fighter, its wings and fuselage shot to pieces, still flying triumphantly. As the poster says, "Heroes are forged, not born."[26]

Gradually, Huawei's success in the developing world opened up doors in more advanced economies. In 2003 the company won a contract in Russia for an optical-cable transmission project stretching across eighteen hundred kilometers in Siberia. The same year, it landed a contract to build a backbone transmission network for France. By 2005 more than half of the company's revenue was coming from outside of China. *Time* elevated Ren to its 100 Most Influential People list. As the smartphone age arrived, Huawei began making not only hulking transmission equipment but also its own branded phones, some six hundred million of which are now in circulation. Today, Huawei's red logo and retail stores full of sleek furniture, pale wood, tablets, laptops, and smartphones seem to be as common on Chinese streets as Starbucks mermaids.

Along the way, the company has been dogged by allegations of not just unfair government subsidies—which permeate almost every aspect of China's economy—but also intellectual property theft and economic espionage. The US government and intelligence community blocked Huawei's attempts to invest in or purchase US companies multiple times, and in 2018, Canadian authorities arrested Meng Wanzhou—Ren's daughter and the company's CFO—at the request of the US Department of Justice on charges related to violating sanctions by doing business with Iran. But all throughout its rise, too, Huawei's technology was underpinned by US chips and partnerships with Western companies like Qualcomm and ARM, whose designs were in most of the chips in its smartphones.

Thus the 2019 Entity List designation was an instant, crippling blow. The US export control measures implemented by the Trump administration in 2019—measures that have since been further tightened and strengthened by the Biden administration—caused a huge ripple impact through Huawei's business, decimating billions of dollars in sales almost overnight. As just one example, 15 percent of TSMC's business used to comprise chips manufactured for Huawei, but because of a critical export control policy tool known as the Foreign Direct Product Rule, which enables the US Commerce Department to extend its export control authorities to restrict or prohibit the export or transfer of any chip made anywhere in the world because they are all made with substantial amount of US technology, software, or equipment, TSMC had to drop Huawei as a customer. Since then, in the wake of the Entity List designation, Huawei has struggled to replenish its chips stockpiles from domestic manufacturers like SMIC, who are themselves now on the Entity List.*

The remarkable power of the United States over the global chips industry was demonstrated again in 2022 and 2023 in response to Russia's invasion of Ukraine, when the US government unveiled a series of sweeping sanctions and export controls against Russia, effectively banning the import into Russia of *any* semiconductor from any country. In doing so, the United States again invoked the Foreign Direct Product Rule authority. Combined with the October 2022 export controls on China, these actions have led leading experts to conclude that "because all semiconductor fabrication facilities use at least some U.S.-made equipment, every such GPU on the planet is now subject to U.S. controls."[27] While this has not stopped all flow of chips to Russia—primarily due to China stepping up its exports to fill the void left by Western firms, acts that in turn have drawn new targeted US and EU sanctions against illegal Chinese exporters—it nevertheless has impacted Russia's ability to procure chips at preinvasion levels. Had it not been for Chinese imports, Russia's ability to sustain its war efforts from communications to advanced weaponry would have likely been crippled even more than it already has been.

The actions against Huawei and Russia demonstrate the power the United States can wield internationally. They also demonstrate that, to maintain leverage over China in the next quarter century, the United

---

* In a sign, though, that there's more the United States and the West need to do to police chip manufacturing, Huawei did announce that it had been able to use SMIC to manufacture 7 nm chips for its latest phones—at the time when Apple was rolling out 3 nm chips in its own iPhone 15. Huawei's breakthrough was enabled in part because of loopholes in the export controls that continued to allow the export of certain chipmaking equipment to SMIC since the primary use of the equipment was manufacturing of foundational chips, which weren't covered by the October 7, 2022, rule. The oversight was particularly unfortunate given that TSMC had publicly shown all the way back in 2019 that it was able to manufacture a 7 nm chip using that same equipment, and there was no reason to think that SMIC couldn't succeed in the same fashion. Luckily, it does not appear that such unrestricted equipment can be used to produce the most leading-edge chips, those at 3 nm and below, but some experts believe that SMIC might still attain a 5 nm process using its available equipment.

States needs to ensure China doesn't achieve its much desired "chip breakout."

Luckily, America here has tremendous power.

What does preventing China from achieving "chip breakout" look like? It requires a four-pronged approach:

1. Prevent China from sustaining existing and building and operating additional domestic fabs via allied export control policies on manufacturing equipment;
2. Diversify chip manufacturing away from Taiwan and invest in US, South Korea, Japan, and European chip manufacturing to reduce US economic vulnerability to a war over Taiwan;
3. Make clear to China that if it attempts to seize Taiwan, it will never get the technology and know-how of TSMC, Taiwan's top semiconductor manufacturer; and
4. Spell out that, much as the United States and the rest of the West banded together quickly and decisively around Russia's invasion of Ukraine, any move by China against Taiwan would launch a Western blockade of semiconductor chips to China that would cripple its economy.

The strategy begins with preventing China from accessing the equipment and tools necessary to build fabs. This is, in some ways, the easiest step the United States can take because the supply chains for the most advanced chip manufacturing equipment are so tiny.

Making any piece of electronics today requires six sets of companies, by which I mean all six. Get five out of six and you're just as far away from a functioning device, be it an iPhone or a missile, as you would be if you only had one. The process starts with those that make the software called Electronic Design Automation (EDA) needed to design the chips (American Cadence and Synapsis); then those that manufacture critical components and chemicals needed to build the chips (Japanese companies, e.g., for photoresists: JSR, Shin-Etsu Chemicals, and Tokyo Ohka Kogyo, known as TOK); those that manufacture equipment needed to make chips (Dutch ASML, American Applied, LAM and KLA, and Japan's Tokyo Electron and Nikon); then those that actually design the chips (Apple, NVIDIA, Qualcomm, etc.); and lastly those that manufacture chips (Intel, TSMC, Samsung, Micron, etc.). And finally, production requires the companies that package chips into final products and assemble them into circuit boards for use in electronics, companies like Foxconn, and others in China, Vietnam, Malaysia, etc., as well as the leading so-called printed circuit board companies, known as PCBs, which include Chinese Zhen Ding Tech and DSBJ, Taiwan's Unimicron and Compeq, and Japan's Nippon Mektron.

Each of these design and manufacturing stages presents a critical choke point—particularly given how uniquely small most of these industries actually are—but not every choke point is equal. Design companies, while dominated by the United States, are increasingly also popping up elsewhere—China, Europe, and Japan are becoming critical players. EDA software companies like Cadence and Synapsis dominate but software is relatively easy to steal and pirate, so their supremacy is unlikely to last. Japan has a virtual monopoly on chemical production, photoresist, and masks necessary for manufacturing, but one could see China developing that capability in the future.

The really significant choke point is in the fourth stage. Indeed, the one area where China is unlikely to make significant progress—especially if the United States and allies ramp up their export control measures and their enforcement—is in equipment manufacturing. Equipment such as the Extreme Ultraviolet (UAV) machines produced by ASML are designed to etch transistors on a piece of silicon wafer that are twenty-five thousand times thinner than a human hair—and getting smaller with each equipment iteration. The complexity of designing, manufacturing, and maintaining these machines is immense. In addition, virtually the entire supply chain for building key components of these machines is located in the West, from an American company called Cymer that was acquired by ASML to help produce high-end lasers for UAV machines to highly sophisticated German

ZEISS mirrors that these lasers bounce off of. For China to replicate that entire supply chain in *addition* to designing and building these machines is a task that is more complex than landing a man on Mars. Perhaps one day with enormous efforts and after at least a decade if not more of trying—attempts abetted by a historically unprecedented campaign to steal Western intellectual property via cyber means as well as old-fashioned recruitment of industrial spies and thieves—they could get there, but they'd catch up only as the United States and its allies move further ahead in the development of even more advanced semiconductor technology. This is the critical choke point for curtailing China's ambitions to become independent of Western chips and then, presumably, to advance beyond the West and build an industry that the West itself becomes reliant on.

The US government has recognized this and as part of that the October 7, 2022, and October 17, 2023, actions instituted the most sweeping export controls on American semiconductor equipment manufacturers to date: preventing the export of equipment essential for China's efforts to develop advanced chips, the line of chips usually considered below 16 to 18 nanometers. It has also successfully leaned on the Netherlands and Japan to do the same with their companies—an effort helped by the fact that Japan, in particular, is highly interested in modernizing its military as a response to an increasingly combative China, a modernization that will require American weapons. But the United States and the West could go much further by limiting export of equipment to China entirely, which would deliver a death blow to their industry, as it does not have the capability to produce its own machinery at scale and of the quality needed to be able to produce chips without reliance on US and allied companies.

One downside of the limitations of the current export control measures is that while they are effective at blocking China's ambitions to build an advanced chips manufacturing industry, they also create a perverse incentive for China to double down on expanding existing manufacturing of foundational chips. Given China's demonstrated propensity both to engage in massive industrial subsidies as well as to dump products at lower cost on advanced economies to capture market share and decimate competitors—a playbook the country has used repeatedly with rare earths, solar panels, steel, textiles, and other sectors—it is not surprising that the Chinese are now apparently trying the same with foundational chips, attempting to capture a large part of the overall chips market. If they succeed, it would be as if we had successfully blocked China from producing advanced carbon fiber materials but allowed them to corner the world's market on aluminum—a still disastrous outcome in terms of providing the PRC with enormous leverage over the United States and the global economy. Department of Commerce Secretary Gina Raimondo cautioned in July 2023 that "the amount of money that China is pouring into subsidizing what will be an excess capacity of mature chips and legacy chips, that's a problem that we need to be thinking about and working with our allies to get ahead of."[28]

In fact, this is an area where Chinese companies actually have an edge because the CCP can subsidize these plants regardless of economics of production or their yield metrics. It's a familiar playbook for China (and their US competitors): the Chinese have done that in the past in other industries, like steel. Steel mills, not unlike chip fabs, need to operate at high levels of capacity utilization to cover high capital costs and retain some profit margin. For US producers, this has long presented an enormous challenge at times of weak market demand, and they traditionally reacted by idling factories when they didn't have enough customers to buy all of their yield. China, by contrast, added more and more capacity in steel because the government subsidies allowed them to operate under artificial market conditions. The state-led economy in China is immune to short-term market forces; the country's political environment is tightly linked to its economic growth, meaning that to preserve its hold on power, the Communist Party would typically rather prop up ailing businesses than risk the turmoil and unrest that might come with large-scale layoffs and closings. That political calculation means that China, in effect, subsidizes dumping cheap product overseas, which in turn means the PRC saves its own labor market by undercutting those in the West. The same playbook is now used by China to win the battle for foundational chips.

To prevent this scenario, export controls must be expanded to cover all semiconductor manufacturing equipment to enjoin China from building, operating, and maintaining fabs at *any* process node size, a move that would further increase China's dependence on the West and provide us with the leverage over its economy to, say, deter hostile action in the East China Sea. These export controls must cover not just the fabs of Chinese companies, like SMIC and YMTC, but also the fabs of Western companies like Samsung, TSMC, and SK Hynix that are located in China, since at any time the Chinese government could nationalize those fabs or confiscate equipment in the event of conflict (and let's not forget the unique expertise that Chinese semiconductor workers gain while working at such companies). Losing access to the Chinese market would not come without significant short-term pain for US, Dutch, or Japanese equipment manufacturers, which would have to scramble to find new buyers, but such a move would pay long-term dividends by saving the overall chip manufacturing industry—an industry that the allies are currently investing over a trillion dollars this decade in boosting. Plus, the short-term pain would be mitigated by the fact that the demand in the global chip market does not depend on the location of fabs; even if those foundational or advanced chips aren't being made in China, they'll be produced somewhere and, thus, the overall demand for chip equipment—minus the spurious demand created by illegal Chinese subsidies—would hardly change. At the same time, to cripple China's ability to create its own domestic competitors to equipment makers like ASML, Applied Materials, and LAM, the export controls must cover critical components that go into these complex machines—from high-end lasers and optics to robotic arms and vacuum measurement components. These actions would serve multiple goals, ensuring that China will not be able to sustain a domestic chips industry using only its own indigenous equipment, while simultaneously paying Western equipment makers for their loss of sales in the Chinese market and assuring them that they would not have to face future price-undercutting competition from Chinese toolmakers assisted by subsidies and illegal economic espionage by the Chinese government.

China, of course, is well aware of what the US Commerce Department could do and is trying to apply pressure on US companies in the hopes that industry leaders will convince the US government to relax export controls. China currently buys more than 20 percent of US semiconductor manufacturing equipment and is a very important market for these companies. In 2023 it banned the use of Micron's memory chips in China's critical industries on bogus claims of "cybersecurity risk." Micron announced it stood to lose $4 billion from China's move, and under what appear to be strong-arm pressure tactics from the Chinese government, Micron soon after announced a $602 million investment in packaging in China.

Such symmetric pressure on US industry is only likely to increase as the Chinese semiconductor industry feels the pain of US export controls and sanctions. The answer to alleviating the pain comes in the form of reducing the reliance of Western firms on the Chinese semiconductor industry by investing in our own and allied production capacity. The 2022 Chips and Science Act has been essential to these ends. One of the few major pieces of legislation in recent years to be passed with strong bipartisan support, the Chips Act (as it's often referred to) provides $39 billion in direct investment funds to companies that would build new chips fabs in the United States, another $13 billion for basic research and workforce training, and another $24 billion over five years in tax credits to offset the costs of purchase of semiconductor manufacturing equipment.

The second component of the strategy is diversifying chip manufacturing away from Taiwan. The extreme concentration of global chip production on an island only roughly the size of the state of Maryland is a critical vulnerability not just for the United States but the whole world.

In addition to the prospect of a Chinese invasion—and the likely destruction this would bring to the TSMC fabs—looming like the sword of Damocles over Taiwan, the island is often affected by a slew of natural disasters, everything from typhoons, earthquakes, landslides, and floods. Any one of these other equally foreseeable disasters could cause devastating power outages and supply disruptions. On average Taiwan experiences twenty-two hundred earthquakes each year, of which over two hundred can be felt.[29] (In October 2023 I was attending a dinner with foreign dignitaries hosted at the top of a Taipei skyscraper hotel by the Taiwanese foreign minister in honor of Taiwan's National Day, when the building suddenly shook from a 5.9 magnitude earthquake.) A network of three dozen faults runs right through the island where the Philippine Sea Plate and Eurasian Plate collide, including the Chihshang fault, which saw a series of earthquakes in 1951 that included four quakes larger than 7.0 magnitude. Powerful earthquakes can damage the fab buildings with their sophisticated clean rooms, destruction that could put some or even most of TSMC production out of commission for months, if not years.

But above all the potential that China may blockade or invade Taiwan and hold the United States and the rest of the world hostage by blocking access to TSMC-produced semiconductors is a mortal economic threat that America cannot tolerate. The answer here—as it is with reducing US economic reliance on the Chinese chip industry market—is greater domestic and allied investment. The primary goal behind the Chips Act was to increase the market share of US chips production from the 12 percent we manufacture today. By providing government incentives for US and allied companies, such as Samsung and TSMC, to build fabs in America, we secure the supply chain in two ways, both at the top and bottom end of the process. We ensure that our supply of chips is slowly diversified away from vulnerable Taiwan, while providing American chipmaking tool companies a larger domestic market that can offset any loss of access in China caused by US export control policies. Unfortunately, despite the massive taxpayer investment, the Chips Act will not make America independent of China- and Taiwan-produced chips, but it will—if successful—substantially increase the share of domestic manufacturing of semiconductors, reducing some of our dependencies, and hopefully reinvigorate the industry in the United States, building up workforce and resulting in even more fabs coming to our shores in the future.

In addition, the Chips Act has helped to start a new "Chips Race," with countries like South Korea, Japan, Singapore, Israel, Germany, and France, among others, rushing to follow suit and provide their own subsidies and incentives to global chip companies to build plants in their countries. While the $76 billion top-line number of the Chips Act is a drop in the bucket considering that just one modern advanced fab could cost as much as $10 billion, the total announced and planned investments in this industry through 2030 by the United States and international partners in both the public and private sectors is estimated to be over $1.2 trillion, according to calculations by my research analysts at Silverado Policy Accelerator. That level of investment will transform this industry, diversify it, and advance it at a pace that was unimaginable just two years ago.

What remains missing, though, is a body that can coordinate this massive global investment and push to make sure that the new manufacturing capacity is distributed across all types of chips needed in global industry—logic, memory, analog, and mixed circuit, as well as advanced and foundational. The worst thing that could happen is for everyone to double down on building the most advanced 2-nanometer logic fabs, facilities that could produce the most advanced CPUs and GPUs in the world, while neglecting foundational chips that comprise the majority of the total semiconductor market. The Chips Act created the International Technology Security and Innovation Fund (ITSI), which provides the State Department with $500 million over five years to ensure a more secure and resilient supply chain. This is an important step, as are the multiple commitments the United States is making through the Quad, USMCA—the Trump administration's trade agreement with Mexico and Canada that replaced NAFTA—and other partnerships, but the US government needs to create something like a Chips Investment Coordination Council with allies and partners, to both encourage more investment and coordinate existing projects and ensure they are aligned with the needs of the global market.

The third part of the strategy is making sure the Chinese government understands that Taiwan is not the answer to China's chip breakout plan. While both the CCP in general and Xi personally have numerous historical, political, and economic reasons for invading

Taiwan—reasons that predate the age of computers entirely, let alone the construction of the TSMC fabs—we need to make sure that the attractiveness of TSMC's plants, know-how, equipment, and people does not become a tipping point that Xi uses to justify an invasion. Taiwan has long talked about its "Silicon Shield," the idea that its dominant semiconductor industry would protect it from a Chinese invasion because the mainland economy itself relies on Taiwanese chips. However, as China increasingly becomes desperate to achieve chip independence, Taiwan's Silicon Shield may turn into something more like a "Silicon Honeypot," a reason too appealing for China not to consider as it weighs the pros and costs of potential invasion.

It is essential for US and allied diplomats to make clear to Xi quietly that under no circumstance will China be allowed to control TSMC fabs should it use force to invade the island. Regardless of whether the United States chooses to fight China over Taiwan, it would have numerous ways to cripple the fabs in the event of Chinese takeover—from working with the Taiwanese to destroy the clean rooms and the equipment to working with Western equipment manufacturers to cripple the equipment in person or remotely to instituting an embargo preventing chemicals, photoresists, and masks from heading to Chinese-occupied fabs. Indeed, former Trump national security adviser Robert O'Brien said in March 2023 during a talk in Doha that the United States would likely destroy the facilities rather than let the Chinese take them, comparing such a move to when Britain destroyed the French naval fleet after France surrendered to Nazi Germany.[30] It's also possible—even likely—that war in Taiwan itself would result in unacceptable and long-lasting damage to the fabs, due to prolonged power outages caused by Chinese bombing campaigns. Regardless of the method, the Chinese leadership must be made to know that invading Taiwan will never be an answer to their chip breakout ambitions.

Finally, to further enhance deterrence of an invasion, China must be made aware of the consequences for their economy should they decide to take Taiwan by force. And this is where the various threads of this strategy combine to deliver even greater force: the United States can communicate that any move against Taiwan will cause the United

States and the other Western powers to levy against China the same comprehensive sanctions deployment and chips embargo that we have instituted against Russia after its invasion of Ukraine. It would be an even more powerful threat and promise if our export control measures were successful at preventing China from building their own chips fabs and China were separately convinced that it cannot take Taiwanese fabs by force.

Russia has managed to escape some of the worst impacts of that US semiconductor export ban by procuring black-market chips, including chips manufactured in the United States, from China, but there is no such alternative for China. And its chips consumption demand is orders of magnitude higher than Russia's: while China is importing nearly half-a-trillion-dollars' worth of chips annually, Russia imported only a paltry $500 million in 2021—a much lower volume that, comparatively, is easier to procure on the black market, evading export controls. You simply can't find $417 billion worth of chips falling off the back of a proverbial truck. Using the powerful Foreign Direct Product Rule, the United States can block all allied countries from supplying chips to China in the case of an invasion, a move that would devastate the Chinese economy. While such a threat is unlikely to be sufficient in deterring Xi from attempting an invasion—if for no other reason than he may choose to doubt we'd make good on this threat given the resulting blowback on Western economies—it can significantly enhance the overall effort of convincing him that the costs of the invasion are too high and the likelihood of its success is too low.

Crucially, any realistic threat of a chips blockade in the event of an invasion is dependent on China's continued dependency on the West for its supply of most chips for both domestic and export needs. Thus, it is important to limit current US export control measures to equipment and components, not the chips themselves—except, of course, for the small category of very advanced chips necessary for the training and running of AI models, which should continue to be barred from export to China. The goal is to prevent China from manufacturing its own chips, not to starve it of chips entirely—at least if it doesn't invade Taiwan. The ultimate objective of the strategy is to achieve a greater dependence on the West for China, while reducing our dependence on China and Taiwan.

Beyond chips, though, there are also important actions the West needs to take to secure the so-called rare earth minerals and other critical materials necessary to next-generation computing power, biotech, aerospace, and green energy technologies.

CRITICAL MINERALS

Commodore Matthew Perry's fleet of four US Navy ships steamed into Edo Bay—now Tokyo Bay—in 1853 amid the dawning global ambitions of the United States with the goal of opening trade with Japan, which had been largely closed to the world for two centuries. The settlement of California had begun to open regular trade with Asia, and yet already the United States was worried by the mid-nineteenth century that it was being boxed out of the region by the British.

At the time, the United States knew so little about Japan that the letter Perry carried from President Millard Fillmore was wrongly addressed to its figurehead emperor, not the military government—known as the Tokugawa Shogunate—that actually ran the country. Fillmore wrote, "I have no other object in sending [Perry] to Japan but to propose to your imperial majesty that the United States and Japan should live in friendship and have commercial intercourse with each other." To Perry and the US Navy, opening and securing relations with Japan was central to countering the British Empire, which was quickly securing East Asian ports in China and elsewhere. En route to Edo Bay, Perry had been scouting outlying islands, and he hoped to secure for the United States some combination of the Bonin Islands or what he knew as the Lu-Chu Islands, a chain that stretched from Japan down to Formosa and included Okinawa.[31]

In the years ahead, much of the political geography of today's Pacific, and particularly American possessions in the Pacific, was shaped by the rush to secure commercial trade routes and critical resources—critical resources, that is, like bird poop. On July 5, 1859, the crew of the sealing bark *Gambia* spotted a tiny island about thirteen hundred miles northwest of Honolulu, a coral atoll that lay roughly equidistant between North America and Asia. The *Gambia*'s captain, N. C. Brooks, named the tiny set of islands, about fifteen hundred acres total and rising just a few feet above the Pacific Ocean, for himself—the Middlebrook Islands—and claimed them for the United States under the Guano Islands Act of 1856, a congressional provision that allowed US citizens to take possession of unclaimed islands to mine bird guano, an ingredient critical to manufacturing fertilizer and gunpowder. What is today known as the Midway Islands—islands that would prove such a critical way station in World War II—would be part of a group of ninety-four islands ultimately recognized as US territory under the Guano Islands Act.*

Subsequently, the embrace of steam led the US Navy to establish in the 1860s its first base—a coal refueling station—in the Kingdom of Hawaii, known then to the West as the Sandwich Islands. As Captain Alfred Mahan, the key US naval strategist, noted, the islands represented a vital strategic crossroads: "To any one [*sic*] viewing a map that shows the full extent of the Pacific Ocean, with its shores on either side, two circumstances will be strikingly and immediately apparent. He will see at a glance that the Sandwich Islands stand by themselves in a state of comparative isolation, amid a vast expanse of sea."[32]

Throughout the nineteenth century, the settling of California, the rise of importance of coal as an energy source, and the spread of global commerce marked a turning point for the US Navy, as it evolved from continental defense to a global force to protect American interests the world over. As one military history explains, "Mahan argued that national prosperity and greatness depended on the development of a strong merchant marine; the acquisition of overseas territories; privileged access to foreign markets; and, most important, a strong navy."[33] Soon, Mahan's strategic thesis found a friend in the White House and

---

* Today, there are still roughly ten islands claimed by the United States under the act, including the uninhabited Baker Island and Howland Island, both roughly halfway between Hawaii and Australia, and Jarvis Island, halfway between Hawaii and the Cook Islands, which along with American Samoa are the only US territories in the Southern Hemisphere.

President Theodore Roosevelt ordered a forty-three-thousand-mile, fourteen-month world tour by an intimidating fleet of sixteen US battleships. The Great White Fleet called on twenty ports across six continents, from Brazil to Australia to the Philippines to China to Egypt, and unmistakably announced the arrival of the United States as a global naval power.

Today, a century later, in a different technological age, a very similar race for commerce and critical resources is playing out between China and much of the rest of the world, including the United States. The manufacture of semiconductors, smartphones, aerospace materials, green technology, and many other applications necessary for modern (and future) life relies on a relatively small set of metals and other critical minerals—including copper, nickel, cobalt, graphite, manganese, lithium, and a set of seventeen so-called rare earth elements. In the United States, the federal government maintains a list of "critical minerals" that are prioritized over others to ensure continuity of supply based on their contribution to national and economic security.

This concept of criticality recognizes that there are finite amounts of these critical minerals in the world, with few viable substitutes, that not all minerals can be extracted due to political and economic feasibility constraints, and that the vast majority of critical minerals are processed into downstream products by just a few countries—predominantly China—which can single-handedly turn off the flow for many of these supply chains. With soaring demand for minerals like copper and lithium and nickel to support a range of end uses, including the global goal of a transition to net zero carbon emissions by 2050, these supply chain choke points are both an acute threat to modern economies and poorly understood by the decision makers who need to act urgently to change course.

Lithium

Not that long ago, lithium—discovered in the 1800s and used in the twentieth century primarily to treat bipolar patients and in the production of thermonuclear bombs—was all but irrelevant to geopolitics. An engineer at Exxon, M. Stanley Whittingham, pioneered rechargeable lithium-ion batteries in the 1970s—he and two others would ultimately receive the 2019 Nobel Prize in Chemistry for their discovery—but the market was so small that Exxon ended up giving it up as a business. It wasn't until roughly two decades later that lithium-ion batteries went mainstream, primarily in video cameras; in 2007, as Tesla adopted them for its electric Roadster, lithium suddenly had a critical use.

Lithium has thus emerged as a poster child critical mineral for modern times. On the one hand there is an imminent shortage of supply on the horizon in terms of available lithium ores and concentrates to meet projected demand. On the other, Chinese government-subsidized investment in the value-added downstream processing of lithium ores and concentrates into cathodes and battery parts and ultimately lithium-ion batteries has boxed out nearly all other processing alternatives.[34]

It's a race between companies like China's Ganfeng Lithium, a chemical processor founded in 2000 in Xinju, and North Carolina's Albemarle, a century-old paper company that in 2015 bet its future on the $6 billion purchase of a New Jersey lithium producer. In the decade since, Albemarle has grown into the world's most valuable lithium producer and the market for the metal skyrocketed from $1.6 billion in 2015 to a high of $38 billion in 2022.[35]

That enormous increase underscores how companies seemingly can't get enough lithium—demand is so strong it has even surprised the companies that saw the future coming. "Looking back we underestimated the growth," Albemarle's former CEO Luke Kissam said in 2023. "The Street didn't believe our forecasts. We far exceeded them in terms of revenue and profitability." The company expects to double in revenue again by 2027 and is rapidly trying to expand its lithium mines in the salt flats of Chile's Atacama desert, which rely on vast evaporation ponds, with new technologies that would allow more direct extraction.[36] Next door in Bolivia, a consortium led by Chinese electric vehicle producer Contemporary Amperex Technology Ltd. (CATL) was selected to develop that country's first large-scale lithium project. The gold—or rather lithium—rush is in full swing.

The rise of lithium—which has seen its price jump ten times or more in recent years—is being driven primarily by demand for clean technologies. Global sales of electric vehicles (EVs) increased by 55 percent in 2022, to 10.5 million vehicles per year, and global energy storage installations rose by 68 percent in 2022 to 16 gigawatts/35 gigawatt hours (GWh). Recent market forecasts indicate that consumption by 2028 will be more than double—and possibly more than triple—the level of consumption in 2022.[37]

And it's likely to need to grow even more, even faster.

Growing evidence suggests that such skyrocketing global demand for the environmental technologies that will support the clean energy transition—for example, wind, solar, geothermal, and energy storage and transmission—will require countries like the United States to dramatically increase their supply of the critical minerals like lithium and cobalt, without which there is no green tech.[38] These minerals are essential for battery production, manufacturing of wind, solar, geothermal, and nuclear energy sources, and many of the same energy critical minerals happen to also be required for chip manufacturing, transportation, farming and manufacturing equipment, and many advanced weapons systems. By some estimates, achieving the Paris Climate Agreement's baseline goal of stabilizing global temperature rise below 2°C requires *quadrupling* mineral development for clean energy technologies by 2040.[39] Achieving the even more ambitious goal of a net-zero world by 2050, meanwhile, likely requires a sixfold increase in critical mineral supply.

In places like South America's "lithium triangle," the corner of Argentina, Chile, and Bolivia that accounts for 56 percent of the world's known supply of the mineral central to building the rechargeable batteries that undergird so many clean energy technologies, most of the ores and concentrates are exported to China for downstream processing. In fact, on a global basis, 96 percent of lithium concentrate exports went to China for processing in 2022, spurring job creation and economic growth in China—and, perhaps most crucially, growing the country's economic leverage over the West.

While lithium may be the standard-bearer for the challenge of critical minerals, renewable batteries comprise a host of key ingredients that the United States and Western allies will have to source, mine, and process in order to achieve our strategic goals over the next generation. The strategies we put into place for lithium will have to entail other ingredients too, like nickel (which comes primarily, in descending order, from Indonesia, Philippines, Russia, New Caledonia, and Australia); cobalt (Congo, Indonesia, Russia, Australia, and Canada); graphite (China, Mozambique, Madagascar, Brazil, and Korea); and manganese (South Africa, Gabon, Australia, China, and Ghana).

Rare Earths

Rare earths aren't actually that rare; they can be mined in lots of places, including the United States itself, as well as many of our allies like Canada, Australia, Israel, and Latin American countries. The term itself is a historical accident, a phrase coined by a miner in Ytterby, Sweden, in 1788 when he discovered a strange-looking, heavy black rock amid the area's quartz and feldspar quarries. It was "rare" simply because its amateur geologist discoverer—Lieutenant Carl Axel Arrhenius—hadn't seen it before, and an "earth" at the time was simply the geological term for any rock that could be dissolved in acid.

In 1794 the rock Arrhenius found was named *yttria*, the first of ultimately four such rare earth elements discovered around and named after the Swedish island town: yttrium, ytterbium, terbium, and erbium. In the decades ahead, scientists, chemists, and engineers found other similar heavy metals and worked to understand just how many of these trace elements actually existed—disentangling one from another, since they often were found together—and ultimately settled on seventeen distinct rare earths.

Rare earths proved important to the Cold War and nuclear weapons, and for much of the twentieth century, the rare-earth industry, such as it existed at all, comprised a single mine in the United States—the Mountain Pass Mine in the Mojave Desert and Clark Mountains along California's Nevada border. The mine, originally discovered by uranium prospectors in 1949, produced about twenty-five hundred tons of rare earths annually and its element europium provided the brilliant red for American cathode-ray televisions in the 1960s. On the military side, the US Air Force used the mine's samarium to enable more powerful radars. At the same time, the Soviet Union found that scandium allowed for a stronger, lighter aluminum that boosted the performance of MiG-29 fighters; later, yttrium proved key to the development of laser range finders for use with guided bombs and missiles.[40]

In the 1980s new onerous environmental regulations by the Nuclear Regulatory Commission (NRC) caused US production of rare earths to seem increasingly untenable. (The industry has long argued that rare earths were actually misclassified by the NRC and should have been subject to far less stringent regulations.) And in the 1990s, the environmental impact and mismanagement of the Mountain Pass Mine began to weigh on its production and owners, as pipeline spills and toxic wastewater contaminated nearby groundwater.

Meanwhile, China's rare-earth industry was on the rise—the country, which has a particularly large reserve of rare-earth elements, realized earlier than the United States did how critical these elements would be to building the future. Rare earths became a cornerstone of Deng Xiaoping's high-tech development initiative known as 863 Program, which sought to "gain a foothold in the world arena; to strive to achieve breakthroughs in key technical fields that concern the national economic lifeline and national security; and to achieve 'leap-frog' development in key high-tech fields in which China enjoys relative advantages or should take strategic positions in order to provide high-tech support to fulfill strategic objectives in the implementation of the third step of China's modernization process."[41]

In 1987 Deng Xiaoping famously said, "The Middle East has oil. China has rare earths," a sentence that has only become more profound in the decades since as America's reliance on Middle Eastern oil has declined but its reliance on rare earths has only increased. Ironically, China's success in the field has come in no small part thanks to US know-how, including most notably through the Chinese purchase of the Indianapolis-based Magnequench, a division of General Motors, which made so-called neomagnets from the rare earth neodymium.

The invention of neomagnets, known as "permanent magnets," had been an enormous scientific breakthrough by GM and Hitachi in the 1980s—stronger and lighter than any magnets yet known—and became a core technology in everything from audio speakers and earphones to automobiles and MRIs to hard disks and wind turbines, as well as, not least of all, the precision-guided weapons that dominated news coverage of the first Gulf War.

In the 1990s General Motors began to sell "noncore" subsidiaries, and in 1995, an investment consortium led by Archibald Cox Jr.—the son of the key figure in Watergate's Saturday Night Massacre—and two Chinese state-owned firms purchased Magnequench for $70 million. Because the 260-person firm's magnets were used by then in some 85 percent of the Pentagon's smart bombs, the US government's CFIUS committee reviewed the sale and allowed it to go through with the stipulation that the company remain in the United States for at least five years. The now-majority Chinese owners—members of Deng Xiaoping's family no less—quickly used Magnequench to purchase other US magnet manufacturers, duplicated the production line in China, and almost to the day and hour of the expiration of that initial covenant, shuttered the US facility in the early 2000s. From then on, the United States was reliant on purchasing its smart-bomb magnets from China, which according to one estimate had more than one hundred neomagnet-producing companies by 2007.[42]

The United States remained so uninterested in rare earths as the twentieth century ended that, in 1998, it sold off the last rare earths in the National Defense Stockpile. In 2002 the Mountain Pass Mine closed, a victim of its own mismanagement and pressure from the EPA and the Bureau of Land Management, which argued the mine threatened the endangered desert tortoise. At the time, it seemed a good bargain to off-shore production. As one column explained, "In the eyes of the U.S. government and major manufacturers, it no longer made sense to acquire rare earths from a U.S. source subject to stringent environmental regulations. Instead, the hard business of extracting useful minerals was exported to other countries, where environmental damage was safely out of sight. China happily obliged, allowing environmental harm to proliferate so long as the costs of rare earth mining were kept down."[43] (In 2005 the China National Offshore Oil Corporation actually bid, unsuccessfully, for the closed mine's parent company, Unocal.)

Today, China—which officially declared rare-earth elements a strategic resource in 2011—accounts for about a third of all known rare-earth reserves, and its lax environmental standards and generous government subsidies have allowed it to dominate the mining and processing market.[44] Its rare-earth mines, primarily located in Inner Mongolia, account for about 65 percent of the global extraction of such elements.[45] And it's even more dominant on the processing side, handling about 85 percent of all the world's rare-earth processing. This lead on the processing side is facilitated, in part, by the fact that few countries are interested in setting up refineries that are typically dangerous and pollutive—especially given the strong Not In My Back Yard (NIMBY) lobbies present in most democracies.

And China hasn't been afraid to use that leverage. Amid a 2010 dispute, when Japan seized the crew of a Chinese fishing trawler that collided with a Japanese coast guard vessel near the disputed Senkaku Islands, China cut off shipments of rare earths to the country—exposing a sudden economic vulnerability that caused Japan to set aside millions for rare-earth exploration and recycling programs that would decrease its reliance on China. Prices rose in some cases tenfold on the global market, and then–secretary of state Hillary Clinton declared it a "wake-up call."[46]

The Japanese incident helped move along the restart of the Mountain Pass Mine, which had been lurching between owners toward a reopening and finally began mining again in 2012. The mine's resurrection couldn't come soon enough, and, in fact, we almost lost the Mountain Pass Mine entirely. James Litinsky, the CEO of MP Materials, told me the story of how in the 2010s he—almost by accident and with no government assistance or encouragement—saved the US rare-earth industry. A young Chicago-based hedge fund owner, Litinsky knew nothing about mining or rare-earth business, but he saw an attractive opportunity to invest in the distressed debt of a company called Molycorp, which at the time owned the Mountain Pass Mine. The company was terribly mismanaged and ultimately had to file for Chapter 11 bankruptcy protection. Litinsky, in despair about his investment, saw no choice but to gamble on buying up the assets of the company—including the mine and its operating licenses—and go into the mining business himself to avoid a large loss. The mine was on the literal verge of shutdown and its last handful of employees about to be laid off—a move that would have meant the loss of the California mining license and, had that license been revoked, there would be little chance of Mountain Pass resuming operations anytime in the foreseeable future due to the slow regulatory process. (It might well be easier to deter China from invading Taiwan than to receive a new mining license from California.) Litinsky saw that cliff ahead and paid the remaining employees to keep the mine barely operational and avoid losing that crucial license. He then went to China to strike future deals to process his extracted minerals, which enabled him to finance the restart of the business and eventually grow it into America's only rare-earth mining concern. The fact that this all happened with no US government involvement—despite the dire implications for US national security, and specifically, the Pentagon's ability to secure critical materials for the manufacture of its weapons systems—is a case study for how unfocused the US national security community has been on this vital issue. It literally took an accidental investment by a tenacious thirtysomething hedge fund operator, determined not to lose his investors' money, to save an indispensable industry in America.

Today, Mountain Pass Mine is now operated by MP Materials Corp. and single-handedly accounts for about 15 percent of the world's rare-earth mining; however, for years it still shipped much of its mined ore to China for processing. In February 2022 the Pentagon awarded the mine's owners a $35 million contract to process ore on-site, and MP Materials is building the country's first rare-earth magnetics factory since Magnequench closed in Fort Worth, Texas.[47] Ironically, one of its first customers will be General Motors—the company that sold off Magnequench three decades ago. Mountain Pass's owners say they hope the mine will soon be able to supply all of the

Pentagon's rare-earth needs. As Halimah Najieb-Locke, the Pentagon's deputy assistant secretary for industrial base resilience, told *Politico* in 2022 as the US-based industry rebounded, "You don't know how much everything is interconnected until you lose access to one piece of the puzzle."[48]

Underscoring this insight, in the second half of 2023 China announced that it will restrict export of gallium, germanium, and graphite, minerals critical to semiconductor manufacturing, green technology, and weapons systems, in a move widely assumed to be a retaliation for the US export controls on its chips industry. China accounts for 83 percent of the world's production of germanium and is the single largest source of US imports of the metal. It also provides 84 percent of the world's refined gallium and 70 percent of synthetic graphite.

Today, many US military systems are built with rare earths from China, including magnets in the F-35 Joint Strike Fighter, which rely on Chinese-processed neodymium, praseodymium, and dysprosium. The defense industrial base's reliance on China isn't limited to rare earths, either. As retired air force brigadier general Robert Spalding notes, the propellant of US Hellfire missiles is imported from China.[49] As it turns out, those are just one part of a larger set of future-focused technologies where the United States faces critical vulnerabilities.

CHINESE INVESTMENT IN MINING AND PROCESSING

Mining of mineral ores is highly concentrated in a small number of countries. For example, Indonesia, the Philippines, and Russia together supply roughly 54 percent of the world's nickel, while the Democratic Republic of Congo supplies approximately 70 percent of world cobalt mine production. Accessing these minerals is challenging, and doing it in an environmentally friendly way is even more so.[50*]

* In the electric-vehicle world, this conundrum is known as the "nickel pickle." Tesla has noted that the intense mining needed to produce the components for EVs means that EVs cause more carbon emissions during their manufacturing phase than conventional

China has already made extensive investments in the mining operations in these regions, giving the country disproportionate power over the rest of the world when it comes to critical mineral supply. For example, almost all of the Congo's cobalt mines are controlled by the Chinese mining company China Molybdenum, giving it 70 percent of the world's cobalt mining market and even more of the processing market.

Globally, between 2018 and 2020, China's net foreign direct investment in mining overseas totaled nearly $16 billion—investments that, if anything, have only grown since. China's largest lithium producer, Ganfeng Lithium, completed a partial acquisition of another major lithium mining project in Argentina in 2021, and the following year, Chinese-owned Zijin Mining announced plans to invest $380 million in a new lithium carbonate plant in Argentina's northern province of Catamarca. As part of the Belt and Road Initiative, other Chinese-owned companies have made similar investments in Colombia's copper and zinc markets—part of an effort to meet what is estimated to be a doubling of copper demand over the next thirty years—as well as in a Peruvian copper mine, where China hopes to boost output by almost 50 percent.[51]

As a Wilson Center working group concluded in 2022, "the United States faces a troubling scenario when it comes to the supply chain for critical minerals." Further, they write, "Rapidly increasing demand, under-developed national resources, intense international competition, and years of neglect in this issue area place the U.S. at a distinct disadvantage vis-à-vis China in securing access to the metals and Rare Earth Elements that are vital for the energy transition and for geopolitical ambitions."[52*]

If anything, such stark language actually underplays how much of a challenge these elements could pose for US technology, innovation,

---

gasoline-powered vehicles, and that it takes about two years of driving for an EV's total emissions to fall below those of a gas-powered vehicle.

* Few people—even among geopolitical strategists—realize just how far-flung and interconnected many critical supply chains are today. In the early days of the Russian invasion of Ukraine, the world woke up to the fact that the war affected Ukrainian facilities that produced three critical noble gasses—krypton, xenon, and neon—used to make certain microchips.

and security in the years ahead. As Silverado Policy Accelerator research found, "Presently, the United States is 100-percent net import reliant on its supply of at least 13 of the 33 critical minerals . . . and it is more than 50 percent net import reliant for at least an additional 13 of these critical minerals." All told, China was the leading supplier for nearly 40 percent of the critical minerals tracked by the US government in 2022.[53]

China's dominance in this area is also a massive vulnerability for the United States, as it impedes our ability to make more aggressive moves on chips and other economic deterrence measures because we lack our own supply of critical minerals that would make us immune to Chinese retaliation. In the days after the Trump administration added Huawei to the Entity List and cut off its chip supply, Xi Jinping made a hastily arranged stop at a rare-earth supplier in southern province of Jiangxi with his top trade negotiator. "It sends the message: 'Keep in mind we have the ability to affect the production of many major products in the United States,'" Anthony Marchese, chairman of Texas Mineral Resources Corp, told the *Wall Street Journal* at the time.[54]

Solutions to increase our independence and self- and friend-reliance are under way, but more is needed—faster. Minerals and metals like lithium are at the center of the race to control the twenty-first century, turning them from a "mere" business concern into geopolitical strategic resources, just as coal or guano were in the nineteenth century and oil and gas were in the twentieth. It's a story with strong parallels to the shifts of the chip industry, where a US dominated field was allowed—with a great deal of private-sector enthusiasm—to shift to Asia, but rather than ending up in a friendly place like Taiwan, the rare-earth and other critical minerals sector ended up in China.

The problem of critical minerals is one the US government is waking up to. Early on in the Biden administration, the president signed Executive Order 14017 on Securing America's Supply Chains, which included calls for an assessment of critical minerals supply chains. That report and many others identified the need for specific materials, including critical minerals, to meet the demand for clean energy technology manufacturing and deployment and acknowledged that demand is outpacing supply for many minerals and that single sources of concentration in the supply chains are an economic and national security vulnerability. Now, we need to take the next steps—we have recognized the problem but not the solution. Despite this urgency, the United States has been slow to advance the permitting reforms and government investments and incentives integral to creating more resiliency in the supply chains for the minerals most at risk of disruption due to supply constraints and geopolitical tensions.

The urgency of the issue is not being met with a proportionately urgent response—particularly in the area of permitting for new mining and refining projects where America's outdated process results in endless delays and court injunctions that can stall a project start by more than ten years. The Department of Energy is investing in R&D for new technologies and doling out loans to expand US EV battery manufacturing capacity, but the United States is still woefully behind on mining and processing, particularly when compared to China.

True, the US government has focused attention on the chance to work with allies and partners to facilitate more on-shoring and "friend-shoring" of mining extraction and downstream processing. It established the Minerals Security Partnership with a range of allies and partners to drive new investment in responsible critical mineral supply chains to support economic prosperity and climate objectives. While this initiative offers some promise, it has been moving at a painfully slow pace.

The Inflation Reduction Act (IRA) that Congress passed in 2022 also supports the growing demand for electric vehicles with provisions that incentivize investment in lithium extraction and battery manufacture at home in the United States, as well as with key trading partner countries. This legislation, in turn, has spurred new pacts with Australia and Japan to enhance coordination and strengthen and diversify critical minerals supply chains and modernize production processes by prioritizing high labor and environmental standards. The United States and the European Union are also in negotiations toward a new Critical Minerals Agreement (CMA), which, like the Japan agreement, would allow EVs that include critical minerals mined or processed in those countries to qualify for special tax credits. The new CMAs are mostly symbolic, however, and designed to meet IRA tax credit criteria; they fall short on zeroing out tariffs among countries for critical minerals or related items or establishing binding financing mechanisms for new exploration and refining. There are important steps being taken, but much more action is necessary.

This challenge can be solved with a multipronged approach that begins with a whole-of-government strategy that looks at what we need to do both at home and with allies and partners abroad. The cross-cutting importance of critical minerals to national and economic security and across so many end-use applications means that it is not just one agency's responsibility to solve this problem. In fact, nearly every US agency is impacted by or working on the resiliency of critical mineral supply chains, from the Department of Energy to the Department of Defense (not to mention the agencies and entities at the state and local levels). Much like America's national security strategy, we need a short-, medium-, and long-term strategy on how to secure the needed supply of critical minerals for US needs—both defense and civilian. And we need every agency to develop an action plan informed by that strategy. It is only with the utmost coordination and organization that the United States will be able to realize its objectives in the timeframe necessary to meet demand and limit exposure to China's increasing impatience with our own moves to cut off the critical chips that they need. Such a strategy must incorporate the following elements.

First, the US government must pass permitting reform that both streamlines the process for obtaining approvals to expand an existing mine or open a new mine (without sacrificing environmental protection) and caps the timeframe for judicial review. Companies need some certainty that their highly capital-intensive investments will actually be put to work.

Second, the United States should move to develop new mining and refining capacity that meets higher labor and environment standards. This is a move necessary to provide an alternative to older, dirtier forms of production, but it's one that is likely to come at a higher cost, at least until these newer, cleaner technologies can mature and be scaled. All incentives are in the end carrots or sticks, and on this issue, the United States has opportunities to deploy both. As a stick, governments can help enable that innovation by ensuring short- to medium-term higher costs are offset by trade measures that remove the cost advantage enjoyed by imports from countries that dole out massive industrial subsidies. For example, the US government and our allies could make use of countervailing duties, that is, tariffs that correct the price advantage for imports that have been subsidized by a foreign government. These taxes could be placed on Chinese-processed minerals and the products that contain them, which are subsidized by the Chinese government and processed in environmentally hazardous ways, often in violation of China's own environmental laws. These efforts to combat China's economic subterfuge, if carried out in concert with other major economic powers, would exert profound pressure, bringing the price of these minerals to a level competitive with other sources of production. And—just perhaps—this strategy would encourage China to clean up its environment act. After all, we are all sharing one planet and pollution produced in China ultimately affects all of us everywhere. Another way to solve this problem would be to institute a ban on the import of any mineral or processed mineral from a country that fails to adopt and enforce laws that have comparable levels of effectiveness on labor and environment compared to laws in the United States.

Third, as a carrot, Western governments should invest in domestic and allied industries to help build refineries that adhere to the highest levels of environmental standards and become a gold standard that is desired by downstream industries because they can show that their inputs have a lower carbon footprint and are not as environmentally degrading as those from countries like China. We have a track record and examples to follow here—like the massive existing chemical and petrochemical industries in the United States that, despite serious past environmental issues, have dramatically cleaned up their act following US government regulations and tough enforcement and today operate at levels that are among the cleanest in the world.

There is no reason why processors of critical minerals can't achieve the same level of success in the United States and other allied nations. In fact, US and Australian companies are already working to extract lithium in a clean and efficient way in California's so-called Lithium Valley, a rural area around the Salton Sea to the northeast of San Diego.[55] Piggybacking on the area's existing geothermal plants, which bring very hot, lithium-rich brine to the surface to drive electricity-generating turbines, these companies now use clean chemical processes to extract that lithium from the brine.

The environmental control industry that forms the foundation of this work is one that has also become extremely beneficial to the US economy. Over three million Americans work to ensure that our industry is adhering to the highest levels of clean production. We can also encourage partners to do the same, including investing in their own industries to help co-locate processors and mining operations. Currently miners who operate in Latin America and Africa often ship their minerals to China for processing, not only increasing cost and climate emissions amid rising global reliance on China for supply but also allowing China to capture most of the value chain from even those foreign resources. US export credit agencies like the United States Agency for International Development, the Export-Import Bank, and the United States Trade and Development Agency, along with their allied partners and global institutions like the World Bank and IMF, can play a critical role in providing investments globally for such endeavors, including by supporting American companies like Albemarle in expanding their operations around the world.

Fourth, as the United States continues to deepen relationships with allies and partners, largely driven by the ongoing conflict with Russia and the broader US-China economic race, critical minerals supply chain resilience should be among the top priorities for engagement. The alphabet soup of US trade initiatives—the Indo-Pacific Economic Framework (IPEF), Americas Partnership for Economic Prosperity (APEP), US-EU Trade and Technology Council (TTC)—along with bilateral initiatives such as the Australia-United States Climate, Critical Minerals and Clean Energy Transformation Pact and multilateral initiatives including the G7 Five Point Plan for Critical Minerals Security and the Minerals Security Partnership have made cooperation on critical minerals core priorities. But these pledges need to be followed by concrete actions that deliver on them.

Fifth, the United States needs to invest in technologies that reduce the need to extract minerals from the ground. This could include innovative new technology to mine tailings in a safe way, uncover new man-made chemical substitutes, and recycle minerals after products reach end of life. Companies like US Strategic Metals—North America's only nickel and cobalt processor—are already investing in recycling but need to supercharge their efforts to get to scale. Looking closely at adding more nuclear energy, which has the smallest reliance on critical minerals, to the US energy mix would also help alleviate the supply crunch.

Building on the various efforts above, a critical minerals club of like-minded countries should emerge that would use its collective market power and combined resources to create the critical mineral supply chains of the future. An agreement could include a detailed evaluation of the current supply and demand landscape and the reasons for its imbalance (e.g., policy gaps or deficits in infrastructure), followed by the creation of an early warning mechanism to react to supply disruptions; catalog current and announced investments in critical minerals development to identify segments that will require more outlays, and then mobilize funding; combine resources to develop and scale cleaner technologies, including nonextractive alternatives like chemicals substitutes and recycled minerals; and use the weight and influence of these initiatives to advance state-of-the-art, sustainable mining practices that begin with local community collaboration and incorporate environmental protection, worker safety, and community health.

RECIPE FOR INNOVATION

The third key ingredient in the recipe for enabling American innovation is people. Nothing happens without them. And America needs both more people and, specifically, more of the world's best people.

We need to shift our political thinking on immigration and approach the issue from a more strategic perspective.

The main reason why China has become one of the world's leading economies isn't because it's particularly productive, wealthy, or innovative. It's just enormous. The PRC has been able to marshal the power of what was for a while the largest population on the planet to first become the world's factory and then move up the industrial and manufacturing commercial value chain.*[56] China's strength is in numbers—and, as we saw in a previous chapter, increasingly its weakness too.

But the United States faces many of the same challenges. As a developed country, America is now falling into the birth-rate trap seen all over the world. Americans are not having enough babies to continue growing our population, and thus, our economy. According to the CDC, birth rates have been below the threshold of population replacement rate—twenty-one hundred births per one thousand women—each year since 2007 and continue to trend downward. The problem began even earlier, in 1972, when the birth rate fell below that critical threshold for the first time. While advanced developed economies the world over are seeing declining birth rates, life in the United States also makes it uniquely challenging to have children. The country suffers from a lack of affordable child care options, no standard parental leave, expensive health care, and a deficit of other basic social safety net programs familiar to nearly every other advanced economy; indeed, there's much more we could do to make it structurally easier for American families to have children.

But by itself, making it easier for Americans to support families isn't enough to alter the country's demographic and economic trajectory. Continuing our economic growth will require reimagining immigration, a policy issue that has traditionally been one of America's greatest sources of strength but that in the last generation has become a partisan battleground. Since the founding of the country, immigration has been a key driver of economic prosperity and military

* There's actually still a great way China *could* grow—if China's workforce achieves half the productivity of the United States, it would be double the size of the US economy, and if it ever equaled US productivity, it would be quadruple the size of the US economy.

strength and a huge contributor to our national spirit of innovation and entrepreneurship—all of which also contributes immensely to our national security. (Conversely, uncontrolled migration can threaten it.)

It's easy to overlook just how profound an impact immigrants have had (and continue to have) on America's economy despite making up just about 14 percent of the US population. To take just a single snapshot of the country's most elite business club—companies that have had a trillion-dollar market cap—immigrants have played central roles in all of them, from Apple's Steve Jobs, the son of a Syrian immigrant, to Tesla's Elon Musk, born in South Africa, to Microsoft CEO Satya Nadella, who was born in Hyderabad, to Google/Alphabet's CEO Sundar Pinchai—another Indian immigrant who took over after the passing of the reins of its founders, including Russian-born Sergey Brin—to Jen-Hsun "Jensen" Huang, a Taiwanese-American who is one of the three cofounders of NVIDIA, to Amazon's founder Jeff Bezos, the stepson of an immigrant from Cuba.

Widen the aperture beyond that most elite club and you still see the outsized impact of immigrant founders and CEOs who have been responsible for creating and leading some of America's most iconic and innovative companies. Take, for instance, eBay founder Pierre Omidyar, Moderna CEO Stéphane Bancel, and Instacart CEO Fidji Simo, all three immigrants from France. Or the co-CEO of Oracle Safra Catz, who was born in Israel, Yahoo cofounder Jerry Yang, also from Taiwan, the cofounders of Stripe, John and Patrick Collison, both Irish immigrants, Uber cofounder Garrett Camp, who moved to the Bay Area from his native Canada . . . the list goes on. In fact, as mentioned earlier, in addition to myself, three out of the nine people I hired to be part of the CrowdStrike launch team—a team essential to building it into one of the largest security companies on the planet—were immigrants, including my chief architect (Romania), chief scientist (Germany), and head of infrastructure (Soviet Union). Two people I brought in who later would successively replace me as chief technology officer were respectively a foreigner (Australia) and a son of immigrants (Soviet Union). It's not an exaggeration to say that without them CrowdStrike would not have become the success that it is today.

Look at the next generation of startups and the same pattern holds true. In 2016, just as the current tech wave was taking off, one study found that immigrants founded forty-four—more than half—of the eighty-seven "unicorn" tech startups then valued at over a billion dollars, companies that had come to employ about thirty thousand people.[57] The outsized entrepreneurial muscle and energy of immigrant founders has been roughly consistent across thirty years of tech IPOs: the National Venture Capital Association found that between 1990 and 2005, there was an immigrant founder involved in 25 percent of all venture-backed companies that became publicly traded and that between 2006 and 2012, immigrants started 33 percent of US venture-backed companies that made it to an IPO. Another study found that 44 percent—almost half—of the 2022 Fortune 500 list of the nation's biggest companies were founded by immigrants or the children of immigrants.[58] As entrepreneurship writer Scott Galloway wrote, "Every year there's a draft for human capital. And every year, the U.S. gets the top picks."[59]

This ability to recruit, retain, and foster talent is one of America's great superpowers—and one China is a long way from replicating.

More broadly than relying on the strength of our numbers, we can approach immigration strategically in two other ways. First, we need to ensure the United States remains the beacon of opportunity and land of invention for the rest of the world, a position that weakens our strategic adversaries over time. We've seen enormous benefits accrued to America as immigrants come here to start companies, in terms of overall wealth, jobs, and keeping our country on the cutting edge of technology, and we should want to remain the place where the world invents—a paradigm that not only ensures that the best Chinese minds would prefer to come here but that smart people from the rest of the world don't choose to go to China to invent the future.

And yet, the system is breaking down. While our higher education system remains the best in the world and continues to attract the best and brightest from all over the world, we don't do enough to support those same students, whose education we've invested in, as they seek to remain in the country and contribute to our success. As we've seen with the chips industry, when these young people go back home, not only do they create leading competitors to our companies overseas—like TSMC and Korean chips companies—but they can also empower our adversaries like China. Our nonsensical policies are literally arming our enemies with the weapons they can use to fight and control us.

Anyone who comes to the United States, earns a university education in a useful scientific field, and clears a security check—for we know that Chinese military and intelligence agencies have an aggressive program to infiltrate American companies and universities to steal our intellectual property—should be immediately offered a path to permanent residency. Similarly, we should also expand merit-based immigration for people who have already been educated in important fields and want to come to America to contribute to our economy and innovation.

Unfortunately, the US process for securing a work visa is lengthy and cumbersome. H1-B visas, which are commonly a proxy for high-skilled immigrant workers, are capped at eighty-five thousand per year, with sixty-five thousand set aside for foreign workers and twenty thousand allocated for foreign students graduating from American universities. Most years, the visa hits capacity in the space of a few days, and demand far outstrips supply.

Intelligently broadening needs-based immigration can alleviate the massive employment shortages faced by the United States in sectors like hospitality, travel, services, health care, and agriculture (which will continue in future years as our population ages) and help unlock new levels of heretofore impossible economic growth. One of the things I've heard from semiconductor chip companies trying to build high-end fabs in the United States after the passage of the Chips Act is that the shortage of high-end welders and other trades professionals is hampering their ability to get these projects going and completed on time. Similar issues are affecting our defense industrial base, which lacks high-tech manufacturing workers to build up much needed capacity to make submarines, surface ships, and missiles. The broad-based multifront war on immigration we've witnessed over the last several decades in our overcharged political climate, combined with the lingering effects and bottlenecks of the COVID-19 pandemic, is having devastating downstream effects on legal immigration. Indeed, the American economy today is missing about two million legal immigrants who would have arrived in the country over the three years from 2020 to 2022 had prepandemic trends continued. The resulting labor shortage has been a big contributor to the postpandemic inflation dogging the economy.

A growing working-age population means a growing economy. From 1965 to 2015 America's working-age population grew on average 1.4 percent per year as economic growth averaged 3 percent; however, the Pew Research Center "estimates that at current immigration rates, the working-age population will grow just 0.3 percent per year in the coming two decades. With half a million fewer immigrants per year, it grows just 0.1 percent, and with 1 million fewer, the working-age population shrinks by 0.1 percent per year."[60] Today, we're barely holding even; in 2020 and 2021, economists calculated that the US working-age population experienced zero growth.[61] As Douglas Holtz-Eakin, a former George W. Bush official and the head of the center-right American Action Forum, says, "At some point we either decide to become older and smaller or we change our immigration policy."[62]

Another smart policy change would be to allow American companies that already employ foreign nationals overseas for critical research and development tasks to offer them green cards if they wish to move to the United States. Importantly, a policy like this would likely have little impact on American jobs since these people would already be employed by US companies. Another interesting idea proposed in recent years to try to break the perpetual logjam on immigration reform in Washington is to delegate immigration visa granting to the states, enabling them to decide which types of workers are needed the most for their local economies, while still having the federal government control security checks and overall admission numbers.[63]

But regardless of how it gets done, we desperately need an immigration policy that attracts the best and brightest from around the world to come and settle in America, to help invent the latest cutting-edge technologies and start new companies that employ American workers. We should never forget that this country was built by people who have immigrated here (unfortunately, some also who did not do so by their own choice). Finally, in the immortal words of Lin-Manuel Miranda's *Hamilton*, "Immigrants—we get the job done!"

THEN, ONCE YOU HAVE THE CHIPS, THE MINERALS, AND THE PEOPLE, the United States needs to focus on enabling innovation in four key areas one might call "emerging strategic technologies." These are technologies that will accelerate the future growth and productivity of our economy and make our lives healthier and more fulfilling: artificial intelligence and autonomy, biotech and synthetic biology, aerospace, and climate-focused so-called green tech. Each of these four areas will be key to the global economy (and security) over the next generation. We need a real national commitment and recognition from the US government of the strategic importance of these technologies, which will transform our daily lives if they're pioneered here in the United States and the West and *really* transform our daily lives if they're pioneered first and controlled by China.

In each of these areas, we need vital government investment—especially in basic R&D, which industry itself rarely has the resources to fund—as well as tax credits and other incentives for these industries to build operations in the United States. We cannot lose sight of the fact that much of the innovation that we rely on for our daily life—semiconductors, the internet, GPS, cell phones, electric cars, and many medical innovations such as treatments, drugs, and vaccines—would not have come about without taxpayer funding.

Industrial policy may have gotten a bad reputation in recent decades in America, but the reality is that the best eras of American economic growth have come alongside smart industrial policies. We have been doing—and are continuing to do—industrial policy since at least World War II. Whether one looks at the budgets of the National Institutes of Health ($45 billion), the National Science Foundation ($10 billion), or the Defense Advanced Research Projects Agency ($4 billion), just to name a few of the agencies involved in funding basic research, we invest huge numbers in research and innovation, and that's not even counting the $76 billion that was recently passed for the Chips and Science Act. We must do a better job of prioritizing these investments—and aligning them better with the private sector funds—in areas that are most important to our economic growth and national security.[64] One way to make such investments more palatable to the taxpayer is to require recipients of scientific grants to provide the US government minority equity positions in any future entrepreneurial endeavors that might arise from such funded research. If the grants and loans are viewed more as investments that could ultimately become highly lucrative for the taxpayer, rather than just a handout to industry, it will be easier to allocate funding for these efforts in the future. (In fact, future grants can be funded, at least in part, by the proceeds from earlier investments.)

ARTIFICIAL INTELLIGENCE AND AUTONOMY

The list of key "emerging strategic technologies" begins with the one that explosively captured the world's attention in late 2022: artificial intelligence. The release of ChatGPT, which quickly became the fastest-adopted application in history up to that point, reaching one hundred million users in just two months after its release, offered a glimpse at AI's truly transformative potential.

AI itself is not all that new—the first neural network-based model, the algorithms from which the ChatGPT-style LLMs are built, was invented by Frank Rosenblatt in 1958. The algorithms have evolved since those early days, but the bigger change is how those models are built. Today, they're trained on the world's largest supercomputers and are being fed internet-scale data sources. According to one source, Microsoft—the key investor behind OpenAI, the company that created ChatGPT—spent $1.2 billion on creating a huge cluster of machines as part of its Azure cloud service, powered by NVIDIA GPU chips, for training the OpenAI models. GPU chips are a type of logic chip originally designed to render graphics in increasingly sophisticated computer games in the 1990s—one of those "$0 billion" markets identified by NVIDIA—that have proved uniquely powerful for the parallel computing necessary for training AI systems. (That breakthrough is what made NVIDIA the world's seventh trillion-dollar company.) And it's that combination of parallel computing GPUs and internet-scale data that turbocharged AI in the 2020s. As exciting as it is to imagine the potential of these models to rapidly accumulate the known universe of human knowledge to answer questions and invent new technologies—such as drug treatments for diseases—the profoundly disturbing dark side of these models is that they could also make it easier for terrorist groups to learn how to build weapons of mass destruction or for states like China to integrate smarter automation into their weapons platforms and give them a qualitative military edge.

In this instantly critical field, the United States once again holds all the power. First, most of the innovation in this sector is coming from US startups like OpenAI and Anthropic. Second, most of the world's GPUs are designed in the United States and then hoovered up by the behemoth US cloud companies like Microsoft, Amazon, Google, and Facebook/Meta. And most importantly for our purposes, the new US export controls on China prevent Chinese companies from buying those same advanced GPUs, blocking them from setting up the massive compute clusters necessary for generating and running really good AI models.

That makes those huge AI models national security treasures. While this is one strategic area that does not need much government financial support—the potential revolutionary opportunities of these technologies has led the private sector to happily invest billions in new AI startups and the computers needed to train models—the main focus for the government should be on protecting these corporate AI models from falling into the hands of our adversaries, be it nation-states like China or Russia or even terrorist groups that may use them to cause us harm.

Beyond simply constraining China's ability to procure the GPU chips necessary to train these models, we must also prevent the PRC from stealing the Western models being developed at huge cost by companies like OpenAI/Microsoft, Google, and Facebook. While the electrical and computing power necessary to create a really good LLM in the first place is enormous, the resulting LLM is just a huge terabyte-size file that contains numeric weights and biases—parameters trained by neural networks—and, thus, can be easily stolen via cyber intrusions or a malicious insider who walks out with a model saved on a USB drive. Luckily, since all of the companies on the planet currently capable of building the most sophisticated of these models are located in the United States, the US government can partner with them to increase their levels of cybersecurity, defend their networks, and do more to vet their employees against potential recruitment by foreign intelligence services. We simply must learn the painful lesson of the semiconductor and critical materials industries: having spent billions of dollars inventing these technologies, we must not squander our advantage yet again and let our adversaries get them on the cheap—by theft.

Closely related to the AI revolution is the transformation we are witnessing in autonomy. Robotic systems, such as drones, have already transformed the modern battlefield—in the air, land, and sea. Factory automation is revolutionizing modern manufacturing. It is not a stretch to imagine all aspects of our modern life being assisted by ubiquitous connected sensors or actuators, powered by AI models, which enable autonomous and swarm activity. All one has to do is watch the astonishing videos from Boston Dynamics of its robots performing dance routines and completing obstacle courses to realize that the future of pervasive autonomous robotics is not far off. The key technology driving all of these advances will be those same powerful AI models—all the more reason that the United States must maintain its AI edge.

Biotech and Synthetic Biology

Next on the scientific front, if the last fifty years of the computing age were characterized by humans programming silicon chips, the next thirty years will likely be characterized by us programming our DNA—a biotech revolution that can bring fundamental changes to the human body in terms of longevity or extending our abilities, even merging man with the machine. Our capacity as humans seems set to change over the next generation in ways it hasn't in millennia. We stand on the verge of exciting—and scary—advancements in synthetic biology, such as being able to rapidly grow human parts and organs on demand or create custom-designed organisms in a lab. The positive and negative potential of this technology, which is likely to become widely accessible in the medium-term future, on the human race cannot be underestimated.

It is now also clear that the future of medicine will be revolutionized by AI. Artificial intelligence is much more capable than humans of processing large amounts of data and finding imperceptible patterns. Once trained on a massive repository of symptoms and diagnoses, it can be the perfect tool for analyzing radiology and MRI results, helping doctors to diagnose patients and developing new compounds for drugs. The holy grail of biotech's use of AI is to develop a process to transform *function* (i.e., "I need an antibiotic drug that can kill this type of bacteria") into *structure* (i.e., "here is a protein structure for that drug") and then to *sequence* (i.e., "here are the amino acids that fold into that protein structure"). Once you have a sequence, it is possible to manufacture the compound based on it.

The other corollary goal is to go through the same process backward, deriving from the sequence of a compound what it actually does. Today we have been able to go from sequence to structure and back, but the critical step of going from structure to function and vice versa remains a huge challenge that can likely only be solved with AI. Unlocking that step will enable the production of custom treatments for diseases that will likely dramatically extend longevity and quality of life. But such breakthroughs would not be without danger too, since they could also be used to produce deadly pathogens.

Beyond medicine and human health, advances in synthetic biology bring enormous promises to other national security areas like energy and material sciences. In the coming decades, we may see new energy sources emerge to replace fossil fuels and augment renewables, as well as bring about a new form of batteries known as bioenergetics. Bioenergetics is a promising field of biochemistry and cell biology that studies how energy is acquired, flows, and is stored by living organisms. Being able to reproduce those processes—such as photosynthesis—with advancements in synthetic biology, literally growing new bacteria-based organisms that can efficiently store and release energy, could revolutionize the global economy just like the discovery of oil refining transformed the twentieth century.

Similarly, the exciting new field of biomanufacturing offers great promise in industrial applications, agriculture, food, and beverage processing, as well as medicine. New biomolecules can be created that one day could replace energy-intensive and CO_2-emitting processes like the manufacturing of cement or improve upon other critical materials like carbon fiber. One day, new synthetic biological materials might replace pesticides and improve the efficiency and safety of our agricultural industries.

The US government needs to continue to support investments in the development of these critical areas, while ensuring we are building proper safeguards to prevent malicious actors from using them to do potentially catastrophic harm to individuals—or even all of civilization. And once again, control of the AI models, and the means to train them, will help solidify the US lead in biotech and synthetic biology.

Space Tech

Over fifty years after America won the space race against the Soviet Union, achieving man's landing on the Moon, we are in the midst of yet another space race—this time against China. But this new race is focused on the satellite networks and communication systems that ring our planet and, notably, the rocket technology to get them into orbit and beyond. China has made remarkable progress in this area, helped by voluntary and involuntary assistance from US companies. In the mid-1990s, Loral Space & Communications provided critical technology to China that helped the PRC to improve the reliability of its nascent space rocket program. In the decades that followed, numerous Western (and even Russian) space technology companies have been hacked by the Chinese military to steal additional vital intellectual property and trade secrets. These efforts, in conjunction with purchased technological and expertise support from Russia, have undoubtedly contributed to major advancements in the Chinese space program, allowing China to become only the third nation in the world after the Soviet Union and the United States to launch a human into space, in 2003. This achievement was followed by the deployment of the global BeiDou satellite navigation system in 2018, the Chinese equivalent of our GPS system, and the launch of a permanently crewed space station in 2021. In recent years, China has routinely led the US in rockets launched into space, but thanks to the reusable Falcon rockets from SpaceX, the United States once again has a narrow lead.

Maintaining the lead in space technology is critical to preserving our strategic military and economic advantage. Space has long been the so-called fifth domain of warfare—after land, sea, air, and cyber—a recognition highlighted by the creation of the US Space Force in 2019 as an independent service under the US Air Force. Space-based systems are used for everything from GPS-based navigation for weapons guidance to vital military communications—enabled by technologies like game-changing Low-Earth Orbit commercial satellite networks such as Starlink or more traditional geostationary military communications satellites—to intelligence, surveillance, and reconnaissance (ISR) platforms dependent on highly sensitive signals intelligence, optical and synthetic aperture radar satellites designed, built, and launched by the National Reconnaissance Office (NRO). Modern warfare is unimaginable without a high reliance on space resources. Thus, countries will have a huge military advantage if they stay at the cutting edge of satellite design manufacturing technology and develop cost-effective, rapid, and mass capacity space launch services utilizing reusable rockets. On the economic front, the space market has already grown to nearly half-a-trillion dollars—up from $280 billion in 2010—and is likely to grow to $1 trillion by 2030 according to McKinsey forecasts.[65] Beating China and preserving our lead in this critical national security industry will serve us well in both the defense and economic spheres.

Once again, luckily, space is an area where the United States has many advantages. By diversifying funding away from traditional defense contractors in recent years into new startups characterized by Silicon Valley technology and a "move fast" mindset (like SpaceX, Blue Origin, and Rocket Lab), NASA and the Pentagon have injected new blood and fostered massive innovation in the space industry. From reusable rockets and spacecraft to the groundbreaking Starlink communications platform, it is once again American companies that are on the cutting edge of space technology. SpaceX in particular has accomplished the remarkable achievement of owning half of all satellites in orbit—and launching many others—in just four years after its first Starlink launch. The company has also captured the majority of the global "space lift" market, responsible for over half of all mass sent into orbit in 2023.

This is yet another area where AI models and their ability to assist with rocket and satellite design, as well as the invention of new, lighter, and more durable materials, can provide a major advantage to America. In short, despite Chinese progress, America still holds a vast lead in space technology, and we need to continue prioritizing investments in this area and encourage NASA and the Defense Department to continue taking risks on new startups with innovative ideas.

Climate/Green Tech

Lastly, one of the most urgent tasks for humanity comes in the form of the technological innovation required to move away from fossil fuels, enable green technologies, and counter (and perhaps even reverse) the effects of the looming climate crisis. Each stage of this effort has important geopolitical implications, from reducing our reliance on unreliable and sometimes unstable allies in the Middle East—or, in Europe's case, outright adversaries, with the continent's reliance on Russian oil and gas—to mitigating the destabilizing human migration and political upheaval that will come amid rising global temperatures. We find ourselves in competition with China, again, for many of the rare earths, lithium, cobalt, nickel, and other critical components of batteries, wind turbines, solar panels, nuclear reactors, carbon capture and other key technologies that industry needs for these innovations.

As suggested earlier, China has been thinking ahead on this challenge in a way we haven't, locking up mineral reserves around the world and subsidizing their own mining and processing industries. Without some quick action, we risk becoming beholden to them—trading our destabilizing dependence on Middle Eastern oil for an even more destabilizing dependance on green energy from an assertive, aggressive, and adversarial China.

But beyond securing China-independent supplies of critical materials and processing capacity, we need to make sure that the United States does not lose the race to China in designing and manufacturing battery technologies, electric vehicles, next-generation safe nuclear power plants, solar panels, wind turbines, green hydrogen, and other forms of green tech power generation, as well as technologies like carbon capture. The 2022 IRA went a long way toward providing incentives and funding to promote domestic manufacturing in these critical areas—albeit at the expense of our allies in Europe and Japan, who were incredulous, sometimes quite hypocritically, that the United States would engage in such a massive industrial subsidy without coordinating with them. As a result, many countries had to provide billions in matching investments to keep their companies from fleeing to the United States, ultimately benefiting not just their own industries but the world. In the end, the IRA radically transformed the global investment landscape in green tech, even if the path could have been better planned and coordinated to reduce tension between the allies.

It's a sad truth that most of China's advances in green technologies have come from stolen intellectual property and economic espionage against American and other Western companies. I have been personally part of investigations into cyber espionage attempts targeting the wind, solar, nuclear, and automotive industries (among others), which is why I understand that any recipe enabling innovation in the West is only part of the puzzle. We also have to stand ready to defend those innovations, industries, and technologies. In addition to the 2019 tariffs that the Trump administration imposed on various Chinese imports in retaliation for China's brazen and indiscriminate IP theft, the United States should go one step further and introduce sanctions on Chinese companies that we can show have requested or benefited from such illegal acts and ban their imports to the United States entirely. We can also ask our allies to do the same, and make US aid assistance to developing countries contingent on following suit. In this area, we need to use the Chinese legal warfare playbook against the PRC. To paraphrase what Chinese officials told one senior US trade negotiator working to counter China's efforts to destroy the US solar technology manufacturing industry, "Go ahead and sue us, by the time the case gets resolved at the WTO, you will have no domestic solar industry to speak of."

Using China's own logic, they can sue us for sanctions against their companies, but by the time those cases get resolved, the pivotal time for value creation from stolen intellectual property will have passed.

CHAPTER 7

Step Two—Defend Innovation

Just months into Russia's invasion of Ukraine, Marine One touched down at 12:51 p.m. on May 3, 2022, in Troy, Alabama, not far from the state's sprawling Lockheed Martin missile plant. President Biden hopped out of the helicopter and, after a fifteen-minute motorcade through deserted forest roads, arrived at the four-thousand-acre, fifty-two-building plant ready to thank the employees for helping defend freedom. Russia's "three-day" invasion had faltered that spring in no small part due to the weapons that rolled off the factory production lines in this seventeen-thousand-person city in Pike County. "I came for a basic reason from the bottom of my heart to say thank you, thank you, thank you—thank you for what you do, thank you for what you continue to do," the president told the plant's six hundred employees, who together manufacture four of the nation's key missiles—the antitank Javelin, the Terminal High Altitude Area Defense (THAAD) missile, the Joint Air-to-Surface Standoff Missile (JASSM), and the Joint Air-to-Ground Missile (JAGM).

The Javelin, in particular, had helped stop Russia's armored advances that spring—the lightweight $178,000 missile, which could be fired by a single person and hit targets up to two and a half miles away, had become a favorite of Ukrainian defenders.[1] The missile easily ripped through Russian T-72 and T-90 tanks, and Lockheed even apparently had a customer-support call center set up in Orlando to field phone calls from the battlefield as Ukrainian fighters struggled with finicky weapons.[2] The missiles quickly became so associated with the war that one Ukrainian-Canadian artist raised over half a million dollars for the Ukraine defense effort through the sale of his painting "Saint Javelin," depicting the Virgin Mary holding one of the iconic launchers.[3]

Standing before the factory crowd that May afternoon, Biden—who had traveled to Alabama with the deputy defense secretary and vice chair of the Joint Chiefs of Staff—raised a triumphant hand together with Linda Griffin, who was the plant's longest-serving employee and who over a quarter century had touched every single one of the fifty thousand Javelins that had come off the assembly line since the missile had been introduced to the military's arsenal in 1996. "Every worker in this facility and every American taxpayer is directly contributing to the case for freedom," Biden said, telling the crowd that Ukrainian parents were even naming their children "Javelin" or "Javelina."[4]

The victory lap celebrating America's defense industrial base, though, proved short-lived. As the Ukraine war continued, officials only grew more nervous about how quickly the Ukrainians were using those Javelins on the battlefield—and about how slowly they were coming out of the Troy factory. At the time of Biden's visit, the Lockheed plant was producing about thirteen thousand missiles a year—pretty close to its maximum annual capacity of twenty-one hundred Javelin missiles, four hundred sixty-eight JASSM and LRASM missiles, eleven thousand JAGMs, and ninety-six THAAD missiles. This meant that the roughly seven thousand Javelins that the United States had rushed to the European battlefield by the time of Biden's visit—about a quarter of the US military's entire stockpile of the weapon—represented more than three years' worth of the factory's production. It was not a comforting calculation.

Indeed, perhaps the hardest lesson for the United States in the first year of the Ukraine war was how hard—and expensive—it is to defend freedom. The Russia-Ukraine war has shown that great power conflicts take considerably more resources, and can last a lot longer, than anyone expected. It has also revealed that our stockpiles and weapon caches aren't anywhere close to the levels where they need to be. Despite having the world's largest defense budget and despite spending two decades in near-continuous combat in Iraq and Afghanistan in the twenty-first century—fighting, it's worth noting, against adversaries who lacked air forces, artillery, or even meaningful numbers of armored vehicles—the United States has turned out to be ill-equipped for a prolonged war against another organized military.

Defense contractors like Lockheed and Raytheon were shocked to see Ukraine race through thirteen years' worth of Stinger production and five years' worth of Javelins in the first eight months of the war.[5] Artillery stockpiles evaporated at a rate that stunned US officials. Over the first year of the war, every three weeks Ukraine expended the amount of ammunition that the United States typically goes through annually—firing roughly seventy-seven hundred artillery shells a day, whereas the United States only produced about fourteen thousand a *month*. "You're not delivering the ordnance we need," Admiral Daryl Caudle excoriated defense contractors during a January 2023 meeting.[6]

In March 2023, as America's main artillery munitions plant in Scranton raced along through a yearlong expansion necessary to boost production to seventy thousand shells a month, Ukraine told the European Union that it anticipated needing two hundred fifty thousand shells a month going forward.[7] Lockheed Martin, meanwhile, doubled its annual HIMARS launcher production from forty-eight to ninety-six, and Raytheon began a plan to produce about sixty Stingers a month, jump-starting a production pipeline that had been almost entirely shutdown.[8] "What the Ukraine conflict showed is that, frankly, our defense industrial base was not at the level that we needed it to be to generate munitions," Undersecretary of Defense for Policy Colin Kahl told Congress in March 2023.

Across the board, the Ukraine war made it clear the United States needs to catch up—and that, despite two decades of near-constant wars in Iraq and Afghanistan, the country wasn't actually prepared for war in the twenty-first century. In any potential conflict with China, America would begin running out of key war matériel, like missiles or ammunition, in just a few weeks. Worse, after shuttering so much manufacturing after the end of the Cold War, we currently lack the defense industrial capacity to easily replace those stockpiles.

Indeed, inventing the future and ensuring that the United States and the rest of the West remain economically competitive over the next generation isn't enough on its own—we must also secure and defend those innovations and our economy. This requires rebuilding and securing our military advantage—in terms of traditional sea, land, and air forces, together with evermore cutting-edge cyber and space capabilities—as well as building a robust trade strategy that can defend a level global economic playing field.

THERE ARE, ACTUALLY, TWO SEPARATE CRITICAL PROBLEMS WITH how America now produces weapons—they're too expensive and we don't (and can't) build enough of them. These challenges are interrelated, of course, but not entirely so.

Ironically, in preparing to fight what the Pentagon calls a "peer adversary" like China—or like we *thought* Russia was—we failed to assemble the mix of weaponry that would actually be necessary to fight China. Simply put, America has become addicted to exquisite expensive weapon platforms, manufactured in small numbers, while neglecting simpler and cheaper ones we would need to use in volume.

Over the last thirty years, we have increasingly prioritized the development of high-tech, highly capable weapon systems—systems so wallet-numbingly expensive that they limit our ability to purchase them in large quantities. A combination of poor Pentagon oversight, waste, and lack of competition in the increasingly consolidated defense industry has meant that procurement costs have ballooned, but we are also not making smart decisions regarding which programs are truly necessary and where a cheaper but more plentiful solution will do the trick.

The F-35 fighter program is expected to cost nearly $2 trillion over its lifetime—a price tag calculated not just in the dollars out the door but also in what we're not able to buy instead. Originally designed to replace the F-16, the F-35 is now so expensive to operate—it costs about $36,000 an hour to fly, by one measure triple the cost of an F-16—that the US Air Force actually thinks it needs to develop another aircraft to serve as the day-in, day-out workhorse of the US fleet.[9*]

The air force's F-22 program has had a similar arc. Originally, the air force intended to buy 750 fighters, but the ballooning cost caused it to first cut that target to 339 and finally to just 187 at a cost of more than $200 million per plane. Keeping them flying through this decade will require $9 billion and require retiring the thirty-two oldest planes, leaving the fleet even smaller.[10]

Or take the $13.3 billion aircraft carrier USS *Gerald R. Ford*, the first of the new *Ford*-class carriers and the most expensive ship ever constructed—a project that took more than double the term of originally planned construction and cost a third more than original estimates.[11] The second ship in the class, the USS *John F. Kennedy*, is scheduled to join the fleet in 2025; the third, the USS *Enterprise*, perhaps in 2028. Each of these last two ships are estimated to cost around $12.8 billion, pending any overruns or delays.

The ten existing *Nimitz*-class nuclear-powered carriers that *Ford* is beginning to replace, as part of the navy's goals to continue to maintain eleven aircraft carriers, cost about half what the *Ford*-class ships do in inflation adjusted dollars. And any one of the *Nimitz* carriers is still more powerful and capable than any carrier possessed by any nation on earth.[†12]

Official estimates are that the next-generation hypersonic missiles, a priority for the Pentagon, will be much more expensive than the $1.3 million per unit subsonic Tomahawk cruise missiles that are the mainstay of the US military's long-range strike capabilities; the navy has

* "You don't drive your Ferrari to work every day, you only drive it on Sundays," said then–air force chief of staff Charles Q. Brown, now the chairman of the Joint Chiefs, in 2021. "This [F-35] is our 'high end.' We want to make sure we don't use it all for the low-end fight."

† The *Nimitz*-class carriers were built from 1968 to 2006, and the last two, built in the 1990s and early 2000s, cost about $4.5 billion each in 2000 dollars.

announced that it will purchase just sixty-four rounds at a mighty cost of over $56 million each.[13] How many targets in a conflict are going to be worth a $56 million missile shot? And then there is the question of what advantages it brings compared to conventional missiles. Yes, hypersonic missiles are highly maneuverable at high speeds and are better suited to operate in contested environments where strong ballistic and cruise missile air defenses can neutralize incoming conventional missiles. But any air defense system can be overwhelmed by sheer numbers of incoming missiles and it would likely take considerably fewer than forty-three Tomahawk missiles (which together cost as much as one hypersonic Conventional Prompt Strike missile) to take out most even well-protected targets. Hypersonics do also offer the advantage of range, given the planned ability to launch them from *Zumwalt*-class destroyers and *Virginia*-class attack submarines prepositioned far away from the conflict zone, limiting the danger to those strike platforms. But given the enormous cost—and the minuscule number of missiles that the United States can afford as a result (compare that to the more than four thousand Tomahawk missiles the United States is believed to have in its arsenal[14])—and the fact that the latest conventional missiles can be launched from the relative safety of over one thousand miles away, one starts to question the wisdom of spending tens of billions of dollars of limited defense resources on the procurement of hypersonic missiles, at least until technology drives their unit cost substantially down from where it is today. In a world of unlimited defense resources, they would surely be found useful. Unfortunately, that is not the world we find ourselves in today and we have to make hard choices about our top priority needs and simply nice-to-haves.

While Pentagon procurement has long seemed broken—programs like the B-1 bomber attracted opprobrium decades ago—it's hard not to conclude that the US military finds itself increasingly unable to develop, procure, and field even critical systems in a timely manner. There is no more clear example of this decline than the air force's generation-long struggle to replace the KC-135 refueling tanker, a low-profile aerial resource central to the military's ability to project power all over the world (and one that would be absolutely critical to any Pacific war). As tanker pilots promise, "You can't kick ass without tanker gas."[15] The Pentagon has spent more than a quarter century trying to develop a replacement for the four hundred KC-135 aerial refueling tankers that began service when Dwight Eisenhower was president, planes that will be some eighty years old by the time they're retired close to the middle of this century.

The KC-135 replacement effort started around 9/11 but ran into so many difficulties—problems so dire that they cost at least one CEO his job and sent two officials to jail—that the first Boeing KC-46 Pegasus tanker only entered limited use in February 2021, at which point it was still so troubled that a key general labeled it a "lemon."[16] Part of the problem in replacing the KC-135 was that the F-22 fighter program topped the air force's wish list, a plane so expensive it pushed everything else to the side, delaying even the start of the tanker replacement effort. Those delays mean, as defense reporter Shane Harris calculated, that sometime in the middle of this decade the last boy or girl will be born who will grow up to pilot a KC-135 tanker that could have been flown by their great-grandfather.[17]

None of this is an argument to not buy expensive platforms or to limit research in advanced weapons technology—sometimes they are absolutely necessary—but for a generation we've allowed very expensive choices to drive out of our budgets and the national industrial base the volume-based weapons that would form the day-in, day-out workhorses of a modern great power war. This is particularly true of the weapons that would form the backbone of attacking an invading amphibious fleet coming across the Taiwan Strait. We need a much more rational way of approaching weapons procurements that balance a few truly exquisite capabilities—the hugely expensive weapons that do give us a meaningful edge in battle—while being realistic about balancing those out with much cheaper systems that we can buy in large quantities and quickly replenish in the case the war evolves into a longer attritional conflict. To be able to confront China, particularly when it comes to munitions, the United States and its allies are going to need thousands of missiles in any meaningful conflict.

We've allowed the lust of defense contractors, eager to build the highest-tech, fanciest (and, ergo, the most expensive and profitable) weapons systems they can, to blind us to the reality of what fighting a war with China would mean. Yes, it would involve lots of exquisite cyber and space capabilities; yes, we'd need stealth fighters and fast attack submarines; but we would also need lots and lots and lots of self-propelled mines, maritime drones, anti-ship missiles, air defense systems, artillery shells, guided rockets, and small arms ammunition, and we've let much of that capability languish since the end of the Cold War. It is telling that despite all the media attention on Javelins and HIMARS systems, the backbone of the fight in Ukraine for both sides has been traditional cannon and tube artillery—Western 155mm howitzers on the Ukrainian side and Soviet-era 152mm artillery and Grad multiple-launch rocket systems on the Russian side. This is a lesson that we actually need to learn from China: when it first increased its military investment and undertook modernization in the 1990s and early 2000s, it overemphasized procuring huge quantities of so-called Anti-Access/Area Denial (or A2/AD) weapons, including mines and anti-ship missiles, meant to make giant US Navy aircraft carrier strike groups think twice about approaching its coasts. We need to learn more from how China positioned itself against the United States: it has been relying on cheap, plentiful weapons.

The one other system, in addition to artillery, that has proven indispensable to both Ukrainian and Russian forces in this war has been unmanned aerial vehicles—drones. Both sides have used them extensively to monitor the battlefield around-the-clock in real time, to identify targets, to guide and correct artillery strikes, and to drop munitions to kill vehicles and personnel. And no drone platform has proven to be as popular with Ukrainian and Russian troops alike as China's Mavics, produced by the company DJI, the largest drone manufacturer in the world. At the cost of a few thousand dollars, both sides can afford to purchase them by the hundreds of thousands, and not hesitate to lose them on a daily mission. Despite the provision of various types of more sophisticated—and much more expensive—Western drones to Ukraine, I've been told by Ukrainian personnel that none of them have caught much interest from the rank and file. Nothing came even close to the dollar-for-dollar capability and versatility of China's DJI systems.

As it turns out, in example after example, system after system, we're paying the price today for what's come to be known in defense circles as "The Last Supper."

It is one of the world's great ironies—and, frankly, scandals—that the United States boasts the planet's largest defense budget and yet also, as the Ukraine war has persisted, finds itself critically short of numerous necessary armaments. After interviewing US military leaders a year into the war, the *Washington Post* expressed concern about the "brittleness" of the domestic defense industrial base. "The slow pace of U.S. production means it would take as long as 15 years at peacetime production levels, and more than eight years at a wartime tempo, to replace the stocks of major weapons systems such as guided missiles, piloted aircraft and armed drones if they were destroyed in battle or donated to allies," the *Post* warned.[18]

One of the major problems is that there just aren't enough defense contractors left.

In 1993 Norman Augustine, then the chief executive of Martin Marietta Corporation, one of the largest military contractors, received an invitation to a dinner with Defense Secretary Les Aspin, who was helping President Bill Clinton figure out how to shrink military spending. After dinner in the secretary's dining room, the group of about twenty-five moved into an adjacent conference room, where Deputy Defense Secretary Bill Perry gave a presentation. "Secretary Perry made a presentation using a graph that was projected on the screen. And it was a stunning graph," Augustine recalled. "The Defense Department was saying there are way too many companies in the defense industrial base—that we can't afford them and that we couldn't have a bunch of companies with half-full factories and not enough money to invest in research and development, huge overhead, high costs. And we need to consolidate the industry."[19]

In category after category, the Pentagon said it would have enough work for fewer companies; instead of three companies making bombers, they would need only one; instead of eight shipyards, they would need just four; ditto for tactical missile manufacturers, which would fall from eight to four. Rocket motors would have to go from five companies to two.[20] Perry, who followed Aspin as defense secretary in 1994, was blunt in his comments: "We expect defense companies to go out of business. We will stand by and watch it happen."[21]

The dinner gathering was quickly dubbed "The Last Supper," and for many defense executives, it was.

The fallout of that dinner was felt across the country; mergers accelerated quickly. Martin Marietta bought the aerospace programs from GE and General Dynamics and then merged with Lockheed, creating the modern-day Lockheed Martin.[22] Northrop quickly bought Grumman. By 1997, the nation's dozen largest defense contractors had shrunk to just four.[23] The five largest aerospace companies—Lockheed Martin, Boeing, Northrop Grumman, Raytheon, and Litton—took the place of what had been fifty-one separate companies in the mid-1980s.[24] (Litton was acquired by Northrop Grumman in 2001.)

In 1985, at the peak of the end of Cold War I, there were three million workers employed across the defense industry, but the "peace dividend" of the end of Cold War I saw the Pentagon procurement budget plunge by two-thirds, and for much of the 1990s, the industry shed an average of one thousand jobs a day. As the *Washington Post* wrote in 1997, "By the end of his second term, it may emerge that President Clinton's most enduring legacy in national security will be his role in creating a handful of extraordinarily powerful defense contractors."[25] By 2021 there were only around 1.1 million workers employed in defense manufacturing, while the Pentagon budget ballooned to the highest levels in history.[26]

To Augustine, that 1993 night in the Pentagon immediately forecast today's problems in the defense industrial base: "It pointed to how fragile our defense industrial base was going to become," he recalled. "But there was another factor that to me was also important: That in those areas there would not be competition. I happen to be a strong believer in competition. The free enterprise system, I think, has served our country well. And apparently we were in such a financial position where we weren't going to be able to afford that."[27]

Now, amid the Ukraine war, we are belatedly recognizing what Augustine realized almost in real time in 1993: the defense industrial base has shrunk and grown so concentrated in the decades since the end of the Cold War that the United States now lacks any meaningful redundancy and is at risk of single points of failure. Whereas six contractors used to build the rocket motors for guided missiles employed throughout the military by the army, navy, marines, and air force—missiles like Raytheon's SM-6 anti-ship missile, a weapon critical to any future fight in the Pacific, as well as Stingers and Javelins, important to both Ukraine and a future Pacific conflict—today just two manufacture the necessary parts. Worse, in late 2022 a fire affected the production line at one of those two manufacturers, Aerojet Rocketdyne. And the Aerojet disruption was hardly the worst-case scenario: only one company, Williams International, builds the turbofan engine used in most US cruise missiles.[28]

Bigger weapon systems would be even harder to replace. For example, CSIS's Mark Cancian has calculated that at current production rates it would take a decade to replace the country's stock of Black Hawk helicopters, a half century to rebuild its aircraft carrier fleet even at "surge production rates," and nearly two decades to rebuild our submarine fleet. And, in a war, we, of course, would not have that much time. "As evidence of the importance of prewar naval modernization, every Navy capital ship—every fleet carrier and battleship—that fought in World War II was authorized before Pearl Harbor," Cancian writes.[29]

America's roiling political dysfunction isn't helping, either. David Norquist, the head of the National Defense Industrial Association, notes that the ongoing inability of Congress to pass reliable annual appropriations bills has undercut the opportunities to build smarter and more consistent weapons pipelines. As he says, "In 13 of the last 14 years, we've had long continuing resolutions that specifically prevent new starts or increased production rates. These trends are not consistent with creating the defense industrial base required for great power competition."[30] Reforming where we are today, spurring additional competition, and helping to make sure we're adequately investing in sufficient production will require a multitude of changes—including a more thorough process for multiyear contracts that will allow defense manufacturers to invest in new assembly lines.

The consolidation across the defense industry, mixed with globalization, has also made supply chains worryingly weak and insecure—we need to make sure that we can manufacture what we need right here in the United States. That will likely require some hard choices, as meaningfully increasing our already eight-hundred-billion-dollar annual defense budget to respond to these needs is not likely to be politically feasible. We simply do not have extra funds to go around, given that our still-rising national debt already exceeds $30 trillion and the annual interest we pay on it is projected to exceed $1 trillion annually before the end of the decade, projections that may accelerate in an era of prolonged high interest rates, as US Treasury bonds mature and get reissued at much higher rates. Nor, frankly, should we need to increase that defense budget, given that the Peter G. Peterson Foundation calculates that the United States in 2022 spent more on defense than China, Russia, India, Saudi Arabia, United Kingdom, Germany, France, South Korea, Japan, and Ukraine combined, a number even more shocking since all but two of those countries are aligned with the US militarily.[31]

Instead, we will have to make tough choices about what weapons platforms and munitions we can afford to build, operate, and maintain going forward—choosing how we balance the need to maintain the critical capability to deter Chinese aggression in the Indo-Pacific, deal with ongoing global counterterrorism threats, support Ukraine and NATO allies in Europe against current and future Russian aggression, maintain peace on the Korean Peninsula against North Korean threats, and contain Iran in the Middle Eastern theater, to name just a few of our military priorities. The challenges are numerous but our spending—despite the huge top-line number—is not providing the needed capability to maintain America's leadership and secure global trade flows.

Countering Russia and China also requires us to think more creatively and thoughtfully about the weapons we do have. The war in Ukraine could continue on for years—the current invasion, after all, is really just a continuation and escalation of a conflict that's been ongoing since 2014. The Ukrainians are certainly thinking of this as a long-term challenge. During my visit to Kyiv in the summer of 2023, the young driver who took us to the train station at the end of the trip had recently returned from the front because he just had a newborn son; he told me that he hoped the war would be over before his son would be old enough to be sent to the front, eighteen years from now. For a country that sees—rightly—this conflict as one that is nearly a decade old already, it's a sobering but hardly crazy thought.

Thus, we need to be thoughtful about the military resources we are sending to Ukraine and consider their impact on how we would prosecute a potential conflict in the Indo-Pacific. Many of the simpler systems we have sent to Ukraine—from Bradley infantry fighting vehicles, Humvees, and M1 Abrams tanks—are not of particular importance to what would likely be a largely air and naval engagement in the Taiwan Strait. (If China is able to disembark significant numbers of troops on the island, and we are locked in a ground tank and infantry battle on the island, Taiwan is likely lost anyway.)

Any successful Taiwan defense strategy will focus on preventing a Chinese air and maritime assault in the first place and attacking an invasion force as it crosses the strait. Some of the advanced weapons systems we have sent to Ukraine would be highly relevant to a Taiwan fight—including air defense systems like Patriot missiles and NASAMS batteries that would be essential to preventing the Chinese Air Force from establishing air superiority over the island, so-called MANPADS such as Stinger missiles, useful for shooting down low-flying rotor and fixed-wing aircraft, and even HIMARS rockets, which could be extremely helpful to Taiwan's defense since they are capable of firing the newest stealthy Long-Range Anti-Ship Missile—missiles that also come out of that Lockheed facility Biden visited in Alabama.[32] Unfortunately, our supply of these systems—and the industrial capacity to produce more to meet critical needs—is severely lagging.

We need to get serious—and Taiwan even more so—about what a war with China would look like. CSIS estimated that such a conflict might devour five thousand missiles over the first three weeks—including four thousand JASSMs, equal to about ten years' worth of the production of that Troy, Alabama, plant, as well four hundred Harpoon anti-ship missiles and four hundred Tomahawk cruise missiles. "If our whole strategy right now, especially in the Pacific, is deterrence, we want to deter conflict—a key part of deterrence is that you have the weapon systems and you have enough of them pre-positioned in key locations so that any actor who is considering the aggressive use of force knows that we mean business," CSIS's Seth Jones said. "That's not where we're at right now."[33]

Moreover, Taiwan isn't Ukraine. In the latter case, resupply routes have been kept steadily humming through the worst of the fighting thanks to the fact that Poland and Slovakia, both NATO members, directly border Ukraine. On my trip to the Ukrainian border from Warsaw to board a thirteen-hour train to Kyiv, I passed miles upon miles of trucks just parked on the side of the road waiting to pass customs clearance to enter Ukraine with critical supplies. The island of Taiwan won't have such an option. Resupplying Taiwan would be infinitely more complex, especially since China will almost certainly try to institute an air and naval blockade of the island as it launches its invasion, a blockade that could even presage an invasion by several months, forcing Taiwan to draw down its resources even before the fighting actually starts. That very likely scenario means it's all the more important that sufficient numbers of weapons systems (as well as food, energy, and other vital logistics) already be stockpiled on the island.

China has inherent personnel and manufacturing advantages that will become clearer with each passing month of any potential attritional war. Any battle over Taiwan cannot wait for a multiyear ramp-up of weapons production, which is why any attempt to transform Taiwan into a "porcupine" of missiles and mines may already be woefully off schedule. Today, it takes between thirteen to eighteen months from the moment the military places an order for munitions until they're actually produced and delivered—a stunningly long turnaround for a future war scenario.[34] (And as a CSIS report worryingly notes, "These lead times are generally to deliver the *first* missiles—not the *last* ones.")[35]

Arms sales to Taiwan are already worrisomely backed up: while the United States has made arrangements since 2009 to sell Taiwan about $30 billion in weapons, nearly two-thirds of those promises ended up caught up in the country's slow-moving munitions system. In late 2022 the United States calculated that the years-deep backlog of weapons for Taiwan already included about $19 billion worth of munitions—including 208 Javelins and 215 Stingers, both ordered all the way back in December 2015, that had yet to reach the island.[36] (That fall, Gen. Wang Shin-lung, the vice minister for armaments at Taiwan's Ministry of National Defense, politely said only, "Taiwan would like to request that the weapons the US sells to Taiwan be delivered as scheduled.") A new billion-dollar contract in April 2023 for four hundred Harpoon anti-ship missiles won't all arrive in Taiwan until March 2029—potentially after the timeline for a Chinese invasion attempt.[37] On my fall 2023 visit to Taipei, the issue of delays in weapons procurement was raised by every single senior official I had met, from the foreign minister to the chief of the general staff to the national security adviser.

We are actively making that backlog worse by cumbersome regulations in what's known formally as the Foreign Military Sales system.[38] "The Foreign Military Sales program is risk averse, inefficient, and sluggish. This reality is particularly concerning because U.S. allies and partners need to play a critical role in deterrence and warfighting against countries such as China," a 2023 CSIS report concluded. "In one case, the decision to sell a specific weapons system to Taiwan through FMS, rather than a direct commercial sale, added two years to the delivery date—on top of a two-year production timeline—for a total of four years." The program has good intentions—it's meant to provide transparency and ensure that high-tech tools aren't going to the wrong countries—but as CSIS found, it is failing known partners like Taiwan: "In trying to prevent military technology from falling into the hands of adversaries, the United States has put in place a regulatory regime that is too sluggish to work with critical front-line countries."[39]

Around the globe, we need to rethink our strategy on what weapons and forces we build, and we need to deter China by concentrating more in places where we still have strategic asymmetric advantages. For instance, our submarine force is much stronger and more advanced than China's and the Chinese antisubmarine warfare capabilities are woefully inadequate; we should be ramping up our production of highly capable silent submarines that can stealthily get up to the coast of China and inflict enormous damage on the PLA Navy and its ports with torpedo and missile strikes, should the need arise.

We also need to harden our bases in the region, particularly in Japan and Guam, because of the high risk that they will be struck with Chinese long-range missiles within the first hours of any large-scale campaign, attacks that right now would likely result in our forward bases being out of commission for a month or more. We need to assess the vulnerability from Chinese cyber disruptions of critical life support systems—such as energy and water—on those bases, attacks that could have a negative impact on their operations in the crucial initial days of the conflict. In 2023, public reports surfaced about cyber intrusions into key US critical military and civilian infrastructure in the Indo-Pacific region and the US mainland by a Chinese nation-state actor known as Volt Typhoon. While these intrusions have not proven destructive yet, the intelligence that the Chinese can collect through such reconnaissance operations ahead of an actual military conflict can enable them to rapidly execute disruptive and destructive attacks against these targets when the need arises. In addition to building up the cyber resiliency of such networks, we need to look at low-tech backup systems—such as large stockpiles of bottled water and diesel generators—that could be brought into service in case primary systems are affected by cyberattacks.

Furthermore, we need to concentrate on building up our forces to hit Chinese targets away from shore too. This would include, for example, shutting down Chinese shipping through the critical Strait of Malacca, which would quickly inflict economic paralysis on China's mainland because of the volume of its energy needs that pass through the strait on oil and gas tankers. It could also include using cyberattacks to shut down the oil and gas pipelines that come over the Chinese border from Russia.

The other critical lesson to learn from the war in Ukraine is how Russian electronic warfare (EW) is having a disproportionate impact on the battlefield—from the GPS spoofing steering guided munitions such as the Guided Multiple Launch Rocket System (GMLRS) rounds fired by HIMARS off-course to the radio frequency jamming disabling drones and limiting their use over the battlefield for intelligence, surveillance, and reconnaissance. It is also curtailing the Ukrainian delivery of munitions, such as grenades that are being dropped from drones on Russian trenches, personnel, and vehicles. In a conflict with China, we should also expect that our space-based communications assets will be targeted via spoofing, jamming, cyberattacks, and perhaps even via kinetic missiles strikes by China's highly developed antisatellite weapons program.

The newly created US Space Force needs to prioritize not only building resiliency in our systems against these disruptions and attacks but also making sure that our huge reliance on space for communication, intelligence collection, and navigational guidance does not leave us entirely blind if those systems are successfully disabled. It is critical to ramp up training of our and allied military personnel on scenarios where GPS, satellite imagery, and space-based communication channels are unavailable and investing in alternative capabilities—such as inertial and optical navigation, which is not reliant on space assets, and hard-to-jam shortwave communications. The other important implication is that US operations and doctrine should not become overly reliant on unmanned systems like drones, especially drones that are unable to operate autonomously in the absence of a communication link with an operator, as such systems can be disabled with jamming. This doesn't mean that unmanned vehicles are useless—far from it, as the war in Ukraine has shown they can be extremely important—but we need to appreciate that they are not a cure-all for our battlefield needs and can be lost in huge numbers. Ukraine, for instance, was losing over ten thousand drones per month throughout 2023. Until AI improves sufficiently to allow for a high degree of autonomous operation of these devices in the face of adversarial action, manned systems are unlikely to disappear from the battlefield.

But most of all, we need to be building more, faster. Currently, we're not positioned to rebuild our stockpiles of critical weapon systems anywhere near the necessary pace or agility—let alone build the weapons in the next few years that might be most useful in *deterring* war in the first place. We should be ramping up production rapidly to make sure we are not left in a disastrous position should war break out in the Indo-Pacific region. But perhaps more important even than concerns about stockpiles of individual weapons systems and munitions is the need to rationalize defense spending to make sure that while we are building up our depleted stocks from the supplies we've provided to Ukraine—as well as giving multiyear contracts to the defense industry to invest in extra production capacity—that in these budget-constrained times we are also investing in the necessary air and naval capabilities needed for the fight in Asia. This would include submarines, destroyers, fixed-wing and rotor aircraft, and most importantly large stockpiles of anti-ship missiles, self-guided smart underwater mines, and large numbers of reconnaissance and attack drones.

Arguably the most important thing we have learned from the Russian war in Ukraine is that great power wars can last a long time. Consequently, we need to make sure that we have both the inventories and the production capacity to replenish the losses we would inevitably sustain. This does not mean, as some have argued, that we should not assist Ukraine with military hardware to enable them to defeat Russian aggression. That help must also be a priority, not just for humanitarian reasons but also to stand up for the principle of preservation of territorial integrity and not allowing the precedent permitting great powers to arbitrarily change borders by force. Ultimately, there is also the simple realpolitik logic that helping Ukraine destroy Russian offensive military capacity without the sacrifice of any American lives goes a long way to achieving our strategic goal of containing Russia.

As ALREADY IMPLIED IN THIS BOOK, A BETTER-COORDINATED STRATegy to protect and defend Western innovation must also include more aggressive actions in the cyber realm. China's economic rise over the last twenty years has relied on cybertheft and economic espionage as a core part of the strategy, a critical and long-standing violation of international norms that has brought enormous economic damage to US and Western companies, as well as our national security and that of our allies. A 2015 deal to curtail such activity during the Obama administration was violated by the Chinese within months, as I discovered and publicly announced at the time, and it's long overdue that the United States move to address this threat.[40] As a starting point, we have to retaliate forcefully against sectors that are benefiting from such thefts. For instance, if we see a hack from Chinese state-sponsored hackers into a Western solar power company, we should be willing to sanction Chinese solar power companies writ large—even if we don't know the recipient of what was stolen. Such signals are critical to the message that we will not allow China to benefit from ill-gotten theft of economic and trade secrets.

For most of the last three decades, US cybersecurity policy and cyber strategy treated cyberattacks as if they emerged from the ether, unconnected to the geopolitical conflicts and competitions that structure the global security order. As a result, much of the US cyber strategy has focused on managing the effects of cyberattacks through defense and narrow deterrence of actors in cyberspace rather than addressing their geopolitical root causes.

Deterrence, as it has been put into practice in the cyber domain, has been similarly ineffective at preventing cyberattacks on the US homeland. In the past four years, the US government has sanctioned and indicted government officials and contractors from all of its four primary adversaries: China, Iran, North Korea, and Russia. Yet these states regard the cost of these measures as relatively minor—sometimes even treating such indictments as a badge of honor and allegedly awarding medals to sanctioned cyber operatives—and continue to carry out or condone cyberattacks at an unrelenting pace. More aggressive sanctions that would threaten the underpinnings of economic growth in these countries, such as sanctions against industrial national champions, would likely achieve a greater effect. But because the United States does not approach these attacks in their broader geopolitical contexts, it has failed to mount appropriately tailored responses. As I have argued for more than a decade, we cannot treat cyber as a technical problem; more fundamentally, *we do not have a cyber problem—we have a China, Russia, Iran, and North Korea problem*. It is not a coincidence that nearly all state-sponsored cyberattacks against the United States originate from these four countries. They do not hold any special monopoly on the use of cyber power; rather, they are the primary adversaries we face on the geopolitical stage, adversaries willing to use cyber to achieve asymmetric advantage over us that they often can't in the physical domain. They are the worst actors on the international stage across multiple realms, the ones most likely to use cyber and noncyber means to try to threaten our economic and national security. Numerous other countries have advanced offensive cyber capabilities—from Israel to France to Singapore—but we worry little about them turning these technical means against us due to the nonadversarial nature of our relationships with these states. Finally, in addition to using their military and intelligence agencies to do everything from steal US government, allied, and commercial secrets to conducting more disruptive operations, these four countries also tend to host many of the world's cybercriminals, providing them with a safe haven from prosecution as long as they direct their activities toward the West.

Like all complex geopolitical challenges, cyberthreats can be addressed using the right combination of incentives, disincentives, and compromises. The question for the United States and its allies is whether they are willing to prioritize progress on issues in cyberspace over progress on other geopolitical objectives—and what they are willing to give up for the sake of that progress. Considering the ever-increasing major ransomware attacks and supply chain hacks, the US government must urgently answer that question. Then it must back up its rhetoric on cyberattacks with hard-nosed diplomacy and the imposition of hard costs that can change its adversaries' behavior.

Cyber defense as it is currently practiced cannot mitigate cyberthreats on its own. Our nation's attack space across public and private networks is simply too vast to defend effectively. Moreover, often adversaries succeed in breaking into networks not due to a particularly brilliant technical exploit or malicious code but because they've been able to successfully use social engineering to induce an employee working at a target organization to click on a link, open an attachment, or even give up their login credentials over the phone. As an appointed member of the US government's Cyber Safety Review Board (CSRB)—a unique private-public organization that is roughly the cyber equivalent of the National Transportation and Safety Board (NTSB), which investigates transportation accidents—I participated in the 2023 review of a cyber extortion group called Lapsus$.[41] Our board had determined that Lapsus$ and a number of other related groups, which consisted of teenagers who often had very limited technical skills, had nevertheless succeeded in breaking into major technology companies like Microsoft, Uber, and T-Mobile using primitive social engineering techniques—techniques as simple as calling up employees and business contractors and scamming them out of their credentials. Unfortunately, there are no foolproof technical solutions to gullibility. Thus, in addition to beefing up defenses, we have to ramp up our deterrence.

This means implementing measures that raise the costs to hostile regimes of carrying disruptive and destructive cyberattacks, as well as cyber-enabled theft of data for financial or economic gain, while denying them the benefits of doing so. In addition to indictments of military and spy agency operatives, the United States should sanction and indict foreign companies and their executives that benefit from cyber-enabled economic espionage, sending the message that the theft of intellectual property and trade secrets comes at a hefty price. And, since pseudo-anonymous cryptocurrency transfers now fuel so much of global cybercrime, the United States should continue working with its allies to sanction and shut down cryptocurrency exchanges that cater to criminal operations or that do not perform "Know Your Customer" and "Anti Money Laundering" due diligence on the transactions they facilitate.

Moreover, drawing—and holding—firm lines in cyberspace means rethinking the public messages on cyber intrusions and making it clear that some behaviors, even behaviors we may dislike, are acceptable because they're within the bounds of long accepted norms of nation-state activities and, whether we admit it publicly or not, behaviors that our own intelligence agencies and the military conduct routinely themselves. By more clearly defining what is acceptable, we can more easily make clear what is expressly unacceptable and what behaviors will draw quick severe consequences and repercussions.

The above applies to Russia as much as it does to China. We need to be more careful—and calibrated—in what Russian behavior to complain about, particularly in cyberspace. Cyber is a critical issue, but it's one where US policymakers have blurred lines that we should try to preserve clarity in. We need to be clearer about what's acceptable cyber behavior and what's not, defining rules of the road that aren't hypocritical and that we agreed to abide by as well. We should focus our complaints and reactions to digital attacks and moves that are true redlines: such as theft of intellectual property and financial resources, blackmail, or indiscriminate disruptive attacks on infrastructure.

As one example of overheated rhetoric, US policymakers complained loudly about Russia's intrusions into dozens of companies and government agencies as part of the SolarWinds Hack in 2020—a brilliantly executed and wide-ranging supply chain exploit that, contrary to the chicken-little "act of war" pronouncements by some policymakers, was by all appearances a fairly typical cyber espionage campaign, similar to what the US itself conducts routinely.[42] Shame on *us* for letting it happen, rather than shame on *them* for trying.

Similarly, in 2022, as Russia launched its full-scale invasion of Ukraine, it simultaneously attacked the American Viasat satellite communications company—a move widely condemned as unacceptable by the West. Why? It was, by all accounts, a narrowly targeted attack aimed at a military communications system in wartime, seemingly the very definition of a type of cyberattack that you would determine is lawful to conduct in time of war. While there was some civilian spillover, Russian hackers did not brick or disable every Viasat customer modem; rather, they targeted modems deployed in Ukraine and rolled out the malicious update against that specific subset of users. Russia could have just as easily destroyed the entire Viasat network and all of their customer terminals; by overreacting to the limited attack, the West inadvertently sent a message that Russia's hackers shouldn't bother with such damage-limiting careful planning in the future. Why even bother with the extra effort of tailoring an attack to limit collateral damage if you're going to be condemned either way?

In a way that the public didn't notice, the United States actually did draw precisely this distinction regarding the Russian attempt to influence the 2016 presidential election. While the Justice Department publicly named and indicted the Russian GRU hackers—a team called "Fancy Bear" by the cyber-actor-naming convention I invented at CrowdStrike—who broke into the Democratic National Committee server and leaked stolen documents to WikiLeaks, the United States did not indict the "Cozy Bear" Russian SVR hacking team that similarly penetrated the DNC network and whose members' identities were also uncovered by Western intelligence. The difference? The Cozy Bear team restricted their activities to routine political intelligence gathering. The problem wasn't the hack; it was how the Russian teams used the information they'd stolen. In this case, the behavior the United States wanted to punish and discourage was the "dump and leak" influence attack on our elections. In espionage parlance, the problem was the dissemination, not the take. This is precisely the type of nuance we need to embrace, discuss, and make public.

Clearly defining our norms and expected behaviors in cyberspace will help more sharply draw the boundaries of our Cold War II with

China, since its behavior continues to be outside any such bounds. More—much more—needs to be done to inflict significant pain on the companies and industries in China benefiting from this type of theft, and thus this is the area where we must invest in defending innovation through peacetime fights at the trade negotiating table.

DEFENDING OUR ECONOMIC ADVANTAGE

One of the most egregious examples of China's directed cyber economic espionage was its almost literally part-by-part theft of the components necessary to build the Comac C919 airliner. The effort grew out of the Chinese government's recognition that by the mid-2020s the looming demands for air travel by China's middle class would outstrip the country's ability to source the necessary aircraft from Western suppliers like Airbus or Boeing. Instead, the Chinese needed to jump-start their indigenous aircraft manufacturing industry—one of the ten priority "leap-frog" industries identified in official economic planning documents.

China's answer was the C919, a narrow-body airliner manufactured by Comac; the plane had its maiden flight in 2017—three years behind the initial schedule—and relied heavily on Western parts. Its wing anti-icing system came from Germany, its wings from Japan, its engine thrust reverser from France, and its flight control system, engines, weather radar, landing gear, auxiliary power unit, and more all came from the United States. Even its tires came from the West—from Michelin—as did the flight simulator necessary to learn how to fly the plane. It was a long way from the domestic manufacturing triumph China desired—a fact underscored by China's deals in 2017 for three hundred Boeing planes, at a cost of $37 billion, and in 2019 for another three hundred Airbus planes (this one at the cost of $45 billion).

That ongoing need for external aviation sources is surely why, just two years after the Comac C919 development program launched in 2008, a government-sponsored hacking group began targeting

Western suppliers' trade secrets. The group, which CrowdStrike called TURBINE PANDA, was well-known to us: we believed it was a part of the Ministry of State Security (MSS), the Chinese foreign and domestic intelligence agency that resembles a partial combination of the CIA and FBI. Not coincidentally, this was also the agency behind the brazen 2015 theft of millions of US government security clearance records from the Office of Personnel Management.

In 2019 CrowdStrike outlined the Comac-focused economic espionage we detected and collected in a report titled *Huge Fan of Your Work*, which traced how Beijing used a mixture of official and unofficial cyber actors—including not just MSS officers but also hackers sourced from China's underground hacking scene and company insiders—to selectively and carefully steal the know-how to build the aircraft domestically. We included a full-page org chart for the hacking group, from the MSS division director, Zha Rong, on down through five bureaucratic layers to the actual people behind the keyboards. Between 2010 and 2015, these Chinese hackers had successfully breached suppliers like AMETEK, Honeywell, Safran, Capstone Turbine, GE, and others.

As our report said, "The actual process by which the CCP and its SOEs (State-Owned Enterprises) provide China's intelligence services with key technology gaps for collection is relatively opaque, but what is known from CrowdStrike Intelligence reporting and corroborating U.S. government reporting is that Beijing uses a multi-faceted system of forced technology transfer, joint ventures, physical theft of intellectual property from insiders, and cyber-enabled espionage to acquire the information it needs. Specifically, SOEs are believed to help identify major intelligence gaps in key projects of significance that China's intelligence services then are likely tasked with collecting."

The thefts were remarkably well-coordinated. For example, targeting of the Los Angeles–based Capstone Turbine began just a month after Comac chose the company as the manufacturer of the plane's engines.

The US government went after some of the hackers involved, issuing detailed indictments in 2017 and 2018, and in 2018 arrested one of the MSS intelligence officers concerned, catching Xu Yanjun in Belgium and extraditing him to the United States where he was sentenced to twenty years in prison, the first-ever Chinese intelligence officer to face charges Stateside. It was a huge success for the United States and an ever bigger embarrassment for China, but ultimately there's a lot more we should be doing to force China and its companies to think twice before relying on stolen intellectual property.

The Comac C919 is now entering service—it received its airworthiness certificate from the Civil Aviation Administration of China in September 2022—and had its first commercial flight, with China Eastern Airlines, in May 2023, on a trip from Shanghai to Beijing. Each flight, though, and each plane that rolls off China's assembly line is its own thumb in the eye of Western manufacturers. According to Comac, the company hopes to be a feisty upstart competitor to Boeing and Airbus, capturing both a third of the Chinese narrow-body market by 2035 and a fifth of the global market overall.[43]

Its success would come at the cost of US and European jobs (at Boeing, Airbus, and other plane-part manufacturers), jobs lost due to China's unfair competitive practice. After all, it's certainly cheaper to research and develop cutting-edge technologies if the government hands you your competitors' blueprints. In response to such blatant actions, the United States should sanction Comac and threaten sanctions against any airline (including domestic Chinese ones) that purchase it. Comac—and other Chinese companies—would certainly think twice about participating in such schemes if they believed that doing so would dramatically limit their business access to the international market.

And this is where defending innovation moves from the hard power realm of military, cyber, intelligence, and law enforcement to the soft power realm of trade agreements.

It's clear now that the biggest mistake the United States made in the 1990s and early 2000s in accommodating China was allowing that country into the World Trade Organization—an organization that effectively operates as a club of rule-abiding nations—when it was clear even then that China had no interest in following the rules and was planning to undermine the entire system from within. Prevailing wisdom at the time was that bringing China into the world trading system would help to open the Chinese market to the benefit of Western exporters and investors, while also moving the PRC's nonmarket economy more toward an open, capitalist model. The Clinton administration supported this "engagement approach," one backed by large business interests, but there were deep divisions in Congress over this path and whether it would lead to a more prosperous and secure future for the United States and the world generally. Critics pointed to China's dismal record of labor abuses and human rights violations, its continued threats against Taiwan, and its party-governed economy as harbingers of an outcome the United States would one day regret.

Of course we now know that despite making numerous commitments in its protocols of accession, China has failed to live up to them, remained steadfast in its adherence to market-distorting principles, supported widespread labor abuses, engaged in forced labor manufacturing and genocide of the Uyghur population, and embraced a set of industrial policies that have led to an offshoring of Western manufacturing and jobs and an unsustainable exploitation of natural resources from Argentina to Zimbabwe. The critics had been proven right.

Understanding how we screwed up China's WTO accession and how to better align our geopolitical approach to trade—and the tools and leverage we have to do so—requires a bit of history, knowledge of US government org charts, and understanding the role of one of the least-understood corners of the White House.

As it turns out, one of the key tools that the United States already possesses for the necessary economic push to defend innovation is the Office of the US Trade Representative (USTR)—a cabinet-level agency that isn't well-known outside of DC policy circles but possesses a surprisingly powerful and nimble force for advancing US interests on the global stage. While most tuned-in Americans can rattle off the names of the secretary of state or secretary of defense, very few can name the US trade representative, but the post has grown quietly in recent decades into one of the government's most important geopolitical and economic tools.

As much as we think of the Constitution and Bill of Rights as the nation's founding documents, the country's history of international trade treaties is actually longer and older. John Adams began negotiating the first, with France, in 1776, a document eventually known as the Treaty of Amity and Commerce and signed in 1778. The realm of trade exists at a blurry line between the legislative and executive branches, and over the last seventy years—particularly as global commerce thrived in the postwar era—the field evolved from one-to-one trade and commerce treaties to the more modern and comprehensive free trade agreements.[44]

Recognizing the rising importance of trade and the need for more trade agreements, Congress pushed for John F. Kennedy to name a special representative for trade. This resulted in the creation of the Office of the Special Trade Representative in 1962 as an agency within the Executive Office of the President, that is, the White House, much like the Office of Management and Budget and, in Kennedy's era, the Office of Emergency Planning, which headed the nation's Cold War civil defense efforts.

Congress steadily expanded the agency's authorities throughout the 1960s and 1970s, and in 1979, it was formally renamed the Office of the US Trade Representative and assigned its modern legal responsibilities. As far as federal agencies go, USTR is remarkably small, made up of approximately two hundred trade negotiators, lawyers, and support staff. It's also miniscule compared to the size of foreign trade ministries. For instance, a country like Japan might have two hundred staff members within its trade ministry devoted exclusively to agricultural issues, whereas USTR's two hundred staff are responsible for the whole sweep of US trade policy. USTR's relatively smaller size has worked to its benefit by allowing for quick decision making and far less bureaucracy than in larger agencies, where critical decisions can be marred by unending delays in approvals.

Within the government, USTR's small size and its seasoned, civil-service professional staff have given it a reputation as agile, creative, and even a little bit scrappy. Interpersonally, trade negotiators have a reputation for being type-A personalities who are maniacally focused on getting stuff done. And they're blunt: while State Department diplomats are often hemmed in by protocol and decorum, there's a frankness in international trade negotiations that's relatively unique within foreign policy.

Today, USTR is responsible for negotiating and enforcing all elements of US trade policy. Its primary role is to set and enforce policy, but its purview extends far beyond tariffs to include responsibilities like crafting protections against the theft of American intellectual property and enforcing sanitary measures for foodstuffs. The agency's objective is to promote domestic economic growth through both boosting US exports and protecting domestic industries from unfair competition. But as a geopolitical tool, trade is about more than just dollars and jobs: trade agreements present a mechanism for delineating and articulating our values and include environmental, labor, or other human rights provisions that make market access contingent on the trading partner taking steps to eradicate child labor from supply chains or clean up environmentally unsound industries.

All of this means there's a certain political creativity inherent to the work of USTR. On the one hand, the enforcement of trade policy depends on interagency cooperation; on the other, trade policy itself has to balance the interests of several different constituencies, from private sector businesses to Congress to White House leadership. Unsurprisingly, then, there's a high premium on pragmatism and flexibility. USTR's strategy often reflects the political contingencies and realities of a specific moment: the goal is to find a way to get a particular objective done now, not to craft some elegant policy structure that will endure for all time as policies and politics are ever changing. In this respect, trade policy tends to be much more maneuverable and agile than other types of foreign policy.

In addition to setting and enforcing US trade policy, USTR is also responsible for holding other countries accountable for sticking to their agreements. Its main leverage point in that effort—the big stick it carries to enforce trade agreements—is the tariff. If USTR believes another country isn't abiding by the terms of a trade agreement that it has signed with the United States, it can launch an interagency investigation; if a dispute settlement body finds violations are occurring, USTR can then raise tariffs in response, choking off market access for foreign companies. This process, which is written into most trade agreements, is known as "dispute settlement." It gives USTR real teeth to enforce trade agreements—a power, notably, that distinguishes trade agreements from many diplomatic documents, which often lack effective enforcement mechanisms. (Contrast that, for instance, to the UNCLOS ruling that China's territorial claims in the South China Sea are invalid—Beijing has largely ignored it and has suffered no meaningful consequences for its ongoing actions in the region.)

Importantly, though, these dispute settlement processes are discretionary mechanisms. They depend on the White House choosing to use them, rather than being triggered automatically by law. And it's here that we have allowed our trade relationship with China to veer off course.

The primary multilateral forum for the USTR and America's broader trade interests is the WTO, which became the modern successor in 1995 to the legal agreement known as the GATT, the so-called General Agreement on Tariffs and Trade, established after World War II. The story of the modern economy—the rise of the global middle class, globalization, and complex interconnected supply chains—can be traced through the GATT and WTO's hard and successful work lowering tariffs around the world: from 1947 to 1999, average international tariffs fell from 22 percent to 5 percent.[45]

In the modern era, though, the WTO has increasingly proven to be an imperfect arena for combating major threats to US economic interests—especially the threats presented by China, which gained accession to the WTO in 2001. Importantly, this inability to confront China isn't a bug. There are structural conditions within the WTO that prevent it from cracking down on China's illegal trade practices.

In order to gain WTO membership, countries are supposed to meet a certain set of legal and operating standards that ensure that all member countries are operating on a fair, level economic playing field. This includes, for instance, promises that member countries aren't going to arbitrarily stop imports from one another at the border, or that all of them will afford foreign companies the same IP protections that they afford domestic companies. Fundamentally, the WTO is based on the principle of reciprocity: a country will extend the same benefits to all the member countries that it extends to individual members, and those countries will in turn extend those benefits to it—a principle known as Most Favored Nation or MFN status.

When a country doesn't follow through on these agreements or otherwise engages in unfair trade practices, there's a formal mechanism within the WTO for settling disputes—but it's a cumbersome mechanism that takes a long time to run its course, typically around a decade. While most members have followed the dispute settlement process they negotiated, in some cases, WTO members will short circuit the longer practice by imposing unilateral trade restrictions on other members and seeing if they are challenged. And members on the receiving end of those restrictions may retaliate before a case even gets to the dispute settlement body. For those cases that do end up in the WTO's dispute settlement review, a WTO panel or the Appellate Body may find that a suspension of tariff benefits is necessary to address the offending member's practices. What is interesting is that the prevailing member may choose to impose tariffs based on a value amount that is not based on the product that is the subject of the review.*

The logic of these levers is built around their deterrent capability—when targeted against a democratic country with a market-based economic system, these measures will provoke domestic economic pain. The industries that bear the brunt of the retaliation are meant to respond by pressuring the government to stop the sanctioned trade practices, and, in turn, the government will yield by responding to that domestic political incentive. It works against governments who care

* This asymmetrical tariffing means that, if country A engages in trade practices that harm country B's steel industry, but country A doesn't have a substantial domestic large steel industry to punish, the victim can take steps to put the squeeze on a different, more important industry in country A.

about their constituents and citizens. But in a country like China—which has a nonmarket economy that's almost entirely integrated into an authoritarian political system—that same logic doesn't apply. China can pursue its practices without regard for profit or normal domestic political pressure. In other words, China's idiosyncratic mix of nonmarket economy and authoritarian politics makes it uniquely resistant to the sort of short-term economic pressure that the WTO relies on to keep member states in line.

As a result, China has ridden roughshod over the WTO's rules over the last two decades, but WTO member countries have faced an exceedingly difficult time holding China accountable for its behavior within the WTO framework. Every time the United States and its trading partners get to the table at the WTO with China, they essentially renegotiate China's original accession agreement.

They are continually giving away new concessions to China, but what are they getting in return?*

Indeed, China has done vanishingly little to comply with the commitments it undertook during the WTO accession process, including moving toward a market economy, respecting foreign intellectual property rights, reciprocally opening government procurement to foreign bidders, curbing massive industrial subsidies, or eliminating discriminatory technology standards. In February 2023 USTR submitted its annual report to Congress on China's WTO compliance, with a quote from trade representative Katherine Tai: "More than 20 years after it acceded to the World Trade Organization, China still embraces a state-led economic and trade approach that runs counter to the open, market-oriented principles endorsed by all members of the organization. China's approach makes it an outlier and continues to

* It was this sense of futility that led the Trump administration to take a hard line on WTO reform—a hard line that initially left the institution nearly on life support but that has actually ended up paving the way for serious discussions about reform. One relic of that Trump-era policy that remains to this day is an impotent Appellate Body, unable to act because it lacks a quorum to approve new candidates. As a result, the normal "dispute settlement process" is only half intact, without an option for appeal, a paralysis that calls into question whether members must still follow the rules if there is no final arbiter of disputes.

cause serious harm to workers and businesses in the United States and around the world. This report details the scale of China's non-market policies and practices and is a reminder that the international trading system must continue to work together to defend our shared interests against these harmful actions."[46]

There's indeed a bigger question here about whether the WTO can operate at all with member states who have nonmarket economies—or if it needs to be entirely overhauled in order to function with China as a member. In the meantime, the good news is that the United States and its trade representative don't have to rely exclusively on multilateral agreements negotiated through the WTO to pursue American goals. USTR has a whole host of other levers at its disposal to advance US interests and combat China's unfair trade practices, from pursuing comprehensive bilateral or regional free trade agreements without China to working through smaller fora like the Organization for Economic Development (OECD), a coalition of thirty-eight developed nations, on specific issues such as systemic steel overcapacity.

US-led efforts under the Obama administration to set up the Trans-Pacific Partnership (TPP) provide one example of how the United States can use trade agreements to create new trade and investment flows with like-minded countries in a particular region without having to grant China the same benefits. Agreements like the TPP are examples of so-called FTAs, which are an exception to the normal MFN principle of the WTO—benefits extended to partner nations under a regional FTA do not apply to other WTO countries. In other words, only the members of that regional agreement would incur its benefits, whereas an agreement within the WTO would benefit every member of the organization, including China. President Obama's announced "Pivot to Asia" strategy was supposed to be as much economic as it was military. While the US did not end up joining the TPP after Congress punted on its ratification and the Trump administration subsequently pulled out of the negotiated agreement, those negotiations and relationships with countries such as Vietnam and Japan have endured and have paved the way for the Biden administration to seek certain beneficial trade outcomes through its launch of the Indo-Pacific Economic Framework (IPEF) negotiations.

While IPEF is important from a geopolitical perspective—and will likely help to ensure smoother trade and enhanced investment among its partners—the fact that it does not include tariff negotiations means it will not necessarily yield the market power required to pressure China to change its economic practices. Instead, the United States might actually move the needle on trade practices with China by pursuing a new "IPEF+" agreement that would bring together China's major trading partners—but not China—and include a reduction in tariffs and a common external policy toward countries that engage in certain unfair and discriminatory practices.

From the above discussion, it should be obvious that the United States has plenty of tools that it could use more aggressively and smarter to coerce change in China's unfair trade practices. With such a large toolbox, and so many measures implemented to combat China's uncooperative policies, how does history keep repeating itself in industry after industry, from solar to steel to new-energy vehicles? The problem has been that the United States has been slow to wake up to the Chinese economic threat and slow to act against its worst and most abusive trade practices.

To date, the United States has led global efforts to hold China accountable at the WTO, through regional efforts, and through unilateral measures authorized under US trade laws, but there's more to be done. Some such work has already started. In particular, there are three provisions that Robert Lighthizer, the USTR under the Trump administration, used smartly to specific effect to target unfair Chinese practices.

Namely, Ambassador Lighthizer used Section 301 of the Trade Act of 1974—which grants USTR a range of authorities to investigate and to enforce US rights under trade agreements and respond to certain foreign trade practices—to launch a seven-month investigation into China's "forced technology transfers," wherein it relied on joint venture requirements or foreign investment restrictions to wrongly gain access to US corporate trade secrets, as well as its practices abusing intellectual property protections, cyber-enabled economic espionage, and other unfair practices. USTR concluded, "A key part of China's technology drive involves the acquisition of foreign technologies through acts, policies, and practices of the Chinese government that are unreasonable or discriminatory and burden or restrict U.S. commerce and are part of a multifaceted strategy to advance China's industrial policy objectives."[47]

To anyone who had been paying attention, the findings hardly came as a surprise, but it was still striking to see China's assault on free and fair trade laid out in stark official language. The USTR's report pointed to how, for instance, China requires any company trying to bring a new-energy vehicle to the domestic market do so through a joint venture with a Chinese organization that caps the foreign ownership at no more than 50 percent—and then requires that joint venture to demonstrate "mastery" of the technology, a standard that all but forces the US company to hand over trade secrets to the Chinese partner as part of an "unfair technology transfer regime." The report concluded, "After carefully weighing all the evidence adduced in the course of this investigation, the investigation supports findings that China's acts, policies, and practices are unreasonable or discriminatory, and burden or restrict U.S. commerce."[48]

The USTR report came after years of the US government raising concerns about these practices in numerous forums with China, complaints that went unaddressed. The trade representative's findings laid the foundation for the United States to impose sweeping tariffs targeting the largest value of imports ever stemming from a single investigation; all told, US tariffs were levied on over $500 billion of Chinese imports. The Trump administration struck a "Phase One" deal with China in 2020 following the Section 301 action, but—to no one's surprise—as of this book's publication, China has failed to live up to those commitments too. Had the United States been able to convince partners like the EU to join in on the tariffs, the collective market power could have been a game-changer.

Another of the key global complaints about China's unfair economic policies is its tendency to dump excess capacity on foreign markets at depressed prices. China's heavily subsidized industrial policies particularly distort capital-intensive sectors like steel, solar, and aluminum—sectors that require high levels of capacity utilization to operate profitably, which normally forces companies to carefully rationalize capacity with production. Instead, China's steel, solar, and aluminum sectors run with outsized excess capacity with little regard for market-driven profitability, and the resulting glut of manufactured products are exported at depressed prices, displacing market share from good-faith actors. Not surprisingly, this means that Chinese exports to the United States boast the highest number of offsetting antidumping and countervailing duties than any other country. What's even more concerning is that this Chinese playbook is now being expanded and used in advanced technology sectors, such as semiconductors, where the government is investing billions in new fabrication facilities without any rational tie to global demand.

This type of behavior can be addressed by the USTR's Section 201 policy tool, which allows the president to impose costs on foreign industries that are causing documentable harm to US industries. The Trump administration used these authorities in 2018 to target Chinese solar manufacturers (and believe it or not, washing machine manufacturers too).

Lastly, there's Section 232 of the Trade Expansion Act of 1962, which gives the government broad power to adjust imports—including through the use of tariffs—if excessive foreign imports are found to be a threat to US national security. The Trump administration used this tool in an attempt to help the US steel industry in 2017 and 2018, finding that cheap Chinese steel imports were undercutting the long-term viability of an industry vital to US defense interests and recommending a new 24 percent tariff that the government assessed "would enable domestic steel producers to use approximately 80 percent of existing domestic production capacity and thereby achieve long-term economic viability through increased production."[49]

And then we come to the human rights concerns: China has also rightfully come under fire for its forced labor practices, particularly in the Xinjiang Uyghur Autonomous Region. Under the cloak of political "reeducation," China has forced over one million Uyghurs—a Muslim ethnic minority in northwest China—and other ethnic minorities into forced labor camps, using the facilities to produce goods such as textiles, agricultural products, and even polysilicon needed for solar panels. These goods then make their way into global supply chains at the expense (and even the lives) of the imprisoned workers. It was precisely this type of labor and human rights abuse that critics of China's WTO accession were afraid of—for good reason.

In response to these egregious violations of human rights, the United States has taken strong steps to enforce protections against forced labor, using targeted trade actions that aim to eradicate this type of labor from supply chains by seizing goods from China at the border if there is no proper documentation regarding how and where they were manufactured. Those measures have sent clear signals to producers and suppliers to better monitor their own supply chains and that just because a practice is acceptable in China doesn't mean it's acceptable to the US market.

The United States can also levy additional antidumping or countervailing duties on Chinese imports that help level the playing field for US domestic producers by offsetting the value of the dumping or Chinese government subsidies—a practice the US has already employed in solar and other fields. These types of measures can result in hefty tariffs—sometimes several hundred percent—but they are also difficult and time-consuming to pursue. Many domestic producers are fighting for changes to make this process more nimble and the remedies more immediate. (Again, these measures are especially powerful if carried out in conjunction with US allies and trading partners and can be implemented in ways that are consistent with WTO rules.) Furthermore, the United States must work with other partners to greatly reduce our reliance on certain critical Chinese imported goods, like rare earths, for which few alternatives currently exist. Securing supply chains is not something America can do alone; it requires coordinated action and ultimately hard choices (or government mandates) for businesses that will have to wean off the Chinese market and comparatively lower price point.

In short, our political and business leaders allowed themselves to get conned by the near-term economic benefits of increasing trade with China—and the apparent operational efficiency and profitable benefits of outsourcing our critical supply chains and manufacturing base there—while neglecting the longer-term downsides. Those near-term economic benefits were certainly large and important to our economic growth over the last two decades, and we should not be discounting them entirely, but as time has passed, the longer-term consequences have become clearer and, increasingly, far outweigh the gains.

What actually happened was that China used its membership in the WTO to benefit from the low or zeroed out Most Favored Nation tariff rates enjoyed by WTO members while simultaneously pursuing an industrial policy that hollowed out the manufacturing base of countries like the United States and the European Union. The WTO long worked because everyone operated from the same playbook and followed the same cooperative, gentlemanly set of rules and economic practices. But the WTO rules were not negotiated in contemplation of China's continued nonmarket and mercantilist policies, and their intended protections and safeguards have fallen woefully short of what the United States and others envisioned when giving China the green flag to join the organization.

The downsides, of course, are not just the economic and national security risks of our increased reliance for important goods on an adversarial country. More broadly, we underestimated the impact of this unequal trade relationship on the number one national security threat facing the United States (and the world) this century: the increasingly likely prospect of a devastating and world-changing war with China over Taiwan, a China that we have helped to massively enrich over the last three decades and which, in turn, has taken that newfound economic power and built up a military capable of challenging and inflicting horrendous losses on us in the Indo-Pacific.

Enriching China through trade may turn out akin to what enriching imperialist Japan or Nazi Germany would have been in the 1930s—a devastatingly shortsighted, naive, and foolish decision. It's become increasingly clear that doing so without protecting our core interests—ensuring our resiliency in critical supply chains, assisting our manufacturing base, and punishing China for stealing our intellectual property and engaging in unfair competition—was shamefully negligent.

ECONOMIC RECIPROCITY

Doing business with China and Chinese companies comes at a cost that's much higher than might appear on the surface. The US government and business community need to stiffen their backbones in dealing with China and Chinese investments here at home. We are lax about allowing Chinese investment in the United States, including in educational institutions and cultural centers, without demanding any reciprocity for ourselves inside China.

As a first-order response, we need to begin to force a more equal economic reciprocity. We have allowed China to invest too freely in US and Western markets without demanding the right to do so in theirs. China places all sorts of restrictions on Western companies operating there—like insisting on localized data storage and forcing US companies to operate as "joint ventures" inside China—that we don't require in turn of Chinese companies operating in the United States. Perhaps most obviously, we've allowed a vast asymmetry to grow even in cultural outreach and connection. Take TikTok. While the privacy case against the Chinese-owned social media phenomenon is overblown—much of the data TikTok collects is publicly available, not just from TikTok but from dozens of other social media and data aggregator sites that Americans regularly, and often unknowingly, share their data with—the real threat from TikTok is that it represents the rise of what amounts to a popular propaganda outfit controlled by an adversary state. TikTok is a media company, first and foremost, and it controls what you see—and, crucially, what you don't see—on its platform via the use of undisclosed algorithms that can be changed at will and without users' knowledge.

According to TikTok's own numbers, about half of all Americans—some 150 million people—use the service actively on a monthly basis.

By contrast, of course, no such American social medium or traditional media service is available in China. Facebook is actively banned in the PRC (as it is in a rogues' gallery of other authoritarian nations, like Iran, North Korea, Myanmar, Russia, and Turkmenistan) and the platform formerly known as Twitter is blocked for regular users; in China, the domestic heavily censored microblogging site Weibo predominates instead.

This isn't just a matter of "we're an open society and China isn't"; there are more important principles at stake. Just as we wouldn't have allowed a media company run by imperial Japan to operate the newsreels in movie theaters during World War II or a Soviet media company to sponsor and direct the Sunday night broadcast on CBS and NBC during Cold War I, we should not allow Chinese control of media in the United States. This is not a case of constitutionally protected free speech—constitutional protections are not extended to foreign corporations, and there are also long-standing, court-approved rules around concentrated media ownership. The FCC prohibits the ownership by any single entity, including even American citizens, of television stations that collectively reach more than 39 percent of American TV households. Why would we allow a foreign corporation—a Chinese one in particular—to have a reach that exceeds even that FCC threshold? There's a long-standing American legal principle, going back to the days of Thomas Jefferson, that the Constitution is not a suicide pact. Our values and our openness are not, either. Countries that do not open up their systems to our information deserve no such openness from us.

Furthermore, outside of the TikTok issue, we have some important opportunities to decrease our economic and national security interdependence with China, including diversifying raw materials, manufacturing, and supply chains away from China. That doesn't necessarily mean "on-shoring" everything to the United States—which is neither feasible nor cost-effective. Rather, it means helping our allies and our companies build factories and supply chains in Mexico, India, Vietnam, Indonesia, Malaysia, Chile, Argentina, or other countries that are less likely to be geopolitically adversarial.

Crucially, this is not an argument for decoupling—complete decoupling would be economically devastating and is not feasible. But we should demand reciprocity by China in all areas of economic investment in return for its access to US markets. The demand for strict reciprocity, in fact, is not only about fairness in trade—it is the only way to open up China to US investments that does not put US companies at a disadvantage.

As outlined above, there is no single silver bullet to confronting China economically, but there are things the United States can do—alone and with partners—to ratchet up the pressure on China to bring its economic practices more in line with international norms and level out the competitive playing field for businesses around the globe. If China actually played by the rules (whether as a result of coercion or voluntarily), it would be in a markedly weaker position than it is today.

CHAPTER 8

Step Three—Say Yes to Our Friends

When the United States went to war with Huawei, the first two Western victims were both named Michael. Neither was American and, indeed, despite their years of suffering as part of the US quest to rein in Huawei and Chinese tech, most Americans still have never heard of them.

The Trump administration and US Congress had been attacking Huawei throughout 2018, but largely only through fiery rhetoric about the national security threat the Chinese telecom giant represented. Behind-the-scenes pressure from the US government had scuttled a significant partnership between Huawei and AT&T, and in February FBI director Chris Wray had publicly warned against buying Huawei phones. In August President Trump signed a ban on government employees and contractors using Huawei and ZTE products. Then, in late November, the Justice Department and the FBI went for a dramatic escalation.

Specifically, law enforcement agents figured out that Meng Wanzhou, Huawei's forty-six-year-old CFO and the daughter of its legendary founder, had booked a ticket on Cathay Pacific Flight CX838, Hong Kong to Vancouver, where she had a layover before continuing on to Mexico and a meeting with the newly elected Andrés Manuel López Obrador, at which she hoped "AMLO" would embrace Huawei and open Mexico to its products. It was clearly a high priority trip for Meng: she was in the air from Hong Kong even as AMLO was sworn in in Mexico; their meeting was supposed to be one of his first pieces of official business.

US officials scrambled to get Canada to arrest her upon arrival. Meng—known in business circles as Sabrina—had traveled regularly to the United States, including in 2014, 2015, 2016, and 2017—but had apparently stopped doing so after public reports of a US criminal investigation into Huawei's business dealings with Iran. (Her altered travel schedule was particularly noticeable since one of her children attended a boarding school in the United States.) The Justice Department had obtained a sealed arrest warrant for her in August, and now the DOJ and the FBI quickly contacted their Canadian counterparts after determining her travel plans. The US-Canadian law enforcement partnership is one of the closest and most collegial in the world, and the Surrey Detachment of the Royal Canadian Mounted Police (RCMP) quickly sprang into action, working to obtain a provisional arrest warrant for Meng and swearing out the necessary affidavits, which outlined how Meng had participated with a Huawei subsidiary known as Skycom to surreptitiously do business with Iran that violated US sanctions.

When Meng's flight landed, a carefully coordinated three-hour-long law enforcement ballet unfolded, as border officers questioned her, confiscated her electronics—a Huawei phone, an iPhone, a rose gold iPad, and a pink MacBook—and locked them in a secure bag that would block any attempts to wipe them remotely. Finally, the RCMP formally arrested her. "Me?" she responded. "Why would I have an arrest warrant?"

That same Saturday night, Xi Jinping, Donald Trump, and Canadian prime minister Justin Trudeau were attending a celebratory closing dinner at the G-20 summit in Buenos Aires. It's unclear if either Trump or Trudeau knew about the arrest that night, but within hours, the relationship between the three countries would chill considerably. Alerted to the arrest by the FBI, the Canadian Security Intelligence Service, that country's rough equivalent of the CIA, wrote a prophetic analysis: "The arrest is likely to send shock waves around the world."[1]

Back in Shenzhen, the home of Huawei's global headquarters, Joe Kelly was awakened Sunday morning China time by a phone call. A veteran of British telecommunications, Kelly headed the company's international media affairs. On the other end of the line was a reporter: *Sabrina has been arrested in Canada at the request of the US government. Do you have any response?* Kelly sighed and offered the only comment he could muster: "I haven't had my coffee yet."[2]

Huawei's response—once Kelly had brewed some coffee and rallied with company executives—was corporate outrage, but China's official response was downright vindictive, a nasty reminder that decades of efforts by legal activists to push China more toward a Western-style independent judiciary had failed (and actually led, not a little bit ironically, to the imprisonment of many of those same activists).

Any attack on Huawei was seen as an attack on the leadership of the Chinese Communist Party and would face a fierce response.

MICHAEL KOVRIG, IN PARTICULAR, HAD AN UP-CLOSE SEAT TO THE decline of the rule of law in China and the rise of Xi's increasingly authoritarian state. Reform activists and a not insignificant number of Western policymakers and officials had long hoped that China would lurch slowly toward the rule of law, evolving from the capricious and brutal one-man-rule of the Mao era toward something that resembled an independent judiciary that exerted meaningful checks on abuses of power and process by the government and CCP leaders.

And indeed, China had periodically embraced political reforms known as *dangzheng fenkai*, "separating the party and the government," and attempted to build a true civil service, but party leaders never allowed the reforms to advance too far—and the balancing act grew harder as the country evolved economically. "For decades, Chinese leaders have pledged to build robust legal institutions that can deliver good governance and social stability," Xi biographer Chun Han Wong writes. "But as China's economy took off, its fledgling legal system struggled to keep up with the social distensions kicked up by widening wealth gaps and the spread of corruption."[3]

In 2014 Xi himself announced an effort to reform the judiciary, creating more room for an independent court and prosecutors and removing the "unspoken rules," including bribes and favors, that often led to appearances (and actuality) of backroom deals for the elite. "The judicial system is the last defense for social justice," he told the Fourth Plenary session of the Eighteenth Communist Party of China Central Committee. "If it fails, people will widely question [the country's ability to realize] social justice and stability will hardly be maintained."[4]

But Xi's words didn't reflect what was actually going on in the country. In 2015—less than a year after his reform message—more than three hundred Chinese lawyers and activists were arrested in what came to be known as the "709 crackdown," named for the crackdown's launch date of July 9. The arrests and detentions decimated what was known as the *weiquan* movement, the "rights-defense" activists who tried to use the court system to push for reform, expose abuses of power, and promote human rights. Some were formally arrested; others just disappeared. Human rights lawyer Wang Quanzhang—who had been beaten by court officials weeks earlier in June 2015 while trying to represent a Falun Gong member—was held incommunicado for three years.

That December, another prominent human rights lawyer, named Pu Zhiqiang, went on trial in Beijing. Pu was one of the leading voices of the *weiquan* movement, represented numerous dissidents and journalists over the years, including the artist Ai Weiwei, and had been part of the pro-democracy movement in 1989 that led to the Tiananmen Square massacre. Ironically (but perhaps not surprisingly) he'd actually been arrested even as Xi launched his fig leaf of a reform effort, taken into custody alongside four other lawyers who had attended a meeting of dissidents commemorating the twenty-fifth anniversary of the massacre. The Beijing Public Security Bureau announced Pu had been arrested for "creating disturbances and illegally obtaining personal information," and when the US embassy protested, a foreign ministry spokesperson snidely replied, "I think lots of people have the same feeling with me, that some people in the United States have hearts that are too big and hands that are too long. Washington should address human rights problems at home and stop trying to be the world's policeman or judge."[5]

Pu's Beijing trial was guarded by rows of police, clad all in black and wearing N95 respirators to protect against the city's smog, and attracted public protests; Western embassy officials, there to monitor the protests, watched as police waded into the gathered crowd, punching, kicking, and throwing cameras to the ground. Canada had relied on Michael Kovrig, one of its embassy diplomats, to monitor the trial. After an eight-day trial, Pu was given a suspended three-year prison sentence; writing up the trial, the protests, and the melee by police for the Canadian embassy, Kovrig said Pu's sentence was "lighter than what many observers had feared."[6]

Over many years, Kovrig had become a careful student of China's reform movement. Born in Canada, he'd served a decade as a Canadian diplomat—including four years in Afghanistan and stints in the New York UN mission, Hong Kong, and Beijing—and, after his time in Beijing, eventually went to work for a Brussels-based think tank known as the International Crisis Group.[7] Through his overseas postings and his time as a desk officer for Canada's Department of Foreign Affairs, he'd seen China's false starts with respect to the justice system. The World Justice Report had steadily dropped China's standing in its international rule-of-law index—whereas in 2014, China ranked 76th among then-99 tracked countries, it fell year after year, until in 2021 it would be 98th out of 139 tracked countries.

Kovrig was working for the International Crisis Group on a research trip to Beijing in December 2018 when he became its next victim—disappearing from his hotel room, the next pawn in Beijing's games and abuse of the legal system.

As the *Wall Street Journal* later reconstructed, Xi had been briefed on Meng's arrest. During that meeting, the Ministry of Public Security presented a list it had assembled of Canadians inside China and proposed two for him to prosecute in retaliation.[8]

KOVRIG AND ANOTHER CANADIAN, MICHAEL SPAVOR, WERE ARRESTED and held on trumped-up charges just days after Canada detained Meng Wanzhou.* The Foreign Ministry informed Canada's embassy that both men were charged with endangering state security, but it was clear that they were official hostages. China never produced real evidence against either of them. Spavor, a native of Calgary, had spent years in China working to build cultural exchange programs with its belligerent and closed-off neighbor North Korea—he'd even been part of the team that accompanied NBA star Dennis Rodman to meet Kim Jong Un in 2013 and jet-ski with the dictator. He had disappeared from the Chinese border city of Dandong on December 10 as he prepared to fly to South Korea on a routine trip.

Ultimately, "the two Michaels," as the Canadian media came to call them, were held by China for 1,019 days; while officially China said their ongoing detention was totally unrelated to Meng's case in Vancouver, everyone could see that the Canadian men were hostages. Canada engaged in secret negotiations, via a former McKinsey managing partner named Dominic Barton, whom Chinese officials told Canada was just a "lapdog" for the United States.[9] (Barton would become, later, the Canadian ambassador to China, where he would continue pressing for the Michaels' release.) Meng was placed under home arrest, at one of her two giant Vancouver mansions, out on $10 million bail and monitored around-the-clock by a large private security team, as her multiyear extradition legal battle played out, but Spavor and Kovrig received nothing close to such luxuries: they were interrogated for up to eight hours at a time, the lights in their cells kept on twenty-four hours a day.

* In late 2023, Michael Spavor filed a lawsuit against Michael Kovrig and the Canadian government, alleging that he was unwittingly entangled in a spy case, an allegation both deny.

Worse, this wasn't even the first time that China and Canada had faced off over a US arrest warrant—and not the first time China had used a resident of Spavor's town of Dandong as a geopolitical pawn.

In 2014 a Canadian couple named Kevin and Julia Garratt had gone out for a seemingly routine dinner with a Chinese friend in Dandong. A devout Christian couple in their fifties with an entrepreneurial streak, they had spent nearly all of their adult lives in the sprawling border town that sits just across the Yalu River from North Korea. The Garratts had come to China from Canada in the 1980s as English teachers, and lived in six different Chinese cities over the years—raising four children along the way—before settling in Dandong. There, they ran a coffee shop and supported a North Korean orphanage. For tourists and expats, the Garratts' business, Peter's Coffee Shop—just a short walk from the Sino-Korean Friendship Bridge across the border—was a hub of Western conversation and comfort food. "After time in North Korea a decent cup of coffee was one of those things I was really looking forward to," one Australian tourist wrote in early 2014. "Peter's was a perfect place."[10]

After dinner that August night in 2014, the Garratts got into an elevator that took them from the restaurant down to the building lobby. The doors opened onto a swarm of bright lights and people with video cameras. The Garratts initially thought they'd stumbled into a party of some kind, maybe a wedding. But then some men grabbed the couple, separated them, and hustled them toward waiting cars. Everything happened fast, and very little made sense. As the vehicles pulled away, neither Kevin nor Julia had any idea that it was the last they'd see of one another for three months.

It wasn't until the two arrived at a police facility that they each realized they were in real trouble. And it wasn't until much later still that the couple would understand why they had been taken into custody: they'd been taken hostage after the arrest of a Chinese expat living in Canada named Su Bin, who the FBI had fingered as aiding a massive cybertheft of US defense secrets. Su Bin, who owned a Canadian aviation consulting firm, had worked with Chinese government hackers to plunder hundreds of millions of dollars in design plans for the C-17 transport plane and other US military aviation systems. Acting at the request of the FBI, Canadian authorities detained Su Bin and—like with Meng—began extradition proceedings. That was when the Garratts were seized in Dandong; they were charged with an almost mirror image of the US case against Su Bin. As their lawyer told the *New York Times*, "the Chinese made it clear that the Garratt case was designed to pressure Canada to block Su Bin's extradition to the US."[11]

Su Bin eventually realized that his extradition proceedings might last longer than a US prison sentence; he decided to waive extradition. FBI agents flew to Vancouver in the bureau's Gulfstream jet to pick him up, and on the flight back to California, he made small talk with the agents. He complimented the FBI's plane. Making chitchat, one of the agents asked him if he had a favorite jet. "Not the C-17," Su deadpanned.[12]

On March 22, 2016, Su Bin pleaded guilty. His thirty-five-page agreement was perhaps the most detailed firsthand explanation of China's spying apparatus ever released in public. "It was the first time we'd had that kind of success—the first time we'd had someone owning their part in an intrusion like this," said FBI supervisory special agent Justin Vallese, who ran the FBI cyber squad in Los Angeles that brought the case. Su Bin declined to speak publicly, though, in court. "I lost my words now," he said at his sentencing, where a judge handed him forty-six months in federal prison and ordered him to pay a $10,000 fine. With time served, he was released in October 2017. The case against the Garratts rapidly unraveled in the wake of Su Bin's decision to waive extradition; Julia left China in May 2016, and Kevin was released that September, after paying $20,000 in fines and penalties.[13]

The combination of the case of Meng and the "two Michaels" unfolded in a similar parallel. For over a thousand days, the Huawei case dragged on; in the summer of 2021, Canada's *Globe and Mail* newspaper launched a massive national letter-writing campaign to pressure the Chinese embassy. Behind the scenes, Canada, the United States, and China were all engaged in a fierce lobbying effort to resolve the cases. At one point, China did, according to the *Wall Street Journal*, engage in talks about a prisoner swap, following the arrest by FBI agents of five Chinese researchers in the United States—a deal that ultimately expanded to include sixteen people across China, Canada, and the United States—but the deal fell through when Meng refused a plea agreement.[14]

Finally, on September 24, the US government announced it had negotiated a deferred prosecution agreement with the Huawei executive allowing her to return to China, and, via a video feed from Vancouver, she admitted to a New York court that she'd misled bankers about Huawei's work in Iran. A special chartered Air China plane arrived to take her home, and within a minute of her taking off, the two Michaels boarded another plane in Tianjin, accompanied by Canada's ambassador to China, and took off for Alaska.

In the end, all four Canadians made it home, but the United States didn't make it particularly easy for Canada along the way. And, given the history, Canadian authorities—or authorities in other friendly Western countries—might well look askance at the next time the Americans asks them to arrest a high-profile Chinese target. The United States, in fact, has taken no clear action to prevent China from running the same playbook the next time—or laid out the consequences it would impose if China did.

And then there are the Australian lobsters.

After the Australian prime minister called in April 2020 for an international investigation into the origins of COVID-19 pandemic, the Chinese ambassador to Australia Chen Jingye ominously hinted at the economic backlash. "Maybe the ordinary [Chinese] people will say 'Why should we drink Australian wine? Eat Australian beef?'" he told the *Australian Financial Review*.[15] It and other outraged statements from the Chinese government had all the subtlety of a mafia capo wandering into the neighborhood deli and saying, "Nice little business you got here—shame if anything happened to it."

In the weeks and months that followed, China instituted new import inspections on Australian rock lobsters—inspections that, given the difficulty of transporting live marine crustaceans, were tantamount to a ban—and instituted new bans on timber and barley shipments from Australia. Given that in 2018 and 2019, China had accounted for about 94 percent of the Australian rock lobster market, the new trade restrictions were clearly meant to devastate the country's lobster industry.[16]

China also invoked punishing tariffs on Australian wine—tariffs that in some cases reached 212 percent—and exports stopped almost overnight. One winemaker, Jaressa Estates in the South Australian wine growing region of McLaren Vale, had been selling about seven million bottles a year to China, some 96 percent of its total business, and saw that number drop to zero. "The country's biggest overseas market vanished almost immediately. Sales to China plummeted 97 percent that first year. Storage tanks overflowed with unsold vintages of shiraz and cabernet sauvignon, pressuring red grape prices," the *New York Times* reported.[17] "Now that its economy is entrenched as the world's second largest, the threat of losing access to China's 1.4 billion consumers is a stick that few countries or industries can afford to provoke."

It was a brutal lesson for Australia. As one winemaker told CNN, perhaps Australia shouldn't be so quick to cross China in the future—and it should have approached questions about COVID-19's origins with more delicacy. "Australia's only a little nation. We should have absolutely supported it, but we didn't need to lead the charge," the vintner said.[18] All told, Australia saw some $13 billion worth of exports targeted.

Outside the egregious Australian case, China has begun to wield the economic stick more regularly. For example, it halted salmon imports from Norway after the Nobel Peace Prize went to Chinese dissident Lio Xiaobo, punished Taiwan in 2022 with new restrictions on exporting pineapples, apples, and fish, and went after Lithuania when the Baltic country tried to strengthen ties with Taiwan.[19] Indeed, while Taiwanese farmers were left with ponds packed with unsold groupers and island restaurants rolled out new "freedom-themed" pineapple courses to blunt the impact of the loss of mainland sales, the wide-ranging Chinese move against Lithuania was unprecedented—extending not to just to obvious products like milk or peat but also against products manufactured with semiconductor chips made in

Lithuania. As the *New York Times* wrote at the time, "China's drive to punish Lithuania is a new level of vindictiveness." The consequences for Lithuania were so dire that the German-Baltic Chamber of Commerce reported that the country's high-tech industry faced an "existential" threat.[20]

In each of these cases, there were some heroes who tried to step into the breach—Japan increased its purchases of Taiwanese pineapples and Australia successfully pivoted its rock lobster exports to Hong Kong, where, amazingly, smugglers carried them into mainland China for consumption—but the most powerful voices in the global trade discussion largely stayed silent.[21] The European Union filed a perfunctory WTO complaint on Lithuania's behalf but, as the *New York Times* reported, "otherwise largely left one of its smallest and weakest members to fend for itself," and behind the scenes its officials urged Vilnius officials to appease China. "To use a Chinese phrase, they are killing the chicken to scare the monkey, particularly the big German monkey," one European think tank leader said. "Many European leaders look at Lithuania and say, 'My God, we are not going to do anything to upset China.'"[22]

And while some US officials held performative tastings of Australian wine, the United States failed to step in to stabilize or support Australia, Norway, Taiwan, or Lithuania. There were no high-profile "Berlin Airlifts" of pineapples to US grocery stores, tanker convoys of Australian Shiraz rolling up the Capital Beltway, or "Buy Baltic" public service announcements to encourage consumers and corporate leaders to look to Lithuanian suppliers. There was no coordinated effort to build a coalition to implement an emergency adjustment of tariffs on Australian wine or lobster, let alone to help the affected industries find new commercial buyers.

Perhaps it's easy to write off such American reluctance as our own strain of protectionism—maybe the government didn't want to be accused of undercutting Hawaiian pineapples or promoting foreign competitors to California Zinfadels—but the truth is that even at home the United States has failed to stand up for our industries when China targeted them. We didn't support American airlines and hospitality companies when China pressured them to remove Taiwan's name from their maps; nor did the United States government stand up meaningfully for the free speech of NBA players who criticized China.

China is learning, again and again, that bullying works, mastering the twenty-first century toolkit of economic statecraft and warfare. As Bethany Allen, a journalist who has covered China for a decade, now with *Axios*, writes, "If we speak the language of markets . . . then China hasn't just learned that language. It has learned to speak it louder than anyone else."[23] The CCP's "authoritarian style of state capitalism," Allen argues, means it "is willing to draw on its full arsenal of leverage, influence, charm, deception, and coercion." And China has begun to deploy those tools all too frequently—leading to very real questions about whether anyone, companies or nation-states, can afford to be economically reliant on China.

We need to do better—for ourselves and our allies.

Strong allies are not going to help only out of self-interest, they're going to do it because they want to follow their values and principles—and we have to make it easier for countries who want to help us counter China. That's what friendship means. Absent that friendship, China can divide us and take each country, Western or otherwise, on in turn. We need to create the umbrella and space where countries, companies, and individuals feel comfortable taking on the worst aspects of China's attempts at hegemonic thought and action.

Critical to any global strategy to counter China is building and securing the series of bilateral relationships and multilateral institutions and alliances that helped the West win Cold War I. We have to make it easy for our allies—and desired potential allies—to say yes to such alliances. China is surrounded by many relatively small and weak countries that need real reassurances, both security and economic, that if they side with the United States in a regional coalition they won't be out in the cold. Even countries like South Korea, Japan, and Australia that by most measurements would be considered "large"—all of them are G-20 countries with advanced economies and trillion-dollar-plus GDPs—are small compared to the behemoths like China and the United States, especially if they're left geopolitically isolated.

"Vulnerable states are likely to look for something more, some greater assurance that *they specifically* will be effectively defended against an opponent as powerful as China," former Pentagon strategist Elbridge Colby writes. "They will want a concrete, credible pledge from the United States (and potentially others) not to leave them in the cold but rather to effectively defend them in *these* circumstances."[24]

Saying "yes" to our allies—giving them the cover, protection, and friendship necessary to make difficult choices—will require on a geopolitical level (1) delivering some tough love to certain allies and would-be allies (including Taiwan itself) as well as (2) taking some strong medicine and resetting our own relationship with some key partners we haven't adequately supported in the past. On the corporate front, we must also (3) support and help American and other Western companies unwind and decouple vital supply chains from China while (4) encouraging countries around the world that are on the fence between the United States and China to choose to build their future around the West.

Succeeding across all four of these realms will ensure that our allies feel they are protected from coercive Chinese retaliation—whether it's military, diplomatic, or economic—and that they can make their own choices about their future without facing security threats or crippling trade disruptions. We need to create a stronger sense that the West is united and that the United States is clearly willing to support its friends in the face of Chinese aggression.

We need to do better to say yes to our friends.

TOUGH LOVE

Countering China also means being clear with our friends—Taiwan first and foremost among them. The message should be simple: Americans can't be expected to fight for Taiwan's freedom if Taiwan itself won't. The truth is that Taiwan historically hasn't been all that serious about its own defense: it has long fallen prey to magical thinking that the island's economic links with China will prevent a conflict, and, if that fails, that the big powerful US military will rush to its rescue.

Part of that strategy has been massive investments in the development of semiconductors—the so-called Silicon Shield, which rests on the idea that China will not invade Taiwan as long as it is reliant on the island's chips. The trouble with that strategy, of course, is that Taiwan itself has undermined it by assisting in the development of China's semiconductor industry, aiding the reduction of the mainland's reliance on TSMC's island fabs, and, as the rising tensions show, the chips might actually be a primary reason China today covets Taiwan. Consequently, Taiwan needs to get serious about investing in its military capabilities and its fighting force, learning and incorporating the hard-won lessons of Ukraine's battle against Russia.

As tiny an island as Taiwan may seem, it actually stands a good chance of repelling a Chinese invasion with the right preparation. Taiwan is home to twenty-three million people, including six million military-age males (as well as a similar number of military-age females, who comprise 15 percent of the active-duty military but are exempt from conscription). It also has the ability to manufacture numerous weapons systems itself because of the island's advanced industrial base. China's military is, on paper, the largest in the world, with between two million and three million personnel, about a million of whom are in the ground forces. However, any possible invasion force would be but a fraction of that size, and an amphibious invasion is just about the most logistically complicated military campaign one can imagine—a typical offensive strategy would call for a three-to-one advantage to seize and hold territory. Most importantly, the terrain of the island of Taiwan makes it a natural fortress, an absolute hellish place to invade. From those stormy and unpredictable currents in the Taiwan Strait to its rocky and shallow water beaches to the mountainous terrain, cleaved with fast rivers that create natural and easy-to-defend choke points for invading forces trying to get across, to the island's tens of thousands of tunnels and bridges, there are few other places on earth that could be turned into as an impregnable stronghold as Taiwan.

And yet, Taiwan has largely pursued a half-hearted and nonstrategic approach toward military reform, modernization, and overall defense strategy—including relying upon a four-month active-duty conscription term for its military. (That brief conscription term was extended to twelve months in 2024, but it can be deferred until 2026.) They have also expended limited defense budget resources on the procurement of fancy and expensive weapon systems, like amphibious landing ships to defend outer islands and M1 Abrams tanks, vehicles that likely wouldn't be of much use in an event of an invasion of the mountainous landmass from the mainland.

Taiwan's air force, meanwhile, has spent billions buying hundreds of advanced F-16 fighter jets that can be operated from just several dozen island airfields on the island. While they have built some underground tunnels to protect the planes from Chinese missiles, rockets, or bombers in an initial preinvasion strike, the air force would still be reliant on operational runways that would surely be a primary target for the PLA. As their backup plan, Taiwanese pilots regularly practice taking off and landing on the island's numerous highways, but the delicate landing gear and large, low engine air intake under the nose of an F-16 means it is imperative to operate such jets only on clean and well-maintained runways—free of so-called foreign object debris (FOD)—and wartime highways, hastily converted into makeshift runways, are unlikely to meet that standard. And this is before one mentions their lack of fueling, maintenance, and ordnance storage facilities that would be required for operating a combat fighter fleet.

Taiwan's most wasteful and, arguably, least valuable military program, though, is the recently launched indigenous submarine, the *Hai Kung*—"narwhal" in English—at the eye-watering cost of over $1.5 billion. President Tsai proudly announced the accomplishment, one that fulfilled a key campaign promise, during a National Day ceremony I attended in October 2023. The submarine, though, is far less than meets the eye: the domestically designed boat, based on the outdated 1960s designs of the Dutch Navy, albeit somewhat modernized and upgraded, lends little benefit to Taiwan's defense. The Taiwan Strait is too shallow to operate submarines, and the Taiwan military's plans of using the *Hai Kung* submarines to keep the supply lines open out of the country's east coast ports, a "lifeline" to the Pacific in the event of war, seem unrealistic. China itself is building a capable fleet of over fifty diesel-electric and nuclear attack submarines, as well as numerous sub-hunting destroyers and frigates, that would outmatch the Taiwanese fleet. Still, Taiwan has announced plans to build a total of eight boats at a total estimated cost of up to $16 billion—precious dollars that could and should have been used to procure cheaper, more numerous, and asymmetric defensive systems.

The main trouble with Taiwan's strategy is that the Taiwanese seemingly do not put a high likelihood on the scenario of an all-out invasion and are much more concerned about "gray-zone warfare tactics," such as the harassment of Taiwanese ships and planes at sea, incursions into the island's airspace, and attempts at economic trade blockades. Even if their analysis is correct and the likelihood of invasion is low, an invasion still presents the clearest existential threat to their island, culture, and way of life—a threat graver in every respect than any other potential crisis scenario. Yes, it's problematic if China invades Taiwan's small outlying islands, which sit very close to the mainland, and—in the ideal world—it would be nice for Taiwan to have the military capability to launch an amphibious assault on such islands to retake them. A strong, modern air force armed with large numbers of F-16s is ideal if your goal is to counter and repel incursions into your airspace by China. However, none of those capabilities matter if the scenario you are confronting is the invasion of Taiwan itself—in an actual war scenario, expensive amphibious landing ships would be sunk in port and the island's small number of runways capable of launching combat aircraft would surely be cratered by huge Chinese missile barrages in the opening act of a cross-strait invasion, limiting and even perhaps all but grounding Taiwan's F-16 fleet before it even got into action.

In short, Taiwan's military priorities haven't caught up to the acceleration of the Chinese threat, and the Taiwanese are not investing fast enough in the right types of systems to deter it—instead, Taiwan continues to focus on platforms and munitions that could help it confront other less dire scenarios. The island's priorities are misaligned to the threat for two main reasons.

First, Taiwan's perception of the likelihood of outright war is low. In a May 2022 survey, 45 percent of Taiwanese respondents indicated that they were not at all or only slightly concerned about China invading Taiwan, with another 30 percent only moderately concerned with such a prospect.[25] The second factor, which is just as important, has to do with how the island's military is organized and its history. Over the seventy-five years since Chiang Kai-shek fled with his KMT nationalist forces to Taiwan, the military has gotten used to a considerable amount of independence from civilian control. Moreover, it continues to still be viewed suspiciously by the Taiwanese public, who remember the long period of brutal military dictatorship known as the White Terror, during which thousands were executed and tens of thousands imprisoned for opposition to the government. The military ranks remain filled with generals sympathetic to the KMT, a party that has evolved and now favors appeasing China as a way to avoid war and stands in contrast to the more independence-minded DPP party. The DPP, for its part, has limited national security expertise and is timid about pushing the military on defense policy issues. As recently as twenty years ago, there were still very real concerns in Taiwan that the military might orchestrate a coup and oust the democratically elected DPP out of office.

Taiwan has tried to reform this system and in 2002 established the post of minister of defense, a move meant to ostensibly provide more civilian control of the military, but in the two decades since all of the ministers who have lasted more than a few months have been former generals and admirals. This has contributed to an insularity and cultural outlook that makes it very difficult even for DPP presidents to reform the military and focus it on the most urgent threat, the survival of Taiwan against an invasion. In addition to not believing in the threat of invasion, many Taiwanese generals have vigorously protected the expensive procurement programs that give them prestige and power (not unlike generals and militaries everywhere, to be sure). The one flag officer who tried to break the mold is Admiral Lee Hsi-ming, who served as chief of the General Staff in the period of 2017 through 2019. Recognizing that Chinese invasion is the primary threat to the island, Lee tried to move the defense establishment toward an asymmetric defense strategy but, as he told me with great exasperation in his voice over drinks in Taipei, he was stymied by the national defense establishment and lack of support from the National Security Council. A former submariner himself, he nevertheless thought the indigenous submarine project was a counterproductive use of limited defense resources. Such subversive thinking ultimately led him to retire in frustration without being able to accomplish most of the changes he had advocated.

Another great challenge Taiwan's military faces is the training quality of the conscripted men. As mentioned, Taiwan had only a four-month mandatory military training for young men, which did little to prepare the drafted men for war. A common refrain about the training regimen was that it taught conscripts how to clean barracks, not to shoot rifles. As one conscript told CNN in 2023, "We were assigned simple tasks, and we spent most of the time helping with cleaning and washing the cannon carts. If war breaks out today and I am told to work as an artilleryman, I think I will just become cannon fodder."[26] With the strict gun control laws in Taiwan, most of the population has never shot a gun, much less cleaned and learned how to care and maintain it—skills particularly essential considering the island's humid and rainy tropical climate. Shockingly, these basic skills, drilled into every US soldier going through training, are not currently taught to the Taiwanese conscripted force.

Today, Taiwan needs to act like it is running out of time—because it might be. It needs to adopt a strategy that turns the island into the twenty-three-million-person equivalent of a porcupine, including a heavy investment in large numbers of anti-ship missiles, drones, and mines that could overwhelm an invading force even before the armada gets across the Taiwan Strait. It needs to build up a large well-trained and armed population that would meet any Chinese invasion on the beaches, airfields, and in the ports, using significant inventories of artillery systems, antitank guided missiles and loitering munition drones. Ukraine had years of low-level combat against Russia and its proxies in eastern Ukraine to prepare its military and rethink its doctrine ahead of the 2022 invasion; Taiwan almost certainly won't have that luxury and will need to make similar reforms and investments ahead of time. For all the reasons outlined above, if Xi orders his military to undertake an operation against Taiwan, he will go for the whole enchilada—not a half-hearted attempt to capture partial territory, such as outlying islands. There will be no off-Broadway premiere and shakedown tour for full-scale war in the Indo-Pacific, which was the role that the Donbas conflict played for Ukraine since 2014.

In addition to significant investment in anti-ship and anti-landing defense capabilities and a serious and focused reserve-force training program, Taiwan needs to invest in short- and medium-range air defenses that would prevent China from establishing air superiority over Taiwan's skies and would also impede PLA airborne forces from landing at key port and airfield facilities on the island. Taiwan also needs to make sure that it has large stockpiles of basic munitions—missiles, shells, rockets, and small-arms rounds—that are stored safely in reinforced bunkers or mountain caves, where they cannot be destroyed by the opening salvo of Chinese bombing or missile strikes.

It also needs to be ready to rapidly rig its ports for detonation to complicate their seizure and use for delivery of additional Chinese forces to Taiwan and to supply logistics to any landed invasion force. In the worst-case scenario, the Taiwanese government might have to order the rapid deployment of large obstructions—such as the scuttling of container ships—in the mouth of the critical Tamsui River. If Taiwanese national defense leaders dither too long in making such decisions, they could face disastrous consequences. Indeed, perhaps the most critical decision the Ukrainians made in the opening moments of the Russian invasion—aside from President Zelensky's inspiring choice to defiantly stay and fight in Kyiv—was the timely order to destroy the runways at Hostomel Airport near Kyiv in the early hours of the invasion, which prevented the Russian airborne forces from executing a landing operation at the airport and driving into Kyiv in an attempt to kill or capture key government leaders in a rapid decapitation strike. All of the subsequent well-documented problems regarding the unpreparedness of the Russian military to occupy Kyiv stem from that fateful and swift decision by Ukrainian forces to destroy their own infrastructure. Had the Hostomel airborne assault succeeded, Russia's war against Ukraine—and indeed, all of Ukraine—would be in a very different place today.

Taiwan also needs to invest more in the resiliency of its computer networks from cyber disruption, as well as ensuring it has redundant and resilient communications systems that would not be affected by cyber or space attacks. Given the overwhelming reliance of Taiwan's access to the internet on undersea cables—cables that China has already cut "accidentally" on multiple occasions—the Ministry of Digital Affairs must ensure that the internal communications on the island will remain up even if access to the rest of the world is severely degraded. Needless to say, the Taiwanese must also regularly exercise and practice for such a scenario. Luckily, as inaugural minister of digital affairs Audrey Tang, a former open-source software developer, told me, Taiwan "benefits" from numerous typhoons that impact communications and provide a natural opportunity to exercise disaster response. As she quipped, natural typhoons help the island to prepare against "Volt Typhoons," a reference to the Chinese state-sponsored hacker group that has been targeting critical infrastructure across the Indo-Pacific region. In turn, if Taiwan steps up, we need to as well. We should be planning for a Chinese invasion of Taiwan too—in part to discourage it!—and preparing for that possibility by pressuring Taiwan through our economic and military and diplomatic engagements to start doing the right things. For instance, Ukraine has been helped in its war by the deep US engagement with Ukraine's intelligence and military—deep partnerships and training exercises the United States does not currently maintain to the same extent with Taiwan, given America's long-standing half-in, half-out One China policy that prevents high-level engagement. Instead of feel-good high profile and provocative diplomatic visits by members of Congress to the island, such as the visit by then–House speaker Nancy Pelosi in 2022, which triggered a simulated blockade of Taiwan by China, it is much better to engage in low-key but more impactful engagements with the Taiwanese, such as military exchanges, joint planning, and undisclosed training exercises.

Elsewhere, we need to hold some pointed conversations with Europe, which has prevaricated in the last decade about its path between China and the United States, hoping that it won't have to choose. Specifically, there are some stark divides between Baltic countries like Lithuania, Estonia, and Latvia—which have taken strong principled stances against both Russia and China—and larger European countries, such as Germany and France, that have sent more mixed signals.

It is certainly the case that much of Western Europe does not share our interests in the Indo-Pacific. Political and business leaders in many of these countries have told me privately that they—not being Pacific powers themselves—see it as inevitable that China would one day conquer Taiwan and establish itself as the dominant power in Asia, and that they accept that outcome and would prefer to keep on trading with China and focusing on their own domestic economic interests. Many of them want nothing to do with our China rivalry. Consequently, we need convince the Europeans that it is not just in our interest to deter China, it is in theirs as well.

We must articulate that in the event of a war in the Indo-Pacific, Europe will not be able to sit on the sidelines. For one, if China retaliates against the US mainland, it would result in the triggering of the NATO Article 5 collective defense requirement and likely would bring NATO into a war with China.*

But even if the war is limited to the Indo-Pacific and European countries decide to sit it out militarily, Europe—and the rest of the world—will be massively affected economically. There certainly is not a circumstance in which most Western allies could continue normal trade with China while Americans and other Indo-Pacific allies—not

* Incredibly, European allies might have some wiggle room to avoid war even if China targets Hawaii. Article 6 of the NATO treaty defines it as covering only European and North American territories "in the Mediterranean Sea or the North Atlantic area north of the Tropic of Cancer," a definition that leaves out the fiftieth state. Indeed, since the 1960s the US State Department has admitted that the "collective defense" requirement wouldn't apply to attacks on Hawaii. This geographic loophole also allowed NATO to avoid getting drawn into the Falklands War between the United Kingdom and Argentina in 1982.

just potentially the Japanese but also Australians—are fighting and dying in the Pacific.

Europe would have no choice but to instantly decouple from China, as devastating as that would be for their economy, both financially and in terms of the disruption of daily life. Thus it is very much in the Continent's strategic interests, too, to avoid facing such turbulent choices by helping us deter China. Through my conversations with prime ministers and foreign ministers of European nations at the annual Munich Security Conference, it has become clear to me that we have not made this point forcefully enough, if at all. Most of them cannot imagine a world where the United States goes to war with China over Taiwan. What struck me most in those conversations in 2023, though, is how similar they were to the conversations I had—even with many of the same people—on the weekend of February 18 to 20 at the 2022 Munich Security Conference, just four days before Russia invaded Ukraine, and how many of my interlocutors also refused to believe that this would come to pass.

STRONG MEDICINE

Just as there's more we need to ask of certain allies, there's more the United States needs to do to support our partners. We have made life difficult for some of them, and we don't always back up our friends when we should. We need to make it easier for our friends to say yes to countering China.

When Canada followed our request to arrest Huawei's CFO, it quickly felt the consequences of that favor in the form of China's detention of the two Michaels. But beyond expressing verbal solidarity, the United States did not engage in any of the aggressive diplomacy one would expect had the two Canadian hostages held American passports—despite the fact that their detainment in China was a direct result of Canadian support for our policy. How can we expect allies to stand together with us in confronting Chinese aggression when we refuse to do the same for them? The Three Musketeers principle behind NATO's Article 5 mutual defense concept—"all for one and one for all"—needs to apply to more than just military invasion. We have to stand together with all of our partners—be it Canada, Australia, Lithuania, Norway, or the Philippines, which have all faced Chinese pressure and retaliation—and treat any aggression against them as if it were directed at us. That is not only the right moral choice and what should be expected of a true partner and friend, it is the only approach that will convince other countries to side with us in the competition against China.

Beyond ad hoc responses to these types of pressure on our friends when they stand up to China—especially but not only when they're acting at our request—we need to figure out a new alliance framework to deter such actions from China in the future. China needs to know that bullying won't work.

On the security front, there's little value in the Indo-Pacific in a replacement for SEATO, the twenty-year attempt to build a Southeast Asia alliance like NATO that ended in 1977 after never achieving a working military structure. (One British diplomat called the alliance a "zoo of paper tigers."[27]) Today, too many of the countries across the Indo-Pacific are already protected by bilateral security pacts with the United States to bother joining a larger formal security alliance. For example, given that both Japan and the Philippines have their own security pacts with the United States, it's not entirely clear what domestic political appetite there would be for, say, the Philippines to be treaty-bound to defend Japan if it is attacked.

Instead of a military security alliance in the Indo-Pacific, we should be looking to build a new—and global—economic security alliance. America should lead the way in creating a new organization—call it something like the Treaty of Allied Market Economies (TAME), an "economic NATO" alliance of European and Indo-Pacific nations with open-market economies. Together, the partners in this alliance would respond as a unified block to political and economic pressure from China—or any other economic aggressor, for that matter. The alliance's "Article 5" collective economic defense mechanism would trigger a combination of trade barriers, sanctions, and export controls that could be used in a coordinated manner to equalize pressure and retaliate against any aggressor unfairly singling out a member of the alliance. In some ways, this alliance would look similar to the coordinated but independent action that the West—including the UK, European Union, Canada, and Japan—took in levying unprecedented sanctions against Russia after its Ukraine invasion. As an additional carrot to joining such an alliance, like-minded members could all share increased trade benefits in the form of tariff cuts, regulatory cooperation, and enhanced investment terms. Beyond formal joint economic punishment of an aggressor, such an alliance could also plan for and commit to repairing and replacing real economic harms that member countries face when hit with retaliatory tariffs or trade wars—e.g., a promise by member states to make Australian lobstermen whole if their market in China is torn away. Such "trade diversion" often occurs in the market anyway. As one market closes, another opens—and we know that, in part, because of China's actions against Australia. Markets are adaptable and most goods can flow elsewhere, especially if protectionist tariffs don't stand in the way. It's why Australia, for instance, weathered some of China's aggressive moves better than anticipated. In particular, the Australian coal industry—which was also hit with punishing bans—turned out just fine because coal is such a fungible and high-demand product. "Once China banned imports of Australian coal in mid-2020, Chinese utilities had to turn to Russian and Indonesian suppliers instead. This, in turn, took Russian and Indonesian coal off the market, creating demand gaps in India, Japan, and South Korea—which Australia's stranded coal was able to fill," *Foreign Policy* noted. "The result of decoupling for one of Australia's core industries was therefore just a game of musical chairs—a rearrangement of who traded with whom, not a material injury."[28]

One of the reasons that NATO has never had to invoke Article 5 against another nation-state attack—the only time it's ever been used was after September 11 against al-Qaeda—is precisely because of how strong all other countries know the response from the combined NATO force would be. The same is true on the economic front. As Daleep Singh, a National Security Council official who helped coordinate the US response to Ukraine, says, "The best sanctions are the ones that never have to get used."[29] China might very well think twice before weaponizing its trading strength if it understood the combined—and severe—penalties it might face in taking such action and that even if it did launch a trade war, it wouldn't necessarily inflict much economic harm to begin with.

There's enough evidence of China's willingness to inflict economic pain for political gain across Asia and Europe that a well-crafted TAME organization would likely attract a long line of participants—many countries across the globe are becoming increasingly concerned about Chinese belligerent behavior, and there is safety in numbers. While it is unlikely that some large countries with significant economic dependence on China, such as France and Germany, would rush to join this new alliance, states that have already found themselves on the receiving end of Chinese coercion in the past—such as Australia, Norway, Sweden, Japan, the Czech Republic, Lithuania, the Philippines, and Taiwan itself, among others—are prime candidates for initial membership. Over time, as TAME membership grows in numbers, combined economic power, and market size, it will become a magnet too attractive for other market economies to avoid, especially if China continues to engage in brutish bullying tactics around the world. TAME creation, however, requires American leadership. The only way such an alliance can come into existence is if the United States—as the world's largest economic power—shows the way and commits using its enormous economic leverage over aggressor states like China on behalf of smaller aggrieved allied countries. Just like with NATO's sacred Article 5 commitment, only if we are willing to commit to sacrifice on behalf of others could we expect to receive reciprocal commitments from them.

GET WOULD-BE FRIENDS OFF THE FENCE

The Pacific and Indian Oceans represent the future of our geopolitical security and the world's economic center of gravity. Building a shared vision for the future of Asia among the nations that rim them will be among the most important projects facing the coming generations of US diplomats. Much like the "strong medicine" conversation the United States needs to have with Europeans to convince them that it is in their interest to deter China, we need to convince our Asian partners of the same truth.

A key counterbalance to China can be our broader relationships across Southeast Asia. Figuring out how to appeal to and partner with countries like Vietnam, Indonesia, and the Philippines—and position them alongside steady long-standing allies like South Korea and Japan—will be critical to creating the alliances China will notice. The United States has been pouring new resources and energy into the so-called Quad, our reinvigorated partnership with Japan, India, and Australia, and it's no coincidence that the we created in 2021 another new security pact, AUKUS, which includes Australia and the UK. AUKUS emerged as a tactical arms deal to provide Australia with nuclear-propelled submarines based on highly sensitive UK and US technology—a deal that unfolded after Australia opted out of procuring French diesel submarines. The original French deal had not only unattractive economics for Australia and limited national security benefits compared to the advantages of building a closer partnership with the world's primary superpower—the United States—but it had technical downsides as well. Nuclear submarines have much longer range and can operate underwater for much longer than traditional diesel submarines—nuclear subs are effectively limited only by the supplies of food and water on board. Diesel subs need to come up to the surface every few days to recharge batteries, which makes them more vulnerable to detection by overhead reconnaissance assets. AUKUS was originally formed as an important pact to enhance the submarine capabilities of Australia, a key ally in the Indo-Pacific, allowing it to contribute to overall security in the region. It has since been expanded to cover Australian investments in building additional shipyard capacity in the United States—itself a vital expansion of our defense industrial base—and the ability for US nuclear subs to permanently base in Australia, adding to our military assets in the region. It also now involves the joint development of other "military capabilities to promote security and stability in the Indo-Pacific region," capabilities that will include joint development of autonomous underwater vehicles, AI and autonomous weapons, hypersonic missiles, and electronic warfare tools, as well as the development of quantum technologies.[30]

The pivot to Southeast Asia should also heavily feature the strengthening of relations with India, another 1.4-billion-person country that aspires to global power status. The economic rise of India—the world's largest democracy—over the last quarter century has been remarkable, but in certain ways much more fraught and fragile than China's, beset as India is by greater internal political divisions and a challenging domestic political and religious landscape. Prime Minister Narendra Modi's summer 2023 state visit to Washington, DC, was marred by awkward questions about the backsliding of democracy under his leadership. Moreover, the Canadian government's accusation in the months following that the Indian intelligence services had orchestrated the assassination of a Canadian citizen in British Columbia—an immigrant involved in a separatist Sikh movement in India—threatened to unravel the slowly developing partnership between India and Western countries. But the truth is that both China and the United States have a vested economic interest in India's continued growth, with its huge emerging markets and rising consumerism providing new markets for industries. As the world's most populous country with a rapidly growing economy, India's geopolitical heft will continue to increase as the century progresses. India, which has its own nuclear arsenal, has made clear that it wants to triangulate its relations and pursue its own course to global power status. It is wary of China, wants international respect, and doesn't want to be vassal of the United States—nor, as India has made clear, does it want to be tied to a NATO-like Pacific security structure that would obligate it to act on our behalf. (After all, unlike the United States, India shares a sometimes tense land border with China.) At the same time, India is interested in Western military technologies; as it views China's growing naval effort in the South China Sea and its own namesake ocean with great suspicion, it is keen to modernize its own sea capabilities, like submarines and advanced surface ships. The United States can provide more defensive weapons and deeper military integration, as well as a closer economic integration, including lowering of trade tariffs and ensuring India is treated more like an equal partner. Already, the Pentagon is touting a rapidly deepening partnership with the Indian military; as one US official told a briefing, "We now have working groups on everything ranging from cyberspace and critical technologies to maritime security, and India is leading in those forums together with the U.S. and like-minded partners."[31]

That mix of wariness and desire for a secure independence is shared by other countries in the region, like Vietnam, the Philippines, and Singapore. They see the benefits of closer cooperation with the United States, but they want to conduct it on equal terms—even if they don't have the power or scale to dictate terms that India might. Thus, securing the Indo-Pacific region will necessitate the construction of fruitful concentric circles of partners, where we recognize individual strengths and needs of each country to build a shared vision for the future of Asia.

Across the Pacific, the United States is scrambling to make up for lost time and repair long-ignored relationships. Indonesia is the world's fourth most populous country, and for decades we barely had a strategy for dealing with it. The United States is reentering engagement with Indonesia with baggage from its shameful support of Indonesia's brutal dictator Suharto and his death squads—a regime that from 1968 to 1998 killed at least five hundred thousand and perhaps as many as a million Indonesians. However, China's brutishness is also making Jakarta much more wary of Beijing. From China Coast Guard vessels blocking Indonesian oil exploration in the South China Sea in 2021 to Chinese fishing boats hoovering up fish in what Indonesia considers its Exclusive Economic Zone near the northern Natuna Islands, there are plenty of irritants in that bilateral relationship for the United States to exploit. Doubling down on investments in Indonesia, encouraging migration of Western factories from China to Indonesia and other regional countries through more favorable tariff and tax treatments, building partnerships on the exploration and processing of its nickel reserves (the world's largest) and other critical materials: all of these are opportunities we should seize to build closer partnerships with a nation that will undoubtedly play a big economic role in the twenty-first century.

Officials in the Biden administration have been hopscotching across the Pacific, from Fiji to Vanuatu, and opened a new embassy in the Kingdom of Tonga. But the results have been mixed, in part because of our own political challenges. In May 2023 the congressional brinksmanship over the federal debt limit led Biden to cancel a planned visit to Papua New Guinea, a stop that would have made him the first-ever US president to visit the Pacific island, where he was supposed to meet with leaders of eighteen islands. Secretary of State Antony Blinken went in Biden's stead and proclaimed, "America's future is here in the Pacific."[32]

Sometimes, our outreach occurs too late. For example, in March 2023 US officials were stunned by a draft agreement between China and the Solomon Islands that appeared to open the islands to Chinese military bases and stipulated that the nine-hundred-island chain would rely on Chinese help in dealing with security challenges. Former Australian prime minister Kevin Rudd called the move "the worst Australian security-policy failure in the South Pacific since World II, almost certainly making Chinese warships a more permanent feature in the Coral Sea."[33]

The key strategy for winning these countries—or, if not fully bringing them to our side, at least keeping them out of China's pocket—is to emphasize a very simple message: *China is only out for China, it is driven by a Hobbesian, zero-sum view of geopolitics.* The United States and our Western allies are self-interested too, sure, but we play for the good of a larger global security order. This is not a battle of democracy versus authoritarianism, or communism versus capitalism, this is a battle over a predictable, secure, rules-based future versus bowing to China's whims. After all, while our overly moralistic messaging of democracy and human rights promotion may play well at home in Western countries, it often goes over like a lead balloon in much of the rest of the world. In contrast, no country and no people—regardless of their preferred system of government—want to be taken advantage of on the international stage. It's in that fundamental contrast—China's rule by law versus the Western rule of law—that we have a tremendous opportunity to highlight China's neocolonialism and self-serving debt-trap engagements. This is not as a hard message to deliver as it might have been even a few years ago, given the bribery scandals and failing infrastructure stories that have increasingly become associated with the Belt and Road Initiative.

But as we build up our own reputation, it is also vital to take down China's. We should not miss an opportunity in our diplomatic engagements around the world to talk about China's territorial disputes, aggressive actions in the Indo-Pacific region, and violations of major political agreements. Examples are legion, from the decades-early unwinding of the "One Country Two Systems" agreement with the British following the transfer of Hong Kong to the 2016 UNCLOS arbitration tribunal ruling over Philippines maritime rights in the South China Sea. Other Chinese behavior that should concern many nations around the world includes its support for Russia in its illegal invasion of Ukraine, detention and prosecution of Uyghur Muslims in Xinjiang, failure to deliver quality projects via its Belt and Road Initiative infrastructure, and more. Many countries around the world are suspicious of America and Europe—not least because of our various shameful histories of slavery and colonialism. But this is not a battle for perfection. Other countries do not need to love us (as much as we would like them to) and most of them, for reasons good and bad, never will. But as long as they hate China more, they may prefer to partner with us.

We must act like—and actually be—the more trustworthy partner, the one it's easy to say yes to.

CHAPTER 9

Step Four—Say No to Distractions

IN FOREIGN POLICY CIRCLES, THERE'S ALMOST NO MORE CUTTING joke than "the Asia Pivot." During his time in the White House, Barack Obama—raised in Indonesia and Hawaii—laid claim to being "the first Pacific president," deploying the phrase throughout a trip to Asia in November 2009. In fall 2011 he and Secretary of State Hillary Clinton embraced what they hoped would be a sweeping change in American geopolitics, reorienting the country from its long-standing transatlantic focus to the east. In October 2011 Clinton declared the era "America's Pacific Century" in a *Foreign Policy* article, saying, "The future of politics will be decided in Asia, not Afghanistan or Iraq, and the United States will be right at the center of the action."[1] The following month, during another trip to Asia, Obama formally declared a "Pivot to Asia," one that would be marked by the new Trans-Pacific Partnership trade agreement and US engagement in the East Asia Summit. "Our enduring interests in the region demand our enduring presence in the region. The United States is a Pacific power, and we are here to stay," Obama told the Australian parliament. "So let there be no doubt: In the Asia-Pacific in the 21st century, the United States of America is all in."[2]

And for a short time, the pivot seemed real, supported by new trade agreement with South Korea, deployments of US Marines to Australia, a new first-in-a-half-century trip by the secretary of state to Myanmar, and more. A few weeks after Clinton's trip, North Korean dictator Kim Jong Il died, a transition that only underscored the extent to which Asia, and East Asia specifically, seemed now to be the global center of gravity. In 2012 Clinton embarked on another historic visit (this time to Laos), and Obama himself that year became the first sitting US president to visit Cambodia and Myanmar.

But then reality interceded. Month after month, year after year, the Obama administration seemed to be pulled back to Europe and the Middle East. There was the civil war in Syria, the attack on the US consulate in Benghazi, the Russian seizure of Crimea and fomentation of an insurgency in eastern Ukraine, the rise of ISIS, the Saudi war against Yemen, and more. Much as the United States struggled to escape the pull of events elsewhere in the world and maintain the focus on Asia, the results were not promising. The Trump administration tried, too, to "Pivot to Asia," with a similarly mixed record of success. There's a likely apocryphal story about how, when asked for his view of Western civilization, Mahatma Gandhi replied, "It would be a very good idea." During a rooftop dinner at Arizona State University's Washington, DC, campus in 2019, Jake Sullivan—who had helped launch the Obama effort eight years earlier—updated the joke: when asked about the Asia Pivot, he replied, "It would be a very good idea."

And so it was that almost exactly a decade after Obama's Australia speech that an October 2021 NPR headline read, "Long Promised and Often Delayed, the 'Pivot to Asia' Takes Shape under Biden."[3] It was going to be a centerpiece, in fact, of the Biden administration's winter 2022 release of its comprehensive National Defense Strategy. But then another speed bump: a land war broke out in Europe. The Biden administration ended up delaying the release of the National Defense Strategy for months. And then, in October 2023, the barbaric

Hamas terror attacks on Israel lit the Middle East on fire in yet another major conflict.

THE UNITED STATES WILL NEVER BE ABLE TO FULLY ESCAPE ENGAGEment with the rest of the world—between its far-ranging commercial and security interests, the country remains (and should remain!) too central to too many multilateral institutions, international alliances, security agreements, trade routes, and geographic regions to focus only on the Pacific. While it is critical to marshal as many of our diplomatic, economic, and military resources as possible to confront the top challenge of our century—avoiding a catastrophic war with China while preserving our dominant position in the Indo-Pacific—we cannot completely ignore other global problems. But we do need to change *how* we think about those problems and challenges.

Much as the United States organized its foreign policy during Cold War I around countering the Soviet Union ideologically and militarily, we need in the coming decades to view the rest of the world through a simpler lens than we do today. Namely, we should be closely reevaluating our entanglements in Europe, the Middle East, and Latin America, and asking the question: Does this impact our ability to contain and deter China or does it distract us from that critical objective?

This is about making hard choices we haven't forced ourselves to make over the last generation. America needs to admit it can't do everything and can't be everywhere. Just as we need to emphasize saying yes to our friends, making it easy for countries to ally with us and counter and blunt China, we need to be more focused about saying no to distractions. We need a stronger focus on evaluating core interests and identifying what's at the heart of our partnerships and alliances around the world and to treat other questions in foreign policy not as one-offs but through the lens of dealing with China.

The most prominent of these questions, of course, concern the three other perennial members of the adversary club: Russia, Iran, and North Korea. Saying no to distractions doesn't mean ignoring or capitulating to their demands—but it does mean being cognizant that those three countries present much smaller challenges to America and our leadership in the world than China does, especially if we manage to successfully separate our dreams and desires from actual core interests. They are second-tier powers that can cause significant regional problems, but not global trouble, and we need to be better about recognizing this fact. We should not ignore the important security threats all three pose in their own way—but we must zero in our attention on resolving and stabilizing the geopolitical rivalry of those three relationships so we can focus our sustained attention on China.

Most importantly of all, we must also reevaluate and view our engagement with Russia through the lens of countering China.

The last thirty years have witnessed Russia's failure (and, frankly, unwillingness) to anchor itself in the West. Unlike the cases of Germany and Japan, which landed on stable perches in the Western order after being vanquished during World War II, the United States tried to cater to Moscow's craving for respect following its loss in Cold War I by inviting Russia to join the G-7 club of developed nations (it has since been kicked out) and by establishing the NATO Russia Permanent Joint Council in 1997 to assuage the Russian Federation's concerns about NATO enlargement in eastern Europe. As late as 2009 Hillary Clinton touted a possible "reset" with Russia, presenting Foreign Minister Sergey Lavrov with a red button intended to be labeled "reset." The fact that the Russian word on the button, *peregruzka*, actually meant "overload" ended up being prescient, as despite all the Western engagement Russia continued to nurse its various grievances, succumbing to toxic nationalism and imperialism.

US policymakers should nevertheless appreciate that Russia—the world's ninth most populous country, one that encompasses 11 percent of the world's landmass, a territory almost twice as large as the world's second-largest country by landmass, Canada—is not likely to disappear and that we need a strategy for managing that relationship, if for no other reason than to reduce tensions between the two largest nuclear states while making it more difficult for China to benefit from Russia's weakness. Of course the United States would love to see a democratic Russia, its transformation into a country anchored in the Western alliance, one that doesn't threaten its European neighbors and participates fully and cooperatively in trade partnerships, respects human rights and the rule of law at home and abroad, and develops a practicing free press and robust civil society. That, after all, was the dream that some harbored throughout the 1990s and early 2000s, but it was always just that, a dream—one never attainable even during the best times of the relatively friendly Boris Yeltsin.

As much as history has begun to mythologize the Yeltsin thaw, it's worth remembering he opposed our policies on Iraq, Iran, and Kosovo (not to mention the expansion of NATO) and demonstrated highly corrupt and antidemocratic tendencies from the start of his tenure. Instead, the reality that the foreign policy community has long refused to confront—a refusal that continued right up until Russia launched its self-defeating and genocidal invasion of Ukraine in 2022—is that our geopolitical interests are not compatible with Russia's, regardless of who is sitting in the Kremlin.

Too often we tend to personalize politics, thinking that if only there can be a leadership change at the top of another nation, a geopolitical relationship can be drastically altered. But such shifts rarely occur since countries have core interests that persist even across leadership transitions. Paradigm-altering leaders are the exception rather than the rule on the global stage. Post-Soviet Russia remained a significant diplomatic irritant, even under Yeltsin's leadership, and post-Saddam Iraq hasn't become the key ally in the Middle East that the George W. Bush administration predicted.

We mistakenly view the radical change that takes place under leaders like Mikhail Gorbachev as entirely the result of their personality, when in fact their remarkable leadership reflects the emergence of the right person at a unique moment when societal change is already under way. Dramatic shifts in national posture and policy are usually driven less by personality than by the recognition of fundamental change in a geopolitical or domestic situation. Soviet foreign policy dramatically changed direction when Gorbachev took over from the previous geriatric Communist Party secretaries Chernenko (1984–1985), Andropov (1982–1984), and Brezhnev (1964–1982). Gorbachev never wanted to lose Cold War I to the United States, nor did he want the collapse of the Soviet Union, but he recognized when arriving in the Kremlin in 1985 that the system had atrophied and was collapsing under the weight of economic inefficiency, corruption, unaffordable military spending on the Afghanistan war, and the arms race. He tried to reform the system from within—with the *perestroika* and *glasnost* programs—and adjust the foreign policy by building a better relationship with the Reagan administration to pause the unaffordable arms race, but in the end he lost it all: Cold War I, the Soviet Union, and his own position. He took these gambles and actions not because he was seeking to tear down the Iron Curtain and embrace a market economy by pursuing a radically different domestic and foreign policy, but precisely because he felt these changes were necessary and his best chance to preserve the status quo—the Soviet Union, the Warsaw Pact, and the communist system itself.

Today, we have to appreciate that regardless of who replaces Putin—and someday someone will—Russia's core interest in attempting to dominate its near-abroad will almost surely be sustained across leadership transitions. Russia's centuries-old pursuit of being a great power to be respected and reckoned with on the world stage is deeply rooted in the Russian psyche—it's a feeling that dates back to at least the times of Ivan the Great, the first self-proclaimed tsar, who ended the Mongol-Tatar domination of Russia in 1480 and, following the fall of Constantinople to the Ottoman Empire in 1453, adopted the idea of Moscow as the third Rome. It was reinvigorated and permanently seared into Russian mindset by Peter the Great, the first self-proclaimed Russian emperor, who Westernized and modernized Russia, turned it into a naval power, and defeated one of the great powers of the day, Sweden, thereby expanding the Russian empire to capture today's Baltic states of Estonia and Latvia, as well as parts of modern Finland and modern Ukraine. This imperialistic drive has survived the tsars, the Russian Revolution and rise of the Bolsheviks, and the Soviet Communist Party. It will very likely survive Putin too.

Two generations of Russian elites have refused to come to terms with the country's diminished post-Soviet stature. While we often cite

Russia's renewed international aggression as dating to Putin, it's worth remembering that in December 1992, Russian foreign minister Andrei V. Kozyrev stood before European foreign ministers in Stockholm and blasted them with a Cold War–style diatribe, threatening that Russia would force former Soviet republics to join a new Moscow-led alliance. Secretary of State Lawrence S. Eagleburger later said he had "heart palpitations" listening to the speech, and the ministers were only let in on the joke a half hour later, when Kozyrev returned to the podium and said "just kidding," explaining the speech was meant to illustrate the Russia the world would face if right-wing nationalists took power in Moscow.[4*]

Regardless of how Putin meets his statistically and actuarially inevitable end, Russia is not likely to transform into a liberal democracy in the foreseeable future. Nor is it clear that even if Putin falls ill or is cast aside that the next leader of Russia would be any better, more cooperative, or more open to Western ideals. Those choices are ultimately up to the Russians themselves and our ability to influence them has always been and will remain extremely limited. And even if such an unlikely scenario were to come to pass, we must recognize that even a liberal reformist Russian president would undoubtedly continue to pursue policies that are seen as being in the interest of preserving Russian greatness and independent power on the international stage as demanded by the Russian populace and elites, strategies and goals that will inevitably bring almost any future imaginary Russia into tension with America. No Russian president—no matter if they are an authoritarian dictator or a Russian version of Thomas Jefferson—would willingly and happily accept being a junior and relatively powerless partner or ally to the Western alliance. For that to happen, Russia would have to come to terms with its own loss of geopolitical power, something that it has shown little interest in doing. Thus, the United States needs to accept that we may be dealing with an aggressive and recalcitrant Russia for many decades—maybe even longer.

---

* Kozyrev eventually found the course of Russian politics disconcerting enough in the twenty-first century that he relocated to America.

At the same time, Russia is too big and geopolitically important as a major nuclear power to turn it into a permanent, isolated international pariah. Nor, as examples of perennial irritants and troublemakers from North Korea to Iran show, is that necessarily a productive path in the first place. After all, seventy years of attempted isolation of North Korea—a tiny and much less developed country in comparison to Russia—have not only not led to the transformation of its brutal dictatorial regime but indeed have made the regime more threatening as it acquired nuclear weapons and land- and submarine-based ICBMs to deliver them. It's hard to imagine that any similar effort to isolate Russia is a sound long-term solution that will create a less threatening Russia. Instead, as Russia, increasingly cut off from the West, becomes beholden to China as a trade partner and key international patron, we're watching an intriguing unequal relationship develop—one that just may present a unique opportunity one day. Russia has already diverted flows of energy and mineral exports from past markets in Europe to China, its consumers are increasingly reliant on Chinese imports that have replaced no longer accessible Western ones, and Chinese currency is playing a major role in transactions on Moscow's stock exchange. These changes, and others, are giving Beijing growing influence over Moscow and turning Russia effectively into a vassal state of China—a geopolitical reality that will eventually become a major irritant to Russian leaders and populations alike.[*5]

For all the rhetoric among Russian Moscow- and St. Petersburg–based elites over the past decade about Russia's "Turn to the East," they continue to see themselves as European and not Asian, and so the only thing worse in their minds than being a junior partner to the West would be being in a position of subservience to China. After all, not many Russians are rushing to teach their kids Mandarin instead of the traditional

* It is also a notable—and historically fraught—reversal of roles, given that the Soviet Union spent decades viewing communist China as its own "poorer cousin." "Beijing sees its relationship with Moscow as being of paramount importance for several reasons," Alexander Gabuev writes in *Foreign Affairs*. "Their economic relationship is perfectly complementary: Russia is rich in natural resources but needs technology and investments, while China can offer technology and investments but needs natural resources."

foreign-language choices of English, French, or German, and few are interested in vacations or real-estate investments in China when they're used to France, Italy, or Spain. Even as they have found European vacation and shopping destinations increasingly difficult to access due to sanctions, Russians are flocking in droves to Istanbul and Dubai, not to China. (Cultural exchanges between the two countries also remain fairly limited.) Thus, the current warm relationship between Moscow and Beijing is not only a historical aberration—the two countries have fought numerous territorial conflicts, the last one wrapping up as recently as 1969, when Vladimir Putin was eighteen—but one that is merely a political expediency for both countries. Their marriage of convenience today is a simple joining of forces to confront their mutual adversary—the Western alliance led by the United States. It is not necessarily particularly durable. Beijing has already begun to drive a hard bargain with Moscow, taking advantage of its need to sell energy to negotiate substantial discounts, as well as refusing to overtly supply large quantities of desperately needed weapons and ammunition for Russia to use in its war on Ukraine. To date, China has tolerated Russia's independent relations with India and Vietnam and grudgingly respected the Kremlin's significant role in Central Asia, but as China comes to understand and wield its enormous leverage over Russia, it will seek to shape Russian foreign policy in ways that serve its own interests. As Sergey Radchenko and I wrote in *Foreign Affairs*, "such heavy-handed Chinese policy will give the Russian political establishment ample reason to rethink their own inveterate hostility toward the West. Moscow will eventually recognize that it can extend its international influence and increase its leverage with other powers (including China) by restraining its aggressive impulses in Europe."[6] How or when that scenario comes to pass, and whether Putin is atop the government then, is still unknown, but it's hard not to think that in the not-too-distant future Russian elites will realize that Chinese coercion will only hasten Russia's collapse as a great power.

As we await that recognition, Washington should "encourage Russians to at least imagine a future in which Russia is an influential, independent player on the global stage that seeks to peacefully and profitably coexist with the West," Radchenko and I wrote.[7] Our goal is not to bring Russia in from the cold and turn it into an ally against China—such "reverse Kissinger" moves are unattainable dreams that Russia has no interest in playing along with—but instead to foster Russian neutrality, a geopolitical state wherein Russia stands as a non-aligned independent force equidistant from the West and China. To achieve that end, the United States must communicate to Russia what it already knows to be true: China is merely looking after its own interests and cares about Russia only insofar as Russia is an instrument to achieve China's goals. We can appeal to Russians' sense of their own country's historical greatness by highlighting to them the benefits of an independent path, one that doesn't turn them into a junior partner or adversary of either the West or China. The carrot we can offer is a renewed economic and security relationship with the West, a relationship Russia can use to balance its trade and security dealings with Beijing and reduce China's leverage over the medium and long term. But to benefit from those rewards, the Russian Federation must permanently end its aggression against Ukraine and cease threatening other neighboring countries. We must be mindful that Russia may never become a true democracy with a rule of law, free and open press, and independent judiciary, but such a high bar should not be a precondition for a Russia that is willing to participate in the wider world in a cooperative and nondestructive way. In some ways, the US goal when it comes to Russia remains, after seventy-five years, what George Kennan articulated at the start of Cold War I: the US must once again embark on a strategy of "patient but firm and vigilant containment of Russian expansive tendencies." As Kennan himself recognized, "the Soviet Union will not last, but Russia will."[8]

We need to realistically identify our long-term interests regarding Russia and work toward that goal. At a minimum, we want Russia to be a country that obeys and participates in international norms—not invading its neighbors, not using chemical or radiological weapons for assassinations, and not undermining democracy abroad through cyber and covert intelligence operations. Russia is unlikely ever to be our friend, but it also doesn't need to be our enemy—in fact, we can continue to have significant disagreements and conflicts in the diplomatic and geopolitical realms. The goal, rather, should be to keep those disagreements from triggering actual conflict—either directly with us or with our partners and allies.

There are, moreover, many areas where we need Russian engagement. We're not going to solve climate change without addressing Russian fossil fuel use and extraction; we're not going to open up the Arctic and the Northern Passage trade routes to Asia without Russia; we're not going to keep the Iranian and North Korean threats under control without Russian assistance. Most importantly, the world will become a much more dangerous place if the United States and Russia are unable to showcase leadership in the area of nuclear weapons arms control and adhere to their commitments to ban the testing of nuclear weapons. Should that long-standing arms-control regime fall, more and more states are likely to procure nuclear weapons—dramatically increasing the risk of a world-changing nuclear conflict.

Fortunately for the United States, the poor leadership of Yeltsin and Putin has destroyed Russia's ability to present an existential conventional threat to the West either economically or militarily. By being unwilling or incapable of confronting their country's runaway corruption and its reliance on an economy built on extractive industries—fossil fuels like oil and gas, yes, but also other materials like aluminum, nickel, gold, and diamonds—they've condemned Russia to the fate of a shrinking economic power; the war in Ukraine on top of ongoing corruption has caused Western business to think twice about operating inside Russia, just as it has jolted Europe to diversify the continent's energy sources away from reliance on Russian oil and gas. All of these are moves that will reduce Putin's ability to coerce Europe. Moreover, the war in Ukraine has demonstrated the extent to which corruption and the atrophying of military leadership over the past several decades have doomed Putin's military reforms and wasted hundreds of billions of dollars. Tactically, the Russian military has shown itself incapable of modern combined-arms combat and has been forced to rely on contract mercenaries like the Wagner Group and its recruitment of convicts for human-wave attacks for the little success it has been able to achieve. It will take Russia a generation, under the best of economic circumstances (which are obviously not what it faces today) to rebuild and restock the decimated Russian military, which has lost thousands of tanks, armored vehicles, and artillery pieces, as well as hundreds of fighter aircraft and helicopters.

Now, with a much stronger hand than the United States or Europe had even five years ago, we need to ensure that Russia—which from 2014 to 2022 has managed in so many instances to wrest our attention from the east—doesn't continue to distract us from dealing with China.

Obviously, we cannot pull out of Europe or abandon Ukraine (as some China hawks, like John Mearsheimer have argued we should), as such a drastic move would both endanger our Russia containment policy and make it much harder to extract help and concessions from European countries when it comes to confronting China—a continent that feels abandoned and overwhelmed is hardly one happy to help us elsewhere. We must achieve a balance and view our steps against Russia through the lens of the fight with China. This strategy calls for several key steps: continuing to provide military aid to Ukraine to help it defend itself against current or future Russian aggression; enabling and strengthening our allies, like Baltic and eastern European states, to allow them to feel secure against any possible threat from Russia; and setting the terms for future Russian engagement.

The Ukrainian military is undergoing a crash course in the modernization of its arsenal, doctrine, and training according to NATO standards, while simultaneously fighting a brutal war against Russian invaders. They have fought admirably and courageously, defending their country from being overtaken by the Russians and clawing back a lot of the territory originally captured. But our task of helping Ukraine transform what used to be a backward Soviet military into a potent NATO-aligned fighting force is not yet over. While much has already been done to supply Ukraine's army with Western armored vehicles, tanks, and artillery pieces, as well as shift the country to Western short- and medium-range air defense systems, more work remains to transform its air force away from obsolete Soviet-era MiG and Sukhoi fighter jets to Western platforms such as the American F-16 and Swedish Saab JAS 39 Gripen. The Ukrainian Navy must also develop capabilities to deter the Russian Black Sea fleet from threatening Ukraine's coastline and enforcing blockades against the vital ports of Odesa and Izmail. Not all of this can be done by the United States—we have to prioritize critical capabilities, such as anti-ship missile stockpiles, for the potential fight in Asia—but we can do more to help secure for Ukraine other foreign-made anti-ship cruise missiles that are of no use to us, such as the French Exocet or Turkish ATMACA cruise missiles.

We must also push Ukraine to invest in its own indigenous defense industry. Prior to 2022 Ukraine was on the verge of making great progress toward developing its own Hrim-2 short-range ballistic missile, a weapon with a reported five hundred kilometer range, as well as the Neptune anti-ship missile, which was successfully used to sink the Russian cruiser *Moskva* in April 2022. With financial support from the West, Ukraine can and must build significant stockpiles of these systems to increase its own security and conventional deterrence. I was shocked during my visit to a military drone factory in Kyiv in the summer of 2023 to witness a single machinist there, wearing a T-shirt and flip-flops, working to produce only one military drone a month. Ukraine surely can and must do better than that in mobilizing its economy and population to produce critical munitions—drones, missiles, and artillery shells. In addition to providing durable security for the country, a stronger indigenous Ukrainian defense industry can become an important source of economic prosperity for the war-ravaged country as it can market its weapons systems for export, having demonstrated their efficacy on the battlefield against Russia.

Similarly, it is important to reassure other countries bordering Russia or Russian occupied territories—from the Baltic states, Poland, and Romania to Transnistria in Moldova—of their own security against potential Russian invasion. To date, these countries have little faith in the ability or willingness of the major European powers Germany and France to defend them, and so it is important for us to deploy small battalion-size, trip wire–style units—ideally jointly with other NATO partners—to these countries to assure them that the United

States is committed to their defense. In exchange, we should ask for their help in confronting Chinese economic aggression—perhaps by joining TAME, our proposed economic alliance, and by reducing their own dependence on China in critical national security areas like telecommunications.

Looking ahead, we need to start to define what we want from a new relationship with Russia—what steps can Moscow take to reenter the global economy and reengage with the future? We have to put options on the table—they may not take them up today, they may not take them up two years from now, but they may do so in ten years—and define, openly and explicitly, that our current sanctions and export controls are not going to be in place forever. Our goal is not to destroy a country with 140 million people and turn Russia into permanent adversary. Instead, we need to outline the rules of the road that we expect Russia to abide by—an outline that could include harsh steps, like reparations to Ukraine and verifiable destruction of chemical weapons, but that nonetheless includes a balanced selection of carrots and sticks necessary to chart a future with Russia.

Part of that roadmap has to be deep engagement with a future generation of Russians—including the provision of visas and educational opportunities for those who might find themselves in positions of power at home a generation from now. And, taking into consideration those who don't ever want to return home, are highly educated, and can contribute as immigrants to the building of our own country, we should make it easier for Russians to settle in the United States and help advance our economy and scientific knowledge.

Building that roadmap for future engagement is critical, in fact, to undermining Putin's main argument to his country—that the West is out to destroy Russia—and, longer-term, softening his hold on power. We need to build a counternarrative that says we're willing to sit down and talk whenever Russia is ready to reverse course and drop its imperial ambitions.

So where do our interests align? One obvious area is limiting stockpiles of nuclear weapons through renegotiating the last strategic arms control treaty—a START II treaty. Addressing climate change, from the Arctic to the green energy revolution, is another area where we must cooperate. Even if Russia stops being a major exporter of carbon fuels, it is going to continue being a massive exporter of aluminum, nickel, palladium, titanium—all critical ingredients we need for any transition to green technology and for enabling advanced manufacturing. A surprising number of US industries and manufacturers are actually reliant on Russian resources, from solar panels to nuclear power. Boeing would love to keep buying Russian titanium; the semiconductor industry needs neon gas that it had been purchasing from Russia and Ukraine prior to the war. Without steady and predictable access to Russian resources, many of the key aspects of daily life will quickly become uneconomical. That, though, is also an opportunity: we can work to encourage and turn Russia into a major provider to the world of natural resources that are not destroying the planet but actually helping to save it. That's good for them. That's good for us. And it will be bad for China.

THERE ARE ALMOST NO COUNTRIES IN THE WORLD THAT THE AVERage American misunderstands more than Iran and North Korea, dictatorships in a multidecade-long pursuit of nuclear weapons. Both exist in the American mind as caricatures—one a backward regime led by fanatical mullahs, hell-bent on destroying Israel, the other a Potemkin personality cult led by a brutal but goofy dictator with a missile fetish and bad fashion sense. In both cases, the caricatures lead us to misunderstand the countries and what matters to their rulers.

In this regard, we face the challenge of two brutal regimes that have come to believe—rightly or wrongly—that their hold on power is dependent in part on their virulent anti-Americanism. By portraying their countries as being in an existential fight with the "evil imperialist Americans," they attempt to distract their populations from the terrible economic problems they face on a day-to-day basis. Both are also driven by extreme insecurities—they are convinced that the United States is pursuing a policy of regime change, a belief reinforced by our historical proclivities for such missions, as well as by our periodic and often counterproductive global democracy-promotion rhetoric, which they see as directed at weakening their dictatorial rule. It is doubtful that we can change these mindsets and situation in the foreseeable future, so our policy toward both countries needs to be focused on protecting our allies and minimizing the criminal and destabilizing activity that these regimes engage in across the world—whether it's Iran's extensive support to terrorist groups across the Middle East or North Korea's arms trafficking, currency counterfeiting, or cryptocurrency theft.

Architecting future relations with North Korea and Iran will involve some hard choices and recognizing that both countries are, effectively, permanent nuclear or nuclear-threshold states, as is the case with Iran. For decades, the United States has pretended to ignore North Korea achieving nuclear power status—even though the DPRK is now moving steadily toward building at least two legs of a nuclear triad, land- and submarine-launched ICBMs. And now the bungling of JCPOA, the Iran nuclear deal, has placed Iran within easy shot of its own nuclear weapons. We have to appreciate that in the history of the nuclear age, no nuclear power with operational and deliverable nuclear weapons has ever relinquished them. (Ukraine, Belarus, Kazakhstan, and South Africa—the only countries to have ever given up these weapons—either had no operational control over them, as was the case with Ukraine, Belarus, and Kazakhstan, or they didn't have a delivery system, as was the case of South Africa.) But even if there was a roadmap to denuclearizing, both Iran and North Korea actually believe their hold on power and regional security is contingent on their nuclear ambitions, and US foreign policy—unintentionally—has done much to confirm these concerns in the twenty-first century. Both Iran and North Korea see the US efforts of Iraq and Libya as case studies for what they want to avoid; in Iraq, we got Saddam Hussein to give up his nuclear program after the 1991 Gulf War and then invaded his country again in 2003 and allowed Iraqis to execute him, and in Libya, we got Muammar Gaddafi to give up his nuclear program in 2003 and then armed and supported the rebels who overthrew his regime and ultimately brutally killed him.

North Korea, in particular, has a significant nuclear arsenal—and any hope that we ever might have had to change or prevent that is long past. North Korea detonated its first nuclear bomb in 2006 and in 2017 was able to test a thermonuclear hydrogen bomb; today, it's estimated to have around fifty bombs and a large missile arsenal to deliver them, with ICBMs that could reach US territory (although the accuracy of those weapons is questionable at best).

The good news is that two decades of North Korea as a de facto nuclear weapons power has not significantly altered the security situation in Asia. It did not, contrary to some predictions, cause South Korea or Japan to go nuclear—in no small measure due to their belief in the US security guarantees. Nor did it make North Korea an appreciably more respected or powerful state in the region. It also, importantly, did not make the DPRK significantly more bellicose—at least by the special sliding scale of North Korean rhetorical standards. The last act of North Korean aggression against South Korea that resulted in loss of life was its sinking of the naval corvette ROKS *Cheonan* and the artillery shelling of Yeonpyeong Island in 2010—an event the United Nations called one of most significant since the 1953 Korean War armistice and which resulted in the deaths of around fifty people, including two civilians. Notably, though, this incident took place under the rule of Kim Jong Il, and his son Kim Jong Un, who took over from his father in 2011, has not repeated such active aggression even as he's engaged in highly bellicose and colorful rhetoric and a major conventional and nuclear military buildup.

Within this context, it is clear that denuclearizing North Korea is not a realistic policy. Our priority going forward with North Korea must be to make sure that we maintain a credible deterrent in the region to defend our allies—especially South Korea and Japan—and that we also contain to the best of our ability North Korean ambitions to engage in illicit arms trafficking, currency counterfeiting, and bank and cryptocurrency thefts.

Ironically, the Trump administration showed that the United States can sit down in bilateral and high-level talks with North Korea. The world didn't end. We can have a tough negotiation but need to think through what the goals of that negotiation should be. True, the Trump administration set out too aggressively, pretending that denuclearization was a realistic end goal, whereas we need to acknowledge that nuclear weapons are a fundamental internal and external security guarantor of the Kim family's brutal dictatorship.

Our goal with North Korea should be simple: reduce tensions on the peninsula, specifically those related to the threats posed to South Korea and Japan by North Korean missile programs and acts of blackmail. This may be done by offering North Korea economic integration and investments in return for verifiable agreements on nonproliferation of nuclear and missile technology to other states, a ban on atmosphere-polluting nuclear testing, a framework for a responsible and nonthreatening testing of long-range missiles, and a mutual scaling down of the military presence on the DMZ.

Our focus needs to be on reintegrating of North Korea into the society of nations and accepting that, while we may abhor the regime and its treatment of its citizens, our ultimate and driving goal is to reduce the chance of war on the peninsula and the attendant risk to US public and strategic interests worldwide.*

Similarly, much of North Korea's misbehavior in cyberspace—including frequent global bank robberies, financial frauds, ransomware schemes, and other destructive and malicious operations—and its prolific global counterfeiting, arms trafficking, and drug trafficking operations all comprise criminal activity designed to procure funds for a regime that's cut off from all normal economic trade, banking systems, and commerce. We need that behavior to stop, and the economic integration offered in a deal like this—with the possibilities of tourism, trade, and industrial production drawing on North Korea's rich mining resources—would offer a path to providing the regime with much-needed cash in ways that contribute to the global economy rather than undermine it.

---

* Success may even allow for the United States to scale back and withdraw some of the twenty-seven thousand American troops that have been a presence in South Korea over a period of decades, a deployment that causes tensions with the South Korean population and comes at a high annual financial cost.

Global reintegration with North Korea would—we hope—lead to improved lives for North Koreans, who currently face brutal conditions and widespread starvation. But even if it doesn't, and the regime chooses only to reward itself and North Korean elites with its newfound economic benefits (not only a distinct possibility but perhaps the most likely outcome), America should nevertheless pursue such a deal, since it would significantly improve our security and allow us greater focus on the threat that truly matters to American lives: China. We simply cannot afford to let the perfect be the enemy of the good.

Iran's nuclear ambitions date all the way back to the Shah in 1973, and it's pursued that goal without crossing the threshold of achieving an assembled and tested nuclear weapon for longer than any nation on earth. And along the way it has weathered devastating economic sanctions, the threat of air strikes and assassination campaigns by Israel, and cyberattacks, among other hurdles. The decision by the Trump administration to pull out of the Obama-negotiated nuclear deal, the Joint Comprehensive Plan of Action (JCPOA), has left Iran finally on the precipice of acquiring nuclear weapons. It already possesses the knowledge for how to enrich uranium to the required greater than 90-percent level, and Israeli and American intelligence services believe it has mastered the detonation designs for the weapon and likely has made significant progress in miniaturizing such a device for placement atop a missile. The only thing that stands in the Iranians' way of actually building and testing a weapon is an order from the Ayatollah Khamenei, Iran's Supreme Leader, to do so.

For whatever reason, the Islamic republic hasn't taken that final step. Perhaps it's fear of retaliation from Israel (and perhaps the United States) or maybe fear that crossing the nuclear threshold would likely push their regional opponents Saudi Arabia or Turkey to immediately pursue nuclear weapons.*

---

* This, after all, is one of the main reasons that Israel has maintained an *amimut* or "nuclear opacity" policy since it first acquired its nuclear weapons in the 1960s, essentially refusing to acknowledge itself publicly as a nuclear power and maintaining, over many years, that it "will not be the first country to introduce nuclear weapons to the Middle East."

Regardless of why Iran hasn't so far embarked on nuclear "breakout," America's ability to stop Iran from crossing the threshold and becoming a nuclear power state is likely highly limited, at least short of either war or a diplomatic breakthrough that gets Iran to rejoin something like the JCPOA with its temporary limits on the scope of Iran's nuclear program. Nor are future cyberattacks, sabotage operations, or aerial or missile strikes on nuclear sites likely to permanently cripple Iran's nuclear ambitions—indeed, the risk is that any such strikes would accelerate the Iranian nuclear program by creating an incentive for the Ayatollah to retaliate.

That's not to say that the United States should not continue to engage in diplomatic negotiations to try to delay that breakout point for as long as possible, perhaps in the hopes that a successor government may come along in the future that would recognize a changed world and choose a different path. However, we should be preparing for a circumstance when a nuclear-armed Iran will one day emerge in the Middle East.

Just like North Korea becoming a nuclear armed state, Iran turning nuclear—while certainly not a welcome development by any measure—is unlikely to drastically remake the Middle East. At least, not as long as the United States maintains sufficient deterrence and prevents other countries in the region from going nuclear (making the risk of nuclear conflict in a powder keg and unstable region much more likely), which might require providing a mutual defense agreement to Saudi Arabia, just as we've done with South Korea and Japan.

But above all, the priority for both Iran and North Korea is to make sure they don't proliferate their nuclear know-how to other countries, as Pakistan had famously done to both countries in the 1980s and 1990s, when the "father" of its nuclear weapons program, A. Q. Khan, helped jump-start the nuclear programs of Iran, North Korea, and Libya. Such additional proliferation would truly be a nightmare scenario for the United States—and indeed the whole world. Perhaps one of the greatest diplomatic achievements of the last half century was the establishment in 1968 of the Non-Proliferation Treaty (NPT), an international protocol that aims to prevent the spread of nuclear weapons and its technology.* The two decades following the United States' and Soviet Union's development of nuclear weapons in the 1940s rapidly saw four other countries build nuclear weapons: the United Kingdom, France, China, and Israel. Had it not been for the NPT and the durable taboo on nuclear weapons it successfully established, we would likely live today in a world where many dozens of countries possessed these world-ending bombs, dramatically increasing the chance of an accidental or intentional detonation that would deliver horrific death and destruction and increase the risk of a civilization-ending general thermonuclear war. Each new weapon and each country that joins the nuclear weapons club makes the horrific prospect of nuclear war that much more likely. For the sake of the safety of the entire planet and perhaps even our survival as a species, we have no choice but to work as hard as possible to limit the number of nuclear weapon–wielding states to the best of our ability. It's bad enough to have to live with nuclear-armed North Korea—and perhaps one day soon a nuclear-armed Iran—but it would be a geopolitical catastrophe to see those countries drive the introduction of nuclear weapons to still more countries, either through those rogue states proliferating this technology to other countries or as a direct nuclearization response to the perceived threat they present, as might someday be the case for neighboring states like Saudi Arabia or South Korea. We must work hard to avoid both scenarios—through security guarantees for threatened allies and partners and through strengthening regional deterrence, as well as making it clear to both rogue nations that any attempts at proliferation will result in devastating consequences.

Ultimately, the key to dealing with Iran and North Korea is to recognize that the United States has not just finite budgets and military capability but finite bureaucracy and time. The interagency process through which policy is made and agreed upon in the United States is slow and unwieldy—there's only so much we can get through the system at once and so much that can occupy the attention of senior leaders. The National Security Council has only so many directors and senior

* Today, some 191 countries are party to the NPT, all but five in the entire globe: North Korea, India, Israel, Pakistan, and South Sudan.

directors and there are only so many times you can bring together the two primary tools of the interagency process at the White House—the so-called Principals Committee meeting, featuring cabinet leaders, and so-called Deputies Committees, featuring the subcabinet leadership—in the Situation Room to discuss and decide on pressing issues before they're presented to the president for action. We must make room in that bureaucracy and free up time and attention to focus on the long-overdue "Asia Pivot," to make it a reality. That means we can only do so much on the issues of Russia, Iran, or North Korea—or indeed on any of the other numerous conflicts around the world, from instability in Venezuela, conflicts in Ethiopia and Sudan, civil wars in Syria, Libya, and Yemen, among three dozen other global conflicts.

It is important for us to focus on what truly matters. Beyond managing the rise of China and deterring any attempt by the Chinese to take Taiwan by force or coercion, our narrow core interests when it comes to the three other primary state adversaries are at their most basic just this: to contain Russia while waiting for the day when it realizes, hopefully, that being an isolated rogue state and vassal to China is not in its strategic interests; delay for as long as possible Iran's crossing the nuclear weapons threshold and counter its regional aggression and support for genocidal terrorists; and maintain deterrence against North Korean aggression and curtail the DPRK's proliferation attempts. On other issues, we have to share the stage and leadership burden with allies, from sanctions policy against Russia to conflict resolution diplomacy in Africa and the Middle East.

Perhaps counterintuitively, this also means that we should welcome greater Chinese diplomatic engagement in the world—at least in certain circumstances. There was much hand-wringing in US foreign policy circles when in 2023 China negotiated a diplomatic rapprochement between Iran and Saudi Arabia, but Sen. Chris Murphy, the head of the Senate Foreign Relations Committee's Middle East panel, was right to take this development as a positive. "Not everything between the U.S. and China has to be a zero-sum game," Murphy said. "I don't know why we would perceive there to be a downside to de-escalation between Saudi Arabia and Iran."[9]

Indeed, given our lack of leverage over Iran, we could have likely never negotiated an agreement like that ourselves, and the deal was helpful for a time in reducing tensions in the Middle East. Besides, if the Chinese decide to spend their time and efforts negotiating peace agreements in the Middle East and elsewhere, more power to them—their bureaucratic time and attention is finite too, so such engagement means they're spending less time focusing on taking over Taiwan. We can't do it all—and that necessarily means that others, be it friends or foe, have to fill in the hole that our lack of attention to certain issues will inevitably leave.

In the end, as important as so many of these other international issues feel on a daily basis, if we get China wrong, none of the other questions will end up mattering.

Conclusion

PRESIDENT JOHN F. KENNEDY WAS INFINITELY RELIEVED WHEN HE realized that Nikita Khrushchev was building a wall through the center of Berlin in August 1961. For more than a dozen years, the divided German city had been the central flash point of Cold War I, a tiny bastion of Western democracy deep inside East Germany, enveloped on all sides by the communist Iron Curtain. During Truman's presidency, a Herculean airlift had barely kept West Berlin alive amid a Soviet blockade, and just months earlier in June 1961, in Vienna, Khrushchev had bullied Kennedy, still reeling from the embarrassment of the Bay of Pigs fiasco, over the future of the city.

Month by month in that first year of Kennedy's presidency, the clouds over Berlin gathered—and with them, the ominous threat of a nuclear exchange. It would be near impossible for the United States and NATO to defend Berlin from a full-on Soviet onslaught, and Kennedy had to weigh whether he could lead his nation into war to protect the German city. On May 27, 1961, US ambassador to the Soviet Union Llewellyn Thompson wrote a secret telegram to the secretary of state estimating that the world was on a trajectory where the "chances of war or ignominious Western retreat are close to 50–50."[1]

In Vienna, the Soviet leader berated Kennedy, telling him, "It is up to the US to decide whether there will be war or peace." Kennedy responded, "If that's true, it's going to be a cold winter." The Pentagon began dusting off its plans for a first strike against the Soviet Union, outlining how fifty-five long-range bombers would devastate its nuclear capability and knock out eighty-eight "Designated Ground Zeros"—seventy-two bomber bases and sixteen ICBM facilities—in a surprise attack that would unfold in just fifteen minutes. The attack, the Pentagon estimated, would "eliminat[e] or paralyz[e] the nuclear threat to the United States sufficiently," while sparing many Soviet cities and thus preventing an "irrational urge for revenge" by the Soviet Union, an assessment of dubious quality.[2]

On July 25, 1961, Kennedy announced a major buildup of US military forces in Berlin, as well as in Germany and across wider Europe, and warned against a Soviet move on the city. "The immediate threat to free men is in West Berlin, but that isolated outpost is not an isolated problem. The threat is worldwide," Kennedy told the country in a national televised address the same day.

> We have given our word that an attack upon that city will be regarded as an attack upon us all. For West Berlin—lying exposed 110 miles inside East Germany, surrounded by Soviet troops and close to Soviet supply lines, has many roles. It is more than a showcase of liberty, a symbol, an island of freedom in a Communist sea. It is even more than a link with the Free World, a beacon of hope behind the Iron Curtain, an escape hatch for refugees. West Berlin is all of that. But above all it has now become—as never before—the great testing place of Western courage and will.

Kennedy cautioned the Soviet Union, "I hear it said that West Berlin is militarily untenable. And so was Bastogne. And so, in fact, was Stalingrad. Any dangerous spot is tenable if men—brave men—will make it so. We do not want to fight—but we have fought before." The US president promised, "We cannot and we will not permit the Communists to drive us out of Berlin, either gradually or by force."[3]

Then, just a little over two weeks later, a massive East German operation began to unfold, as troops and construction teams erected a barrier that would end up dividing the city for more than a quarter century. In Washington, as US intelligence and diplomats figured out the plan, the president expressed a surprising reaction: relief. "Why would Khrushchev put up a wall if he really intended to seize West Berlin?" Kennedy wondered. "There wouldn't be any need of a wall if he planned to occupy the whole city. This is his way out of his predicament. It's not a very nice solution, but a wall is a hell of a lot better than a war."[4]

Kennedy's intuition proved correct: although Cold War I would continue through the dark chapter of the Cuban Missile Crisis the following year, the Berlin Wall came to represent the beginning of a turning point as a certain level of stability entered the geopolitical picture. While there would be tense moments ahead, and many more proxy conflicts and casualties, the Berlin Wall and the Cuban Missile Crisis brought to a close the extreme danger of Cold War I's first fifteen years. The wake of the Cuban Missile Crisis saw, for instance, the installation of the so-called red phone, the US-Soviet hotline (or what the Soviets called the "Soviet-US" hotline) to allow the leaders to communicate and ease hostilities in future crises. And, with time, détente took root. The United States and the Soviet Union were able to find a sustainable solution for the long term—including cooperation in certain realms and more clearly articulated arms-control agreements and spheres of influence that each side could live with. It didn't mean that the hostility was gone or the Cold War over, but the world didn't lurch from one crisis to another.

Today, Taiwan is the Berlin of Cold War II. If Taiwan didn't exist as a flash point in the US-China relationship, the entire arc of the next decade would look different. If the Chinese desire or ability to take Taiwan were to disappear one day, the points of major contention between America and China would still be present but become far more limited, focused on areas such as supply chain resiliency, trade disputes, support for our adversaries, cyber misbehavior, and human rights. Significant and important concerns, to be sure, but not ones that would present a real danger of dragging the two countries into an unimaginably destructive war. That distrust and challenge could be managed, just as Cold War I was managed for decades after the establishment of a relative equilibrium and mutual acceptance of core interests.

If all Taiwan represented to the United States and the world was us losing some relative power in Asia, many Americans would probably say, "Well, why should we care about Asia?" Let's let China be the regional superpower and be done with it. But Taiwan represents much more than that—and a failure to secure and fight for Taiwan would make the world more unstable and a global conflict even more likely. In short, we need today to do the same dance with Taiwan that Truman, Eisenhower, and Kennedy performed at the start of Cold War I with Berlin: protect and preserve it as a bastion of Western alliance and avoid provoking a devastating global conflagration until an era of stability can take hold.

We need to recognize political realities: the CCP may persevere for decades and even generations to come, and even if the Chinese government becomes more democratic, many of our problems with China will not automatically disappear. Along the way, our strategy must be to keep trying to convince China that it's going to be better off working within the existing global order, respecting territorial sovereignty, engaging fairly in global trade, and putting an end to the practice of economic and military coercion of other nations. We must be realistic that these objectives might not be achievable for a long time; China may remain adversarial and belligerent for years, and Cold War II could remain tense. But diplomatic efforts to employ a carrot-and-stick strategy to punish the malevolent behavior and reward improvement can produce a détente as China's escalating systemic weaknesses force it to compromise, just as the Soviet Union found itself having to do during sustained periods in 1970s and 1980s. However, it is equally important to emphasize that if Chinese leaders choose the *other* path—conflict and war—it will lead to disaster and the potential destruction of the Communist Party.

As I said in the Introduction, over the next decade, the United States and its Western alliance must walk an incredibly thin and delicate line. Every morning, we want President Xi to wake up and think,

"Today's not the day to invade Taiwan," but also to imagine that tomorrow could be, only to have him to wake up one morning in five, seven, or ten years to the same calculation that Khrushchev made in August 1961 about Berlin: the window to invade Taiwan has closed entirely. Stalling day by day is a winning strategy. Slowing China's advance down a month here and a year there is critical, as is letting China make its own mistakes. Just as it was in Cold War I, time is on America's side in Cold War II. But we must use that time wisely.

We want to match the response to Deng's old strategy of "Hide your strength, bide your time," with one of our own: "Tone down aggressive rhetoric but engage in aggressive deterrence," a twenty-first-century update of sorts to "speak softly but carry a big stick."

Conflict is not inevitable, but the likelihood is high, and we need to do everything we can to avoid it.

Above all, we must avoid two different but related worst-case scenarios—the two possible outcomes of the scenario from the Prologue, where China decides that today *is* the day to invade Taiwan. There is no question that a conflict between China and the United States would be disastrous for both countries and the global economy; even a relatively limited war would likely involve horrendous death toll—including tens of thousands of US military personnel and civilians—and include attacks on US territory, including the US mainland itself. It would cause enormous, devastating implications for the global economy, destroying or interrupting trillions of dollars in economic activity, paralyzing supply chains as shortages of goods, such as semiconductors manufactured in Taiwan, ripple across the world. A larger, escalating war involving two nuclear powers in a region comprising four of the other seven global nuclear powers—Russia, India, Pakistan, and North Korea—is a recipe for true calamity, whether intended or accidental.

But if war is the worst, worst-case scenario, there's another still-terrible worst-case scenario that must be avoided too: China seizes Taiwan *without* a war.

What are the implications if China is allowed to conquer Taiwan without the United States coming to the island's aid? First, it will be a disaster for the Taiwanese, as China will do to them what it has done to Tibet, Xinjiang, and Hong Kong. (In summer 2023, China's famous wolf-warrior ambassador to France predicted that China would have to "re-educate" the Taiwanese population "to eliminate separatist thought and secessionist theory.")[5] More broadly, though, such an outcome would rapidly reconfigure the geopolitical power structures across Asia, the Pacific, and beyond. The dominance and influence of the United States would drastically diminish. Many nations—with their faith in our security guarantees and willingness to protect them severely damaged—would by necessity rebalance their relationship with both us and China. Yes, some would likely invest more resources in reforming their defense programs and military to beef up deterrence—Japan, the Philippines, South Korea, Vietnam, Australia, and India would feel particularly vulnerable—as a newly confident and geographically uncorked China starts to project its military power across the region in a more aggressive way than the PRC has been able to do till now, but those countries, and others across Asia and the Pacific, would also find more ways to accommodate the newly emerged preeminent regional superpower, a superpower able to assert more control over all the regional maritime trade routes. Our leverage in the most economically important part of the world—and indeed elsewhere—would decline and China's increase.

Beyond trade, though, the unopposed seizure of Taiwan would herald the emergence of an even more bellicose China, one confident that might makes right. Think of the extent to which China is already telling the world not to criticize or even question it—whether it's over the genocide and persecution of the Uyghurs or over the origins of COVID-19 pandemic—and imagine that coercion and aggression amplified a hundredfold. A reinvigorated, more nationalistic China would not tolerate any objections to its policies and go out of its way to punish any country, organization, or person—with economic, diplomatic, or military coercion—for engaging in or even tolerating such rhetoric. It is a world where, as Zbigniew Brzezinski once suggested, corporate and world leaders would ask first, "What would Beijing think of this?" rather than "What would America think of this?" or

"What is the moral thing to do?" Recall wild controversies that have plagued organizations from the NBA to Marriott that have criticized Chinese policies or accidentally run afoul of its political sensitivities and imagine them again amplified a hundredfold across not just social but national and international political domains. Today, the Chinese retaliation against these organizations is only limited to their market access in China. In the future, a more powerful China may pressure other countries to take such actions on their behalf.

Ultimately, the world where China can cheaply take control of Taiwan means a world that is less free. Many countries—from global giants like the United States and India on down, size-wise, to the smallest Pacific island nations—will have less freedom of action, freedom of decision making, freedom of speaking out for human rights, and other core values. It will mean a world where China will be more powerful and subsequently less just, where it is shaping, creating, and dictating the global world order, diminishing the role of the United States and the Western alliance in the process. It would not be a world we would very much like living in.

Perhaps even more crucially, though, it will be a much more dangerous world. Failing to stop China from conquering Taiwan is more likely to cause an even more devastating conflict down the road. Having succeeded with Taiwan, China may push its luck with other territorial disputes—with countries like Japan, the Philippines, India, and Vietnam, some of which we are treaty-bound to defend. Simply put, easing China's way to a takeover of Taiwan is hardly likely to be the end of its regional and, indeed, global bullying campaign.

Those worst-case scenarios, both terrible, are why the single organizing principle of US foreign policy over this next "decisive decade"—or, in Cold War I terms, "window of vulnerability"—must be *Sinae deterrendae sunt*. China must be deterred.

To achieve this goal, we should organize—through steps outlined in the pages of this book—toward a goal of a best-case scenario. While it's easy in some ways to imagine the specific outcomes of what a loss to China this century looks like, it might seem harder to imagine the acceptable outlines of a "victory" that would not entail an—unlikely—complete defeat of China or the disappearance of the CCP.

Ultimately, America's goal is to buy time—delay, delay, and delay—for the Taiwanese. Taiwan must build up its own forces, mobilizing, training, and arming itself and showing China that a war will be too costly and its outcome very likely a disastrous defeat of the invasion fleet.

Our job is to buy Taiwan that time. If we can convince Xi, day by day, week by week, year by year, just like we had convinced Mao and his successors, that attaining "reunification" with Taiwan is not yet possible, and certainly not by force, we just might move the ball far enough down the road where Taiwan and its dream of de facto independence and democracy can outlive him. That doesn't mean that the problem will be solved should Xi leave office, one way or another—as this book shows, the CCP's ambitions to possess Taiwan predate Xi and will very likely long outlast him—but Xi is clearly a throwback to the old mold of Chinese leader, one who is more likely to take risks and promote his own legacy than anyone since Mao. If he is replaced by a more responsible or weaker successor or if Taiwan is put on the back burner by the regime in favor of focusing on domestic issues, that would give us—and Taiwan—crucial time to build and secure sufficient defenses in the region that would make even the most aggressive Chinese leader believe that an invasion is an impossibility.

Then, once the biggest thorn in the US-China relationship—the decades-long unresolved question of Taiwan—recedes from the top of the agenda, we can work on building a more productive relationship with China. That new relationship should not replicate the mistakes of the past—the false hopes that engagement will lead to democratization and liberalization of the country—nor should it be based on the premise that the CCP will one day collapse. (Any of these things would, of course, be welcomed if they occurred, but we should not build a strategy around hopes and dreams.)

Along the way, we must maintain America's critical advantages and the strength of the Western alliance—deterring a calamitous war with China while preserving our dominant advantages in the Indo-Pacific and globally. This requires sustaining and strengthening our balance of power vis-à-vis China—in military capability, as well as semiconductors and the key technological applications that run on top of them, from AI, biotech and synthetic biology, space technology, to green technology. On top of that, we must invest in talent-based immigration that will, combined with China's upcoming demographic collapse, help us to neutralize the PRC's numerical advantages over time. (Crucially, we must organize to counter China without creating a new Red Scare and ensure that our political and economic efforts against the country aren't allowed to slide into xenophobia and rekindle the racism that long dogged our engagement with Asia in past generations.) Left to their own devices, the systemic challenges that the Chinese economy suffers from—challenges for which the CCP doesn't appear to have any solutions—will make China's bid to become the world's biggest and most powerful economy much less realizable.

In one word, this strategy is all about leverage: we must increase our leverage over China and decrease its leverage over us. Crucially, it is not about decoupling, for the complete disconnection of our economies is not only unrealistic but would increase the risk of danger as China would feel less connected to the West and freer to disregard our interests. Instead, a successful economic strategy needs to be focused on bringing China tighter into our orbit by increasing its dependence on our supply chains while giving us more room to maneuver by simultaneously decreasing our critical dependence on the PRC. It is a strategy of unidirectional entanglement—the pursuit of one-way selective decoupling that also increases the coupling in the other direction to achieve the kind of equilibrium that incentivizes peace. Of course, we should be fully aware that China is trying to implement the exact mirror strategy. The winner of this race will very likely determine the future of the twenty-first century.

A win for us, we hope, would deliver a world not unlike the one inherited by JFK's successors in the latter half of the twentieth century, a world overshadowed by a cold war but one that didn't daily threaten catastrophe. It would substantially reduce tensions and the risks of conflict globally if even a CCP-ruled China is ultimately convinced that it is better off working within the established rules of the existing international order—including respecting the territorial integrity of other nations and engaging fairly in global trade.

Tensions and flash points between China and the United States are unlikely to disappear, just as they didn't between the United States and Soviet Union after the Berlin Wall went up and the Cuban Missile Crisis was resolved, but the United States and China might find themselves in a position to compete without direct conflict for decades—or longer. We may never be best friends with China—there's hundreds of years of history, dating long before Xi and even the CCP, that make clear China's relationship with the West ebbs and flows—but we may still create a productive, albeit still cold, relationship. A China we can live with and a China that can live with us means a better, more secure world. We will still face an imperfect and unjust world—one where brutal and adversarial authoritarian regimes exist and even prosper—but it will be a world that is on balance wealthier, more peaceful, and better equipped to deal with other pressing global challenges.

To get there, we must heed the advice and wisdom of the first two presidents of Cold War I, the two men who preceded Kennedy and dealt with the early chapters of the Berlin challenge. Harry Truman, as he left office, said, "When history says that my term of office saw the beginning of the Cold War, it will also say that in those eight years we have set the course that can win it." His successor, Dwight Eisenhower, said, as he left office, that his proudest accomplishment was keeping the peace, adding, "People asked how it happened—by God, it didn't just happen, I'll tell you that."[6]

Focusing and executing on a strategy and keeping the peace is hard, but both are critical to our success ahead. Devastating war or the establishment of the "Chinese Century" is not inevitable, but the risks are high. We are a World on the Brink. All of us—each and every one—should get up each morning and think about how we can contribute to avoiding the worst-case scenarios.

Acknowledgments

Thirty years ago, America welcomed a new immigrant family that left Russia with not much more than a couple of suitcases. In those intervening decades, I have been lucky to have experienced the American Dream in its fullest form—a journey that started for me as a student, then a startup employee, an entrepreneur, a national security professional, and now a philanthropist. Some of the proudest days of my life were becoming a naturalized citizen of this great country and later being asked to contribute in a small way to enhancing its national security, as an adviser to the Departments of Defense and Homeland Security. Throughout that time, I've been passionate about finding ways to give back to this country that gave me a home and an opportunity to build a successful and meaningful life.

I see this book as part of that lifelong effort. Since those fateful events of Operation Aurora in January 2010, I have been concerned about the negative impact that China's actions have had on the ability of this country to continue to grow economically and provide the same opportunities to other Americans—whether they are native-born or naturalized immigrants. As the decade went on, I also became increasingly anxious about the prospect of a devastating war breaking out between these two large countries and the urgency of finding ways to avoid it. I have spent many years thinking about these issues, and I want to express deep appreciation to the numerous China, Taiwan, and other national security experts who have provided me with invaluable insights and ideas and have been willing to challenge and debate my own thoughts over the years.

I'm gratefully indebted to the reviewers of the draft manuscripts and other immensely valuable feedback providers, including the entire brilliant team at Silverado Policy Accelerator. I specifically want to recognize Maureen Hinman, Sarah Stewart, Marc Raimondi, Ian Ward, Jen Ayers, Dr. Sergey Radchenko, Ivan Kanapathy, Patrick Gray, Vartan Sarkissian, Ronnie Wiessbrod, Heather Adkins, Alex Ionescu, Dr. Thomas Rid, Sandra Joyce, Matthew Spence, Dan Invegaldson, Tammy Haddad, Gillian Tett, Jim Schwartz, Thorsten Benner, Thomas Shugart, Jack Watling, Chris Miller, and Jamil Jaffer. Thank you for dedicating the time to read, provide feedback, discuss, and analyze the ideas presented in this book. Similarly, thank you to Howard Yoon, Ben Adams, Shena Redmond, Irina du Quenoy, and the rest of the team at PublicAffairs who helped turn this idea into a book.

I could not have asked for a more experienced and hardworking partner to write this book with than Garrett Graff, to whom I owe a deep debt of gratitude. I want to thank him for his calm and patient guidance of this first-time author and his constant but gentle pressure against my reluctant nature to infuse more of myself and my background into this book. From the initial concept, which he first suggested might work better as a long magazine article, he persuaded me to expand the ambition and scope. This led to this labor of love that resulted in printing these pages. I sincerely hope you found them intellectually stimulating, even if you did not agree with all of what I said.

To my parents, I will never stop thanking you for having the courage to uproot your life, sacrifice everything to leave Russia, and bring me to this country, thus giving me the opportunity to not just succeed but to live. For who knows—if I had stayed in Russia, perhaps I would be yet another one of Putin's victims, being forcefully mobilized to die in the grassy fields of Ukraine.

Last but certainly not least, to my wife, thank you for bearing with me and providing extraordinary support, patience, and understanding throughout this long journey. Your encouragement has been a source of strength and motivation. This book would not exist without it.

Source Notes

Introduction

1. Associated Press, "Salesman: Hackers Use Chinese Company's Servers," *CBS News*, February 11, 2011, www.cbsnews.com/news/salesman-hackers-use-chinese-companys-servers.

2. Rush Doshi, *The Long Game: China's Grand Strategy to Displace American Order* (New York: Oxford University Press, 2021), 313.

3. Ibid., 333.

4. Elbridge Colby, *The Strategy of Denial: American Defense in an Age of Great Power Conflict* (New Haven, CT: Yale University Press, 2021), 1.

5. John Richardson, *A Design for Maintaining Maritime Superiority*, Department of Defense, Washington, DC, January 2016, available at https://news.usni.org/2016/01/05/document-cno-richardsons-new-u-s-navy-guidance.

6. Michael Doyle, *Cold Peace: Avoiding the New Cold War* (New York: Liveright Publishing, 2023), 12–14.

7. Ibid., 46.

8. Xi Jinping, "Achieving Rejuvenation Is the Dream of the Chinese People," speech, National People's Congress of the People's Republic of China, November 29, 2012, Beijing, www.npc.gov.cn/englishnpc/c23934/202006/32191c5bbdb04cbab6df01e5077d1c60.shtml.

Chapter 1: The Road to the Brink

1. Dmitri Alperovitch, "Revealed: Operation Shady RAT" (white paper, McAfee, 2011), https://web.archive.org/web/20110804083836/www.mcafee.com/us/resources/white-papers/wp-operation-shady-rat.pdf.

2. Gregory Poling, *On Dangerous Ground: America's Century in the South China Sea* (New York: Oxford University Press, 2022), 210.

3. International Institute for Strategic Studies, "13th Asia Security Summit, Singapore, 30 May–1 June 2014: The Shangri-La Dialogue," August 8, 2019, https://issuu.com/iiss-publications/docs/shangri-la-dialogue-2014.

4. AMTI Leadership, "Highlights from Shangri-La Dialogue 2014," Asia Maritime Transparency Initiative, May 28, 2015, https://amti.csis.org/highlights-from-shangri-la-dialogue-2014.

5. Sally K. Burt, *At the President's Pleasure* (Leiden, Netherlands: Brill, 2015), 53.

6. Herbert P. Bix, *Hirohito and the Making of Modern Japan* (New York: Harper Perennial, 2000), 359. Chiang's own fighting took a huge toll: he drowned half a million Chinese and displaced five million when he destroyed the dikes along the Yellow River in June 1938, an effort that allowed his forces to stop the Japanese advance at the four-month battle of Wuhan that summer.

7. John Pomfret, *The Beautiful Country and the Middle Kingdom: America and China, 1776 to the Present* (New York: Henry Holt, 2016), 281.

8. Ibid., 322, 354.

9. Ibid., 331.

10. John S. Service, *The Amerasia Papers: Some Problems in the History of US-China Relations* (Berkeley: Center for Chinese Studies, University of California, 1971), 161–162. The quote from Mitter in the footnote comes from Rana Mitter, *Forgotten Ally: China's World War II, 1937–1945* (Boston: Houghton Mifflin Harcourt, 2014), 330.

11. Daniel Kurtz-Phelan, *The China Mission: George Marshall's Unfinished War, 1945–1947* (New York: W. W. Norton, 2018), 3.

12. Ibid., 242.

13. Ibid., 237.

14. Kevin Rudd, *The Avoidable War: The Dangers of a Catastrophic Conflict between the US and Xi Jinping's China* (New York: PublicAffairs, 2022), 5.

15. Pomfret, *Beautiful Country and the Middle Kingdom*, 6.

16. Rudd, *Avoidable War*, 21.

17. Ibid., 20.

18. Margaret MacMillan, *Nixon and Mao: The Week That Changed the World* (New York: Random House, 2007), xviii.

19. Pomfret, *Beautiful Country and the Middle Kingdom*, 11.

20. "Chinese Porcelain," George Washington's Mount Vernon, accessed August 11, 2023, www.mountvernon.org/library/digitalhistory/digital-encyclopedia/article/chinese-porcelain; Pomfret, *Beautiful Country and the Middle Kingdom*, 10–11.

21. Marie-Stéphanie Delamaire, "Who Owns Washington? Gilbert Stuart and the Battle for Artistic Property in the Early American Republic," in *Circulation and Control: Artistic Culture and Intellectual Property in the Nineteenth Century*, ed. Marie-Stéphanie Delamaire and Will Slauter (Cambridge, UK: Open Book Publishers, 2021), chap. 3; Pomfret, *Beautiful Country and the Middle Kingdom*, 11.

22. Pomfret, *Beautiful Country and the Middle Kingdom*, 13.

23. Ibid., 23, 39.

24. Ibid., 27.

25. Ibid., 20.

26. Ibid., 31.

27. Ibid., 35, 56.

28. Ibid., 36, 84.

29. Ibid., 70–71, 79.
30. Ibid., 92–101.
31. Ibid., 137.
32. Ibid., 116.
33. Ibid., 167.
34. Ibid., 131.
35. Ibid., 133, 134.
36. Ibid., 151.
37. Ibid., 148.
38. Rana Mitter, *A Bitter Revolution: China's Struggle with the Modern World* (Oxford: Oxford University Press, 2005), 37.
39. Pomfret, *Beautiful Country and the Middle Kingdom*, 149, 163.
40. Denny Roy, *Taiwan: A Political History* (Ithaca: Cornell University Press, 2003), 111–112.
41. Pomfret, *Beautiful Country and the Middle Kingdom*, 406.
42. MacMillan, *Nixon and Mao*, xix.
43. Pomfret, *Beautiful Country and the Middle Kingdom*, 404.
44. Ibid., 421, 424.
45. Ibid., 445; MacMillan, *Nixon and Mao*, xx.
46. MacMillan, *Nixon and Mao*, 246.
47. Ibid., 245–261.
48. "Text of Nixon Toast at Shanghai Dinner," *New York Times*, February 28, 1972, www.nytimes.com/1972/02/28/archives/text-of-nixon-toast-at-shanghai-dinner.html.
49. Pomfret, *Beautiful Country and the Middle Kingdom*, 459.
50. "40 Years of Friendship: From the Personal to the Political, President Carter Reflects on Our Nation's—and His Own—Relationship with China," Carter Center, January 9, 2019, www.cartercenter.org/news/features/p/china/president-carter-on-normalizing-relations-with-china.html.
51. Ibid.
52. "China Policy," Office of the Historian, US Department of State, accessed August 11, 2023, https://history.state.gov/milestones/1977-1980/china-policy.
53. Taiwan Relations Act, H.R. 2479, 96th Congress (1979), www.congress.gov/96/statute/STATUTE-93/STATUTE-93-Pg14.pdf.
54. Evan Osnos, *Age of Ambition: Chasing Fortune, Truth, and Faith in the New China* (New York: Farrar, Straus and Giroux, 2014), 13.
55. Pomfret, *Beautiful Country and the Middle Kingdom*, 449–451.
56. Ibid., 501.
57. Ibid., 480.
58. Orville Schell and John Delury, *Wealth and Power: China's Long March to the Twenty-First Century* (New York: Random House, 2013), 5.
59. Ibid., 6.
60. Chun Han Wong, *Party of One: The Rise of Xi Jinping and China's Superpower Future* (New York: Avid Reader Press, 2023), 153.
61. *Frontline*, "Transcript: The Tank Man," aired April 11, 2006, on PBS, www.pbs.org/wgbh/pages/frontline/tankman/etc/transcript.html.

62. Ibid.

63. "Tiananmen Square Protest Death Toll 'Was 10,000,'" *BBC News*, December 23, 2017, www.bbc.com/news/world-asia-china-42465516.

64. "George H. W. Bush, Press Conference, June 5, 1989," University of Southern California US-China Institute, June 5, 1989, https://china.usc.edu/george-hw-bush-press-conference-june-5-1989; Pomfret, *Beautiful Country and the Middle Kingdom*, 524.

65. Bill Clinton, "Address Accepting the Presidential Nomination at the Democratic National Convention in New York," speech, July 16, 1992, New York, American Presidency Project, www.presidency.ucsb.edu/documents/address-accepting-the-presidential-nomination-the-democratic-national-convention-new-york.

66. Pomfret, *Beautiful Country and the Middle Kingdom*.

67. Osnos, *Age of Ambition*, 22, 24.

68. Poling, *On Dangerous Ground*, 166.

69. Rush Doshi, *The Long Game: China's Grand Strategy to Displace American Order* (New York: Oxford University Press, 2021), 69.

70. Pomfret, *Beautiful Country and the Middle Kingdom*, 565.

71. Graham Allison, *Destined for War: Can America and China Escape Thucydides's Trap?* (Boston: Houghton Mifflin Harcourt, 2017), 7.

72. Joseph Stiglitz, "The Chinese Century," *Vanity Fair*, December 4, 2014, www.vanityfair.com/news/2015/01/china-worlds-largest-economy; "The Chinese Century Is Well under Way," *Economist*, October 27, 2018, www.economist.com/graphic-detail/2018/10/27/the-chinese-century-is-well-under-way.

73. Osnos, *Age of Ambition*, 14.

74. Pomfret, *Beautiful Country and the Middle Kingdom*, 6.

75. Robert Zoellick, "Whither China? From Membership to Responsibility," speech, National Committee on U.S.-China Relations, September 21, 2005, New York, www.ncuscr.org/wp-content/uploads/2020/04/migration_Zoellick_remarks_notes06_winter_spring.pdf.

76. Elizabeth Economy, *The Third Revolution: Xi Jinping and the New Chinese State* (New York: Oxford University Press, 2018), 17.

77. United Nations Conference on Trade and Development, Review of Maritime Transport, 2015, https://unctad.org/system/files/official-document/rmt2015_en.pdf.

78. William Branigin, "U.S. Military Ends Role in Philippines," *Washington Post*, November 24, 1992, www.washingtonpost.com/archive/politics/1992/11/24/us-military-ends-role-in-philippines/a1be8c14-0681-44ab-b869-a6ee439727b7/.

79. Stanley Meyer, "Incident at Mischief Reef: Implications for the Philippines, China, and the United States," Strategy Research Project, US Army War College, January 8, 1996, https://apps.dtic.mil/sti/pdfs/ADA309432.pdf.

80. "Asia Now," *Time*, March 8, 1999, http://web.archive.org/web/20010220044944/www.time.com/time/asia/asia/magazine/1999/990308/spratlys2.html.

81. Bureau of Oceans and International Environmental and Scientific Affairs, *Limits in the Seas: China's Maritime Claims in the South China Sea*, no. 143, December 5, 2014, 6, https://2009-2017.state.gov/documents/organization/234936.pdf.

82. Jeremy Page and Trefor Moss, "South China Sea Ruling Puts Beijing in a Corner," *Wall Street Journal*, July 12, 2016, www.wsj.com/articles/south-china-sea-ruling-puts-beijing-in-a-corner-1468365807.

83. Chun Han Wong, "China to Continue Construction on Disputed Islands," *Wall Street Journal*, July 18, 2016, www.wsj.com/articles/china-flies-military-aircraft-near-scarborough-shoal-1468852659.

84. Asia Maritime Transparency Initiative, "China Lands First Bomber on South China Sea Island," Center for Strategic and International Studies, May 18, 2018, https://amti.csis.org/china-lands-first-bomber-south-china-sea-island/.

85. Hannah Beech, "China's Sea Control Is a Done Deal, 'Short of War with the U.S.,'" *New York Times*, September 20, 2018, www.nytimes.com/2018/09/20/world/asia/south-china-sea-navy.html.

86. Niharika Mandhana, "How Beijing Boxed America Out of the South China Sea," *Wall Street Journal*, March 11, 2023, www.wsj.com/articles/china-boxed-america-out-of-south-china-sea-military-d2833768?mod=article_inline.

87. Ibid.

88. Ibid.

89. Thomas C. Schelling, *Arms and Influence* (New Haven, CT: Yale University Press, 2020), 66.

90. Poling, *On Dangerous Ground*, 1.

91. See for instance, Thomas Shugart, "China's Artificial Islands Are Bigger (and a Bigger Deal) Than You Think," *War on the Rocks*, September 21, 2016, https://warontherocks.com/2016/09/chinas-artificial-islands-are-bigger-and-a-bigger-deal-than-you-think.

92. Economy, *Third Revolution*, 38.

93. Jun Osawa, "China's ADIZ over the East China Sea: A 'Great Wall in the Sky?,'" Brookings Institution, December 17, 2013, www.brookings.edu/articles/chinas-adiz-over-the-east-china-sea-a-great-wall-in-the-sky.

94. Mandhana, "How Beijing Boxed America Out."

95. Doshi, *Long Game*, 263.

96. Ibid., 2.

Chapter 2: Distracted and Disoriented

1. "Prime Minister Vladimir Putin Met with Leading Russian Writers," Government of the Russian Federation, October 7, 2009, http://archive.government.ru/eng/docs/5108/.

2. Joseph Marks, "The Cybersecurity 202: U.S. Officials: It's China Hacking That Keeps Us Up at Night," *Washington Post*, March 6, 2019, www.washingtonpost.com/news/powerpost/paloma/the-cybersecurity-202/2019/03/06/the-cybersecurity-202-u-s-officials-it-s-china-hacking-that-keeps-us-up-at-night/5c7ec07f1b326b2d177d5fd3.

3. Mikhail Frunze, "Unified Military Doctrine and the Red Army," *Krasnaya Nov* 1 (1921): 94–106, available at www.patriotica.ru/history/frunze_doctrine.html.

4. National Security Agency, "Reading Gentlemen's Mail," March 12, 2018, www.nsa.gov/portals/75/documents/news-features/declassified-documents

/history-today-articles/03%202018/12MAR2018%20Reading%20Gentlemens%20 Mail.pdf.

5. Barack Obama, "Remarks by President Obama and President Xi of the People's Republic of China in Joint Press Conference," September 25, 2015, Washington, DC, White House, https://obamawhitehouse.archives.gov/the-press-office/2015/09/25 /remarks-president-obama-and-president-xi-peoples-republic-china-joint.

6. Jeffrey Goldberg, "The Obama Doctrine," *Atlantic*, April 2016, www.the atlantic.com/magazine/archive/2016/04/the-obama-doctrine/471525/.

7. Christina Wilkie, "Biden Sees No Need for 'a New Cold War' with China after Three-Hour Meeting with Xi Jinping," CNBC, November 14, 2022, www .cnbc.com/2022/11/14/biden-sees-no-need-for-a-new-cold-war-with-china-after -three-hour-meeting-with-xi-jinping.html.

8. Xi Jinping, "Secure a Decisive Victory in Building a Moderately Prosperous Society in All Respects and Strive for the Great Success of Socialism with Chinese Characteristics for a New Era," Xinhua News Agency, October 18, 2017, www .xinhuanet.com/english/download/Xi_Jinping's_report_at_19th_CPC_National _Congress.pdf.

9. Erin Banco et al., "'Something Was Badly Wrong': When Washington Realized Russia Was Actually Invading Ukraine," *Politico*, February 24, 2023, www .politico.com/news/magazine/2023/02/24/russia-ukraine-war-oral-history -00083757.

10. Rush Doshi, *The Long Game: China's Grand Strategy to Displace American Order* (New York: Oxford University Press, 2021), 17.

11. Ibid., 185.

12. Garrett M. Graff, "The New Arms Race Threatening to Explode in Space," *Wired*, June 26, 2018, www.wired.com/story/new-arms-race-threatening-to-explode -in-space/.

13. Doshi, *Long Game*, 39.

14. Ibid., 40.

15. Graham Allison, "Lee Kuan Yew: The Sage of Asia," *Caixin*, trans. the Belfer Center for Science and International Affairs, March 28, 2015, www.belfercenter .org/publication/lee-kuan-yew-sage-asia.

16. Doshi, *Long Game*, 29–30.

17. Ibid., 31.

18. Ibid., 48.

19. Ibid., 72.

20. Deng Xiaoping, "We Must Adhere to Socialism and Prevent Peaceful Evolution towards Capitalism," November 23, 1989, available at Marxists.org, www .marxists.org/reference/archive/deng-xiaoping/1989/173.htm.

21. Kai He, *Institutional Balancing in the Asia Pacific Economic Interdependence and China's Rise* (New York: Routledge, 2009), 36.

22. Doshi, *Long Game*, 75.

23. Ibid., 60.

24. Ibid., 85.

25. Ibid., 79.

26. Ibid., 148.

27. Ibid., 156.

28. Zbigniew Brzezinski, "A Geostrategy for Eurasia," *Foreign Affairs*, September 1, 1997, www.foreignaffairs.com/articles/asia/1997-09-01/geostrategy-eurasia.

29. "China's Coercive Tactics Abroad," US Department of State, accessed October 4, 2023, https://2017-2021.state.gov/chinas-coercive-tactics-abroad/#United Front.

30. Michael H. Hunt, *The Genesis of Chinese Communist Foreign Policy* (New York: Columbia University Press, 1996), 220.

31. Ibid., 220.

32. Ibid., 221.

33. "China's Coercive Tactics Abroad."

34. Bethany Allen-Ebrahimian, "In Tanzania, Beijing Is Running a Training School for Authoritarianism," *Axios*, August 20, 2023, www.axios.com/chinese-communist-party-training-school-africa.

35. "Two Arrested for Operating Illegal Overseas Police Station of the Chinese Government," US Department of Justice, April 17, 2023, www.justice.gov/opa/pr/two-arrested-operating-illegal-overseas-police-station-chinese-government.

36. Bethany Allen-Ebrahimian, "The Chinese Communist Party Is Setting Up Cells at Universities across America," *Foreign Policy*, April 18, 2018, https://foreignpolicy.com/2018/04/18/the-chinese-communist-party-is-setting-up-cells-at-universities-across-america-china-students-beijing-surveillance/.

37. George Kennan, "The Charge in the Soviet Union (Kennan) to the Secretary of State," Document 475, FRUS, 1946, vol. 6, National Security Archive, https://nsarchive.gwu.edu/document/21043-long-telegram-transcript.

Chapter 3: The Taiwan Dilemma

1. "Taiwanese/Chinese Identity (1992/06~2023/06)," Election Study Center, National Chengchi University, July 12, 2023, https://esc.nccu.edu.tw/PageDoc/Detail?fid=7800&id=6961.

2. Kevin Doyle and Al Jazeera staff, "Is Xi Jinping China's New Mao Zedong?" *Al Jazeera*, October 17, 2022, www.aljazeera.com/news/2022/10/17/is-xi-jinping-chinas-new-mao.

3. Peter Hartcher, "'Untouchable': How Xi Jinping Became More Powerful than Mao Zedong," *Sydney Morning Herald*, October 25, 2022, www.smh.com.au/world/asia/untouchable-how-xi-jinping-became-more-powerful-than-mao-zedong-20221024-p5bs8i.html.

4. See Chun Han Wong, *Party of One: The Rise of Xi Jinping and China's Superpower Future* (New York: Avid Reader Press, 2023), 14–19.

5. Nicholas Kristof, "Looking for a Jump-Start in China," *New York Times*, January 5, 2013, www.nytimes.com/2013/01/06/opinion/sunday/kristof-looking-for-a-jump-start-in-china.html.

6. Wong, *Party of One*, 17.

7. Ibid., 17.

8. Ibid., 19–25.

9. Ibid., 27.

10. Ibid., 39.

11. Ibid., 43.
12. Ibid., 44.
13. Kevin Rudd, *The Avoidable War: The Dangers of a Catastrophic Conflict between the US and Xi Jinping's China* (New York: PublicAffairs, 2022), 47.
14. Wong, *Party of One*, 77.
15. John Pomfret, *The Beautiful Country and the Middle Kingdom: America and China, 1776 to the Present* (New York: Henry Holt, 2016), 91.
16. Neville Maxwell, "How the Sino-Russian Boundary Conflict Was Finally Settled," *Critical Asian Studies* 39, no. 2 (2007): 229–253.
17. Alan Wachman, *Why Taiwan? Geostrategic Rationales for China's Territorial Integrity* (Stanford, CA: Stanford University Press, 2007), xx.
18. Ibid., 112.
19. Sergey Radchenko and Vladislav Zubok, "Blundering on the Brink," *Foreign Affairs*, April 3, 2023, www.foreignaffairs.com/cuba/missile-crisis-secret-history-soviet-union-russia-ukraine-lessons.
20. Mao Zedong, "The Chinese People Cannot Be Cowed by the Atom Bomb," January 28, 1955, conversation between Mao Zedong and the Finnish ambassador to the PRC Carl-Johan Sundstrom, archived at wilsoncenter.org, https://digitalarchive.wilsoncenter.org/document/mao-zedong-chinese-people-cannot-be-cowed-atom-bomb.
21. "Discussion between N. S. Khrushchev and Mao Zedong," October 2, 1959, archived at wilsoncenter.org, https://digitalarchive.wilsoncenter.org/document/discussion-between-ns-khrushchev-and-mao-zedong.
22. "Full Text of Xi Jinping's Report at 19th CPC National Congress," *China Daily*, October 18, 2017, www.chinadaily.com.cn/china/19thcpcnationalcongress/2017-11/04/content_34115212.htm.
23. Elizabeth Economy, *The Third Revolution: Xi Jinping and the New Chinese State* (New York: Oxford University Press, 2018), 3.
24. Odd Arne Westad, *Restless Empire: China and the World since 1750* (New York: Basic Books, 2012), 2.
25. Jonathan Manthorpe, *Forbidden Nation: A History of Taiwan* (New York: Palgrave Macmillan, 2005), xi.
26. Ibid., 23.
27. Ibid., 22, 37–39.
28. Denny Roy, *Taiwan: A Political History* (Ithaca: Cornell University Press, 2003), 15.
29. Ibid., 21.
30. Manthorpe, *Forbidden Nation*, xi.
31. Roy, *Taiwan*, 31.
32. Mao Zedong, *China, the March toward Unity* (New York: Workers Library, 1937), 40; Pomfret, *Beautiful Country and the Middle Kingdom*, 233.
33. Roy, *Taiwan*, 62.
34. Manthorpe, *Forbidden Nation*, 202.
35. Ibid., 18–19.
36. Andrew Nathan and Andrew Scobell, *China's Search for Security* (New York: Columbia University Press, 2014), xx.

37. Hal Brands and Michael Beckley, *Danger Zone: The Coming Conflict with China* (New York: W. W. Norton, 2022), 57.

38. Westad, *Restless Empire*, 4.

39. YingHui Lee and Jane Chan, "China-ASEAN Nontraditional Maritime Security Cooperation," *China Review* 21, no. 4 (2021): 11–37.

40. Toshi Yoshihara and James Holmes, *Red Star over the Pacific: China's Rise and the Challenge to U.S. Maritime Strategy*, 2nd ed. (Annapolis, MD: Naval Institute Press, 2018).

41. Francis C. Prescott, Herbert A. Fine, and Velma Hastings Cassidy, eds., *Foreign Relations of the United States, 1949, The Far East: China* (Washington, DC: Government Printing Office, 2010), 460.

42. Manthorpe, *Forbidden Nation*, 25.

43. "China/Taiwan: Evolution of the 'One China' Policy—Key Statements from Washington, Beijing, and Taipei," Congressional Research Service, March 12, 2011, to January 5, 2015, www.everycrsreport.com/reports/RL30341.html.

44. Ibid.

45. "Obama Statement Congratulating Taiwanese President-Elect Ma Ying-Jeou," March 22, 2008, available at American Presidency Project, www.presidency.ucsb.edu/documents/obama-statement-congratulating-taiwanese-president-elect-ma-ying-jeou.

46. "Biden Tells 60 Minutes U.S. Troops Would Defend Taiwan, but White House Says This Is Not Official U.S. Policy," *60 Minutes Overtime*, aired on CBS, September 18, 2022, www.cbsnews.com/news/president-joe-biden-taiwan-60-minutes-2022-09-18/.

47. Paul Mozur and John Liu, "The Chip Titan Whose Life's Work Is at the Center of a Tech Cold War," *New York Times*, August 4, 2023, www.nytimes.com/2023/08/04/technology/the-chip-titan-whose-lifes-work-is-at-the-center-of-a-tech-cold-war.html.

Chapter 4: They Are Weaker Than We Think

1. Erin Banco et al., "'Something Was Badly Wrong': When Washington Realized Russia Was Actually Invading Ukraine," *Politico*, February 24, 2023, www.politico.com/news/magazine/2023/02/24/russia-ukraine-war-oral-history-00083757.

2. Ibid.

3. Brad Lendon, "Russia May Have Lost up to Half of Its Operational Tank Fleet in Ukraine, Monitoring Group Says," CNN, February 9, 2023, www.cnn.com/2023/02/09/europe/1000-russian-tanks-destroyed-ukraine-war-intl-hnk-ml/index.html.

4. Dmitri Alperovitch and Sergey Radchenko, "Another Russia Is Possible: The Kremlin Will Eventually Tire of Its Reliance on China," *Foreign Affairs*, August 29, 2022, www.foreignaffairs.com/russian-federation/another-russia-possible.

5. "Putin Orders Measures to Reverse Mass Wartime Exodus," *Moscow Times*, May 12, 2023, www.themoscowtimes.com/2023/05/12/putin-orders-measures-to-reverse-mass-wartime-exodus-a81124.

6. "Russia's Population Nightmare Is Going to Get Even Worse," *Economist*, March 4, 2023, www.economist.com/europe/2023/03/04/russias-population-nightmare-is-going-to-get-even-worse.

7. "Unprecedented Migration May Be Only Chance to Beat Russia's Population Decline," *Moscow Times*, April 13, 2023, www.themoscowtimes.com/2023/04/13/unprecedented-migration-may-be-only-chance-to-beat-russias-population-decline-study-a80813.

8. Elena Holodny, "The Rise, Fall, and Comeback of the Chinese Economy over the Past 800 Years," *Business Insider*, January 8, 2017, www.businessinsider.com/history-of-chinese-economy-1200-2017-2017-1.

9. Francis C. Prescott, Herbert A. Fine, and Velma Hastings Cassidy, eds., *Foreign Relations of the United States, 1949, The Far East: China* (Washington, DC: Government Printing Office, 2010), document 122.

10. "The Chinese Century Is Well under Way," *Economist*, October 27, 2018, www.economist.com/graphic-detail/2018/10/27/the-chinese-century-is-well-under-way.

11. Hal Brands and Michael Beckley, *Danger Zone: The Coming Conflict with China* (New York: W. W. Norton, 2022), xv.

12. Moreover, Chinese cultural preferences for a son meant that during the height of the one-child policy, parents engaged in selective abortions or even infanticide, a downstream effect that that left today's family-aged population remarkably unbalanced: China has about 104 males for every 100 females, leaving millions of "excess" heterosexual men family-less.

13. David Stanway, "Bringing up a Child Costlier in China Than in U.S., Japan—Research," Reuters, February 23, 2022, www.reuters.com/world/china/chinas-child-rearing-costs-far-outstrip-us-japan-research-2022-02-23.

14. Ruchir Sharma, "The Demographics of Stagnation," *Foreign Affairs*, February 15, 2016, www.foreignaffairs.com/articles/world/2016-02-15/demographics-stagnation; Stanway, "Bringing up a Child." It's possible that even these dire numbers are optimistic. The Pew Research Center suggests that in 2022, China's fertility rate was even lower, just 1.18 children per woman. See Laura Silver and Christine Huang, "Key Facts about China's Declining Population," Pew Research Center, December 5, 2022, www.pewresearch.org/short-reads/2022/12/05/key-facts-about-chinas-declining-population/.

15. Alicia Chen, Lyric Li, and Lily Kuo, "In Need of a Baby Boom, China Clamps Down on Vasectomies," *Washington Post*, December 9, 2021, www.washingtonpost.com/world/asia_pacific/china-birth-control-vasectomy/2021/12/09/c89cc902-50b8-11ec-83d2-d9dab0e23b7e_story.html.

16. Xiujian Peng, "China's Population Is about to Shrink for the First Time since the Great Famine Struck 60 Years Ago. Here's What That Means for the World," World Economic Forum, July 26, 2022, www.weforum.org/agenda/2022/07/china-population-shrink-60-years-world.

17. Sharma, "Demographics of Stagnation."

18. Nicholas Eberstadt and Ashton Verdery, "China's Shrinking Families," *Foreign Affairs*, April 7, 2021, www.foreignaffairs.com/articles/china/2021-04-07/chinas-shrinking-families.

19. "For the First Time since the 1960s, China's Population Is Shrinking," *Economist*, January 17, 2023, www.economist.com/china/2023/01/17/for-the-first-time-since-the-1960s-chinas-population-is-shrinking.

20. Simon Scarr, Ashlyn Still, and Jin Wu, "China's Debt Problem," Reuters Graphics, accessed November 10, 2023, http://fingfx.thomsonreuters.com/gfx/rngs/CHINA-DEBT-GRAPHIC/0100315H2LG/.

21. Engen Tham, Xie Yu, and Ziyi Tang, "Analysis: China's Debt-Laden Local Governments Pose Challenges to Economic Growth, Financial System," Reuters, March 10, 2023, www.reuters.com/world/china/debt-laden-local-governments-pose-fresh-challenges-chinas-growth-financial-2023-03-10.

22. Zhiwu Chen, "How China Keeps Putting Off Its Lehman Moment," *New York Times*, March 26, 2023, www.nytimes.com/2023/03/26/opinion/china-finance-banking-evergrande-crisis.html. As one Hong Kong analyst explains, Chinese "regulators [have] a degree of control over debt problems that their Western counterparts can only dream of," and "the government has virtually unlimited power to head off crises by directing resources—and apportioning pain—as it sees fit, often by ordering banks and other creditors to accept losses for the greater good before things get out of hand."

23. Stella Yifan Xie, Yoko Kubota, and Cao Li, "China's Cities Struggle under Trillions of Dollars of Debt," *Wall Street Journal*, March 6, 2023, www.wsj.com/articles/chinas-cities-struggle-under-trillions-of-dollars-of-debt-c341b6e0.

24. "Housing Should Be for Living In, Not for Speculation, Xi Says," *Bloomberg*, October 18, 2017, www.bloomberg.com/news/articles/2017-10-18/xi-renews-call-housing-should-be-for-living-in-not-speculation#xj4y7vzkg.

25. Zongyuan Zoe Liu and Daniel Stemp, "The PBoC Props Up China's Housing Market," Council on Foreign Relations, March 21, 2023, www.cfr.org/blog/pboc-props-chinas-housing-market.

26. "China's Ghost Cities Are Finally Stirring to Life after Years of Empty Streets," *Bloomberg*, September 1, 2021, www.bloomberg.com/news/features/2021-09-01/chinese-ghost-cities-2021-binhai-zhengdong-new-districts-fill-up#xj4y7vzkg.

27. Yoko Kubota and Liyan Qi, "Empty Buildings in China's Provincial Cities Testify to Evergrande Debacle," *Wall Street Journal*, October 4, 2021, www.wsj.com/articles/evergrande-china-real-estate-debt-debacle-empty-buildings-cities-beijing-11633374710.

28. "China's Property Slump Is Easing, but the Relief Will Be Short-Lived," *Economist*, January 26, 2023, www.economist.com/leaders/2023/01/26/chinas-property-slump-is-easing-but-the-relief-will-be-short-lived.

29. Yen Nee Lee, "The U.S. Will Remain Richer than China for the Next 50 Years or More, Says Economist," CNBC, March 26, 2021, www.cnbc.com/2021/03/26/us-will-remain-richer-than-china-for-the-next-50-years-or-more-eiu.html.

30. Thomas Fingar and Jean C. Oi, "Introduction," in *Fateful Decisions: Choices That Will Shape China's Future*, ed. Thomas Fingar and Jean C. Oi (Stanford, CA: Stanford University Press, 2020), 6.

31. Robert A. Rohde and Richard A. Muller, "Air Pollution in China: Mapping of Concentrations and Sources," *PLoS ONE* 10, no. 8 (August 2015): e0135749.

32. Deng Tingting, "In China, the Water You Drink Is as Dangerous as the Air You Breathe," *Guardian*, June 2, 2017, www.theguardian.com/global-development-professionals-network/2017/jun/02/china-water-dangerous-pollution-greenpeace.

33. Finbarr Bermingham, "Malaysia Leads 'Blowback' against China's Belt and Road Initiative," *Global Trade Review*, August 18, 2022, www.gtreview.com/news/asia/malaysia-leads-blowback-against-chinas-belt-and-road-initiative.

34. Ryan Dube and Gabriele Steinhauser, "China's Global Mega-Projects Are Falling Apart," *Wall Street Journal*, January 20, 2023, www.wsj.com/articles/china-global-mega-projects-infrastructure-falling-apart-11674166180.

35. David Herbling and Dandan Li, "China's Built a Railroad to Nowhere in Kenya," *Bloomberg*, July 18, 2019, www.bloomberg.com/news/features/2019-07-19/china-s-belt-and-road-leaves-kenya-with-a-railroad-to-nowhere#xj4y7vzkg.

36. Finbarr Bermingham, "Baltic Countries Fume as China's Envoy in France Lu Shaye Questions Sovereignty of Post-Soviet States," *South China Morning Post*, April 23, 2023, www.scmp.com/news/china/diplomacy/article/3218016/baltic-countries-fume-chinas-envoy-france-questions-sovereignty-post-soviet-states.

37. Daniel Drezner, "Chinese Diplomacy Steps In It Yet Again," *Drezner's World* (blog), April 23, 2023, https://danieldrezner.substack.com/p/chinese-diplomacy-steps-in-it-yet?utm_source=substack&utm_medium=email.

38. Susan L. Shirk, *Overreach: How China Derailed Its Peaceful Rise* (Oxford: Oxford University Press, 2023), 7.

39. Brands and Beckley, *Danger Zone*, 25.

Chapter 5: We Are Stronger Than We Think

1. Shane Harris, "The Time U.S. Spies Thought Al Qaeda Was Ready to Nuke D.C.," *Daily Beast*, July 12, 2017, www.thedailybeast.com/the-time-us-spies-thought-al-qaeda-was-ready-to-nuke-dc.

2. Matt Duroot, "A Record Number of Immigrants Have Become Billionaires in the U.S.," *Forbes*, April 18, 2022, www.forbes.com/sites/mattdurot/2022/04/18/a-record-elon-musk-eric-yuan-peter-thiel-number-of-immigrants-have-become-billionaires-in-the-us/?sh=4dfeda7a2f4b.

3. See Andrew Higgins and Maureen Fan, "Chinese Communist Leaders Denounce U.S. Values but Send Children to U.S. Colleges," *Washington Post*, May 19, 2012, www.washingtonpost.com/world/asia_pacific/chinese-communist-leaders-denounce-us-values-but-send-children-to-us-colleges/2012/05/18/gIQAiEidZU_story.html.

4. Alexis Lai, "Chinese Flock to Elite U.S. Schools," CNN, November 26, 2012, www.cnn.com/2012/11/25/world/asia/china-ivy-league-admission/index.html.

5. See Bethany Allen-Ebrahimian, "A U.S. University Insured Itself against a Drop in Chinese Students," *Axios*, August 18, 2020, www.axios.com/2020/08/18/university-illinois-chinese-students.

6. "Report: U.S. Doctorate Awards," National Center for Science and Engineering Statistics, Survey of Earned Doctorates, 2021, https://ncses.nsf.gov/pubs/nsf23300/report/u-s-doctorate-awards#overall-trends.

7. Remco Zwetsloot et al., "China Is Fast Outpacing U.S. STEM PhD Growth," CSET Data Brief, August 2021, https://cset.georgetown.edu/wp-content/uploads/China-is-Fast-Outpacing-U.S.-STEM-PhD-Growth.pdf.

8. Chun Han Wong, *Party of One: The Rise of Xi Jinping and China's Superpower Future* (New York: Avid Reader Press, 2023), 89.

9. Donald C. Clarke, "Order and Law in China," GW Law Faculty Publications, 2020, https://scholarship.law.gwu.edu/faculty_publications/1506/.

10. Wong, *Party of One*, 101.

11. Lingling Wei, "China Blocked Jack Ma's Ant IPO after Investigation Revealed Likely Beneficiaries," *Wall Street Journal*, February 16, 2021, www.wsj.com/articles/china-blocked-jack-mas-ant-ipo-after-an-investigation-revealed-who-stood-to-gain-11613491292.

12. Jing Yang and Lingling Wei, "China's President Xi Jinping Personally Scuttled Jack Ma's Ant IPO," *Wall Street Journal*, November 12, 2020, www.wsj.com/articles/china-president-xi-jinping-halted-jack-ma-ant-ipo-11605203556?mod=article_inline.

13. Matt Levine, "The US Might Be Only AA+," *Bloomberg*, May 25, 2023, www.bloomberg.com/opinion/articles/2023-05-25/the-us-might-be-only-aa.

14. In the early days of CrowdStrike, I was pushing for a remote work model long before COVID; I pushed back on my board of directors and convinced them that seeking out the best people from around the country and letting them work remotely in 2011 was a great idea. As a result, the first dozen people that I hired as an initial launch team were based in five states and two countries.

15. Niall Ferguson, "Crypto and the Dollar Are Partners, Not Rivals," *Bloomberg*, May 1, 2022, www.bloomberg.com/opinion/articles/2022-05-01/niall-ferguson-crypto-and-the-dollar-are-partners-not-rivals.

16. Joseph J. Ellis, *Founding Brothers: The Revolutionary Generation* (New York: Knopf, 2003), 15.

17. Joseph J. Ellis, *American Creation: Triumphs and Tragedies in the Founding of the Republic* (New York: Knopf, 2008), 9.

18. While the constitution of San Marino, which dates to 1600, is older, it was never codified as a single document in law. Sean Gorman, "Goodlatte Says U.S. Has the Oldest Working National Constitution," *PolitiFact*, September 22, 2014, www.politifact.com/factchecks/2014/sep/22/bob-goodlatte/goodlatte-says-us-has-oldest-working-national-cons.

Chapter 6: Step One—Enable Innovation

1. Chris Miller, *Chip War: The Fight for the World's Most Critical Technology* (New York: Scribner, 2022), xx.

2. Ibid., xxv.

3. James A. Lewis, *Learning the Superior Techniques of the Barbarians: China's Pursuit of Semiconductor Independence*, Center for Strategic and International Studies, January 2019, p. 6, https://csis-website-prod.s3.amazonaws.com/s3fs-public/publication/190115_Lewis_Semiconductor_v6.pdf.

4. Miller, *Chip War*, 12.

5. Ibid., 21.

6. Rachel Courtland, "Gordon Moore: The Man Whose Name Means Progress," *IEEE Spectrum*, March 30, 2015, https://spectrum.ieee.org/gordon-moore-the-man-whose-name-means-progress.

7. Sam Shead, "Investors Are Going Wild over a Dutch Chip Firm. And You've Probably Never Heard of It," CNBC, November 24, 2021, www.cnbc.com/2021/11/24/asml-the-biggest-company-in-europe-youve-probably-never-heard-of.html.

8. Saif M. Khan, Alexander Mann, and Dahlia Peterson, "The Semiconductor Supply Chain: Assessing National Competitiveness," Center for Security and Emerging Technology, Georgetown University, January 2021, https://cset.georgetown.edu/publication/the-semiconductor-supply-chain.

9. Miller, *Chip War*, 66.

10. Ibid., xx.

11. Ben Cohen, "The $1 Trillion Company That Started at Denny's," *Wall Street Journal*, June 1, 2023, www.wsj.com/articles/nvidia-ai-chips-jensen-huang-dennys-d3226926.

12. Miller, *Chip War*, 245.

13. "Taking Stock of China's Semiconductor Industry," Semiconductor Industry Association, July 13, 2021, www.semiconductors.org/taking-stock-of-chinas-semiconductor-industry.

14. Paul Mozur and Quentin Hardy, "Micron Technology Is Said to Be Takeover Target of Chinese Company," *New York Times*, July 14, 2015, www.nytimes.com/2015/07/15/business/international/micron-technology-is-said-to-be-takeover-target-of-chinese-company.html.

15. "U.S. Secretary of Commerce Penny Pritzker Delivers Major Policy Address on Semiconductors at Center for Strategic and International Studies," US Department of Commerce, November 2, 2016, https://2014-2017.commerce.gov/news/secretary-speeches/2016/11/us-secretary-commerce-penny-pritzker-delivers-major-policy-address.html.

16. Raymond Zhong and Cao Li, "With Money, and Waste, China Fights for Chip Independence," *New York Times*, December 24, 2020, www.nytimes.com/2020/12/24/technology/china-semiconductors.html.

17. Hui Tse Gan, "Semiconductor Fraud in China Highlights Lack of Accountability," *Nikkei Asia*, February 12, 2021, https://asia.nikkei.com/Business/36Kr-KrASIA/Semiconductor-fraud-in-China-highlights-lack-of-accountability.

18. Paul Mozur, "The Failure of China's Microchip Giant Tests Beijing's Tech Ambitions," *New York Times*, July 19, 2021, www.nytimes.com/2021/07/19/technology/china-microchips-tsinghua-unigroup.html.

19. Jan-Peter Kleinhans et al., "Running on Ice: China's Chipmakers in a Post-October 7 World," Rhodium Group, April 4, 2023, https://rhg.com/research/running-on-ice.

20. Dong-Won Kim, "The Godfather of South Korea's Chip Industry," *IEEE Spectrum*, August 27, 2022, https://spectrum.ieee.org/kim-choong-ki.

21. Outlook, "Explained: How Americans In Chinese Tech Firms Might Have to Choose between US Citizenship and Job," October 15, 2022, www.outlookindia

.com/international/explained-how-americans-in-chinese-tech-firms-might-have-to-choose-between-us-citizenship-and-job-news-230218.

22. Jeff Pao, "China-Based US Chip Experts Face Stay-Go Dilemma," *Asia Times*, October 15, 2022, https://asiatimes.com/2022/10/china-based-us-chip-experts-fade-stay-go-dilemma.

23. Garrett M. Graff, "Inside the Feds' Battle against Huawei," *Wired*, January 16, 2020, www.wired.com/story/us-feds-battle-against-huawei/.

24. Ibid.

25. Ibid.

26. Ibid.

27. Martijn Rasser and Kevin Wolf, "The Right Time for Chip Export Controls," *Lawfare*, December 13, 2022, www.lawfaremedia.org/article/right-time-chip-export-controls.

28. Mackenzie Hawkins, "Commerce Secretary Warns of Semiconductor Glut Due to China's Subsidies," *Bloomberg*, July 26, 2023, www.bloomberg.com/news/articles/2023-07-26/raimondo-warns-of-semiconductor-glut-due-to-china-s-subsidies?in_source=embedded-checkout-banner.

29. "What Is the Frequency of Earthquake Occurrence in Taiwan?" Central Weather Bureau Seismological Center, accessed August 13, 2023, https://scweb.cwb.gov.tw/en-US/Guidance/FAQdetail/190.

30. Steve Clemons, "The U.S. Would Destroy Taiwan's Chip Plants If China Invades, Says Former Trump Official," *Semafor*, March 13, 2023, www.semafor.com/article/03/13/2023/the-us-would-destroy-taiwans-chip-plants-if-china-invades-says-former-trump-official.

31. Hyman Kublin, "Commodore Perry and the Bonin Islands," *United States Naval Institute Proceedings*, vol. 78/3/589 (March 1952), www.usni.org/magazines/proceedings/1952/march/commodore-perry-and-bonin-islands; Claude B. Mayo, "An Outline of American Diplomacy in the Far East," *United States Naval Institute Proceedings*, vol. 58/1/347 (January 1932), www.usni.org/magazines/proceedings/1932/january/outline-american-diplomacy-far-east; Charles Oscar Paullin, "Early Naval Voyages," *United States Naval Institute Proceedings*, vol. 37/1/137 (March 1911), www.usni.org/magazines/proceedings/1911/march/early-naval-voyages.

32. Ambjörn L. Adomeit, "Alfred and Theodore Go to Hawai'i: The Value of Hawai'i in the Maritime Strategic Thought of Alfred Thayer Mahan," *International Journal of Naval History* 13, no. 1 (April 2016), www.ijnhonline.org/alfred-and-theodore-go-to-hawaii-the-value-of-hawaii-in-the-maritime-strategic-thought-of-alfred-thayer-mahan.

33. Stacie L. Pettyjohn, *U.S. Global Defense Posture, 1783–2011* (Santa Monica, CA: Rand Corporation, 2012), 26.

34. Andrew Dowd et al., "Lithium at a Crossroads: Ten Takeaways on the Global Lithium Market," Silverado Policy Accelerator, May 2023, https://silverado.org/news/report-lithium-at-a-crossroads-ten-takeaways-on-the-global-lithium-market; "DATA SET—Lithium at a Crossroads: The Global Lithium Market, Industry, and Trade," Silverado Policy Accelerator, May 15, 2023, https://silverado.org/news/data-set-lithium-at-a-crossroads-the-global-lithium-market-industry-and-trade.

35. Julie Steinberg and Rhiannon Hoyle, "A Onetime Paper Maker Is Now the King of Lithium," *Wall Street Journal*, June 1, 2023, www.wsj.com/articles/a-onetime-paper-maker-is-now-the-king-of-lithium-99421b8c.

36. Alexander Villegas, "Albemarle Aims to Expand Chile Lithium Mine in 2028 with New Technology," Reuters, May 11, 2023, www.reuters.com/markets/commodities/albemarle-aims-expand-chile-lithium-mine-2028-with-new-technology-2023-05-11.

37. Global lithium demand is forecast to increase from over 700,000 metric tons (mt) of lithium carbonate equivalent (LCE) in 2022 to 2.8 million mt LCE in 2030, according to Benchmark Mineral Intelligence. "Lithium," Mineral Commodity Summaries 2023, United States Geological Survey, accessed August 13, 2023, https://pubs.usgs.gov/periodicals/mcs2023/mcs2023-lithium.pdf; "Financing the Battery Arms Race: The $514 Billion Cost of Bridging the Global EV Supply Chain Divide," *Benchmark Source*, June 19, 2023, https://source.benchmarkminerals.com/article/financing-the-battery-arms-race-the-514-billion-cost-of-bridging-the-global-ev-supply-chain-divide.

38. "Climate-Smart Mining: Minerals for Climate Action," World Bank, May 29, 2019, www.worldbank.org/en/topic/extractiveindustries/brief/climate-smart-mining-minerals-for-climate-action#:~:text=World%20Bank%20Group-,Overview,demand%20for%20clean%20energy%20technologies.

39. "The Role of Critical Minerals in Clean Energy Transitions," International Energy Agency, 2021, www.iea.org/reports/the-role-of-critical-minerals-in-clean-energy-transitions.

40. "History and Future of Rare Earth Elements," Science History Institute Museum and Library, accessed August 13, 2023, https://sciencehistory.org/education/classroom-activities/role-playing-games/case-of-rare-earth-elements/history-future.

41. "National High-Tech R&D Program (863 Program)," Consulate General of the People's Republic of China in New York, March 3, 2005, http://newyork.china-consulate.gov.cn/eng/kjsw/std/201603/t20160305_5520599.htm.

42. David Johnston, *Free Lunch: How the Wealthiest Americans Enrich Themselves at Government Expense (and Stick You with the Bill)* (New York: Portfolio, 2007), 38–40.

43. Jeffery A. Green, "The Collapse of American Rare Earth Mining—and Lessons Learned," *Defense News*, November 12, 2019, www.defensenews.com/opinion/commentary/2019/11/12/the-collapse-of-american-rare-earth-mining-and-lessons-learned.

44. Ashley Feng and Sagatom Saha, "Chinese Heavy Metal: How Beijing Could Use Rare Earths to Outplay America," *Scientific American*, August 3, 2018, https://blogs.scientificamerican.com/observations/chinese-heavy-metal-how-beijing-could-use-rare-earths-to-outplay-america.

45. Duncan Wood et al., *The Mosaic Approach: A Multidimensional Strategy for Strengthening America's Critical Minerals Supply Chain*, Wilson Center, Supply Chain Initiative, 2021, www.wilsoncenter.org/sites/default/files/media/uploads/documents/critical_minerals_supply_report.pdf.

46. In televised fiction, a Chinese ban on the rare-earth element samarium was a key plot thread in Netflix's *House of Cards*.

47. Mikayla Easley, "Special Report: U.S. Begins Forging Rare Earth Supply Chain," *National Defense*, February 10, 2023, www.nationaldefensemagazine.org/articles/2023/2/10/us-begins-forging-rare-earth-supply-chain.

48. Lara Seligman, "China Dominates the Rare Earths Market. This U.S. Mine Is Trying to Change That," *Politico*, December 14, 2022, www.politico.com/news/magazine/2022/12/14/rare-earth-mines-00071102.

49. Robert Spalding, *Stealth War: How China Took Over While America's Elite Slept*, with Seth Kaufman (New York: Portfolio/Penguin, 2019), 82.

50. Jon Emont, "EV Makers Confront the 'Nickel Pickle,'" *Wall Street Journal*, June 4, 2023, www.wsj.com/articles/electric-vehicles-batteries-nickel-pickle-indonesia-9152b1f.

51. Cecilia Jamasmie, "Zijin Mining to Produce Copper at Buritica Gold Mine," Mining.org, November 17, 2021, www.mining.com/zijin-mining-to-produce-copper-at-its-buritica-gold-mine; "China's Chinalco Starts $1.3 Billion Expansion of Peru Copper Mine," Reuters, June 4, 2018, www.reuters.com/article/us-peru-copper-china/chinas-chinalco-starts-1-3-billion-expansion-of-peru-copper-mine-idUSKCN1J00CI.

52. Wood et al., *Mosaic Approach.*

53. Adina Renee Adler and Haley Ryan, "An Opportunity to Address China's Growing Influence over Latin America's Mineral Resources," *Lawfare*, June 8, 2022, www.lawfaremedia.org/article/opportunity-address-chinas-growing-influence-over-latin-americas-mineral-resources.

54. James Areddy, "Xi Jinping Flexes China's Trade Muscle with Visit to Rare-Earths Hub," *Wall Street Journal*, May 21, 2019, www.wsj.com/articles/xi-jinping-flexes-china-s-trade-muscle-with-visit-to-rare-earths-hub-11558442724.

55. "'Lithium Valley' May Provide California with Its Next Gold Rush," *60 Minutes Overtime*, aired on CBS, May 7, 2023, www.cbsnews.com/news/california-lithium-industry-develops-for-electric-vehicle-battery-needs-60-minutes-2023-05-07.

56. Graham Allison, *Destined for War: Can America and China Escape Thucydides's Trap?* (Boston: Houghton Mifflin Harcourt, 2017), 7.

57. Stuart Anderson, "Immigrants and Billion Dollar Startups," National Foundation for American Policy, March 2016, https://nfap.com/wp-content/uploads/2016/03/Immigrants-and-Billion-Dollar-Startups.NFAP-Policy-Brief.March-2016.pdf.

58. Arun Kumar, "44% Fortune 500 Companies Founded by Immigrants or Their Children," *American Bazaar*, June 10, 2022, www.americanbazaaronline.com/2022/06/10/44-fortune-500-companies-founded-by-immigrants-or-their-children-449902.

59. Scott Galloway, "Migrant," *No Mercy/No Malice* (blog), July 1, 2022, www.profgalloway.com/migrant.

60. Greg Ip, "Trump's Hard Line on Immigration Collides with U.S. Demographics," *Wall Street Journal*, February 22, 2017, www.wsj.com/articles/trumps-hard-line-on-immigration-collides-with-u-s-demographics-1487789388.

61. Giovanni Peri and Reem Zaiour, "Labor Shortages and the Immigration Shortfall," *Econofact*, January 11, 2022, https://econofact.org/labor-shortages-and-the-immigration-shortfall.

62. Nicholas Riccardi, "Less Immigrant Labor in US Contributing to Price Hikes," *Associated Press*, May 7, 2022, https://apnews.com/article/immigration-covid-health-business-united-states-dcfd75981dcd212ef6747eeaf87f4f31.

63. Alex Nowrasteh, "Why We Need State-Based Immigration Visas," CATO Institute, November 20, 2019, www.cato.org/commentary/why-we-need-state-based-immigration-visas.

64. "Budget," National Institutes of Health, accessed November 10, 2023, www.nih.gov/ABOUT-NIH/WHAT-WE-DO/BUDGET.

65. "A Giant Leap for the Space Industry," McKinsey and Company, January 19, 2023, www.mckinsey.com/featured-insights/sustainable-inclusive-growth/chart-of-the-day/a-giant-leap-for-the-space-industry.

Chapter 7: Step Two—Defend Innovation

1. Associated Press, "Biden Visits Lockheed Plant as Weapons Stockpile Strained," WSAZ, May 3, 2022, www.wsaz.com/2022/05/03/biden-visit-lockheed-plant-weapons-stockpile-strained.

2. Alex Horton, "For Ukrainian Troops, a Need Arises: Javelin Customer Service," *Washington Post*, June 14, 2022, www.washingtonpost.com/national-security/2022/06/14/ukraine-javelin-assistance.

3. Bernd Debusmann Jr., "How 'Saint Javelin' Raised over $1m for Ukraine," BBC, March 10, 2022, www.bbc.com/news/world-us-canada-60700906.

4. "President Biden Thanks Employees at Javelin Production Facility in Troy, Al.," Lockheed Martin, May 4, 2022, www.lockheedmartin.com/en-us/news/features/2022/president-biden-thanks-lockheed-martin-troy-employees-javelin-facility.html.

5. Missy Ryan, "In Race to Arm Ukraine, U.S. Faces Cracks in Its Manufacturing Might," *Washington Post*, March 9, 2023, www.washingtonpost.com/national-security/2023/03/08/us-weapons-manufacturing-ukraine.

6. Eric Lipton, "From Rockets to Ball Bearings, Pentagon Struggles to Feed War Machine," *New York Times*, March 24, 2023, www.nytimes.com/2023/03/24/us/politics/military-weapons-ukraine-war.html.

7. Teresa Mettela, Luis Martinez, and Nathan Luna, "US, Allies Scramble to Meet Ukraine's Need for Ammunition ahead of Russian Offensive," *ABC News*, March 10, 2023, https://abcnews.go.com/Politics/us-allies-scramble-meet-ukraines-ammunition-ahead-russian/story?id=97558471; "Ukraine Asks EU for 250,000 Artillery Shells a Month," *Financial Times*, May 3, 2023, www.ft.com/content/75ee9701-aa93-4c5d-a1bc-7a51422280fd.

8. Haley Britzky and Oren Liebermann, "Ukraine Is Burning through Ammunition Faster Than the US and NATO Can Produce It. Inside the Pentagon's Plan to Close the Gap," CNN, February 17, 2023, www.cnn.com/2023/02/17/politics/us-weapons-factories-ukraine-ammunition/index.html.

9. Sébastien Roblin, "The Air Force Admits the F-35 Fighter Jet Costs Too Much. So It Wants to Spend Even More," *NBC News*, March 7, 2021,

www.nbcnews.com/think/opinion/air-force-admits-f-35-fighter-jet-costs-too-much-ncna1259781; John Tirpak, "Brown Launching Major TacAir Study with CAPE, Considering '5th-Gen Minus,'" *Air & Space Forces*, February 17, 2021, www.airandspaceforces.com/brown-launching-major-tacair-study-with-cape-considering-5th-gen-minus.

10. John Tirpak, "Keeping the F-22 Credible through 2030 Will Cost at Least $9 Billion, USAF Leaders Say," *Air & Space Forces*, April 4, 2023, www.airandspaceforces.com/f-22-credible-9-billion-air-force.

11. Kyle Mizokami, "The Troubled Aircraft Carrier USS Gerald R. Ford Is (Finally) Prepared for Combat," *Popular Mechanics*, April 8, 2022, www.popularmechanics.com/military/navy-ships/a39664440/uss-gerald-r-ford-is-finally-prepared-for-combat; "Navy Ford (CVN-78) Class Aircraft Carrier Program: Background and Issues for Congress," Congressional Research Service, updated March 27, 2023, https://sgp.fas.org/crs/weapons/RS20643.pdf.

12. Ronald O'Rourke, "Navy CVN-21 Aircraft Carrier Program: Background and Issues for Congress," Congressional Research Service, May 25, 2005, https://apps.dtic.mil/sti/pdfs/ADA472563.pdf.

13. Justin Katz, "Navy Seeks $3.6 Billion over 5 Years for 64 Hypersonic Conventional Prompt Strike Rounds," *Breaking Defense*, https://breakingdefense.com/2023/03/navy-seeks-3-6-billion-over-5-years-for-64-hypersonic-conventional-prompt-strike-rounds/.

14. Alastair Gale, "Japan to Spend Billions on U.S. Tomahawk Missiles in Military Buildup," *Wall Street Journal*, December 23, 2022, www.wsj.com/amp/articles/japan-to-spend-billions-on-u-s-tomahawk-missiles-in-military-buildup-11671784716.

15. Shane Harris, "Own the Sky," *Washingtonian*, November 1, 2010, www.washingtonian.com/2010/11/01/own-the-sky.

16. Thomas Newdick, "Air Force Says KC-46 Is A 'Lemon' That It's Trying to Make Lemonade Out Of," *Drive*, February 2, 2021, www.thedrive.com/the-war-zone/39047/air-force-says-kc-46-is-a-lemon-that-its-trying-to-make-lemonade-out-of.

17. Harris, "Own the Sky."

18. Ryan, "In Race to Arm Ukraine."

19. Jonathan Chang and Meghna Chakrabarti, "'The Last Supper': How a 1993 Pentagon Dinner Reshaped the Defense Industry," *On Point*, aired March 1, 2023, on NPR, www.wbur.org/onpoint/2023/03/01/the-last-supper-how-a-1993-pentagon-dinner-reshaped-the-defense-industry.

20. Lipton, "From Rockets to Ball Bearings."

21. John Tirpak, "The Distillation of the Defense Industry," *Air & Space Forces*, July 1, 1998, www.airandspaceforces.com/article/0798industry.

22. Lipton, "From Rockets to Ball Bearings."

23. John Mintz, "How a Dinner Led to a Feeding Frenzy," *Washington Post*, July 4, 1997, www.washingtonpost.com/archive/business/1997/07/04/how-a-dinner-led-to-a-feeding-frenzy/13961ba2-5908-4992-8335-c3c087cdebc6.

24. Tirpak, "Distillation of the Defense Industry."

25. Mintz, "How a Dinner."

26. John Tirpak, "For Defense Industry to Surge Production, Here's What It Needs, Leaders Tell Congress," *Air & Space Forces*, February 8, 2023, www.airandspaceforces.com/defense-industry-surge-production-needs-leaders-tell-congress; Mintz, "How a Dinner."

27. Chang and Chakrabarti, "'Last Supper.'"

28. Lipton, "From Rockets to Ball Bearings."

29. Ryan, "In Race to Arm Ukraine"; Mark Cancian, "Industrial Mobilization: Assessing Surge Capabilities, Wartime Risk, and System Brittleness," Center for Strategic and International Studies, December 2020, https://csis-website-prod.s3.amazonaws.com/s3fs-public/publication/210108_Cancian_Industrial_Mobilization.pdf.

30. Tirpak, "For Defense Industry to Surge Production."

31. "U.S. Defense Spending Compared to Other Countries," Peter G. Peterson Foundation, April 24, 2023, www.pgpf.org/chart-archive/0053_defense-comparison.

32. "HIMARS versus Ships—Lockheed Martin Is Looking into Launching LRASM from the Ground," Technology.org, November 29, 2022, www.technology.org/2022/11/29/himars-versus-ships-lockheed-martin-is-looking-into-launching-lrasm-from-ground.

33. Seth Jones, "The U.S. Defense Industrial Base Is Not Prepared for a Possible Conflict with China," Center for Strategic and International Studies, January 23, 2023, https://features.csis.org/preparing-the-US-industrial-base-to-deter-conflict-with-China.

34. Gordon Lubold, Nancy A. Youssef, and Ben Kesling, "Ukraine War Is Depleting U.S. Ammunition Stockpiles, Sparking Pentagon Concern," *Wall Street Journal*, August 29, 2022, www.wsj.com/articles/ukraine-war-depleting-u-s-ammunition-stockpiles-sparking-pentagon-concern-11661792188?mod=article_inline.

35. Jones, "U.S. Defense Industrial Base Is Not Prepared."

36. Gordon Lubold, Doug Cameron, and Nancy A. Youssef, "U.S. Effort to Arm Taiwan Faces New Challenge with Ukraine Conflict," *Wall Street Journal*, November 27, 2022, www.wsj.com/articles/u-s-effort-to-arm-taiwan-faces-new-challenge-with-ukraine-conflict-11669559116?mod=article_inline.

37. "Taiwan to Buy 400 US Anti-ship Missiles to Face China Threat—Bloomberg News," Reuters, April 17, 2023, www.reuters.com/world/asia-pacific/taiwan-buy-400-us-anti-ship-missiles-face-china-threat-bloomberg-news-2023-04-17.

38. "Arm Sales: Congressional Review Process," Congressional Research Service, updated June 10, 2022, https://sgp.fas.org/crs/weapons/RL31675.pdf.

39. Jones, "U.S. Defense Industrial Base Is Not Prepared."

40. Editorial Board, "Will China Keep Its Cyber Promises?," *Washington Post*, October 21, 2015, www.washingtonpost.com/opinions/will-china-keep-its-cyber-promises/2015/10/21/c0c8e422-7775-11e5-a958-d889faf561dc_story.html.

41. "Cyber Safety Review Board Releases Report on Activities of Global Extortion-Focused Hacker Group Lapsus$," Homeland Security, August 10, 2023, www.dhs.gov/news/2023/08/10/cyber-safety-review-board-releases-report-activities-global-extortion-focused.

42. Maggie Miller, "Lawmakers Ask Whether Massive Hack Amounted to Act of War," *Hill*, December 18, 2020, https://thehill.com/policy/cybersecurity/530784-lawmakers-ask-whether-massive-hack-amounted-to-act-of-war/.

43. "COMAC Launches C919 Inaugural Flight," *Aviation Week*, May 5, 2017, https://aviationweek.com/air-transport/aircraft-propulsion/comac-launches-c919-inaugural-flight.

44. Kathleen Claussen, "Trading Spaces: The Changing Role of the Executive in U.S. Trade Lawmaking," *Indiana Journal of Global Legal Studies* 24, no. 2 (Summer 2017): 345–368.

45. Chad P. Bown and Douglas A. Irwin, "The GATT's Starting Point," in *Assessing the World Trade Organization*, ed. Manfred Elsig, Bernard Hoekman, and Joost Pauwelyn (Cambridge, UK: Cambridge University Press, 2017), 45–74.

46. "USTR Releases Annual Report on China's WTO Compliance," Office of the United States Trade Representative, February 24, 2023, https://ustr.gov/about-us/policy-offices/press-office/press-releases/2023/february/ustr-releases-annual-report-chinas-wto-compliance.

47. *Findings of the Investigation into China's Acts, Politics, and Practices Related to Technology Transfer, Intellectual Property, and Innovation under Section 301 of the Trade Act of 1974*, Office of the United States Trade Representative, Executive Office of the President, "Executive Summary," March 22, 2018, https://ustr.gov/sites/default/files/enforcement/301Investigations/301%20Draft%20Exec%20Summary%203.22.ustrfinal.pdf.

48. Ibid.

49. "Presidential Proclamation on Adjusting Imports of Steel into the United States," Trump White House, March 8, 2018, https://trumpwhitehouse.archives.gov/presidential-actions/presidential-proclamation-adjusting-imports-steel-united-states/#:~:text=Among%20those%20recommendations%20was%20a,achieve%20long%2Dterm%20economic%20viability.

Chapter 8: Step Three—Say Yes to Our Friends

1. Fen Hampson and Mike Blanchfield, *The Two Michaels: Innocent Canadian Captives and High Stakes Espionage in the US-China Cyber War* (Toronto: Sutherland House, 2021), 20.

2. Garrett M. Graff, "Inside the Feds' Battle against Huawei," *Wired*, January 16, 2020, www.wired.com/story/us-feds-battle-against-huawei/.

3. Chun Han Wong, *Party of One: The Rise of Xi Jinping and China's Superpower Future* (New York: Avid Reader Press, 2023), 89.

4. "Xi Pledges Reform to Ensure Independent, Fair Judicial System," *China Daily*, October 28, 2014, www.chinadaily.com.cn/china/2014-10/28/content_18817323.htm; Wong, *Party of One*, 90.

5. Edward Wong, "China Rebukes U.S. over Criticism of Civil Rights Lawyer's Detention," *New York Times*, May 7, 2015, www.nytimes.com/2015/05/08/world/asia/pu-zhiqiang-china-detention.html.

6. Hampson and Blanchfield, *Two Michaels*, 40–42.

7. Ibid., 21–22.

8. Drew Hinshaw, Joe Parkinson, and Aruna Viswanatha, "Inside the Secret Prisoner Swap That Splintered the U.S. and China," *Wall Street Journal*, October 2, 2022, www.wsj.com/articles/huawei-china-meng-kovrig-spavor-prisoner-swap-11666877779.

9. Ibid.

10. Garrett Graff, "How the US Forced China to Quit Stealing—Using a Chinese Spy," *Wired*, October 11, 2018, www.wired.com/story/us-china-cybertheft-su-bin.

11. Dan Levin, "Couple Held in China Are Free, but 'Even Now We Live under a Cloud,'" *New York Times*, January 1, 2017, www.nytimes.com/2017/01/01/world/canada/canadian-couple-china-detention.html.

12. Graff, "How the US Forced China to Quit Stealing."

13. Levin, "Couple Held in China Are Free."

14. Hinshaw, Parkinson, and Viswanatha, "Inside the Secret Prisoner Swap."

15. Ben Westcott, "Australia Angered China by Calling for a Coronavirus Investigation. Now Beijing Is Targeting Its Exports," CNN, May 27, 2020, www.cnn.com/2020/05/26/business/china-australia-coronavirus-trade-war-intl-hnk/index.html.

16. "Australian Lobster, Timber Halted by Chinese Customs Checks, Fuels Trade Dispute Concerns," Reuters, November 2, 2020, www.reuters.com/article/australia-china-trade-int/australian-lobster-timber-halted-by-chinese-customs-checks-fuels-trade-dispute-concerns-idUSKBN27I10Q.

17. Claire Fu and Daisuke Wakabayashi, "China Wine Tariff Pushes Australia's Grape Growers into Crisis," *New York Times*, March 16, 2023, www.nytimes.com/2023/03/16/business/china-wine-australia.html.

18. Ben Westcott, "How China Is Devastating Australia's Billion-Dollar Wine Industry," CNN, February 18, 2021, www.cnn.com/2021/02/16/business/australia-china-wine-tariffs-dst-intl-hnk/index.html.

19. Amy Chang Chien, "First Pineapples, Now Fish: To Pressure Taiwan, China Flexes Economic Muscle," *New York Times*, June 22, 2022, www.nytimes.com/2022/06/22/business/china-taiwan-grouper-ban.html.

20. Andrew Higgins, "In an Uneven Fight with China, a Tiny Country's Brand Becomes Toxic," *New York Times*, February 21, 2022, www.nytimes.com/2022/02/21/world/europe/china-lithuania-taiwan-trade.html.

21. Editorial Board, "A Lobster Lesson in Geopolitics," *Wall Street Journal*, November 1, 2021, www.wsj.com/articles/a-lobster-lesson-in-geopolitics-australia-china-trade-dispute-hong-kong-11635804837.

22. Higgins, "In an Uneven Fight."

23. Bethany Allen, *Beijing Rules: How China Weaponized Its Economy to Confront the World* (New York: HarperCollins, 2023), xxiv.

24. Elbridge Colby, *The Strategy of Denial: American Defense in an Age of Great Power Conflict* (New Haven, CT: Yale University Press, 2021), 61.

25. Timothy Rich, "Parsing Taiwanese Skepticism about the Chinese Invasion Threat," Global Taiwan Institute, June 29, 2022, https://globaltaiwan.org/2022/06/parsing-taiwanese-skepticism-about-the-chinese-invasion-threat/.

26. Eric Cheung, "If War Breaks Out . . . I Will Just Become Cannon Fodder," CNN, January 20, 2023, www.cnn.com/2023/01/20/asia/taiwan-mandatory-military-service-conscription-intl-hnk-dst/index.html.

27. John J. Tierney Jr., "Reviving SEATO," Institute of World Politics, August 25, 2020, www.iwp.edu/articles/2020/08/25/reviving-seato/.

28. Jeffrey Wilson, "Australia Shows the World What Decoupling from China Looks Like," *Foreign Policy*, November 9, 2021, https://foreignpolicy.com/2021/11/09/australia-china-decoupling-trade-sanctions-coronavirus-geopolitics/.

29. Erin Banco et al., "'Something Was Badly Wrong': When Washington Realized Russia Was Actually Invading Ukraine," *Politico*, February 24, 2023, www.politico.com/news/magazine/2023/02/24/russia-ukraine-war-oral-history-00083757.

30. For details, see, for example, "FACT SHEET: Implementation of the Australia–United Kingdom–United States Partnership (AUKUS)," White House, April 5, 2022, www.whitehouse.gov/briefing-room/statements-releases/2022/04/05/fact-sheet-implementation-of-the-australia-united-kingdom-united-states-partnership-aukus/.

31. David Vergun, "U.S., India Rapidly Expand Their Military Cooperation," US Department of Defense, June 20, 2023, www.defense.gov/News/News-Stories/Article/Article/3433245/us-india-rapidly-expand-their-military-cooperation/.

32. "Secretary Antony J. Blinken at the U.S.-Pacific Islands Forum Dialogue," U.S. Department of State, May 22, 2023, www.state.gov/secretary-antony-j-blinken-at-the-u-s-pacific-islands-forum-dialogue/.

33. Kevin Rudd, "A Decade of Solomons Blunders Rolled Out the Red Carpet for Xi Jinping," *Asian Financial Review*, April 21, 2022, www.afr.com/policy/foreign-affairs/a-decade-of-solomons-blunders-rolled-out-the-red-carpet-for-xi-jinping-20220419-p5aebh.

Chapter 9: Step Four—Say No to Distractions

1. Hillary Clinton, "America's Pacific Century," *Foreign Policy*, October 11, 2011, https://foreignpolicy.com/2011/10/11/americas-pacific-century.

2. "Remarks by President Obama to the Australian Parliament," White House, November 17, 2011, https://obamawhitehouse.archives.gov/the-press-office/2011/11/17/remarks-president-obama-australian-parliament.

3. Greg Myre, "Long Promised and Often Delayed, the 'Pivot to Asia' Takes Shape under Biden," *Morning Edition*, aired October 6, 2021, on NPR, www.npr.org/2021/10/06/1043329242/long-promised-and-often-delayed-the-pivot-to-asia-takes-shape-under-biden.

4. Norman Kempster, "Just Kidding, Russian Says after Cold War Blast Stuns Europeans," *Los Angeles Times*, December 15, 1992, www.latimes.com/archives/la-xpm-1992-12-15-mn-2214-story.html.

5. Alexander Gabuev, "China's New Vassal," *Foreign Affairs*, August 9, 2022, https://archive.ph/IwbCJ#selection-1435.0-1438.0.

6. Dmitri Alperovitch and Sergey Radchenko, "Another Russia Is Possible: The Kremlin Will Eventually Tire of Its Reliance on China," *Foreign Affairs*, August 29, 2022, www.foreignaffairs.com/russian-federation/another-russia-possible.

7. Ibid.

8. "A Kennan for Our Times: Celebrating the Legacy of George F. Kennan," Wilson Center, February 13, 2018, www.wilsoncenter.org/microsite/3/node/67031.

9. Alexander Ward, "'Win-Win': Washington Is Just Fine with the China-Brokered Saudi-Iran Deal," *Politico*, April 6, 2023, www.politico.com/news/2023/04/06/china-saudi-iran-deal-00090856.

Conclusion

1. Llewellyn Thompson, telegram, U.S. Department of State, May 27, 1961, available at https://nsarchive2.gwu.edu/nsa/publications/berlin_crisis/bcdoc.html.

2. Garrett M. Graff, *Raven Rock: The Story of the U.S. Government's Secret Plan to Save Itself—While the Rest of Us Die* (New York: Simon and Schuster, 2017), 116.

3. John F. Kennedy, "Radio and Television Report to the American People on the Berlin Crisis," July 25, 1961, available at the John F. Kennedy Presidential Library and Museum, www.jfklibrary.org/archives/other-resources/john-f-kennedy-speeches/berlin-crisis-19610725.

4. Kenneth P. O'Donnell, David F. Powers, and Joe McCarthy, *Johnny, We Hardly Knew Ye: Memoirs of John Fitzgerald Kennedy* (Boston: Little Brown, 1972), 303.

5. Finbarr Bermingham, "Chinese Envoy to France Lu Shaye Doubles Down on Taiwan 'Re-education' Aims," *South China Morning Post*, August 8, 2022, www.scmp.com/news/china/diplomacy/article/3188192/chinese-envoy-france-lu-shaye-doubles-down-taiwan-re-education.

6. "A Presidential Farewell: Truman's Farewell Address to the Nation," January 15, 1953, available at the Truman Library Institute, www.trumanlibraryinstitute.org/farewell-address/; Peter Lyon, *Eisenhower: Portrait of the Hero* (Boston: Little, Brown, 1974), 854, as well as quoted in Stephen Ambrose, "Epilogue: Eisenhower's Legacy," in *Eisenhower: A Centenary Assessment*, ed. Guenter Bischof and Stephen E. Ambrose (Baton Rouge: Louisiana State University Press, 1995), 251.

Courtesy of the author

Dmitri Alperovitch is a cofounder and chairman of Silverado Policy Accelerator, a national security think tank. He is also the cofounder of CrowdStrike, one of the world's largest cybersecurity companies. He has been named one of *Foreign Policy*'s Top 100 Leading Global Thinkers and *MIT Technology Review*'s Top 35 Innovators Under 35 in 2013. Alperovitch serves on the Department of Homeland Security's Advisory Council and has previously served as a special adviser to the Department of Defense. He is the host of the *Geopolitics Decanted* podcast.

Garrett M. Graff is a journalist and best-selling historian. A Pulitzer Prize finalist, the former editor of *Politico* magazine and longtime contributor to *Wired* and CNN, and the founding director of the cybersecurity and technology program at the Aspen Institute, Graff is the author of multiple books, including the number one national bestseller *The Only Plane in the Sky: An Oral History of 9/11*, as well as *The Threat Matrix: Inside Robert Mueller's FBI*, *Raven Rock*, about the government's Cold War Doomsday plans, and *Watergate: A New History*, among others.

PublicAffairs is a publishing house founded in 1997. It is a tribute to the standards, values, and flair of three persons who have served as mentors to countless reporters, writers, editors, and book people of all kinds, including me.

I. F. Stone, proprietor of *I. F. Stone's Weekly*, combined a commitment to the First Amendment with entrepreneurial zeal and reporting skill and became one of the great independent journalists in American history. At the age of eighty, Izzy published *The Trial of Socrates*, which was a national bestseller. He wrote the book after he taught himself ancient Greek.

Benjamin C. Bradlee was for nearly thirty years the charismatic editorial leader of *The Washington Post*. It was Ben who gave the *Post* the range and courage to pursue such historic issues as Watergate. He supported his reporters with a tenacity that made them fearless and it is no accident that so many became authors of influential, best-selling books.

Robert L. Bernstein, the chief executive of Random House for more than a quarter century, guided one of the nation's premier publishing houses. Bob was personally responsible for many books of political dissent and argument that challenged tyranny around the globe. He is also the founder and longtime chair of Human Rights Watch, one of the most respected human rights organizations in the world.

• • •

For fifty years, the banner of Public Affairs Press was carried by its owner Morris B. Schnapper, who published Gandhi, Nasser, Toynbee, Truman, and about 1,500 other authors. In 1983, Schnapper was described by *The Washington Post* as "a redoubtable gadfly." His legacy will endure in the books to come.

Peter Osnos, *Founder*